Social Work and Health Care

Policy, Practice, and Professionalism

Joan M. Borst, PhD, LMSW

Grand Valley State University

Allyn & Bacon

Boston Columbus Indianapolis New York San Francisco Upper Saddle River
Amsterdam Cape Town Dubai London Madrid Milan Munich Paris Montreal Toronto
Delhi Mexico City Sao Paulo Sydney Hong Kong Seoul Singapore Taipei Tokyo

Senior Acquisitions Editor: Patricia Quinlin
Editorial Assistant: Carly Czech
Senior Marketing Manager: Wendy Albert
Production Editor: Karen Mason
Manufacturing Buyer: Debbie Rossi
Cover Administrator: Kristina Mose-Libon
Editorial Production and Composition Service: Laserwords

Library of Congress Cataloging-in-Publication Data

Borst, Joan M.
  Social work and health care : policy, practice, and professionalism / Joan
M. Borst.
     p. cm.
  Includes bibliographical references and index.
  ISBN-13: 978-0-205-49807-9
  ISBN-10: 0-205-49807-8
1. Social service--Political aspects. 2. Medical care--Political aspects.
I. Title.
  HV40.B548 2009
  362.1'0425--dc22

                                                            2009018487

11

Allyn & Bacon
is an imprint of

www.pearsonhighered.com

ISBN-10:   0-205-49807-8

ISBN-13:   978-0-205-49807-9

Dedication

The completion of this book was possible due to the love and support of my family and dear friends, both near and far.

I dedicate this book to my parents, John Harvey and Fanny Velthouse Vander Veen, who both died from complications due to chronic illness. Their unconditional love and support continue to enrich my life.

Contents

Introduction

For years I have searched for social work and health care educational literature for advanced undergraduates and graduate students that brings together the history, policy, practice, and professional challenges of social work in health care practice in a sufficiently challenging, approachable, and sequential manner. While social work as it applies to specific content areas is available, it is rare to find one resource that acknowledges that social work in health care requires the integration of policy, practice, and professionalism.

After 20 years of professional social work in health care, a profession that is rooted in a strengths-based, culturally competent, and ecological systems perspective, I know it is essential to acknowledge the influence of multiple systems, the application of the biopsychosocial model, and the interplay and intersections of human diversity through cultures. Heath care demands that social workers be well informed about the relationships between policy, practice, and professionalism, yet, too often, one area of competency is highlighted at the expense of the others. The policies related to health care shape practice and practice must be rooted in professionalism. It is impossible to imagine that a social worker employed in health care is not held accountable for the knowledge and competencies in all areas. Social workers must know the basics regarding policy, practice, and professionalism in health care.

This book draws on the natural continuum of integration of policy, practice, and professionalism and offers examples through vignettes and history to prompt thinking and learning. Starting with the groundwork of policy, the reader learns that policy is often developed only after social problems are identified. The reader visits the history of health policy in the United States and considers the effect of diversity and personal values on the creation of legislation regarding health care and reviews the basics of health insurance coverage and the strategies that control costs and practice. The process of policymaking and the factors that influence the success or failure of a policy help a social worker to advocate, develop, and utilize the practice of policy-based interactions. The book reviews some of the predominant areas of practice in health care and the unique roles and tasks that social workers contribute.

Social work practice builds on the general understanding of policy creation and delivery of services. Again, the diversity between and among cultures sensitizes the reader to the unique needs and worldview that exist for individuals, groups, and communities. While the common needs of humans to minimize pain and live well may exist, the assumptions about how individuals define these issues and the choices they wish to make about their health, illness, and healing are important to avoid. The journey for understanding others is lifelong and there are ways to improve personal and professional competency. Practice in health care is identified as happening with individuals, groups, and communities, but it is also between colleagues, supervisors, team members, the health care system, the community, and the globe. It is clear that health exists within an extensive system of relationships, both personal and professional.

Practice also demands social workers to understand the loss and grief issues associated with health changes and that those losses are experienced and best understood using the biopsychosocial model. Loss and grief happen for patients, as well as for caregivers and social workers. Coping is discussed as an intervention to teach to others, but also as an important way to stay emotionally, physically, and socially strong for the professional social worker.

Professionalism is maintained through ethical practice and supported through competent and professional supervision. As with all forms of practice, prevention of problems is the most cost-effective and least damaging way to live. Self-awareness and the ability to set healthy boundaries help social workers maintain their strengths and offer professional social work support to others.

Readers engage with the biopsychosocial perspective to assess the interrelatedness of systems and the influence of diverse and multiple cultures. The strengths of patients, caregivers, and systems and the complexity of relationships between systems encourage readers to approach health care with the understanding of the need to listen, to support self-determination, to partner with systems to obtain quality resources, and to advocate for improved interventions from all health care providers.

This book focuses on specific issues related to culturally competent practice, with an emphasis on interventions with chronic illness as a frequent and common condition. This text is framed by existing literature from interdisciplinary sources and clinical practice studies, while also focusing on methods of critical thinking and the use of supervision and consultation to foster creativity in health care practice process. It is written in the language of health care, and uses the term *patient*, as opposed to *client*, *resident*, or *consumer*. This is intentional to show the strength of the host setting and the language of the medical culture, and urges social workers to learn the language of this often impersonal and intimidating culture. But it also indicates that despite the problem, diagnosis, and treatment setting, social workers offer a unique perspective to health care that enhances the resilience of the patient and others and brings knowledge of their strengths and power to all of the systems. This policy-based professional practice perspective is powerful to understand and intervene in issues related to the health of populations at risk. Case scenarios provide questions to tease out critical thinking and application. The reader is encouraged to learn the basics of policy, practice, and professionalism and understand how these three concepts are essential to the work of social workers in health care.

Part I

Social Work, Health Care, and Policy

Sara recently turned 50 years old and finds she is thinking about her health more than ever. She feels well and has never been sick. She follows her doctor's advice about annual exams, but worries that she should be doing something more. Her friends are joining health clubs, taking vitamins and prescriptions, and talking about a variety of cosmetic surgery options. Sara finds she is less content with her current health status.

The United States is obsessed with issues related to health. There are daily reminders that many of us are too fat, eat too much sugar, have a high incidence of heart disease and hypertension, and are vulnerable to a variety of chronic illnesses. We are challenged to exercise more, diet more, drink less alcohol, stop smoking, and to buy products and programs to ensure our success.

In addition to the increasing obsession with health, we find we live with a broken system of access to health care services. We are regularly informed of the problems associated with the rising cost of health care for both the employed and the unemployed and the risk of the employed losing their health benefits. We constantly talk about health care for two main reasons: (1) the fear we won't have health care when we need it as a result of an inadequate and inequitable system of health care delivery, and (2) our desire to live longer and better. Our interest in health and how health care is delivered finds its way into many areas: our personal life, our professional life, and our politics.

Health care policy in the United States is one of the most daunting and challenging social problems of our time (LeBow, 2004). We are increasingly aware of what is wrong with the health care system, but we seem to remain paralyzed as a nation to take the radical steps necessary to make improvements. Without the foundation of a functional and reliable system of health delivery, millions of people in the United States will continue to experience frustration, substandard care, or, in many cases, a total lack of access to health care coverage (Gladwell, 2005).

Although challenging, social workers must practice within the confines of this inequitable health care system, and regardless of the dysfunction, social workers must do their best to ensure that ethical and just decisions are made. To best understand this challenge it is helpful to start the process of learning about health care by examining the policies that hold our current system of health delivery together (Dobelstein, 2003).

In the United States, health care continues to be shaped by the history of our nation. Political events and social reactions to community health and illness influence health policy. Challenge yourself to listen to the radio or television, read newspapers or magazines for a day and not see, hear, or read about issues related to health care and health care policy. We think and communicate about policies frequently, and national health care policy is no exception.

References

Dobelstein, A. (2003). *Social welfare: Policy and analysis* (3rd ed.). Toronto: Thomson Brooks/Cole.

Gladwell, M. (2005, August 29). The moral-hazard myth. *The New Yorker,* pp. 44–49.

LeBow, R. H. (2004). *Health care meltdown: Confronting the myths and fixing our failing system.* Chambersburg, PA: Hood.

1

The Development of Health Care Policy

Teaching and Learning Goals

- Identify the barriers and deficiencies in the United States health care system
- Understand the role of values in the conception, creation, and implementation of social policy
- Identify the role of the social worker in health care and policy change
- Understand how the social, economic, and political environment influences the design of health care policy

Social workers understand that policy, practice, and professionalism are inseparable in every setting where social work is practiced. Policy is the foundation for all professional social work practice and evolves and changes based on the social, economic, and political conditions. Social workers rely on policy to guide the delivery of socially just services

3

within society (Dobelstein, 2003). Policy and practice depend on each other, absolutely, to deliver professional social work services.

A friend of mine, also a social worker, recently learned that his mother-in-law was diagnosed with Alzheimer's disease. She lives alone in a big city, a couple of hours away from where he and his family live. He and his wife have three children and the children occupy a great deal of the time that remains in the day after they both return home from their full-time jobs. The news of his mother-in-law's diagnosis brings him a new and personal level of awareness of how dependent he is on social health care policy. He and his wife find they are overwhelmed by the challenge of trying to provide care to his mother while maintaining work demands and the needs of their young family. He shared this insight with me, stating, "We are all just one crisis away from needing social services." When we consider the implications of health care policy in a personal way, it helps us understand the implications of policy and the important role of social programs and services to aid people in need. Do the health policies created in the United States provide people with access to quality health care? Will these policies benefit us and our family members if medical treatment or health supports are needed? Do U.S. health care policies provide social justice?

Many social work students avoid or perhaps dread the study of public policy. Policy is perceived as boring and difficult to understand and to read because it is written in a legalistic style. But the final written form of policy is but one form of policy, and it is the result of many steps of activity that occurs to develop a plan of action intended to alleviate the effects of a social problem (Dobelstein, 2003). Unfortunately, if social workers do not understand and appreciate the development and the results of the policy process, they miss opportunities to adequately engage policymakers and advocate for policy to support well-conceived programs and social service delivery systems that contribute to social justice. Without engagement in the policy process, we risk losing valuable opportunities to improve the social services system. We cannot afford to be naive and believe the myth that the United States has the best health care system in the world (LeBow, 2004). The individuals, groups, and communities we work with in social practice settings rely on social workers to help find accessible and affordable health care and one significant way to do this is by being vigilant about the policies that guide the creation of services (Perez & Martinez, 2008).

It is impossible to cover all areas of social health care policy in the United States, but it is just as impossible to talk about health care practice without acknowledging the policy process used to develop the criteria of how health care is defined, treated, and funded. Policy regulates many aspects of health care: who provides health services, who receives health services, where the services are received, what services are provided and for how long, and the cost of services (Landon, Wilson, & Cleary, 1998). All social work activity in health care is dictated by health care policy. Before we examine ways to deliver professional social work services in the field of health care, it is important to briefly examine the role of health care policy in the provision of health care. This chapter reviews the history and development of social policy and the vital roles social workers employ to influence the design.

Social Justice

Many believe health care is a basic human need and access to affordable health care is a fundamental human right (DiNitto, 2000; Hunt, 2007; Veatch, 1994). This belief is shared by many around the world, including social workers. In the professional policy on the delivery of health care, the National Association of Social Workers (NASW; 2003), states that "all individuals have a right to an affordable, accessible, and quality health care continuum" (p.172).

Social justice is one of the five core values of the social work profession (NASW, 1999) and this value promotes the belief that because everyone directly experiences the need for health care equally, we therefore deserve equal access to health care. In addition, social workers believe the continuum of health services must be available to all in the United States, regardless of their circumstances (NASW, 2003). Sadly, it is recognized that the United States does not have a health care program that offers health care equitably (Bodenheimer & Grumbach, 2005; Crowley, 2008; DiNitto, 2000; Moniz & Gorin, 2007). The United States is the only developed nation that does not have a health care system that guarantees access to health care for all citizens and it is the only country where a citizen can go bankrupt due to the costs associated with health care treatments (LeBow, 2004).

There is overwhelming evidence that the health care delivery system in the United States is unable to respond to the millions of people who need health-related services (Schaeffer, 2007). The inability to respond effectively to societal health care needs indicates the inadequacy of current health care policies. Failure of health care policy results in an overburdened health system and an increasing number of people who exist without access to necessary health care. Inaccessibility to care is often due to lack of insurance or an inability to pay for services. For those fortunate enough to possess some form of insurance, many experience continual reductions in coverage and increases in cost. The uninsured are often forced to seek some form of charity care (Bodenheimer & Grumbach, 2005; LeBow, 2004).

The U.S. system of health care provision fails to provide access to health care to everyone despite attempts to subsidize health care plans for those who lack insurance or economic resources. There are millions of individuals who remain without health care because they do not meet the specific criteria for government-sponsored insurance programs (Bodenheimer & Grumbach, 2005; DeNitto, 2000).

The United States is perceived as the richest country in the world and has the luxury of spending nearly twice as much per person on health care than any other country in the world, but the results of these expenditures are disappointing (Schaeffer, 2007). For example, in 2000, the World Health Organization (WHO) announced global life expectancy rankings and the United States ranked near the bottom of wealthy countries in measures such as life expectancy and infant mortality. The U.S. has the most costly and least equitable health care in the world (Schaeffer, 2007; Stairfield, 2000). Because there are so many uninsured and the cost of health care is rising so rapidly, the current health care system in the United States is one of the country's most pressing social policy issues (LeBow, 2004; Mechanic & Tanner, 2007).

From Social Problem to Social Policy

Policy development happens as a result of social, economic, and political changes in the environment. For instance, changes within families, neighborhoods, and work environments often result in tensions that call for a process of finding resolution through forms of consensus (Mukhodpadhyay, 2007). When communities change and it results in social problems that attract broad attention, the process of policy development is used to create a course of action to identify possible solutions (Marinoff, 1996).

A fundamental role of social policy creation is the attempt to alleviate social problems (Dobelstein, 2003). One way to understand the process and content of a policy is to examine the social problem it attempts to address. Recognition of inaccessible and unaffordable health care as a social problem depends on the values of the society. For instance, do U.S. values support the idea that all people have a right to access quality health care? For some, the answer to this question may seem clear, but to develop policy the question requires definitions for "access" and "quality" and answering additional questions, such as "Who are all people?" If the complex culture of the United States was in full agreement about the right to equitable access to quality health care, the implementation of this concept would become the next challenge (Dobelstein, 2003).

The existence of a social problem is recognized when a large or vocal group of citizens find consensus regarding the identification of the issue and share a desire to find resolution. At times, social problems bring some unlikely groups of people together, but the strength of consensus within a group, motivated to find a solution, often provides the momentum necessary to bring issues to the attention of policymakers. While policy development is often a long process of drafting, approving, funding, and implementation, it begins with the first vital step of recognizing and advancing the issues related to a social problem.

Sometimes social problems exist for centuries before people unite in a way powerful enough to receive adequate attention for policy development. For instance, racism has existed for centuries in the United States, yet little national policy progress was made toward equal rights for all citizens in the United States, despite the Emancipation Proclamation. Attempts to change Jim Crow laws went unsupported and countless other forms of legalized racism were supported until the momentum of protest crystallized into the Civil Rights Movement. The passionate and consistent leadership, the dedication of individuals committed to civil rights, the eventual assassination of Dr. Martin Luther King, Jr., in 1964, and the national exposure to violence perpetrated on innocent citizens broadcast on television propelled the social, economic, and political problems related to racism and civil rights into the national agenda. From the struggle of the Civil Rights Movement, including the deaths, torture, and imprisonment of individuals devoted to equal rights, came some of the most powerful legislative policies on equal rights in U.S. history. The Movement also brought other forms of legalized discrimination to the attention of society and pressured leadership to act, resulting in radical changes in national policy (Fee, Brown, Lear, Lazarus, & Theerman, 2002; Hoffman, 2003; Smith, 2005).

The introduction of a policy, however, does not guarantee the social problem is corrected (Doblestein, 2003; Marinoff, 1996). While the initial steps of civil rights policy development led to laws enacted to protect the rights of minorities in the United States, racism continues today. Racism is evident in innumerable ways, including the evidence that today minorities continue to face barriers to health care that are unrelated to health insurance (Smedley, Stith, & Nelson, 2003). In the United States, legislative bodies can enact policies that provide well-designed plans to address social problems, but just as racism exists today despite civil rights legislation, policy cannot eliminate the personal values that influence the provision of health care (Dobelstein, 2003).

The development of national policies such as Medicaid and Medicare in 1965 were an attempt to assist the poor, disabled, and aging to access health care. However, despite these programs, many people, including participants in the Medicaid and Medicare programs, remain without a reliable source of medical care. In addition, the cost of these social health programs continues to rise, and are unable to keep up with escalating health care costs (Bodenheimer & Grumbach, 2005; DiNitto, 2000). Policies must continue to be developed, reviewed, edited, and retooled to fit the context of social need through the input of concerned citizens and the incremental process of policy change.

Values

It is impossible to overstate the influence of personal and public values in the creation of social policies (Mechanic & Tanner, 2007; Neale, 2007). In a country of millions of people representing generational links to cultures throughout the world, it is difficult to imagine the variety of values that exist in the United States, yet there are many values that a majority of citizens share. Health care often represents a value that is shared universally because most individuals have an interest in maintaining or obtaining "good" health. Individuals who are healthy and live without personal health concerns are likely to know or perhaps care for someone who has a health problem.

The history associated with ancient societies indicates humans have always had a close connection to health, illness, and healing and an interest in health continues today. Humans expend great effort to identify health care problems and find health care solutions. People mortgage homes, fly to other countries, and try radical controversial treatments in an effort to cure disease. Social policies pertaining to health are vital to all regardless of health insurance coverage or economic circumstances.

Discrimination is also a part of the values associated with health. There is a suspicion that people who do not have good health or have inadequate health care are in some way inferior or unwilling to do what is necessary to care for themselves in the same way as those who are insured. Our society continues to see people who live in poverty as deserving of their circumstances and when disastrous or catastrophic circumstances occur, we "blame the victim" (Mechanic & Tanner, 2007; Ryan, 1976).

Due to the uniqueness of values, no one sees a social problem in the same exact way. Individual values play a strong role in the perception and recognition of a dilemma. Many of the political battles in the United States are due to often extreme differences in personal values. For instance, some believe that longevity of life, regardless of the time, expense, or quality of life, must be supported by whatever means available. Some believe that if a person is of sound mind and facing a terminal illness, he or she has a right to end his or her life if he or she chooses. A continuum of values drives the entire policy process. Values influence the identification of a social problem, the selection of a solution to deal with the problem, every step taken through the passage of legislation, and the resulting fiscal support and social programs implemented (Mechanic & Tanner, 2007; Neale, 2007).

It is difficult to develop solutions to social problems under the best of circumstances and implementation of national policies across the continuum of social needs comes with challenges of equity and justice. Everyone encounters life in a unique way despite the similarities of the human experience. So, while health policies are frequently aimed at problem solving for certain populations, it is erroneous to think everyone within that population experiences the problem in the same way.

Once more, racism serves as an example that policy alone does not solve social problems. It is clear that policies, such as the ones that now exist to promote racial equality, often fail to offer immediate, temporary, or permanent solutions. Although the passage of the Voting Rights Act intended that all citizens had the right to vote, it did not ensure all citizens that freedom. Law alone cannot authorize a program of equal access to voting that ensure changes in the values of individuals who are resolved to interfere with the voting rights of others. Legislation did not deconstruct the significant barriers to voting rights supported by racist values. Violence, intimidation, technicalities about identification, and other threatening activities continue to accomplish the task of presenting obstacles to citizens trying to exercise their right to vote. Some citizens eligible to vote in the United States today remain unassured of access to voting because of value-based barriers.

Social Change

Society defines a social problem differently at distinct points in time and the issue of health care is a good example (Mukhodpadhyay, 2007). For much of history, health care was obtained through the process of bartering or paying cash to someone the community recognized as having expertise to heal or care for the sick. Physicians and healers commonly had personal relationships with their patients and did not hesitate to go to their homes. Today, it is rare for a person to pay cash for the cost of an entire period of hospitalization or for a physician to treat a patient at home. Insurance programs, increasing costs, specialties, and technology make the system of health care and payment for health care services far more complex. The time it takes for physicians and patients to develop close professional relationships has payment and cost implications, while treating someone outside the clinical setting is often cost-prohibitive.

Increasing costs is arguably the chief reason why health care delivery is experiencing difficulty (Schaeffer, 2007). An additional challenge to the current health system is the incredible changes in our society (population growth and shifts, increased diversity, media, and globalization). Antiquated health delivery systems contribute to the reality in the United States today. There are more than 50 million people who have no health insurance and inadequate resources to purchase health care (Bodenheimer & Grumbach, 2005). Little or inadequate health coverage is no longer a social problem for the unemployed and the poor alone, it is also true for people who are currently employed and consider themselves middle class (Dhooper, 1997). Until recently, employees relied on the fringe benefits of a job to cover their health expenses. Today, health insurance is not guaranteed as a fringe benefit and if the employer does provide health care insurance to workers and retirees, coverage is often being reduced.

The Influence of Policy

Everywhere professional social workers are employed reveals health care as an important issue of concern to many seeking help. It is a common subject of discussion in people's lives. Many people worry about health and the inability to pay for medical treatments. Others are concerned about older family members who depend on weakening national health care programs such as Medicare. Many worry about inadvertently hurting the people they love and care for because while they act as the sole medical caregiver for family members living with chronic illnesses, they feel unsupported and untrained. People experience all kinds of issues related to health or the health of someone they know. Social workers must be aware that there are barriers for many to health care, even if social work and health care is not their field of practice.

Social workers that choose to practice in one of many health care environments will find themselves trying to deliver effective and affordable services to patients while at the same time coping with extraordinary changes in their professional role (Dziegielewski, 2004). Some social work jobs in health care have disappeared, some are restructured with their roles and responsibilities changed, and some social workers are reeling from a complete shift in their position within a health organization. Significant changes are often connected to attempts to save money for the health system or to reduce an investment in nonmedical care. These experiences can leave social workers feeling frustrated, angry, or unwelcome in patient care (Dziegielewski, 2004). However, in some instances, change may be welcomed. Social workers may see some institutional changes as a personal or professional opportunity to improve patient services.

Restructuring health-related social work positions inevitably raises questions about the entire health care system and the influence of broader socio-economic and cultural transformations occurring in the United States. Everyone who is employed as a professional social worker has some experiences with the effects of policy change, but the impact of these changes are not uniform. There is, however, growing recognition that medical care delivered without attention to the social and emotional needs of the patient and caregivers is unsuccessful and more expensive to society (Mechanic & Tanner, 2007; Moniz & Gorin, 2007).

As challenging changes occur to the social worker employed in health care, health policy changes present an opportunity for improved care if professionals are flexible and creative in their thinking and rally to respond to new challenges. Professional commitment to the NASW Code of Ethics (1999) is the prism used to understand and influence change. Social workers grapple with the significance of changes in health care policy, how it affects social work and social justice, and at the same time look for opportunities to merge professional commitment to the vulnerable and influence organizational transformation.

Understanding Policy

Policy sets the standard for service delivery. The health care delivery programs that employ social workers attempt to provide services that closely follow the standards set in governmental or agency policies. Social workers offer benefits best suited to patient care when the objectives and limitations of their role is clearly understood. It is vital for social workers to know the policies that shape the services offered to individuals, just as it is essential for them to know the policies of the agency that employs them. A patient's access to full benefits is maximized when social workers understand the barriers to patients receiving services and when alternative options to obtain client services are recognized.

Public policy is created and maintained through an incremental process. It includes a series of steps that are constantly repeated within cyclical patterns. Lester and

BOX 1.1 • *The Seven-Step Process of Policymaking*

1. Identification of a social problem
2. Identification of goals and agenda setting
3. Policy formulation
4. Policy implementation
5. Policy evaluation
6. Policy change
7. Policy termination

Source: Lester & Stewart (2000).

Stewart (2000) describe the process of policymaking in the following seven steps: (1) the identification of a social problem for the government, (2) identification of goals and agenda setting, (3) policy formulation, (4) policy implementation, (5) policy evaluation, (6) policy change, and (7) policy termination. Typically, public policy follows rather predictable steps of development, but the core of policy making is the activity or inactivity of legitimate groups and their attempts to access the resources necessary to achieve a goal (Dobelstein, 2003). The incremental nature of policy development and revision to improve access to affordable health care is a great example.

The Role of the Social Worker in Health Care Policy

Marinoff (1996) suggests social workers influence political change and social justice in a number of ways, including (1) education, (2) empowerment, (3) program development, and (4) evaluation. First, social workers play an important role in sensitizing and educating the general public, family, and friends about the importance of their role in politics. In other words, when the public understands that critical thinking, informed voting, and knowledge about policies can contribute to the quality of health care for everyone, it makes a positive contribution toward change. Every time a story is told about health care being unavailable or unaffordable to someone, it becomes better understood that the provision of health care is inequitable. For people living without access to health care, the problems are obvious; however, many who are insured and have access to health care remain personally unexposed to the health-related disasters of others. While it is possible for society to develop policies that improve access to affordable health care, these changes will only occur if people with firsthand knowledge of these issues educate and expose others to the issues. An informed public enhances the likelihood of political involvement, political momentum, and opportunities for policy change (Marinoff, 1996; Perez & Martinez, 2008).

Second, social workers must also seek ways to empower disenfranchised populations to gain personal and political power. For instance, when a community owns a health care clinic and decides how the resources of the clinic are applied to their neighborhood, health access and innovative programming options improve (Baquet et al., 2005). Who are those disenfranchised from access to affordable health care? People who are economically challenged are most likely to have poor access to health care. Economic challenges are faced by the unemployed, the disabled, the underemployed, those at risk of losing their jobs, and the uninsured. Those faced with economic challenges represent a diverse and growing group of people (Gehlert, Mininger, Sohmer, & Berg, 2008; Mechanic & Tanner, 2007). Marinoff (1996) suggests that a power shift is necessary for political change. A shift in power does more than influence the development of policy; it is an attempt to ensure the power to make decisions about health care resides within a community. It gives decision-making power and support to greater community creativity and maintains the social changes necessary to benefit from health care policy.

Third, when a social policy becomes legislation, it may provide resources to support social programs. Agencies must develop a framework to meet the requirements of the policy through procedures and methods that best support service delivery. The mission of the agency influences the provision of services. Agencies must also develop specific and measurable goals about target populations, the type and volume of services, the cost of services, and how to evaluate the program. Existing policies do not always address all the needs of the people using specific agencies. For instance, perhaps a patient at an HIV clinic would benefit from intensive case management from a social worker, but current health care policy does not allow billing for this service. Some social workers are employed in agencies that allow them to provide creative, innovative, and inexpensive ways to contribute to client needs. As programs create measurable goals for service, opportunities to modify agency policies and offer interventions that better fit the needs of clients and patients can occur.

Finally, social workers contribute to the evaluation, revision, and development regarding health policy. Research suggests consistent evaluation of both short-term and long-term goals is vital. Evaluation of goals offers agencies opportunities to adjust and revise programmatic policy, and as necessary advocate for policy change. The system of policy creation relies on the modification, adjustment, and revision of policy and results in incremental change (Anderson & Eamon, 2004; Marinoff, 1996).

Witness to Human Needs

Social workers often partner with the disenfranchised and within these relationships, there is a magnified view of human need. Regardless of the area of expertise or the field of practice, professional social workers seek out opportunities to advocate for individuals, groups, and communities unable to access necessary assistance. Often the needs and barriers of others are undetected by the majority of society.

We are witnesses to human suffering and need and are responsible to give honest and reliable accounts of injustice to those with the power to make change. Social workers often partner with individuals living in social turmoil and despair. We directly see the influence of poor or missing policy and the results of racism and inequity. Social workers look into the eyes of children who are underfed and poorly clothed or perhaps older adults who are malnourished and abandoned. We see apartments without heat or ventilation, or infested with cockroaches. We work in emergency rooms, clinics, nursing homes, rehabilitation centers, and hospice centers and are exposed to inadequate insurance coverage for patients and their families. Working in community agencies and institutions, social workers see the results of the inadequacy of resources. The scenes we observe influence our opinions and values about social policy.

Being Political

Being a witness to injustice comes with certain responsibilities. Social workers do not have the luxury of being politically neutral or nonpolitical. It is important to connect with issues of injustice and to help others understand the prevalence and depth of disparity. We raise political awareness of our families and friends when we share with them the state of the social conditions we experience. Informed voting is vital and social workers have opportunities to be a positive influence for change. "Vote 'yes' for this policy," "Vote 'no' for that change in funding," or "This politician is knowledgeable and committed to this issue" are some of the conversations that help people who are less exposed to social inequalities revise their values and shape their opinions. Social workers who witness the health crises of others can vote, but they can also protest, rally, educate, and work for positive social change through the political system (Perez & Martinez, 2007).

Marinoff (1996) states citizens and residents within the United States can influence the creation of policy in a variety of ways:

1. People can organize around a particular issue by beginning petition drives, starting publicity campaigns, and joining other organizations with similar agendas.
2. Citizens can vote. Never underestimate the vote of one individual. The United States has had many political races where the results were determined by an incredibly small number of voters. The vote remains a powerful tool for the individual citizen.
3. People can send letters, faxes, and emails to legislators stating support or disagreement with political issues. Politicians do respond to a large outpouring of citizen responses. Calling campaigns to legislator offices can also be effective.
4. The public can participate in protests. This can take on many forms, but it is legal for United States citizens to protest. This may mean carrying signs, being part of a parade, or other forms of protest. Check about restrictions if you want to avoid attention by the police. Remember, standing up and sharing a political opinion can lead to unexpected consequences. Family, employers, neighbors, or others may disagree with your action, so be clear about what you are doing and saying and why you are standing up for your beliefs. Also, protest done in the spirit of peace ensures that the issue is not lost because of the public's focus on the protestor's methods.
5. Invite legislators who support or disagree with the issue to speak or to engage in a debate of ideas and solutions. Town hall meetings or other forms of community meetings educate both the public and the legislator (Marinoff, 1996).

BOX 1.2 • *How to Influence the Creation of Policy*

1. Organize around a particular issue
2. Vote
3. Send letters, faxes, and emails
4. Participate in protests
5. Invite legislators to speak or engage in a debate

Source: Marinoff (1996).

Public momentum emerges from citizen participation. When citizens believe they are part of the democratic process, they are empowered (Hoffman, 2003; Mechanic & Tanner, 2007). It is often tempting for the leadership in a political process to take charge, but leadership must be careful not to drown out the voices of the people passionately committed to the momentum for change. Social workers recognize the value and strength of all voices including those most affected by the current policies. In fact, Marinoff (1996) challenges social workers to hear every voice within the political system and to accept leadership from unexpected places.

Frequently, the citizens most involved in social problem identification and the accompanying policymaking process have access to power, both formal and informal. Power is often associated with factors such as social and monetary capital. A person who is respected, or has access to money and powerful connections, is frequently in a better position to wield influence over policy than an isolated individual living within a budget. The values of the privileged can conflict with the values of those who are disenfranchised. It is essential that social workers listen carefully to the values and goals of those feeling powerless to make change and to find ways for individuals to safely offer their voice to the political process (Hoffman, 2003; Marinoff, 1996).

United States Health Care Policy

There is no national policy that demands the U.S. government offer accessible and affordable health care. The absence of a national health care policy makes the operation of the health care system very complicated (Dobelstein, 2003). In the United States, health care currently functions as a form of commerce, yet it is very different from most types of commerce. Dobelstein (2003) states there are no other forms of public policy similar to health care policy and states three distinct reasons why this is true. First, healthcare is often regarded as a basic human right, regardless of the patient's ability to pay. The government is perceived by many as having a legitimate role in providing or ensuring the provision of health services, despite the fact that some forms of medical treatment cost more than families earn in a year, or perhaps a lifetime.

Second, healthcare professionals are bound by both laws and professional values to provide life-saving treatments. This means when a person shows up in the emergency room needing immediate medical attention, they cannot be refused. The public would be outraged to learn of a person dying outside the doors of a hospital. The public perceives it is the duty of medical personnel to help everyone in need as much as possible (Dobelstein, 2003).

Third, unlike most other forms of commerce, consumers are rarely able to "shop around" for the best health care. Most people with health care insurance receive their benefits from employers or from a governmental program. Insurance companies and governmental programs restrict choices over available treatment options and providers of care. In addition, many do not have adequate information about the best forms of medical intervention, do not have the financial resources to gain this information, and are bound by the options based on whether they have or do not have medical insurance (Dobelstein, 2003).

Given these unique features, efforts to reorganize or recreate the current health care system in the United States and rewrite health care policy presents a unique and challenging dilemma for policymakers. Most countries in the world have a form of nationalized medicine and in comparison many of the United States health policy problems are quite unique and distinctive. Over time, attempts of the U.S. to provide health care to specific populations resulted in unique programs; the Veterans Administration health system and the Social Security Act of 1935 are two examples.

The United States Veterans Administration

The United States Veterans Administration (VA, 2007) was developed in 1930 and is managed by the Federal Government under the Department of Veterans Affairs. The role of the VA is to care for active duty and retired military personnel. The mission is immense in part due to the number of people covered by the services of the VA and partly because of the services offered. The VA is recognized as the largest independent, all-inclusive health care system operating within the continental United States (Torrens, 1993; VA, 2007). This health system offers medical services that promote and protect the health of all active-duty personnel and are available wherever the U.S. military is stationed. The system attempts to care for the physical and emotional needs of military personnel while actively involved in health promotion (Torrens, 1993).

The VA health system offers primarily hospital care, mental health services, and long-term care to active and nonactive military personnel through an extensive network of hospitals and clinics. In addition to medical services, the VA also offers many other types of services, such as counseling, mental health, pharmaceutical, and financial benefits (e.g., educational grants, disability compensation, loans) and is one of the largest providers of long-term care for military with disabilities (Torrens, 1993; VA, 2007).

This specialized system of providing health care service to a large population of military must be considered an integral component of the national health care system. The VA benefits from strong political relationships with legislators resulting in predictable access to the United States Congress for support (Torrens, 1993).

The Social Security Act of 1935

The Social Security Act of 1935 is also a good example of how the U.S. developed policy to deliver health care to specific populations with health care needs. Beginning in the 1920s, the Great Depression dramatically changed the lives of most people living in the United States and the country was forced to act assertively to keep people from dying of starvation. Radical and creative thinking was vital and resulted in significant new ways of participating in politics and in the creation of the public social service efforts in the United States. Incredible numbers of people were introduced to poverty and in the absence of supportive federal policies many vulnerable citizens, particularly those living in poverty, older adults, those with disabilities, and children, were susceptible to disease, poverty, and death. Under the leadership of the Franklin D. Roosevelt Administration, Labor Secretary Frances Perkins, a social worker, chaired the Committee on Economic Security in 1934 (Porter, 1999). Based on the Social Security Act of 1935, this committee was charged with the creation and development of a form of social security.

The Social Security Act of 1935 established a mechanism for states to receive annual grants-in-aid from the federal government. This federal program introduced the first major engagement of the federal government in a systemic and nationwide relationship with state and local governments. Titles V and VI of the Social Security Act offered states opportunities to support the needs of some of the most vulnerable citizens. For example, Title V of the Social Security Act provided money designated to assist in the development of full-time local health departments, resulting in the maternal and child health services of the United States Children's Bureau. Title VI of the Social Security Act provided grants for public health that offered local communities discretion in their spending. All money from the federal government needed to be matched by state money (Shonick, 1993). The Social Security Act did not include health care insurance language because of fear that the concept of health insurance in the Act would cause the bill to be defeated (Porter, 1999). Social Security continues to offer health benefits to specific populations with specific needs, but there are growing concerns that the price of health care delivery may bankrupt this health related policy in the future.

Changes in Health Care Policy

Many changes in the provision of health care in the United States have taken place due to social, economic, and political changes. For instance, the result of returning soldiers from World War II brought innovation, the Civil Rights movement highlighted and attempted to change inequity, and initiatives like Healthy People 2010 attempt to educate about and prevent disease. In addition, there are significant changes in the kinds of health care citizens require. Treatment of acute illness has been surpassed by the growing number of people diagnosed with and living with chronic illness.

World War II

Health care in the United States went through significant changes during and immediately after World War II. The return of soldiers from the war, many suffering from the effects associated with amputated limbs and other radical mental and physical injuries, pressured the nation to respond to the battle injuries with technology and science and with new discoveries and advancements. The result of these efforts included the standard application of antibiotics, the use and development of rehabilitation, and the creation of the Veterans Administration and other health-related services (Torrens, 1993; VA, 2007).

Prior to the war, hospitals were places to care for the sick or wounded, but after the war hospitals became oriented toward diagnosis and treatment and included laboratories, operating rooms, modern procedures, new equipment, and innovative techniques. The introduction of modern medical procedures required skilled labor and resulted in the education of aides and technicians. Physicians and nurses were challenged to stay aware of and trained in all of the new and innovative medical treatments. The innovative technology and knowledge led to the advancement of research, development of medicines, and additional ways to influence the treatment of disease. Returning soldiers and their families pressured the biomedical and political world to deliver health services in new and successful ways.

The Civil Rights Movement

The Civil Rights Act of 1964, the War on Poverty legislation, and other civil rights policy are rarely thought about as having a relationship to health care, but the social activism of the 1960s was crucial in addressing some of the most blatant and overt racial segregation activities barring access for blacks to health care in the United States (Fee et al., 2002; Hoffman, 2003; Smith, 2005). Prior to the Civil Rights Act, the U.S. health care system practiced legalized racism. The Jim Crow laws in the United States regularly banned blacks from the "whites-only" health care system (Shin, 2002). For many, our understanding of the Jim Crow laws are frequently identified with symbols like "whites-only" drinking fountains and toilets, but the practice of racism was far more significant and resulted in laws protecting and supporting health institutions in banning all but whites from their medical services throughout the United States.

The provision of health care to African Americans was absolutely segregated. In the post-slavery era, some hospitals in the north and all southern hospitals refused admission and health care to blacks (Shin, 2002). Racial discrimination was as pervasive in the health care system as in other social institutions. The hospitals that did admit blacks through the back or side entrance, maintained "white" and "colored" floors, restricted the number of beds for blacks, and labeled sheets, gowns, and equipment by race. Throughout the United States, black doctors were refused staff privileges and black students were excluded from medical programs and nurse training programs (Quadagno, 2000; Shin, 2002; Smith, 2005).

Prior to the Civil Rights Act, African American health care was often delivered by way of self-help and mutual aid. Even federal programs such as the Hill-Burton Act, used to construct and expand hospitals, supported the segregation of hospital facilities (Shin, 2002). The very few middle-class blacks were able to pay for medical services, while others had to rely on the planters/land owners to pay for their medical care, often resulting in loss of wages or crops for sharecroppers. Beito (1999) reports, "Many white hospitals did not admit Blacks under any circumstances and those that did often placed black patients in the basement, near the coal furnace" (p. 114). The hospitals that did reserve some "colored" beds set aside a ridiculously small portion based on the population needs. For example, in Bolivar County, Mississippi, there was a total of 20 beds allotted to blacks in private and public hospitals meant to serve a black population of approximately 52,000 (Beito, 1999).

The attempts at peaceful protest to end lynching, beating, poverty, lack of educational opportunities, and lack of health care and to gain a right to vote erupted into violent displays that were televised into many homes. In 1964, the Civil Rights Act was enacted and made discrimination based on race, color, religion, and national origin illegal. It made discrimination illegal in all areas, including health care. The War on Poverty, enacted during the Johnson Administration in the 1960s, also served to shift public attention toward social policy issues related to social, educational, and health inequalities (Shi & Stevens, 2005). The U.S. health care system changed drastically and the overt discrimination became less obvious (Smith, 2005). However, although minorities may no longer be refused admission to hospitals based on race, racism continues to be a major factor today in the disparities of access to health care (Hoffman, 2003; Shin, 2002).

Healthy People 2010

The report from the Healthy People 2010 initiative is a product of the United States Department of Health and Human Services (HHS) and it is invested in improving the health of U.S. citizens. The Healthy People 2010 project has two chief goals: (1) to increase quality of life and life expectancy in the United States, and (2) to eliminate health disparities. In addition, the progress of Healthy People 2010 is monitored by focusing on over 450 health objectives, such as the reduction of illness and disability and infant mortality. Other objectives focus on broad issues such as access to health care, strengthening public health, and improving health education in the communities (HHS, n.d.).

Strategies like Healthy People 2010 make the most of collaborations between public health organizations resulting in nonprofit organizations that work together to educate and empower populations to access information and services. History shows that policy, publications, and public awareness all play an important role in achieving improved health for communities and that communities working together is the most effective way to improve health, both for individuals and for society. The strategy is ambitious, thorough, and is evidence that the role of community leadership with the power of national support can play a key role in providing improved health to citizens (HHS, n.d.).

The Emergence of Chronic Illness

Perhaps one of the most significant historical changes in health care is the rather recent development of chronic illness as the most common form of disease. It is worth noting that today issues regarding chronic illnesses represent a significant portion of health care treatment needs. Unfortunately, chronic illness is also the most expensive form of health care.

The diagnosis and treatment of chronic illness is a major change from the historic focus on the treatment of acute illness like infectious disease epidemics. Diseases such as contagious infections like influenza, smallpox, and tuberculosis regularly determined the future of populations, often causing utter devastation to entire regions with little or no warning and no prevention methods or effective treatments. Prior to the emergence of chronic illnesses, accidents and other serious injuries were the most common causes of death. Accidents occurred due to unsafe working conditions and often meant loss of life due to poor infection control and lack of successful surgical techniques.

Today, despite the recent development of some infectious diseases such as acquired immunodeficiency syndrome (AIDS), there is a general decline in death rates due to infectious disease in Westernized countries and an increase in death rates due to chronic and degenerative diseases. While there remains a presence of deadly infectious diseases in some areas of the world, social workers are more likely to work in health care environments where patients are diagnosed with one or more chronic illnesses. Partnering with individuals with health care needs related to chronic illnesses such as high blood pressure, diabetes, heart conditions, human immunodeficiency virus (HIV), and cancer is common. There are many types of chronic illness and the influence and trajectory of each diagnosis is unique to each individual.

Life Expectancy

The quality and quantity of life for many citizens in the United States has improved. In 1900 the life expectancy of men was 47.9 and the life expectancy of women was 50.7. By 1950, the longevity had increased to a life expectancy for men of 65.5 and 70.9 for women. (Centers for Disease Control [CDC], 2004b). Longer life expectancy means many are now more prone to diseases that come with age or poor long-term health choices. In 2004, men could expect to live to an average age of 74.5 and women could expect to live an average age of 79.9

(CDC, 2004b). People live longer despite chronic illness because the most common types of chronic illness tend to impair health slowly and do not cause immediate and sudden death.

There remains, however, a dramatic difference in both general life expectancy and infant mortality between racial and ethnic minorities and whites (Gehlert et al., 2008, Moniz & Gorin, 2007). In 1900, although the life expectancy in the United States was 47.6 years for whites, it was only 33 years for blacks. By 1998, the life expectancy for both blacks and whites rose but remained inequitable: 77.3 years for whites and 71.3 years for blacks (CDC, 2004a).

Diagnosis of chronic diseases often requires persistent and consistent treatment, demands attention for a longer period of time, and involves long-term monitoring. The physical, emotional, and social challenges of people living with chronic illness and working to live a good quality of life matches the skills of a professional social worker.

Summary

As social problems such as the inequity of access to affordable health care for many citizens are identified, opportunities for advocacy, the creation and development of policies, and the delivery of quality services through financed programs occurs, social workers are needed to influence and evaluate the results of public policy. If the policy responds well and the programs deliver services that alleviate the social problem, the results are positive and there will be a measurable improvement in the specific community health goal. The process to a successful health policy is crowded with potential problems. Seldom is the first attempt to solve a social problem through public policy completely successful.

Health does not depend on access to affordable medical care alone; health is often shaped by multiple factors. The environment, genetics, lifestyle, and other sociological variables such as geographic location, age, gender, ethnicity, race, economic class, and sexual orientation all play a role in determining overall health (Keigher, 1999; Mechanic & Tanner, 2007; Rothstein, 2003). Within these social categories, there is a constancy of social inequality so powerful that it affects access to health care and ultimately life expectancy. As noted in the literature (Copeland, 2005; Keigher, 1999), access is further limited by an individual's cultural values, education, social relationships, and culturally insensitive health care systems.

Social workers continue to advocate for effective health care policy and promote and initiate the political debate for equitable, accessible, and affordable health care (Crowley, 2008; Hunt, 2007). The reality of chronic illness, requiring long-term and often expensive care, adds to the urgency of this mission. There are many challenges to obtaining this goal but the work toward creative health policy and programmatic changes will result in an increase in the number of people with access to affordable health care.

Critical Thinking Questions

1. Why do you think the United States is the only developed nation that does not guarantee health care for all citizens?

2. Describe how the different forms of media portray health care in the United States.

3. Imagine you just graduated from college. You have no health insurance and it is unlikely that you will have any in the near future. However, you believe that based on personal issues, this is the perfect time in your life to start a family. What will you do to find health care coverage? What are your options?

4. Imagine that immediately after you graduate you are offered a job that pays $40,000 per year; however, your employer does not pay for health insurance. Now, take your salary and subtract a minimum of 25% for taxes. From the balance, subtract the monthly cost of rent, car payments and insurance, food, gas, etc. Now imagine that on your way to work one day you trip on your front steps and break your arm. What are your options for health care? What is the cost?

References

Anderson, S. G., & Eamon, M. K. (2005). Stability of health care coverage among low-income working women. *Health & Social Work, 30*(1), 7–17.

Baquet, C. R., Mack, K. M., Bramble, J., DeShields, M., Datcher, D., Savoy, M., et al. (2005). Maryland's special populations cancer network: Cancer health disparities reduction model. *Journal of Health Care for the Poor and Underserved, 16*(2), 192–206.

Beito, D. T. (1999). Black fraternal hospitals in the Mississippi Delta, 1942–1967. *The Journal of Southern History, 65*(1), 109–140.

Bodenheimer, T. S., & Grumbach, K. (2005). *Understanding health policy: A clinical approach* (4th ed.). Boston: McGraw-Hill.

Centers for Disease Control (CDC). (2004a). Health disparities experienced by racial/ethnic minority populations. *Morbidity and Mortality Weekly Report, 53*(33), 755.

Centers for Disease Control (CDC). (2004b). Table 11. Life expectancy by age, race, and sex. *National Vital Statistics Reports, 53*(6), 29.

Copeland, V. C. (2005). African Americans: Disparities in health care access and utilization. *Health and Social Work, 30*(3), 265–270.

Crowley, M. (2008). Justice as a frame for health reform. *The Hastings Center Report, 38*(1), 3.

Dziegielewski, S. F. (2004). The changing face of health care social work. In S. F. Dziegielewski (Ed.), *The challenging face of health care social work: Professional practice in managed behavioral health care* (2nd ed., pp. 3–25). New York: Springer Publishing Company.

Dhooper, S. S. (1997). *Social work in health care in the 21st century.* New Delhi, India: Sage.

DiNitto, D. M. (2000). *Social welfare: Politics and policy* (5th ed.). Boston: Allyn & Bacon.

Dobelstein, A. (2003). *Social welfare: Policy and analysis* (3rd ed.). Toronto: Thomson Brooks/Cole.

Fee, E., Brown, T., Lear, W. J., Lazarus, J., & Theerman, P. (2002). The march on Washington, 1963. *American Journal of Public Health, 92*(2), 195.

Gehlert, S., Mininger, C., Sohmer, D., & Berg, K. (2008). (Not so) Gently down the stream: Choosing targets to ameliorate health disparities. *Health and Social Work, 33*(3), 163–167.

Hoffman, B. (2003). Health care reform and social movements in the United States. *American Journal of Public Health, 93*(1), 75–85.

Hunt, P. (2007). Right to the highest attainable standard of health. *The Lancet, 370,* 369–371.

Keigher, S. M. (1999). Reflecting on progress, health, and racism: 1900 to 2000. *Health and Social Work, 24*(4), 243–249.

Landon, B. E., Wilson, I. B., & Cleary, P. D. (1998). A conceptual model of the effects of health care organizations on the quality of medical care. *Journal of the American Medical Association, 279*(17), 1377–1382.

LeBow, R. H. (2004). *Health care meltdown: Confronting the myths and fixing our failing system.* Chambersburg, PA: Hood.

Lester, J. P., & Stewart, J. (2000). *Public policy: An evolutionary approach* (2nd ed.) Belmont, CA: Wadsworth/Thomson Learning.

Marinoff, J. (1996). There is enough time: Rethinking the process of policy development. *Social Justice, 23*(4), 234–245.

Mechanic, D, & Tanner, J. (2007). Vulnerable people, groups, and populations: Societal views. *Health Affairs, 26*(5), 1220–1230.

Moniz, C., & Gorin, S. (2007). *Health and health care policy* (2nd ed.). Boston: Allyn & Bacon.

Mukhodpadhyay, A. (2007). Advocacy for appropriate health policy and effective governance of the health system. *Promotion and Education, 14*(2), 88–89.

National Association of Social Workers (NASW). (1999). *Code of Ethics.* Washington, DC: NASW Press.

National Association of Social Workers (NASW). (2003). *Social work speaks: National Association of Social Workers policy statements, 2003–2006.* Washington, DC: NASW Press.

Neale, A. (2007). Who really wants health care justice? *Health Progress, 88*(1), 41–43.

Perez, L. M., & Martinez, J. (2008). Community health workers: Social justice and policy advocates for community health and well-being. *American Journal of Public Health, 98*(1), 11–14.

Porter, D. (1999). *Health, civilization, and the state: A history of public health from ancient to modern times.* London: Routledge.

Quadagno, J. (2000). Promoting civil rights through the welfare state: How Medicare integrated southern hospitals. *Social Problems, 47*(1), 68–89.

Rothstein, W. G. (2003). Trends in mortality in the twentieth century. In P. R. Lee & C. L. Estes (Eds.), *The nation's health* (7th ed., pp. 11–30). London: Jones & Bartlett.

Ryan, W. (1976). *Blaming the victim.* New York: Vintage Books.

Schaeffer, L. D. (2007). The new architects of health care reform. *Health Affairs, 26*(6), 1557–1559.

Shi, L., & Stevens, G. D. (2005). *Vulnerable population in the United States.* San Francisco: Jossey-Bass.

Shin, M. S. (2002, December). Redressing wounds: Finding a legal framework to remedy racial disparities in medical care. *California Law Review.*

Shonick, W. (1993). Public health agencies and service: The partnership network. In S. J. Williams & P. R. Torrens (Eds.), *Introduction to health services* (4th ed.), Albany, NY: Delmar.

Smedley, B. D., Stith, A. Y., & Nelson, A. R. (2003). *Unequal treatment: Confronting racial and ethnic disparities in health care.* Institute of Medicine (U.S.). Committee on Understanding and Eliminating Racial and Ethnic Disparities in Health Care. Washington, DC: National Academies Press.

Smith, D. B. (2005). Racial and ethnic health disparities and the unfinished civil rights agenda. *Health Affairs, 24*(2), 317–325.

Starfield, B. (2000). Is U.S. health really the best in the world? *Journal of the American Medical Association, 284,* 483–485.

Torrens, P. R. (1993). Historical evolution and overview of health services in the United States. In S. J. Williams & P. R. Torrens (Eds.), *Introduction to health services* (4th ed., pp. 71–93). Albany, NY: Delmar.

United States Department of Health and Human Services (HHS). (n.d.). Leading health indicators: Priorities for action. *Healthy People 2010.* Retrieved August 28, 2007, from http://www.healthypeople.gov/LHI/Priorities.htm

United States Department of Veterans Affairs (VA). (n.d.). *Health care: Veterans health administration.* Retrieved September 3, 2008, from http://www1.va.gov/health/AboutVHA.asp

Veatch, R. M. (1994). What counts as basic health care?: Private values and public policy. *Hastings Center Report, 24*(3), 20–21.

World Health Organization (WHO). (2000). *WHO report on global surveillance of epidemic-prone infectious diseases.* Retrieved September, 3, 2008, from www.who.int/csr/resources/publications/surveillance/plague.pdf

2

Health Policy and
Social Injustice

Teaching and Learning Goals

- Recognize the role of minority status in the receipt of health care
- Understand how policy affects issues of access to health care
- Gain knowledge of past and current social injustice in health care policy

Disparities

There is overwhelming evidence (Bodenheimer & Grumbach, 2005; Gary, Narayan, Gregg, Beckles, & Saaddine, 2003; Gehlert et al., 2008; Gorin, 2000; Kaiser Foundation, 2007; Shavers & Shavers, 2006) that disparities exist for minority populations to access and receive medical treatment in the United States. Disparity is evident in the history of national health policies, in current policies, and in the personal and administrative treatment of individuals. It is no secret that some people have better access than others, and some receive a higher quality of care than others. There is clear data that access and treatment within the health care system is related to some very specific variables. Consider the following scenario.

Scenario 2:1

Anthony Jones is angry. He took off work and spent the entire day sitting in the hospital emergency room with his sister. His sister is on disability due to a back injury and lives in constant pain. She does not see a physician and tries to cope by reducing her movements and taking "regular" pain medicine. While she tolerates the pain most of the time, recently, she states the pain is increasing in severity. When his sister is finally examined by an intern, she is prescribed a form of pain relief that can be bought "over the counter" at any pharmacy. When his sister refuses the prescription and begs for something stronger, the intern infers that his sister is misusing pain medication and may be a drug addict. Mr. Jones is confident that this insult would not have occurred if they were white.

Mr. Jones and his sister received the attention they sought from the medical system, yet the medical staff, the patient, and her brother are certain things did not go well. What do you think happened in this scenario? Does the race, gender, or insurance status make a difference in the experience of the patient in this scenario? Does the race, gender, or age of the medical practitioner make a difference? What actions might have improved the interaction for both the patient and the practitioner?

Disparities in access to health care result from a complex mixture of ingredients. Public and private economic challenges in health care are further complicated by a societal foundation built on systemic inequality. The result of the current reimbursement system for health-related services results in problematic access and treatment barriers particularly for the uninsured, underinsured, and people living in poverty. Discrimination and bias are associated with issues related to membership in a variety of cultural groups (Gorin, 2000; Horton, 2003; United States Department of Health and Human Services [HHS], 2000; Williams & Collins, 1995).

Social workers support a system of health care that provides equitable care to all, regardless of insurance coverage (National Association of Social Workers [NASW], 2003). However, the effort to transform the health care system must include attention to the stereotypes, stigma, discrimination, bias, racism, ageism, sexism, homophobia, and other value-related practices that exist and influence health care delivery in society.

Discriminatory practices are not isolated within health care or to specific professions or groups of individuals. The reality is some groups of individuals in society are more vulnerable than others and this liability can lead to biased treatment in a variety of social interactions. Inequities are also evident in health care. Health care, as with any form of service provision, is provided by people who practice in ways that coincide with their personal values (Grant, 1996). Research suggests that age (Grant, 1996; Salzman, 2006; Starfield, 2004), gender (Spitzer, 2005), race and ethnicity (Copeland, 2005; Hall, 2002; Mechanic, 2005), socioeconomic status (Horton, 2003), and sexual orientation (Lipton, 2004) are some of the common reasons cited for inequity in health care access and treatment.

Age

People living in the United States are living longer than ever before (Federal Interagency Forum on Aging-Related Statistics [FIF], 2004). In addition, individuals age 65 and older represent the fastest-growing population in the United States (Calvin, Frazier, & Cohen, 2007; Salzman, 2006; Yang & Levkoff, 2005). This large and growing segment of the population is experiencing the challenges associated with living with one or more chronic illnesses including heart disease, cancer, stroke, respiratory disease, and diabetes (Calvin et al., 2007; FIF, 2004; Parker Oliver & DeCoster, 2006). In addition, the aging population is living longer with chronic illness, causing significant implications for the health care system (Salzman, 2006).

Whatever disparities already exist in society as experienced by racial and ethnic minorities, women, or by people living in poverty, discrimination in access and treatment to health care is compounded for all people as they age. When someone is old, they are at risk of receiving a different and inferior level of health care (Erlen, 2007; Salzman, 2006). Being old and poor and a racial or ethnic minority equates with being the most vulnerable in the health care system (Hatch, 2005; Yang & Levkoff, 2005).

Nationally, older adults use the most health-related services and this aligns with the onset of many forms of chronic illnesses (Kane & Kane, 2005). Given the significant cost of chronic illness treatment, the issue of providing health care to a growing population of older adults will continue to be an important public policy issue (NASW, 2003; Parker & Thorslund, 2007; Parker Oliver & DeCoster, 2006). For instance, as part of the National Social Security Act, when people reach the age of 65, they are eligible for Medicare, a form of national health care insurance that covers short-term health care needs. The current form of Medicare, however, does not adequately cover some of the significant costs of long-term care needs associated with chronic illness (Hatch, 2005; NASW, 2003). Although 95% of older adults in the United States are covered by Medicare, it is frequently insufficient coverage even when supplemented by additional private insurance coverage or Medicaid (Dunlap, Manheim, Song, & Chang, 2002; NASW, 2003). Inadequate Medicare coverage leaves older adults, many living on fixed incomes, unable to respond to the increasing costs of preventative care, chronic illness treatment, prescriptions, long-term supportive care, and emergency treatment (Erlen, 2007; NASW, 2003).

To save costs, older adults take medications less frequently than prescribed, share prescriptions with a partner, skip medications if they are feeling "OK," or choose to not fill prescriptions (Hooyman & Kiyak, 2008). The cost of residential or in-home care is astronomical and often unaffordable for both older adults and their families. Extended life combined with chronic illnesses like Alzheimer's disease or diabetes is a financial challenge for thousands of families in the United States. Health needs for older adults may be complicated by functional limitations, chronic conditions, and the inability to find affordable health care. When the aging need daily support, many families become the caregivers because there are few affordable options for long-term, personalized, high-quality, and professional care. Wealth, income, and education inequalities are greatest among older adults, with women and minorities reporting the lowest resources (Dunlop et al., 2002). Regardless of economic status, a significant health care crisis, especially a long-term and complicated chronic illness, quickly becomes very expensive.

Aging adults are commonly targeted as vulnerable and are prone to being victimized by slick campaigns promising insurance and medication or support for medical conditions.

Historically, when families lived together in rural communities, older adults were frequently offered some level of health support and protection by their adult children. But as the agricultural system in the United States shrinks, it is far less common for nuclear families to be located in one community. In U.S. society, many older adults exist without adult children living in the same geographical area (Bee & Boyd, 2003; Hooyman & Kiyak, 2008).

Salzman (2006) and Grant (1996) suggest that the aging population is frequently treated based on misconceptions about the concerns and needs of older adults. Myths exist about issues of the inevitability of sleep disorders, depression, cognitive impairment and senility, and substance abuse (Bee & Boyd, 2003; Erlen, 2007; Hooyman & Kiyak, 2008; McInnis-Dittrich, 2005). Older adults are often suspected of seeking medical attention without cause or accused of being hypervigilant for physical symptoms of disease. The same age-related bias experienced in other areas of life can also exist in the receipt of health care.

Although some older adults are particularly vulnerable due to chronic illness and limited health insurance coverage, the very youngest in U.S. society, infants and children, are also at risk of experiencing discrimination in the health care system. Frequently how young children receive health care services is connected to the social status of the parents so children of parents who are living in poverty, or children who are members of racial and ethnic minorities, have similar barriers to health care as do the parents. Barriers to care for sick children include lack of insurance coverage, parents with less health care education, lack of transportation, discrimination, and racism. Some of the most significant health issues for children living in the United States include high infant mortality, failure to be immunized, lack of research regarding age-appropriate health issues, and treatment based on measures (Starfield, 2004).

Gender

Women have been traditionally underserved by health care providers in the United States. One reason for this is that for decades, all clinical trials for medical treatments and other forms of study regarding the trajectory of disease or treatment were based on the exclusive study and findings of male participants (Moniz & Gorin, 2007). Many diseases unique to women were ignored during this time. Scholarly research of the 1950s and 1960s shows that the topic most

BOX 2.1 • *The Barriers and Issues to Health Care for Children Living in the United States*

1. Lack of insurance coverage
2. Less health care education
3. Lack of transportation, discrimination, and racism
4. Failure to be immunized; high infant mortality
5. Lack of research regarding age-appropriate health issues
6. Use of adult health treatments as a child health measure

Source: Starfield (2004).

researched in women's health was not disease or syndrome related, but focused on issues of pregnancy and delivery (Theroit, 2001). Since the 1990s and through the leadership of the National Institutes of Health (NIH), studies pertaining specifically to women's health issues began and continue today (Munch, 2006; United States General Accounting Office, 2000).

Recent research by the Henry J. Kaiser Family Foundation produced a report entitled Women's Health Survey (2004). This report finds that women, as an entire population, are experiencing some progress in access to health care and in acquiring health care that responds to women's unique health needs. While women in the United States are a generally healthy population, about 20% of women experience chronic illness conditions that require ongoing treatment or care and limit their ability to fulfill other roles in their lives.

The Kaiser Foundation (2004) finds that health care for women is affected by several key points: (1) women's health care needs and use of health care services change as they age, (2) health insurance matters for women, but does not ensure their access to health care, (3) health care costs are more frequently identified as a barrier to health care, (4) certain populations of women report more barriers than others, (5) women who are sick experience more barriers to health care, (6) there remains a lack of counseling for women about prevention, health risks, and behaviors, and (7) women take on the majority of health needs and responsibilities for their families.

As women age, their health status can deteriorate and increase the need for ongoing medical care and as women approach midlife, they are more likely to be in fair or poor health, have limitations in activity due to poor health, and have chronic conditions requiring medical attention compared to women in their reproductive years. Sixty percent of women age 65 and older have a chronic condition that requires ongoing medical treatment and 25% of women younger than age 45 are diagnosed with at least one chronic condition that requires ongoing medical care (Kaiser Foundation, 2004).

Women who live on a low income are in poorer health than women with higher incomes (Gehlert et al., 2008; Moniz & Gorin, 2007). The Kaiser Foundation (2004) reports that being a poorly educated, low-income single mother, job changes, and inadequate work hours put many women at greater risk of living without health insurance coverage; this is particularly true for women over age 45. Women living in poverty also experience the traditional barriers to health care such as discrimination, substandard housing, limited family support, language barriers, and transportation problems. Health systems impose unique barriers for caregivers, who are often women. The complications for caregivers include crowded clinics, scheduling problems, and long waiting times to be seen by a doctor (Kaiser Foundation, 2004; Loveland Cook, Selig, Wedge, & Gohn-Baube, 1999; Moniz & Gorin, 2007).

There is little research about the biological, social, and psychological responses to illness and diseases specific to women and this can result in inaccurate or inferior medical treatment. Women receiving health care will benefit from additional research , particularly regarding the difference in socioeconomic status, education, language, and cultural differences between minority women and health care providers (Glanz, Croyle, Chollettte, & Pinn, 2003; Munch, 2006).

More work is needed to increase equity in health care for women. Social workers need to stay alert for opportunities to contribute to women-centered research regarding women's health. We must be aware of the effect of gender in care and how it is influenced by other sociocultural issues (Munch, 2006).

Race and Ethnicity

Evidence suggests that racial and ethic minorities continue to experience less health access, coverage, and care in the United States (Copeland, 2005; Gehlert et al., 2008; Stone & Balderrama, 2008). The Civil Rights Movement ushered in significant national policy changes; however, despite legislation, the goal for equitable treatment for racial and ethnic minority cultures remains unmet. Due to many forms of racial and ethnic inequity, both subtle and overt, minority cultures suffer higher rates of infant mortality, increased rates of chronic illnesses, lower life expectancy, and poorer health outcomes despite treatments when compared to nonminority cultures (Copeland, 2005; Kaiser Foundation, 2007).

Minority cultures are defined in many ways, but the experience of health care inequity affects many populations. For instance, minority populations are broadly identified as African Americans, Native Americans, Alaska Natives, Asian Americans, Pacific Islanders, and Hispanic Americans. Within each of these headings exist many subgroups or communities with unique cultures, traditions, and health care needs (Copeland, 2005).

Kaiser Foundation (2007) reports that racial and ethnic minorities report higher prevalence of health problems associated with chronic illnesses such as diabetes, heart disease, and cancer. Socioeconomic status plays a strong role in the higher rates of illness, but weaker health status persists for racial and ethnic minorities despite differences in income.

The practice of racism cannot be ignored or avoided. Racism is practiced regularly by groups and individuals in society and within health care organizations. Individuals working in health care are at risk of portraying the same racist characteristics as the general public. In addition, health care workers have power in the professional health environment, while patients and families are frequently in a vulnerable and dependent role (McQueen, 2002). The inequity in power adds potential for health care to be distributed based on discriminatory and biased practice. All individuals, including health care workers, notice when individuals are perceived as culturally familiar or unfamiliar. Any ethnic or racial feature that is unique about an individual is potentially used to treat a person differently. Skin, hair, eye color, language, and dress can all be a possible reason for a different level of treatment, or discrimination. Since the majority of people in power within health care are white, educated, insured, employed, and male, the cultural differences between health care workers and patients from minority populations can be an impending barrier to equitable care (McQueen, 2002).

Racial and ethnic minorities are at greater risk of underemployment, holding jobs with little or no insurance or insurance options, and are unable to afford to purchase private health insurance (Lillie-Blanton & Hoffman, 2005). Kaiser Foundation (2007) states that of the more than 46 million individuals who have no health insurance coverage, half are racial and ethnic minorities and are more likely to be uninsured than whites, even after accounting for work status. Lack of or lesser quality insurance coverage reduces access to specialty care, prevention and screening measures, and many other health services that support good quality and longevity of life (Betancourt, Green, & Ananeh-Firempong, 2003; Lillie-Blanton & Hoffman, 2005).

In addition, Gehlert et al. (2008) encourage health care workers to enlarge the lens used to view bias and discrimination. Racism exists in policies and practice at an organizational, structural, and practice level, but racial and ethnic minorities are also subject to social and environmental factors that affect health. The social determinants model of health care aligns discrimination with inequities in housing, education, and employment opportunities. This level of sociocultural discrimination puts minorities at greater risk to suffer disproportionately from many forms of chronic illnesses (Betancourt et al., 2003; Moniz & Gorin, 2007).

Socioeconomic Status

Although reasons for disparity in health care are complicated, one of the most significant variables in the receipt of inadequate health care is socioeconomic status (Betancourt et al., 2003; HHS, 2000). Poverty is a powerful barrier to receiving health care and when poverty is added to minority status it becomes additionally powerful. However, while poverty is the most common determinant of substandard care, anyone who experiences a need for expensive health care is at risk for an economic crisis (Betancourt et al., 2003).

There is a broad continuum of ways that poverty affects access and equity to health care for many populations and lack of insurance and the inability to obtain services results in adverse health outcomes for the discrepancies in health status between the wealthy and the poor (Andrulis, 1998). Women within racial and ethnic minority cultures tend to experience the greatest socioeconomic disparity and are also more likely to experience financial insecurity and job insecurity, stressful life events, lack of access to education, and little to no insurance coverage (Dunlop et al., 2002).

Living in poverty is a strong indicator for shortened life expectancy. A life spent living in poverty means that there is little access to health care and there is also less access to healthy food, less information regarding disease prevention, and a lack of secure and healthy living environments. People struggling to survive for the short term are not interested in long-term health goals. When food and shelter for the next 24 hours are the priorities, exercise and blood pressure are of no concern (Hood, 2005).

Some forms of health delivery are particularly difficult to achieve when living in poverty and residing in temporary housing. Providing health care to people who are homeless is a good example. Consider the following case scenario.

Scenario 2:2

Tommy is currently "living on the streets." He is uninsured. Most likely eligible for some public health insurance coverage, Tommy does not have the documentation necessary to prove his identity to social service organizations. He has no birth certificate, Social Security card, military discharge papers, driver's license, or graduation records. He may have had these documents once, but years of living through the challenges of addiction and homelessness complicated his attempts to save and protect important paperwork. In addition to missing paperwork for identification, he has no address and no telephone number. If Tommy uses the hospital emergency room for his occasional injuries, he has no way to have a prescription filled or to follow the directions to "go home and rest." The hospital is not paid when he receives care. When Tommy spends a night at the community mission, he and the other residents are expected to leave the mission after breakfast, around 7:30 A.M. and are unable to return until 5:00 P.M. This is a hardship for Tommy when he is sick. He must find a place to rest and not attract unwanted attention from the members of the community who could harm him. If medication needs to be taken more than once a day, or if it needs to be taken with food, or refrigerated, Tommy is unable to comply. Follow-up appointments for his health conditions are unlikely to be kept because there is often little reason for Tommy to know the day or time and he has no way to keep a schedule for appointments.

How would health care need to change to benefit Tommy? What can social workers do to assist Tommy within the current health care system? How is this scenario an example of the "social determinants model"?

A person does not have to be homeless to have some of the same problems obtaining good health care, but poverty and a lack of insurance is a lethal combination when someone needs health care. An individual living in poverty is often forced to seek charitable help to receive the necessary and often emergent health care.

Sexual Orientation

The lesbian, gay, bisexual, and transgendered (LGBT) population is at risk of reduced health care and life expectancy (Corliss, Shanks, & Moyer, 2007; Heck, Sell, & Gorin, 2006; Mayer et al., 2008; Steele, Tinmouth, & Lu, 2006). The LGBT community is a diverse population and identification as a sexual minority is a connection with more than a sexual behavior (Mayer et al., 2008; McNair, 2008). Culture identities affect the attitudes, beliefs, and behavior patterns that influence relationships to health care and the effectiveness of treatment. Women with a primary sexual orientation to women are labeled lesbian, men with a primary sexual orientation to men are labeled gay, and individuals with a primary sexual orientation to both genders are labeled bisexual. Transgendered individuals are people with gender identification, expression, or beliefs not traditionally associated with their birth sex (Mayer et al., 2008).

Scenario 2:3_____

David rushed Ronald, his partner of 18 years, to the emergency room several hours ago. He has been waiting to talk to the doctor about Ronald's condition, but the physician has not come back to the waiting room. When David insists on seeing Ronald and attempts to enter the intensive care unit, he is denied entrance because he is not officially designated as a member of Ronald's family. He has been told to wait until Ronald's mother arrives and to speak to her about Ronald's condition.

What could a social worker do to assist in this situation? What is the best solution for this situation? Does this situation serve as an example of a social problem or is it good institutional policy? What values influence the institutional policy? What values will influence a solution?

Sexual minorities have an increased incidence of health disparities due to some unique barriers to the access and use of health systems, including contending with discrimination and violence, the lack of health research specific to sexual minority populations, reluctance to disclose sexual minority status, lack of provider and health care sites that offer a gay-friendly atmosphere, and less access to health care insurance due to "non-married" status (Corliss et al., 2007; Heck et al., 2006; Mayer et al., 2008; Steele et al., 2006). However, despite little research and difficulty in accessing random participation in studies for the LGBT population, available studies show that sexual minorities are at an increased risk of depression and suicide due to societal and self-directed hatred (Corliss et al., 2007; Heck et al., 2006). In addition, the LGBT community may experience increased levels of social and spiritual isolation and impaired family support. Until 1973, health care professionals classified homosexuality as a mental disorder requiring psychiatric intervention (Lipton, 2004; Miller, 2007).

The LGBT population, especially gay men, is challenged to find health care that is focused on more than the history and risk factors associated with sexually transmitted diseases, particularly in relationship to the history of human immunodeficiency virus (HIV). Despite the fact that the estimated number of gay men and lesbians living with a chronic illness other than HIV is somewhere between 500,000 and 1 million individuals, the health system has little to say about other forms of treatment issues in gay men's health because HIV demands all of the attention (Lipton, 2004). Studies committed to HIV transmission for the gay population are similar to the silo of research regarding women and childbirth-related health studies prior to the 1970s; there is more to health care for communities than one area of study. The unique health needs of sexual minorities are only beginning to be discovered (Corliss et al., 2007).

Recent studies suggest higher prevalence of certain conditions for the LGBT population. These conditions include substance abuse, tobacco use, eating disorders, depression and anxiety, stress and intolerance of families and employers, unsafe sexual behaviors, and increased risk for certain cancers and other chronic illnesses (Mayer et al., 2008). Research suggests that lesbians are less likely to visit a physician, less likely to have a regular source of health care, and report experiencing unmet medical needs due to the cost of treatment. In addition, prevention services like mammograms and gynecological exams are less frequently used (Heck et al., 2006; Steele et al., 2006).

The societal norms for sexual minorities are changing, in part due to the Civil Rights Movement and the Women's Liberation Movement. The Women's Movement changed assumptions about gender roles and identity, and empowered the gay community to demand cultural liberation (Mayer et al., 2008). However, there remain significant gaps in understanding the unique health needs and treatments needed for the LGBT community.

One way health care for sexual minorities is improving is through specialty clinics. Free-standing health clinics dedicated to sexual minorities, notably Howard Brown Clinic in Chicago, continue to offer culturally appropriate prevention, care, and treatment and have a rich history in participating in clinical trials. The positive collaborations of these population-specific clinics with national health care organizations add dramatically to the improvement of health knowledge regarding sexual minorities (Mayer et al., 2008). Although this is important progress, specialty clinics are not accessible to all.

Social workers and other health care providers can do some relatively simple steps to improve access issues for sexual minorities. Providers of care can express sensitivity to historic stigma and treatment and be informed about possible barriers to health care specific to the population, the culturally specific health risk factors, and the cultural aspects of medical interactions (Mayer et al., 2008). In addition, very concrete and positive findings conclude that culturally informed provider care can influence health care access; a rainbow flag symbol, a pink triangle, posters, educational materials showing sexual minorities in a positive light, and clinical intake forms with inclusive language of all sexual orientations, can serve to lessen barriers and increase confidence in medical interactions (Steele et al., 2006).

BOX 2.2 • *Barriers to Health Care Access*

1. Health clinics with limited hours of operation
2. Health care inaccessible by walking or public transportation
3. Fees charged beyond the payment of insurance
4. Absence of a supportive family or community
5. Lack of education about disease or about how to navigate the health care system

Source: Smith (2001).

Sociocultural Barriers

In addition to the disparities experienced by populations at risk in the health care system, there are additional barriers to gain access to health care that many people experience. The barriers to access include (1) health clinics with limited hours of operation, (2) health care inaccessible by walking or public transportation, (3) fees charged beyond the payment of insurance, (4) absence of a supportive family or community, and (5) lack of education about their disease or about how to navigate the health care system (Smith, 2001).

Community health clinics have, in large part, taken the place of private doctors' offices. While many private physician offices continue to play an important role, it is challenging for these offices to function if reliant on the rate of reimbursement paid by public insurance, such as Medicaid or Medicare. Patients using public insurance are commonly treated at health care clinics subsidized by federal, state, and local grants to offer creative ways for individuals to be assessed and treated. Some clinics are also subsidized by religious groups or by private philanthropists.

Health clinics offer some benefits, but like doctors' offices, they provide limited hours of operation. Many individuals experience the challenge of getting to an appointment when the hours the clinic are open are the same as common working hours. The hours of clinic operation may act as a barrier to people who work low-paying jobs that do not offer "sick days" or "flex time." People lose their job for not showing up to work. In addition, clinics may not be located in convenient spots. Many people do not own or operate a car. A car is an expensive luxury, but not having this private form of transportation acts as a barrier for a variety of reasons. When someone is sick and needs to get to a clinic, dependent children or bad weather makes waiting for a bus very difficult. Clinics may also be forced to charge fees beyond insurance reimbursement. It does not take much for several small fees, even when adjusted to household income, to take a toll on a tight budget. People living near poverty budget carefully and there is rarely a plan for paying unexpected medical fees. Consider the sociocultural issues in the following scenario.

Scenario 2:4

Clara is a 75-year-old widow who lives in a rural community in Iowa. She was recently diagnosed with breast cancer. Although she has a close relationship with her two adult daughters, they are both married and both live and work on the East Coast. Clara lives frugally in the family farm house and her oncologist's office is over 30 miles away. She is scheduled to begin a series of IV chemotherapy treatments. The oncologist has warned Clara that she may become quite sick due to the cancer treatments. She is very worried about how she is going to manage the months ahead. Her daughters are worried, too.

Identify the social problem(s) in this scenario. What can a social worker do to assist in this situation? What kinds of changes are necessary in the health system to avoid this kind of problem?

Many people live life with relatively few supports. Living alone and isolated when healthy is a radically different experience than living alone when diagnosed with a disease. In current U.S. society there is less geographic closeness with family members, and if family members exist, medical emergencies that call for family support often become a crisis. The crisis can be one of expense, emotion, or lack of options or time. The lack of education about the disease diagnosis and how to navigate the medical system can be due to lack of appropriate information from the health system or the naiveté of patient and family to ask for the information or help needed to plan and cope. All health systems are under pressure to reduce expenditures. This results in reduced time with health staff and can result in fewer opportunities for patients to ask questions or express their concerns.

Sociocultural barriers interfere with access to health care and exist for many populations. Pressure to be a cost-effective health care provider means service adjustments and any reduction to time allotments for appointments are commonly felt by the patient. These changes can be frightening for people with poor health status or chronic illness. The future of our health system will depend on the ability of the United States to develop a system of health care that improves the health of its populations at risk (Smith, 2001). Until then, people will continue to delay getting care, never seek care, or use emergency rooms for care. Emergency rooms are frequently used as a point of entry for health care, because hospitals are often accessible by public transportation, are open 24 hours daily, no appointment is necessary, and health care is obtained despite long waits.

Challenges to Policy

The evidence of disparity is visible in the high number of poor and racial and ethnic minority members in the community who delay and miss receiving health care treatment due to the way our society provides health care services. Beyond blaming the health care system, there are additional factors that influence the discrimination and bias in the provision of health care. Society is responsible for the way health care is provided yet there is overwhelming and growing evidence that millions of people live with unmet health needs.

There are many significant reasons why changing the current health delivery system is difficult. Consider the influence of the following issues: (1) a decision-making process for individuals, agencies, and policies that seeks to determine the "worth" of the patient requiring services; (2) the complexities of intersecting cultures in the United States; (3) the practice of racism in health care; (4) unpredictable funding of programs; (5) problems with the effective delivery of services; and (6) securing competent staff.

Worthy/Unworthy

Developed during the Middle Ages, the Elizabethan "Poor Laws" legalized the concept of categorizing people based on the perception of someone's willingness or unwillingness to work. This policy suggested willingness to work meant a person was "worthy" of assistance and unwillingness to work was equated with being "unworthy." The judgment about someone's relationship to work opportunities became part of the equation in determining the status of someone's future. Unfortunately, this form of determining the "worth" of individuals to receive societal benefits, including health care, continues to be practiced today (Bloy, 2002; DiNitto, 2000; Porter, 1999; Richardson, 1990). Consider the following case scenario and think of issues of "worth."

Scenario 2:5

Margie called the health clinic in crisis 3 days ago. She has two small children and she has lost her job due to complications with her health. She is already behind in her rent and the loss of the job means her fragile system of existence is gone. When Margie called, she cried and demanded that despite the availability of an appointment in 3 days, she needed to be seen immediately. The caseworker, Ben, told her that he would be available during his lunch hour the next day. Margie agreed to come in during that time. Ben waited at the door for Margie to arrive so she would be able to make it past security, but Margie did not show. Two days later Margie called and asked for Ben. She states she needs to see him right away and that she just could not make it the last time they were scheduled. Ben has an opening for tomorrow, but there are several other people waiting to be seen. Margie missed the appointment he gave her so Ben follows agency policy and tells Margie she is on the waiting list to be rescheduled. It irritates him that "some people" just skip their appointments and then expect to just be rescheduled.

What values are used to create agency policy? Can you identify with the values of Ben? What does this form of health delivery have to do with the worth of the person requiring services? Is there a more equitable way to offer appointments at the clinic?

The methods and documentation of worthy/unworthy status during assessments are often subtle and hidden, but chances are good that ethical and well-intentioned social workers occasionally, if not regularly, make decisions about the "worth" of the person receiving services. Choosing one person over another person is a form of rationing health care. Implicit in this act is a determination of worth. A person who makes an appointment and then misses it may find they cannot reschedule for a new appointment until others "on the list" are seen or a certain time period passes or perhaps they're determined to be "noncompliant" and are no longer eligible for services. Although there may be a legitimate reason for the missed appointment, society tends to determine people who come to scheduled appointments as "worthy" and people who do not follow through on appointments as "unworthy." This way of making decisions about allocation of money, services is used regularly.

Social workers are faced with difficult decisions about who to see and what services to offer and unfortunately the needs are often greater than the resources. The process of selecting who receives an appointment, service, or treatment based on objective criteria is part of the rationing of health care. Specialized committees make resource decisions, such as deciding who will receive an organ transplant (Sparks, 2006). These are especially tough decisions due to limited resources. For instance, the decision-making process for eligibility for an organ transplant is based on criteria that make judgments about the ability of the patient to successfully receive the organ, the patient's willingness to be compliant with health care regimes, their use of alcohol or drugs, their support system and living environment, and variables such as age and weight. The rationing of health care takes place when it is recognized there are not adequate resources to meet everyone's needs; some receive the resource, others do not (Sparks, 2006).

Complexities of Culture

A particularly unique challenge in providing health care is the very personal nature of health care. Health care systems create clinical pathways, or fairly predictable ways of recovery from disease or injury, despite the unique nature of each individual. The rich tapestry of an individual's cultural roots influences the kind of health care expected and the way services are perceived as satisfactory.

It is important to agree on what "culture" means. *Culture,* a word frequently used interchangeably with the words *race* and *ethnicity,* is often assigned a very narrow definition. But every culture is complex and people are part of many cultures (Miley, O'Melia, & Dubois, 2009). For instance, if a woman is a mother, she belongs to a culture of mothers. A woman's experience of being a mother comes with a language, events, celebrations, and stories that are unique to the women who share this culture. Of course all women who are mothers, experience being a mother differently, but women who physically give birth often find commonalities with other mothers based on this experience.

There are other forms of culture that influence the experience of being a mother. For instance, if a woman is a racial or ethnic minority, married, a lesbian, working full time, or mentally ill, all of these variables influence the way she experiences the "mother" culture. Think of the simplistic ways "others" are categorized. Frequently generalizations are made about groups of people based on membership in one culture, but social workers in health care quickly learn that every culture adds uniqueness to someone's life (Miley, et al., 2009).

Cultures influence how health care is perceived. Cultural associations determine when it is important to seek health care, when it is justified to spend money on health care, and what to do if diagnosed with a terminal illness. Personal characteristics such as pain tolerance, experience with sports or exercise, or employment history are all forms of culture and these characteristics influence how people will live with health and illness. The cultural complexity of individuals makes the creation of legislation that equitably represents all cultures very difficult.

Racism

Everyone has a culture. But the unique differences or similarities between races are not always met with celebration. Sometimes acts of racism are a form of naiveté, an unintentional action or phrase that means something different to the listener than it does to the person who speaks it. Despite being unintentional, the action is damaging, hurtful, and uninformed. But frequently, racism is the intentional expression of generalized hatred toward an entire race. Racism results in substandard treatment, injurious and insulting language, the denial of rights and services, and can result in reduced quality of life and premature death.

Racism exists in health care policy and practice (Miley, et al., 2009). Laws and policies, as well as training and education, to increase cultural competence and to develop professional awareness regarding race and other issues of diversity in the health system are improving. However, while arguably a decrease in overt expressions of racism has occurred, the dangers of racism remain. Racism can exist in strategic planning, policy and program development, and in the diagnosis and treatment of disease. Racism is practiced, to varying degrees, in all health care settings and when social workers recognize and acknowledge this, they can be effective agents of change.

Funding

A good health care policy is ineffective if it is not funded (Karger & Stoesz, 2010). If a great policy makes it through the legislative process, it does not ensure the policy is funded, or that funding is adequate. Inadequate or nonfunding of a policy results in the inability to start the programs necessary to meet the goals of the legislation.

When health care policies are underfunded, the attempts to complete the assignment of the policy is disadvantaged or abandoned. In addition, when successful programs that complete the assigned health care task are victims of budget cuts, the ability to continue to provide the forms of intervention that made the program successful can no longer continue. This is frustrating for social workers and for people who benefit from the delivery of good services. There are great ideas and programs that make a difference in the provision of health care, but the financial bottom line is a reality for all levels of government and it is of chief concern when making health care decisions.

Delivery

The accurate goals and adequate funding of programs is necessary for health programs and interventions to meet the needs of health policies. In addition, the design of the intervention and thoughtfulness over issues of access, population, and effectiveness are vital. For example, if a program is developed to target the health needs of the poor, but the individuals eligible for the services live in the city and the clinic is located in the suburbs, far from any bus line and only advertised on television, the program will fail. If a program is designed to target the health needs of older adults living in a rural area, but is located in a busy city with inadequate parking, the program will fail. Many things must be considered to ensure a health program is successful. Creating dialogue and asking for input and ideas from people who will use the services is a powerful, positive, and empowering way to create new health care programs.

Competence

Once a policy is funded and the program is designed to deliver the appropriate services to the eligible population in the right location, the program now needs to hire competent staff. Money and ideas are important to the development of a new health program, but the effort is at high risk for failure if competent staff are not selected. For instance, if a program is funded and developed to offer health care services to the Hispanic immigrant community in a city, but none of the staff speak Spanish, there will be predictable and significant problems with the program. If an HIV education outreach program is funded and designed to reach gay youth, but none of the workers are educated about HIV prevention or the gay youth culture, there will be problems.

Competence involves a couple of different components. First, workers must be culturally competent. They must have a level of intimate knowledge about the population they are attempting to reach. This is not to say that social workers and other service providers cannot learn about new cultures. However, it is important that a setting such as a health care clinic reveal through the choices for staff, policies, office decorations, educational literature, and its customs that it is aware and cares about the community it is designed to serve. Showing respect for a community by asking and following through on the input offered will increase the chances of delivering appropriate services.

In addition, staff must be trained to do a competent job. Nothing is more insulting to a community than to offer substandard services. If staff routinely make errors that result in people missing opportunities for financial supports or services, the news of inferior interventions can quickly travel through a community. The consequence can be a tarnished professional reputation. Hiring culturally competent staff and requiring training for staff in cultural competency specific to the community served improves opportunities for staff to display cultural respect and knowledge.

Social Injustice in Health Care Policy

History is filled with many examples of how forms of health care policy attempt to solve social problems, but failed. Despite good intentions, policy support, program planning, funding, competence of staff, and many other points of policy development can miss the goals of alleviating the pain associated with a social problem (Karger & Stoesz, 2010). Missing the goal can be serious and result in the suffering, mistreatment, and death of individuals and although perhaps unintended, the social problem may become worse. It is impossible to document all health care policy failures in history, but a brief review of a few infamous policies will reveal the potential harm policies can cause.

Some policies are based in racism, discrimination, and ignorance. Other policies attempt to improve equity, but unexpected consequences occur and people remain untreated, are treated inhumanely, or are perhaps ignored (Karger & Stoesz, 2010). The following examples are cited to reveal how some policies, intended to be solutions to social problems, resulted in dreadful consequences: the practice of eugenics in Germany and in the United States, the Tuskegee Study, and the unintended consequences of deinstitutionalization legislation.

Eugenics in Germany

The relationship between science and culture was vital in the development of the eugenics movement, a movement intended to improve on the issues related to human heredity (Pernick, 1997). During the 19th century, the introduction of scientific ideas included the powerful work of Charles Darwin. Darwin published the work *On the Origin of Species* in 1859 and the world was introduced to the idea of evolution through natural selection.

Darwin's theory became modified into Social Darwinism, a theoretical application to society with the memorable phrase, "survival of the fittest." and in 1883, Sir Francis Galton introduced the term "eugenics" (Pernick, 1997; Pressel, 2003). Eugenics is the science that proposes societal health improves through the process of controlling heredity through selective breeding. Physicians in the United States and Western Europe in the 19th and

20th centuries subscribed to this theory and by the 1920s Germany had looked to racial hygiene as part of mainstream medicine. The theory of eugenics proposes that "positive" eugenics, or selective and enhanced procreation of desirable members of society, and "negative" eugenics, or the reduction and elimination of procreation among undesirables, strengthened the overall gene pool (Pernick, 1997).

In Germany, shortly after the Nazis came to power in 1933, the Sterilization Act was implemented. This law recognized that select people living with certain medical conditions were a threat to German society. People afflicted with hereditary illnesses such as mental illnesses, developmental disabilities, seizure disorders, addiction, blindness, deafness, or severe physical disabilities were evaluated by a genetic health court. The court had the power to order their sterilization and under the direct order of Adolf Hitler, the sterilization practices quickly evolved into "euthanasia."

Most are familiar with the gruesome medical practices that took place in the Nazi concentration camps during World War II. The concentration camp physician practiced a distorted form of eugenics with the goal of enhancing the "superior" genes of the "Master Race." Through the practice of sterilization, euthanasia, and medical experimentation, the camp doctors failed to see people as individuals with worth, but as specimens belonging to a certain substandard group.

After the war, the Nuremberg Trials brought the medical experiments to light and most physicians were rightfully outraged at the barbaric and inhumane treatment of the prisoners. However, some similarities in beliefs and practices in the health care system existed in the United States. People who are perceived as being weak in society are blamed for burdening the community, perceived as degrading the overall health system, unable to think or make decisions on their own, and are believed to be less worthy than others (Ryan, 1976).

Eugenics in the United States

Although the world was outraged at the news of the practice of eugenics in Germany, the United States was also participating in this form of practice. Native Americans received the same form of inhumane treatment in the United States through health care policies that legalized the practice of sterilization. In fact, the practice of eugenics with the Native American population was referenced at the Nuremberg Trials as a defense for the work of Nazi physicians.

Sterilization was perceived as appropriate because the "population" was deemed inferior or defective. Devastated through battles, wars, slavery, exposure to new European diseases, and federal policies that removed them from their lands, Native Americans suffered greatly. Historians believe that beginning in the 1500s and ending in the 1900s, about 95% of the Native American population died (Stiffarm & Lane, 1992; Weaver, 1998). The treatment of Native Americans included forced acculturation and abandonment of all connections to their culture and isolation on reservations (Weaver, 1998).

Health care in the Native American population was distinctly unique and designed as a "separate" form of health care. Native American health care was never intended to be of the same quality or quantity received by the white population. First offered by the federal government to Native Americans under the auspices of the War Department in the early 1800s, the provision of health care was primarily meant to curb contagious outbreaks of diseases like smallpox (Lawrence, 2000). By 1859 Congress transferred the Bureau of Indian Affairs (BIA) from the War Department to the Department of the Interior. Then, in 1955, the BIA was transferred from the Department of the Interior to the Public Health Service (Lawrence, 2000). The Public Health Service was renamed the Indian Health Service in 1958 and under the management of the Public Health Service the number of patients expected to be treated by each physician rose dramatically (Lawrence, 2000).

During the 1960s and the 1970s, historians estimate that 40% of Native American women in childbearing years commonly received sterilization surgery from the Indian Health Service without their knowledge or consent (Lawrence, 2000; Walters & Simoni, 2002). In trying to understand why these surgical sterilizations took place, Lawrence (2000) proposes several rationales: (1) The number of women on welfare increased dramatically and physicians, experienced at performing large numbers of sterilizations of African American and Hispanic women, believed they were performing a social and economic service; (2) most of the doctors were white European American males who believed that they were helping society by limiting or stopping the creation of babies to low-income minority women who financially burdened the rest of society; (3) fewer low income minority women and children would allow the government to cut Medicaid and welfare programs and would in turn reduce the physicians' personal taxes; (4) physicians increased their personal income by performing sterilizations instead of recommending alternative means of birth control; (5) some did not believe minority women were intelligent enough to properly use alternative means of birth control effectively; (6) civil rights movements often promoted racial and ethnic minorities as troublemakers, and this included Native Americans; (7) some physicians used the opportunity to sterilization as training for professional specializations in obstetrics; and (8) some physicians actually believed they were doing the right thing by helping Native American families become more financially secure by "assisting" them in limiting their number of children.

BOX 2.3 • *Justification for the Practice of Eugenics to Native American Women*

1. Believed they were performing a social and economic service.
2. Believed that they were helping society by limiting or stopping a financial burden to the rest of society.
3. Fewer low-income minority women and children would cut in Medicaid and welfare programs and reduce taxes.
4. Sterilization procedure generated income.
5. Minority women perceived as incompetent to use alternative means of birth control effectively.
6. Civil rights movements often promoted minorities as troublemakers, including Native Americans.
7. Sterilizations used to train for obstetrics specialization.
8. Thought to be the "right thing" to help Native American families become more financially secure.

Source: Lawrence (2000).

The result of the sterilization of Native American women continues to have profound effects for individual women, their families, their communities, and national health care. Individuals, tricked or uninformed about the sterilization process, face a future without opportunity for childbirth. This stunning event in the lives of families left dire consequences for a community already forced to cope with loss of land, culture, independence, and freedom. The harm of sterilization is biological, but it is also emotionally and socially damaging. Families experience damaged and dissolved marriages, challenges to friendships, and "higher rates of marital problems, alcoholism, drug abuse, psychological difficulties, shame, and guilt" (Lawrence, 2000, p. 410).

In 1976, the Indian Health Care Improvement Act passed by Congress gave Native Americans more control over their health care. Native Americans now manage many of their health facilities and started their own health services (Lawrence, 2000; Roubideaux, 2002).

The consequences of eugenic practices, both in Germany and in the United States, resulted in dreadful consequences for people perceived to lack worth in society. Social workers see the results of these concepts when they witness the many inequities in health care systems. Social systems, like health care, continue to devalue people based on characteristics that are viewed as inferior (Pernick, 1997; Pressel, 2003).

The Tuskegee Study

The Tuskegee Study is an event that vividly represents the power of the health care system to discriminate. However, Tuskegee makes a far more powerful statement than that of discrimination, racism, and unethical medical research. It is also an example of how experiments that fail to treat people as individuals with equal rights can lead to unethical and criminal interventions. It is such an outstanding example of racism that this event continues to influence distrustful relationships between African Americans and the U.S. health care system today. All social workers benefit by knowing about this event because it stands as a concrete example of a medical system gone terribly wrong.

The full title of the research study conducted in Macon County, Alabama, in 1932 was "The Tuskegee Study of Untreated Syphilis in the Negro Male." The U.S. Public Health Service conducted this research to study the natural history of untreated syphilis. The study lasted for approximately 40 years, concluding in 1972. In exchange for burial stipends, promises of medical treatment, and a hot meal on "clinic day," 623 African American men were offered ineffective treatments for their diagnosis of syphilis. Even after the widespread availability of antibiotics to successfully treat syphilis, the men in the study were denied this treatment for fear it would damage the research sample and results. In some cases, workers conducting the Tuskegee Study actually prevented men seeking treatment from receiving it.

The study ended in 1972, but only after being publicly exposed. By the time the experiment ended, 28 men had died from the untreated disease, 100 died from disease-related complications, 40 wives had been infected with syphilis, and 19 children contracted the infection at birth (Dawson, 2004). Although the scandal was exposed in 1972, it was not until 1997, 65 years after the start of the Tuskegee Study, that the national government apologized for conducting it. On May 16, 1997, President Bill Clinton offered an apology to the survivors and their families, stating, "The United States government did something that was wrong—deeply, profoundly, and morally wrong. It was an outrage to our commitment to integrity and equality for all our citizens." The Tuskegee Syphilis Study remains a significant example of how the policies guiding scientific research and the racism of society damaged these men, their families, and the community (Mason, 2005).

Deinstitutionalization

Deinstitutionalization was a policy developed in the 1960s by President John F. Kennedy in an attempt to improve the conditions connected to a social problem. President Kennedy had a personal stake in the legislation to improve conditions for individuals institutionalized due to chronic health conditions because he had a sister with developmental disabilities. To set the scene, prior to the 1960s, children and adults that were born with or developed a mental illness or other forms of disability were frequently confined to State-run institutions. There were very few options for families to care for a loved one at home, especially if the disability demanded much time, attention, skill, and cost. In the days before psychotropic medications, people diagnosed with severe and chronic mental illness were difficult for families and society to manage. In some cases, family members believed they were at risk if an unstable family member lived in the home (Cutler, Bevilacqua, & McFarland, 2003).

State-run hospitals were seldom capable of providing treatment. Institutions served the fundamental purpose of safely "warehousing" the disabled residents of the State. Reactions to having a family member institutionalized were mixed. Some families were relieved to institutionalize family members, particularly as the years went on and no change or hope for change existed. Sadly, some families were unable to visit or be with family members due to the great distance needed to travel to get to the hospital. Physicians often encouraged institutionalization of family members, including infants born with obvious birth defects.

The goal of the deinstitutionalization policy was to bring institutionalized family members closer to home and to receive better and more personal treatment within communities. Out of this policy was borne the Community Mental Health (CMH) offices in the counties throughout the United States. Each community was held responsible to make adequate services available (Culter et al., 2003).

The goals of this policy seem fairly simple and sound: bring home a community member living with a chronic disability to live with their family and make treatment and services available in their communities so family and friends can be part of their daily lives. Despite the challenges of reorganizing how support services were provided to people living with severe and chronic mental illnesses, there were clearly people institutionalized at state hospitals who were able to be cared for in a less restrictive environment. Soon states recognized the significant cost savings between the cost of inpatient care for a state facility and adult foster care (AFC) homes. The difference in price to the state was similar to the difference between staying in a hospital overnight and staying in a recuperation center. The cost for individuals to live in AFCs was far less expensive and the cost savings to the state was incredible.

As the state-run hospitals and institutions were emptied and individuals were moved to their communities, there was less funding and institutions began to close sections of the buildings. Before long, employees were terminated and entire hospitals and institutions were closed. This placed pressure on the states to move everyone out on institutionalized care and find appropriate housing in the community.

The very last to leave these institutions were individuals with the most severe and profound forms of illness. Many of the remaining patients presented very complex histories and became a challenge for communities to absorb. The most severe cases were patients with criminal histories, such as arson, murder, or assault. Families were unable or unwilling to take members back into their homes and many adult AFC homes were unequipped and undertrained to provide effective care for these significant challenges. AFC homes, often managed by people as a small business, frequently "mom and pop" operations, offered staffing with very limited mental health training, despite some training provided through CMH support.

The result of inadequate specialized training in communities for the most severely disabled individuals from the State hospitals resulted in a new kind of homeless population. In many cities it is common to find a large percentage of adults with mental illness living on the streets and staying in missions. People who are homeless and mentally ill are vulnerable to crime and frequently develop addictions to drugs and alcohol in an attempt to medicate or sooth the voices and bad feelings experienced. A policy intended to allow people to live in the least restrictive environment resulted in homelessness for people who needed a structured, secure, and treatment-oriented environment the most.

Today, many "health care" activities continue to contribute to social injustice, especially in relationship to the diagnosis and care of populations at risk (Karger & Stoesz, 2010). For social workers, examples in history act as a reminder that when society fails to question and accepts unethical practice because the policy is supported by federal, local, or agency policies, people are hurt and professional ethics are violated.

Summary

The development of social policy plays an important role in providing a way for people to come to consensus and attempt to solve a social problem like the issue of health care delivery. But, despite consensus and legislation of health care policy, significant health care problems remain in the United States.

The United States health care system is faulty and challenged to offer access and adequate health care to a growing number of people. Those most commonly denied adequate health care include people living in poverty, women, children, older adults, and ethnic and sexual minorities, and particularly those who are racial and ethnic minorities, and poor.

The development of good health care policy is difficult. The diversity of values and methods of operation make the complexity of issues such as the rationing of health care, the unique health needs of cultures, funding and delivery of services, and the level of competence of workers influence the creation of effective policy and the programs designed to offer services.

Health care policy problems are not new. There are many examples in history that provide reminders that the passage of a policy does not necessarily result in a solution to the social problem. Procedures and programs that are created as a result of policies can result in ethical problems and inhumane treatment. Social workers will experience these challenges and understand the need for the profession to act as advocates and a voice for justice.

Critical Thinking Questions

1. What are some of the ways people are currently dealing with catastrophic illnesses when they cannot afford the expensive medical treatments not covered through their insurance?

2. What are other examples of health care policy that have failed to meet health needs?

3. What contemporary social problems are unresolved? What role does the absence or presence of policy make in attaining solutions?

References

Bee, H., & Boyd, D. (2003). *Lifespan development* (3rd ed.). Boston: Allyn & Bacon.

Betancourt, J. R., Green, A. R., & Ananeh-Firempong, II, O. (2003). Defining cultural competence: A practical framework for addressing racial/ethnic disparities in health and health care. *Public Health Reports, 118,* 293–302.

Bloy, M. (2002.). The 1601 Elizabethan poor law. *The Victorian Web.* Retrieved September 3, 2008, from http://www.victorianweb.org/history/poorlaw/elizpl.html

Bodenheimer, T. S., & Grumbach, K. (2005). *Understanding health policy: A clinical approach* (4th ed.) Boston: McGraw-Hill.

Calvin, A. O., Frazier, L. & Cohen, M. Z. (2007, May). Examining older adults' perceptions of health care providers: Identifying important aspects of older adults' relationships with physicians and nurses. *Journal of Gerontological Nursing,* pp. 6–12.

Clinton, W. (1997, May 16). *Apology for study done in Tuskegee.* Washington, DC: White House, Office of Press Secretary. Retrieved August 31, 2007, from http://clinton4. nara.gov/textonly/New/Remarks/Fri/19970516-898.html

Copeland, V. C. (2005). African Americans: Disparities in health care access and utilization. *Health and Social Work, 30*(3), 265–270.

Corliss, H. L., Shanks, M. D., & Moyer, M. B. (2007). Research, curricula and resources related to LGBT. *American Journal of Public Health, 97*(6), 1023–1027.

Culter, D. L., Bevilacqua, J., & McFarland, B. H. (2003). Four decades of community mental health: A symphony in four movements. *Community Mental Health Journal, 39*(5), 381–398.

Dawson, G. (2004). Last survivor of infamous Tuskegee syphilis experiment dies. *Journal of the National Medical Association, 96*(3), 285–286.

DiNitto, D. M. (2000). *Social welfare: Politics and public policy* (5th ed.). Boston: Allyn & Bacon.

Dunlop, D. D., Manheim, L. M., Song, J., & Chang, R. (2002). Gender and ethnic/racial disparities in health care utilization among older adults. *Journals of Gerontology, 57B*(4), S221–S233.

Erlen, J. A. (2007). The frail elderly: A matter of caring. *Orthopaedic Nursing, 26*(6), 379–382.

Federal Interagency Forum on Aging-Related Statistics (FIF). (2004, November). *Older Americans 2004: Key indicators of well-being.* Federal Interagency Forum on Aging-Related Statistics. Washington, DC: US Government Printing Office.

Gary, T. L., Narayan, K. M., Gregg, E. W., Beckles, G. L., & Saadine, J. B. (2003). Racial/ethnic differences in the healthcare experience (coverage utilization and satisfaction) of US adults with diabetes. *Ethnicity and Disease, 13*, 47–54.

Gehlert, S., Sohmar, D., Sacks, T., Mininger, C., McClintock, M., & Olopade, O. (2008). Targeting health disparities: A model linking upstream determinants to downstream interventions. *Health Affairs, 27*(3), 339–348.

Glanz, K., Croyle, R. T., Chollettte, V. Y., & Pinn, V. W. (2003). Cancer-related health disparities in women. *Journal of Public Health, 93*(2), 292–298.

Gorin, S. H. (2000). Inequality and health: Implications for social work. *Health & Social Work, 25*(4), 270–275.

Grant, L. D. (1996). Effects of ageism on individual and health care providers' responses to healthy aging. *Health & Social Work, 21*(1), 9–15.

Hall, R. E. (2002). *A new perspective on racism: Health risk to African-Americans. Race, Gender, & Class, 9*(2), 100.

Hatch, L. R. (2005). Gender and ageism. *Generations, XXXIX*(3), 19–24.

Heck, J. E., Sell, R. L., & Gorin, S. S. (2006). Health care access among individuals involved in same sex relationships. *American Journal of Public Health, 96*(6), 1111–1118.

Hood, E. (2005). Dwelling disparities. *Environmental Health Perspectives, 113*(5), A310–A317.

Hooyman, N. R., & Kiyak, H. A. (2008). *Social gerontology: A multidisciplinary perspective* (8th ed.). Boston: Pearson/ Allyn & Bacon.

Horton, R. (2003). Medical journals: Evidence of bias against the diseases of poverty. *The Lancet, 361*, 712–714.

Kaiser Family Foundation. (2007, January). Key facts: Race, ethnicity & medical care. Retrieved September 4, 2008, from http://www.kff.org/minorityhealth/6069.cfm.

Kane, R. L., & Kane, R. A. (2005). Ageism in healthcare and long-term care. *Generations, XXXIX*(3), 49–54.

Karger, H. J., & Stoesz, D. (2010). *American social welfare policy: A pluralistic Approach* (5th ed.). Boston: Allyn & Bacon.

Lawrence, J. (2000). The Indian Health Service and the sterilization of Native American women. *American Indian Quarterly, 24*(3), 400–419.

Lillie-Blanton, M., & Hoffman, C. (2005). The role of health insurance coverage in reducing racial/ethnic disparities in health care. *Health Affairs, 24*(2), 398–408.

Lipton, B. (2004). Gay men living with non-HIV chronic illnesses. *Journal of Gay and Lesbian Social Services, 17*(2), 1–23.

Loveland Cook, C. A., Selig, K. L., Wedge, B. J. & Gohn-Baube, E. A. (1999). Access barriers and the use of prenatal care by low-income, inner-city women. *Social Work, 44*(2), 129–140.

Mason, S. E. (2005). Offering African Americans opportunities to participate in clinical trials research: How social workers can help. *Health & Social Work, 30*(4), 296–304.

Mayer, K. H., Bradford, J. B., Makadon, H. J., Stall, R., Goldhammer, H., & Landers, S. (2008). Sexual and gender minority health: What we know and what needs to be done. *American Journal of Public Health, 98*, 989–995.

McInnis-Dittrich, K. (2005). *Social work with elders: A biopsychosocial approach to assessment and intervention* (2nd ed.). Boston: Allyn & Bacon.

McNair, R. (2008). Recognising the unique health-care needs of sexual minorities. *The Lancet, 371*(9610), 377–379.

McQueen, D. (2002). Patients are not doctors' equal. *British Medical Journal, 324,* 1214.

Mechanic, D. (2005). Policy challenges in addressing racial disparities and improving population health. *Health Affairs, 24*(2), 335–339.

Miley, K. K., O'Melia, M., & Dubois, B. (2009). *Generalist social work practice: An empowering approach* (6th ed.). Boston: Allyn & Bacon.

Miller, R. L. (2007). Legacy denied: Gay men, AIDS, and the Black church. *Social Work, 52*(1), 51–61.

Moniz, C., & Gorin, S. (2007). *Health and health care policy* (2nd ed.). Boston: Allyn & Bacon.

Munch, S. (2006). The women's health movement: Making policy, 1970–1995. *Social Work in Health Care, 43*(1), 17–32.

National Association of Social Workers (NASW). (2003). *Social work speaks: National Association of Social Workers policy statements, 2003–2006.* Washington, DC: NASW Press.

Parker, M. G., & Thorslund, M. (2007). Health trends in the elderly population: Getting better and getting worse. *The Gerontologist, 47*(2), 150–158.

Parker Oliver, D., & DeCoster, V. A. (2006). Health care needs of aging adults: Unprecedented opportunities for social work. *Health and Social Work, 31*(4), 243–245.

Pernick, M. S. (1997). Eugenics and public health in American history. *American Journal of Public Health, 87*(11), 1767–1773.

Porter, D. (1999). *Health, civilization, and the state: A history of public health from ancient to modern times.* London: Routledge.

Pressel, D. M. (2003). Nuremberg and Tuskegee: Lessons for contemporary American medicine. *Journal of the National Medical Association, 95*(12), 1216–1225.

Richardson, M. (1990). Mental health services. In S. J. Williams & P. R. Torren (Eds.), *Introduction to health services* (4th ed., pp. 219–242). Albany, NY: Delmar.

Roubideaux, Y. (2002). Perspectives on American Indian health. *American Journal of Public Health, 92*(9), 1401–1403.

Ryan, W. (1976). *Blaming the victim.* New York: Vintage Books.

Salzman, B. (2006). Myths and realities of aging. *Care Management Journals, 7*(3), 141–151.

Shavers, V. L. & Shavers, B. S. (2006). Racism and health inequity among Americans. *Journal of the National Medical Association, 98*(3), 386–397.

Smith, J. H. (2001). Eliminating health disparities: Our mission, our vision, our cause. *American Family Physician, 64*(8), 1333–1334.

Sparks, J. (2006). Ethics and social work in health care. In S. Gehlert and T. A. Browne (Eds.), *Handbook of health social work* (pp. 43–69). Hoboken NJ: John Wiley & Sons.

Spitzer, D. L. (2005). Engendering health disparities. *Canadian Journal of Public Health, 96,* S78–S99.

Starfield, B. (2004). U.S. child health: What's amiss, and what should be done about it? *Health Affairs, 23*(5), 165–171.

Steele, L. S., Tinmouth, J. M., & Lu, A. (2006). Regular health care use by lesbians: A path analysis of predictive factors. *Family Practice – An International Journal,* 631–636.

Stiffarm, L. A., & Lane, P., Jr. (1992). The demography of native North America: A question of American Indian survival. In M. A. Jaimes (Ed.), *The state of Native America: Genocide, colonization, and resistance* (pp. 23–53). Boston: South End Press.

Stone, L. C., & Balderrama, C. H. H (2008). Health inequities among Latinos: What do we know and what can we do? *Health & Social Work, 33*(1), 3–7.

Theriot, N. M. (2001). Negotiating illness: Doctors, patients, and families in the nineteenth century. *Journal of the History of the Behavioral Sciences, 37*(4), 349–368.

United States Department of Health and Human Services (HHS). (2000). *Healthy People 2010.* McLean, VA: International Medical Publishing.

Walters, K. L., & Simoni, J. M. (2002). Reconceptualizing native women's health: An "indigenist" stress-coping model. *American Journal of Public Health, 92*(4), 520–524.

Weaver, H. N. (1998). Indigenous people in a multicultural society: Unique issues for human services. *Social Work, 4*(3), 203–212.

Williams, D. R., & Collins, C. (1995). U.S. socioeconomic and racial differences in health: Patterns and explanations. *Annual Review of Sociology, 21,* 349–386.

Yang, F. M., & Levkoff, S. E. (2005). Ageism and minority populations: Strengths in the face of challenge. *Generations, XXXIX*(3), 42–48.

3

Health Care Insurance

*Teaching and Learning Goals*_____

- Recognize the differences between Medicare and Medicaid
- Recognize and communicate the conditions that result in the disparity to receive health care
- Understand the challenges to confidentiality
- Understand the barriers that challenge change to the current health care system

Scenario 3:1_____

Markesha is frustrated, confused, and embarrassed. She knows that the last time her mother needed her medication it was paid for in full by her mother's Medicare insurance. After waiting in line for 40 minutes at the huge hospital pharmacy, the pharmacist tells her she owes money this time. Markesha does not have the extra money and she knows her mother is unable to afford any extra expenses. If she cannot get the medication without the payment today, she will have to return home without the medicine. Her mother will be miserable.

What can a social worker do to assist in this situation? How is this scenario related to health care policy? What keeps most people from knowing the actual costs of prescription medications?

The policies and procedures that guide insurance plans change frequently. For social workers working in the health care setting, there is no quick or accurate guide to all insurance reimbursement questions. The treatment or medication that was covered 100% by a specific insurance plan a few months ago may now be covered 80%, and perhaps only if it is required for the patient as part of inpatient care. Working in health care settings where deciphering insurance reimbursement costs is part of the job, social workers often spend hours on the telephone with insurance company reimbursement managers and hospital utilization staff. The goal is to achieve the greatest quality of patient care, the best reimbursement for the health organization, and the least amount of out-of-pocket expense for the patient—a challenging balance to find.

In the United States, people use both government-funded and privately owned and managed health care insurance plans. Criteria for coverage within each plan varies, as does the amount and type of coverage. Social workers develop professional skills and connections with the professionals working in reimbursement settings that facilitate the best and most accurate information available. This information is used to procure the treatments and medical supports patients need. Social workers develop a resource guide to contact people who authorize reimbursed services and advocate for patients to access the best and most affordable services possible.

It is an ethical challenge for social workers to repeatedly observe the fact that some options for health care treatment are available to people with better insurance or more income. After building relationships with patients, social workers often witness the disparity. Social workers frequently get to know patients and the families, particularly if the patient receives treatment for a chronic illness. The reality is insurance coverage is not equal for all and those who would benefit from expensive medical interventions frequently have to do without. The underinsured and the uninsured do not have the same health care options as people with more extensive coverage. While the national health care debate has long acknowledged the facts of disparity, it is difficult to understand that the inequities of health care coverage limit health care treatment. There are a variety of ways people in the United States receive health care coverage. The two most common and well-known public health insurance entitlement programs are Medicaid and Medicare. In addition, people also pay for health care coverage and treatment through private insurance companies and health savings accounts.

Although there are many types of insurance programs with a variety of criteria and regulations, many of them share common language and common function. Social workers function in a health care system that requires helping people find the coverage necessary to pay for medical treatment. Perhaps the patient is insured but does not have the coverage necessary for a treatment ordered by the physician, or the patient may be one of the millions who are uninsured or underinsured. Social workers in health care often know the most current criteria and coverage for the most common insurance programs.

A review of two common public reimbursement systems gives social workers the basics on how these plans are accessed and used and what services they cover. It is also helpful for social workers to know the common policies, terms, and concepts that are used in a health care setting that relate to insurance reimbursement or health care coverage. These terms and concepts include health savings accounts, diagnosis-related groups, managed care, privacy policies, and consent for treatment.

Public Health Insurance

In 1965, the Social Security Act passed in Congress and Titles XIII and XIX, Medicare and Medicaid, became the first national health security nets for some of the most vulnerable of the population: older adults, individuals with disabilities, and dependent children and mothers. These programs are not designed to meet all the needs of these populations, but the plans pay for some of the medical services that were not accessible previously (Moniz & Gorin, 2007).

The United States Department of Health and Human Services (HHS, 2008) manages these programs and attempts to inform consumers and health care providers regarding coverage and entitlement program changes through a number of ways, including a HHS website. Social workers become familiar with the basic eligibility criteria to participate in private and public insurance programs and if someone is eligible or covered by one of these types of insurance, social workers learn how to access the most up-to-date information and process to ensure insurance coverage.

Medicaid

Medicaid is an important form of health insurance because it attempts to offer coverage to some of the many living in poverty. It is a program that offers some health care benefits based primarily on the criteria of income. Medicaid is not offered to everyone; each person must meet the eligibility requirements as designed by the state where they reside (HHS, 2008).

Medicaid is particularly vital because it offers some of the only significant coverage of health costs associated with infants and children living in poverty (Kaiser Foundation, 2007; Moniz & Gorin, 2007). Since its creation, it has become the largest form of health insurance for some of the most vulnerable in the United States (DiNitto, 2000; Kaiser Foundation, 2007; Moniz & Gorin, 2007).

The Medicaid (or Medical Assistance) program was created in 1965 when President Lyndon B. Johnson signed into law Title XIX, an amendment to the Social Security Act. Medicaid became law as a cooperative venture between federal and state governments and is still jointly funded. In this joint venture, states furnish medical assistance based on eligibility criteria. Some of the criteria for Medicaid coverage are mandated by the federal government, but each state has some power to design additional services to best meet the needs of the state (Kaiser Foundation, 2007; Moniz & Gorin, 2007).

Individual states must determine the details regarding the services offered under Medicaid, but there are specific requirements each state must offer to certain groups of people to meet the requirements of federal law. The state determines exact coverage criteria for groups of people, but not everyone in each group are necessarily covered and coverage depends on the requirements of each state. The HHS website suggests that state eligibility requirements cover certain groups of people: (1) the categorically needy, (2) the medically needy, and (3) special groups (HHS, 2008).

The categorically needy include primarily the following groups: (1) some caregivers; (2) children ages 6–19 living at, or under, the federal poverty guideline; (3) families who meet the income and assets requirements of the Aid to Families with Dependent Children (AFDC) programs prior to July 1996; (4) persons receiving Supplemental Security Income (SSI) benefits, such as the aged, blind, or disabled; (5) pregnant women and children with family incomes below specified federal poverty levels; and (6) special protected groups including individuals or couples living in medical institutions (HHS, 2008).

Medically needy are defined as individuals who make too much money to be eligible for Medicaid, but have significant medical costs. Each state determines the eligibility for obtaining Medicaid under these circumstances, and in 2008, only 34 of the 50 states offered Medicaid based on medical needs rather than income. The medically needy may include people who are blind, older adults (over age 65), and other people not covered by health insurance.

Special groups may also be eligible, depending on the state, for options like Medicaid waivers for people with Medicaid managed care programs. For instance, some states may offer time-limited coverage for certain diagnoses such as women with breast or cervical cancers, or treatment for TB. Some state Medicaid programs offer work training programs for those with disabilities who lose their jobs (HHS, 2008).

Some of the most common services covered under Medicaid include physician services, hospital services (inpatient and outpatient), laboratory and x-ray services, certified pediatric nurse practitioners and nursing facilities for those 21 years and older, prevention screening, surgical or medical dental services, services related to a complicated pregnancy, and some home health care if the patient is eligible for nursing facility services (HHS, 2008; Kaiser Foundation, 2007). In addition to these mandated services, states can choose to offer additional services. This additional coverage is optional and varies depending on the state where the person receives Medicaid. For instance, some states offer forms of prescription coverage, rehabilitation, and hospice care. Other states elect to expand coverage to those who experience lack of health care due to socioeconomic conditions or live with severe and persistent forms of chronic illness (Kaiser Foundation, 2007).

A particularly important area of Medicaid is mandated by the federal government: to offer health insurance for medical services to children living in poverty. The states are required to offer the State Children's Health Insurance Program (SCHIP). This program is offered to the children of families who are not economically eligible for Medicaid, but do not have insurance coverage (HHS, 2008). Coverage and eligibility requirements vary from state to state. This Medicaid coverage for children is often the only link children living in poverty have to health care (HHS, 2008).

Medicaid policies for eligibility, services, and payment are exceptionally complex and vary considerably between the states in the amount, duration, or scope of service they provide. The result is that a person who is eligible for Medicaid in one state may find they are not eligible if they move to another state or may be surprised to find that medical or health-related services provided by one state are not necessarily covered under Medicaid in another state. This is very challenging for both patients and social workers who attempt to connect patients with their medical services after relocation. It is particularly difficult when the person moving lives with a significant mental or developmental disability, does not speak English, or does not understand the process for maintaining Medicaid (Kaiser Foundation, 2007).

Some states practice forms of managed care as a way to limit costs based on the average rate of intervention and reimbursement. Managed care is applied in a way that varies by state and may limit the amount of service people are eligible for, the amount of the copay, or the cost of prescription drugs. It can prove frustrating to health care systems, health care workers, social workers, and recipients of Medicaid trying to keep up-to-date and accurate about coverage issues. Although state discretion about eligibility is intended to allow for regional needs to be covered more accurately, it makes for complications in a society where people are mobile and it is common for people to move from state to state (Kaiser Foundation, 2007).

Medicaid is the nation's major source of coverage and financing for the long-term health services needed by people living with chronic illness. The Kaiser Foundation (2007) found that nearly 10 million Americans, especially older adults and people living with severe disabilities, need long-term care and depend on this public health program to cover health care needs. This is a significant problem in the Medicaid system because the program was originally designed to cover acute health care needs. Unfortunately, there are escalating health care needs for people living with one or more chronic illnesses in the United States. Managed care programs that limit services are not designed to meet the often lifelong needs for health care presenting in people with chronic illnesses. Currently, the forms of service needed to obtain long-term care for chronic illness are not covered by Medicaid. The prominence of the cost of health care for chronic illness is high. Continual increases in life expectancies means a growing number of people will require long-term care. The most effective ways to treat chronic illness are not funded by Medicaid.

This public insurance program continues to be the major source of insurance coverage for low-income individuals who need mental health services and substance abuse treatment. Many state Medicaid programs cover certain mental and behavioral health tests and services that are often not billable under other sources of health insurance.

The Medicaid program provides services to many of the most disenfranchised individuals in the United States and may offer the only means of access to the health care system (Kaiser Foundation, 2007). Each state develops its own eligibility standards; determines the type, amount, duration, and scope of services; sets the rate of payment for services; and administers its own program, but must meet the broad federal guidelines established by U.S. statutes, regulations, and policies (HHS, 2008; Kaiser Foundation, 2007).

Medicare

Medicare is the federal health insurance program created in 1965 for people age 65 and older regardless of income or medical history. Before its inception, half of older adults had no health care coverage and millions more had inadequate coverage (Kaiser Foundation, 2007; Moniz & Gorin, 2007; Moon, 2003). Medicare began to deliver services in 1966 as a social insurance program with the primary goal to deliver treatment for acute or short-term episodic illnesses for virtually all people over 65 and to younger people under special circumstances (DiNitto, 2000). In 1972, the program was expanded to include people under age 65 with permanent disabilities. Medicare now covers nearly 43 million Americans (Kaiser Foundation, 2007).

Medicare is different from Medicaid in many ways, but one significant difference is that Medicare is a federally determined program and the management of the program is consistent throughout the United States. This means that regardless of where a person eligible for Medicare moves within the states, they will continue to have the same coverage. This is a luxury people receiving Medicaid do not have.

Medicare is divided into two major areas of support: Part A and Part B. Most people age 65 and older are entitled to Medicare Part A if they or their spouse are eligible for Social Security payments and have made payroll tax contributions for 10 or more years (Kaiser Foundation, 2007). Part A of Medicare pays for inpatient hospitalization, skilled nursing care, and home health care. Part B of the Medicare program pays for outpatient care and physician visits. The program regulations are very specific about the medical providers that are authorized to receive payments, the number of office visits, and the type of service that is covered.

The Medicare program is not a perfect solution to provide health care insurance to older adults, but it does offer supplementary coverage. Medicare does not offer full coverage and the costs to patients are high if they cannot afford additional coverage. However, over the last few decades, attempts to change and improve the program persist. Medi-gap coverage—predetermined payments based on the diagnosis—and a number of managed care plans and payment schedules were used to attempt to make the cost and benefits of the Medicare program viable (Moon, 2003). In 2006, the Bush Administration implemented a prescription drug coverage program to people receiving Medicare. People were given choices to select prescription drug coverage plans that best met their individual needs. The goal was to reduce the high cost of medication to the patient, but regardless of the supplemental coverage, the cost of health care remains high, particularly for the number of services used and the use of technology required for the treatment of chronic illness (Moon, 2003).

As with all insurance programs, most are designed to cover the most common health issues of the day. Until recently, the most common health-related conditions were acute or episodic, so health care plans were designed to cover the expenses associated with these conditions. The dramatic shift in need to long-term care coverage means policies and programs must continue to remodel coverage to cover the expensive health care needs related to chronic illnesses. As with the Medicaid program, the dramatic increase in the diagnosis of chronic illnesses demands a very different way of health care delivery. This is particularly true for the Medicare system because Medicare provides health insurance to 83% of patients who live with at least one chronic illness (Anderson, 2005). Both the prevalence of chronic illness and the ever-growing number of people over age 65 means Medicare services are and will continue to be in high demand, particularly as the "baby-boomer" population ages (Anderson, 2005; Slivinske, Fitch, & Wingerson, 1998). In addition, the U.S. population continues to live longer, and longer life means people who receive Medicare benefits will use the insurance longer than in the past (Moon, 2003). There have been numerous amendments to the Medicare coverage and other public insurance programs in an attempt to make them more responsive to chronic illness needs.

Medicare plays a vital role in ensuring the health of beneficiaries by covering many important health care services. The inclusion of coverage for prescription drugs is a valuable benefit, but there are also gaps in coverage that include important and expensive treatment for dental, vision, and long-term care needs (Kaiser Foundation, 2007). Like most other insurance programs, Medicare continues to implement a managed care system to attempt to reduce costs, but structural changes continue to be called for by federal legislature.

Common Insurance-Related Terms and Policies

As in every profession, there are many acronyms, professional terms, and policies that are common and referred to regularly. There is an expectation that everyone working in the health care environment will know what these concepts are referring to. Many technical words and phrases are used in a medical setting; some are related to forms of medical treatment and testing and are unique to specific diseases and the work in a specialty health care environment (e.g., an HIV clinic). But some of the professional language relates to broader concepts and policies and is applicable to many forms of health care. Managed care, health savings accounts, diagnosis-related codes, and policies protecting patients' privacy and safety are only a few of the most common concepts that social workers in health care are required to understand.

Managed Care

Most professionals who deliver health care in the United States are familiar with the power of managed care over decision making. Managed care is primarily a system of controlling the use of health care services with the goal of saving money through efforts to stop unnecessary tests and procedures. Managed care dominates the environment of health care delivery and represents an attempt to provide integrated, efficient, and high-quality care for the lowest cost. However, this definition is very simplistic; in reality, managed care is very complex and at times presents an ethical challenge for social workers (Dudley & Luft, 2003; Dziegielewski, 2004; Strom-Gottried & Corcoran, 1998).

Before the 20th century, people needing health care in the United States paid for the care with cash or through a form of bartering. Health care functioned as other markets functioned: the provider established bills and was paid by the person receiving the services. Then, in the late 1920s, the third-party payment system began and caused a dramatic shift in how health care was financed. By the 1950s, third-party payments were the dominant way to pay for health care and an appealing alternative to the fee-for-service (DiNitto, 2000; Parker & Burke, 2005). The popularity of third-party payments was in large part due to the government imposition of wage and price controls following World War II. As the cost of health care insurance policies rose and the post-war wage controls took effect, employers found two benefits in offering health care insurance to employees. First, employers could offer fringe benefits to compete for employees during times of governmental wage controls. Second, the federal government allowed employers to deduct the cost of the health care fringe benefit from taxes (Parker & Burke, 2005).

Without limitations, the goal to treat patients as effectively and thoroughly as possible left little incentive to monitor costs of treatment. The cost of health care insurance continued to dramatically increase and by the 1960s and 1970s, insurance companies introduced a form of predetermined payment as an alternative to the patient having unlimited free choice over health care providers and treatment options. This was the beginning of controlling medical treatment decision making by the third-party payer.

✓ Managed care was instituted as a way to restrict choices and contain costs (Bodenheimer & Grumbach, 2005; Dudley & Luft, 2003). The philosophy of managed care is simple; patients are not asked to limit medical services because of inability to pay, but health providers (physicians, social workers, psychiatrists, hospitals, etc.) must limit health care services that have low value (Ginsburg, 2005). By 1995, the influence of managed care was significant, with approximately 73% of people insured through an employer insurance program participating in some form of managed care (Ginsburg, 2005). Originally the development of managed care was a reaction to the out-of-control costs of health care delivery and continues to wield significant influence in efforts to meet this goal (Galambos, 1999; Van Hook, Berkman, & Dunkle, 1996).

It was believed that managed care would result in better coordinated care between inpatient and outpatient care, and the incidence of chronic illness would decline. Managed care reduces cost and availability of procedures, but the concept is difficult and complicated to evaluate (Dudley & Luft, 2003). There are many managed care plans to chose from and some are multitiered with several options for coverage and choice of physician. For now, managed care offers a way to contain costs in the delivery of health care despite the challenges of evaluating data to prove that this form of management improves the quality and coordination of care.

Health Savings Account

Employers struggle with rising health care costs, both as a fringe benefit to employees and in the way it is required by the workers' compensation law. The cost to the employer is changing the discussion about who is responsible for the cost of health care insurance. Is the cost of health care the responsibility of the federal government, the employer, or the consumer? The shift of cost to the consumer is already occurring and it is accelerated by the spread of health savings accounts (HSAs). It is predicted that as many as 25% of privately insured U.S. citizens are likely to enroll in a health savings account, a high-deductible health care plan, by the year 2010.

A HSA is an insurance product, similar to an individual retirement account. Pretax dollars can be saved and medical claims are withdrawn from the balance. In an HSA, the plan is typically managed by a preferred-provider organization and the consumer is expected to pay a significant portion of their health care costs as a deductible, a minimum of $1,000 or more per year per individual, and $2,000 for a family. The goal is to shift part of the increase in health care costs to the consumer. In addition, advocates of HSAs believe that the financial incentives will turn patients into "activated consumers" who put pressure on the health care providers to deliver effective, efficient, and good-quality health care (Lee & Zapert, 2005; Robinson, 2005). It is hoped that as the consumer pays for more health care, healthier lifestyles and activities to prevent chronic illness and injury will increase.

Health saving accounts fit well within the "ownership society" supported by former President George W. Bush in his second inaugural address and his "State of the Union" address in 2006. The society of ownership suggested individuals take ownership of homes, businesses, retirement savings, and health care. This philosophy of financing health care is a radical shift from the collectivist style of insurance programs. The HSA model of insurance provides each individual with a personalized and individual bank of health care reimbursement money. The HSA is viewed as a consumer-directed health plan that offers an alternative to the way consumers pay for health expenses.

There are some significant potential problems with the use of HSAs, primarily because not all consumers are able to make informed decisions about health care. People are not equally experienced or skilled at saving money long term. In addition, not all are equipped to make decisions about the cost and quality of physicians, hospitals, and other forms of health services. The inequity of the personal skills and circumstances in relation to saving money is a threat to the success of HSAs as a way to prevent or effectively treat chronic illness (Lee & Zapert, 2005; Robinson, 2005).

Research (Lohr, Brook, & Kamberg, 1986) suggests that sharing the out-of-pocket costs with a patient does lower health care use, but resulted in a significant rise in high blood pressure and a decrease in the use of tests like Pap smears and mammograms. The fear is that not all patients are confident and capable enough to make decisions about health care procedures. The use of HSAs is still relatively new and there is need for more and contemporary data about the care people receive while using HSAs to finance health care.

HSAs are only one option the U.S. is examining to decrease the economic pressure of increasing health care costs. But relying on market forces alone to improve health care is hazardous. The use of HSAs to improve health care for the millions living in poverty and those who are working at minimum-wage jobs will call for more than relying on individuals to put money aside for health care. The most vulnerable populations do not have the economic capacity to support this form of savings (Lohr et al., 1986).

Diagnosis-Related Groups

Prior to the 1980s, most hospitals and physicians were reimbursed for the reasonable costs of treating a patient, but in 1983, during the Reagan Administration, the U.S. Congress enacted a controversial system named diagnosis-related groups (DRGs). This system altered the way Medicare and other insurance companies reimbursed hospitals and limited and reduced reimbursement to health care providers. The DRG system is similar to a menu of medical conditions organized into almost 500 different diagnosis-related groups. Each group is assigned a reimbursable cost to hospitals and physicians and sets a fixed rate, thus providing a way to control costs. The DRG system defines cost in advance and pays all approved health providers the same amount (DeNitto, 2000; Moniz & Gorin, 2007).

The DRG reimbursement system continues to develop based on a formula of the average cost of a Medicare patient by diagnosis. It sets a cost of care for a specific illness that pays every health provider the same amount, regardless of actual cost. Hospitals keep money that is not actually used for patient care, but are not reimbursed more if the treatment costs more. This system is very complex and there are deficiencies that raise serious questions about the fees that are charged and the reimbursement received, but the DRG system does provide Medicare a way to limit the cost of care for Medicare recipients. As a result, the services offered by a health care provider may be limited because the additional costs for tests may not be reimbursable using the standardized DRG fee (Moniz & Gorin, 2007; Torrens, 1993). For instance, if a patient is admitted for heart surgery and the recovery from surgery is slower than expected, delaying discharge, the reimbursement to the hospital is the same if the patient recovered quickly and went home from the hospital a day early. In other words, a health care provider gets paid the DRG rate for care regardless of the unique health needs of the patient. This form of reimbursement is an incentive for providers to monitor and encourage less expensive forms of care.

The change in the provision of health care was immediate. The predetermined reimbursement rate for patient care capped the charges allowed. The most expensive charges, such as the costs for inpatient care, were immediately reevaluated and inpatient discharge happened much sooner (DiNitto, 2000; Torrens, 1993). As a result, health providers, particularly rural or public urban hospitals, faced financial crises because of the empty hospital beds and the costs associated with the unpaid care for the poor and uninsured. The DRG system benefited some hospitals and health providers because of the choice not to participate in the Medicare program and instead elected to charge patients more than the fixed DRG reimbursement rate (Moniz & Gorin, 2007).

The Health Insurance Portability and Accountability Act

The issues of privacy and confidentiality are fundamental issues for social workers. In health environments, patients receive diagnoses that are private and may have consequences for many parts of their lives. Stigmatizing diseases, such as HIV/AIDS, are likely to affect patients in a variety of ways. Social workers are often a witness to the fear patients experience when there is a risk others will learn about the diagnosis or treatment (Kuczynski & Gibbs-Wahlberg, 2005). Social workers encourage patients to be informed about the people and organizations who access personal medical information. However, patients often feel very little control over their lives at the time of diagnosis, and the sense of empowerment to take control of the security of medical records is weakened.

Patients are commonly concerned about the privacy of medical information, and with good reason. Health care is a maze of people working together for the benefit of the patient, but many who access and work with patient information are behind the scenes and work in supportive and nondirect support services. When patients give personal information to a physician or other identified health provider, many believe the information is confidential, but the truth is, patient health care information is frequently shared with many working within the health care system.

The arrival of electronic computerized medical records raises an additional level of concern about the privacy of patient information. Based on the increased accessibility and ability of health providers to access records via computers, patient advocacy groups like the National Association of Social Workers (NASW) voiced concerns regarding patient confidentiality (NASW, 2003). The result of new communication technology and computerized record keeping quickly increased access to patient records, without sufficient limitations. Advocacy for safeguards resulted in the development of a federal policy named the Health Insurance Portability and Accountability Act (HIPAA) of 1996 (P.L. 104-191). This policy sets clear standards and criteria for providers of health care regarding the right to share patient information. While this policy is an important step in highlighting patients' privacy issues, the policy contains flaws and there remain significant problems with the confidentiality of medical records (Kuczynski & Gibbs-Wahlberg, 2005).

First, compliance with HIPAA requires billing and sharing information with other health care providers be done via the Internet. Despite the cost savings, medical information is potentially at risk by anyone who can gain access, regardless of intention. Security issues are immense and create the possibility of hackers or other unscrupulous organizations gaining access to patient information. Access to Medicare records stored online and breeches in security are a real possibility given occasional accounts of seemingly secure and confidential records of credit card companies and even the Veterans Administration reported as stolen, missing, or illegally accessed (Kuczynski & Gibbs-Wahlberg, 2005). In addition, HIPAA regulations are ineffective when unhindered access to patient records happens, regardless of the wishes of the patient. Ways to access records remain available and are continually developed for drug companies, marketing organizations, law enforcement, public health, or researchers to gain patient information.

Social workers remain strong advocates for patient confidentiality. Patients expect that private information is not accessible to others without signed consent, so it is vital to be aware of the policies of the health provider regarding patient information and inform patients about their rights regarding confidentiality. The introduction of the HIPAA policy brought much-needed attention to the issues of access to private medical information without patient permission and is a vital first step in developing a secure system for patients. Further evaluation of the effects of this policy regarding patient security will influence further policy development and bring incremental change (Kuczynski & Gibbs-Wahlberg, 2005).

The Future of Health Care Policy

Health care delivery in the United States faces a future of extraordinary challenge. The magnitude of this challenge is evident in a number of ways, but three areas that require immediate attention are (1) the extended longevity of the aging generation born soon after World War II; (2) the increasing cost, treatment, and support needs for people living with chronic illness; and (3) the increasing number of uninsured people who experience barriers to health care, including no health care coverage. These issues represent the key elements of the health care challenge. Improvements in health care require leadership and commitment to change and social workers can offer important contributions to this process (Mizrahi & Berger, 2001; Redmond, 2001).

The advancement in medicine and other areas of science is successful in increasing life expectancy for most populations in the United States. Despite increased life expectancy, the cost of providing health care to a population using the Medicare system and an increased risk of chronic illness diagnosis or complications for Medicare recipients places an unprecedented burden on an already taxed health system. The aging of the "baby-boomer" generation—children born soon after the end of World War II—is the largest population; over 77 million individuals are approaching retirement age. This population will put unprecedented pressure on the health care system. With this dramatic shift in the age of the national population comes increased need for understanding the conditions of aging, including caring for chronic illnesses, disease prevention, disease treatment, hospitalization, rehabilitation, home health care, residential care and hospice care, and caregiver support. The effort to meet these needs will require the creation, development, and financial coverage for treatment of long-term care interventions and maintenance of quality of life.

The United States health care system will need national policies that effectively manage, treat, and pay for chronic illness. Although challenging, there are many opportunities to design affordable forms of chronic illness treatment, prevention, and support. The newly retired population, living with chronic illnesses such as HIV/AIDS, asthma, hypertension, and heart disease, now experience increased quality and quantity of life with appropriate treatments, but the treatments are not available to all. Treatments for chronic illnesses are very expensive and often require lifelong care and support services. While chronic illnesses can demand time in inpatient settings, future policies must address the need for long-term residential and home care reimbursement. Caregivers frequently need support and insurance coverage for alternative care settings, such as home health care or other long-term care settings. These care settings continue to be underfinanced and this challenges the health of the patient and the caregivers (Lee & Rock, 2005). The United States must design a health care system that fiscally meets the contemporary needs of the population.

Finally, and of most alarm, the United States must tackle the unprecedented number of individuals who need health care. The U.S. health care system is in crisis and millions of individuals are uninsured (Kaiser Foundation, 2007; Redmond, 2001). In addition, tens of thousands have died as a result of absence or delays in receiving health care (Bartlett & Steele, 2004).

The future model for U.S. health care delivery, particularly for social workers, is going to change. Changes are necessary to grapple with outdated policies and procedures that act as barriers to the provision of quality health care by providers. The evidence of disparity in access to affordable health care is a visible symptom and exposes deep cracks in the national delivery of health care. Making improvements calls for a change in the professional roles and responsibilities of many health providers, including social workers.

Nationalization of the Health Care Debate

Every country in the world provides some system of health care and each system is unique. All systems have advantages and disadvantages, but no health care system is perfect. The system of health care in the United States is no exception. All countries, including the U.S., are influenced by cultures, politics, history, and current economic trends, but most countries make valid attempts to ensure health care to citizens. The U.S. legislature is under increasing public pressure to respond to the unmet health needs of individuals and to make health care more affordable and more accessible. There is undeniable evidence of significant problems in health care delivery and the problems cross socioeconomic status, gender, race, and age. People who experience a health care crisis while adequately insured is increasingly rare (Jost, 2004; LeBow, 2004).

Advocacy groups, lobbyists, politicians, and national legislative bodies discuss and propose possible ways to create alternative and affordable coverage solutions but none of the major attempts to redesign the health care system have successfully made it through the national legislative process. There is a movement of interest toward the creation of a nationalized health care system, but this concept will face a powerful challenge from the lobbyists associated with the health care industry in the United States (LeBow, 2004).

Nationalized health care is a system that ultimately relies on the federal government to pay for the delivery of health care. In exchange, the federal government sets the prices, wages, and rules about health commerce. Criteria for care are frequently based on citizenship and all citizens have similar access to care. Canada is one of many countries that offer a form of national health care.

BOX 3.1 • *Nationalized Health Care Considered in U.S. Legislation*

1. Great Depression
2. World War II
3. Truman Administration
4. Johnson Administration
5. Senate discussions of the 1970s
6. Clinton Administration

Source: Gladwell (2005); LeBow (2004).

A nationalized health care system will have flaws. The most common fears of U.S. citizens are expectations of long waits, a reduction in access to specialists or treatment options, and less skillful health care providers. However, the U.S. stands alone in managing the system of health care as a private and competitive business and will continue to struggle with the issues involved with this form of delivery (LeBow, 2004).

The United States has wrestled with challenges to change health care several times in the last century, but each time the legislation has failed. Despite several attempts to introduce some new type of universal health care, the efforts have been rejected at the last minute. There are six distinct times when a nationalized health care system rose to the top in legislative discussions, outlined in Box 3.1. All of these opportunities to change health care delivery through passage of new legislation were defeated due to political concerns and the powerful ideals that shape the foundation of U.S. policy (Barr, Lee, & Benjamin, 2003).

Barr et al. (2003) acknowledge that many factors influence the current state of health care: the evolution of science and technology, politics, cultural values, and other national priorities. However, the United States is reluctant to change health care policy because of four predominant variables that shape national values: (1) individualism, (2) federalism, (3) pluralism, and (4) incrementalism. These values are critical to understanding the challenges associated with social policy creation (Barr et al., 2003).

First, the "American character" was historically shaped by the ideal of individualism and advanced in images of the determined colonist and rugged pioneer. People capable of success, despite all odds and without assistance, are honored as heroes. There is national pride when someone accomplishes the "American Dream" despite barriers. The concept of asking for or receiving help, however, is rarely honored. Individualism is respected and is closely associated with privacy and the right to live without interference from others, including the federal government. U.S. citizens are perceived as valuing independence, freedom, and confidentiality (Barr et al., 2003).

A second variable, uniquely found in the United States, is national endorsement for the concept of federalism. Federalism is a concept that supports the belief that the federal, state, and local governments have unique and distinct roles in providing services to citizens. The U.S. government is formed to clearly divide the responsibilities between the state and federal governments (Barr et al., 2003; Jost, 2004). The federal government's priority is the nation's defense and the relationships with other countries, while state governments are expected to intervene in local issues such as education, emergency and police protection, and public health care. However, states are not financially equipped to provide health care. Historically the federal government has provided health care through programs like Medicaid and Medicare, but significant changes in the roles of state and federal government must be addressed if the federal government moves to legislating national health care policies (Barr et al., 2003).

Third, pluralism plays a significant role in the debate for new health care policy. Special interest groups that oppose health care policy reform complicate the process of change in the health care system. Numerous special interest groups wield power over the creation and passage of health care policy for a variety of reasons including a fear of higher taxes, loss of control over salaries and fees, and additional administrative burdens. There are political lobbies that represent a variety of perspectives about legislative change, such as the American Medical Association, the American Association of Retired Persons, the National Association of Social Workers, Physicians for a National Health Program, and many others. All groups exert influence over policy, yet the diversity of opinions makes it difficult to achieve broad consensus (Barr et al., 2003; Gorin, 1997; Jost, 2004).

Finally, the value of incrementalism is influential in the outcome of health care policy decisions (Barr et al., 2003). Incrementalism is a process of ongoing policy modification. For a policy to be enacted, it must go through many steps; the policy must be a priority in the legislative agenda, it must be perceived as successfully addressing the social problem, and there must be adequate political agreement. If any of these factors fail to be in place, the policy will not proceed through the legislative system. Issues of funding, strategic programming, staffing, and evaluation also affect the final results. All steps of policy development are influenced by political parties, current public issues and events, the strength of public opinion, and the process of lobbying by special interest groups (Barr et al., 2003).

The reluctance of U.S. politicians to unilaterally and radically alter health care delivery is complex. Citizens report recognition of the problems, believe change is necessary, and hope for greater equality of services, yet the lack of sweeping health care reform continues (Jost, 2004; Mongan & Lee, 2005). Are U.S. citizens really willing and ready to pay more for efficient health care? Perhaps as individuals—once secure about insurance coverage—continue to experience the loss of their coverage through unemployment, renegotiated contracts, or the reduction of benefits, the pressure to change current health care provision will be sufficient to result in change.

Summary

Health care is financed in a complicated variety of ways and social workers working in health care will be challenged to make sense of the changing rules and criteria necessary to advocate for patients. Attempts to contain costs will result in changes to professional roles, rationing systems like managed care, and new ways of organizing who provides supportive health services.

Millions of U.S. citizens, frequently older adults and those living in poverty, are without any access to health care. This is becoming true for more low- to middle-income families as businesses are forced to curtail expenses by drastically reducing or eliminating health care insurance coverage for employees. The cost of treatment and technology make some treatment interventions out of financial reach for millions of people in the United States. Social workers will face ethical challenges as witnesses to the lack of medical care for people in need.

The nation is debating the weaknesses of the current financial reimbursement system for health care and the nationalization of health care is discussed as one of several alternative options. But there is no magic answer to the health care woes in the United States. Given the values of individualism, federalism, pluralism, and incremental change, sweeping health care reform does not seem likely soon.

The future of health care will require social workers to continue to deliver and show evidence of holistic, cost-effective, evidence-based, and humane health care to patients and communities (Van Hook et al., 1996). In addition, social workers will be active in the political scene and bring firsthand accounts of the health care dilemmas faced by people living without health care to the discussion.

Critical Thinking Questions

1. Who are the stakeholders in the current health care system? Name them as they exist in micro, mezzo, and macro systems.

2. What are the main challenges to the current system of health care?

3. What are the challenges of mobility with Medicaid coverage? Compare Medicaid coverage between two states. What are the potential problems for patients who move and are dependent on Medicaid coverage?

4. How has the list of federally mandated services offered through Medicaid become outdated?

References

Anderson, G. F. (2005). Medicare and chronic conditions. *New England Journal of Medicine, 353*(3), 305–309.

Barr, D. A., Lee, P. R., & Benjamin, A. E. (2003). Health care and health care policy in a changing world. In P. R. Lee & C. L. Estes (Eds.), *The nation's health* (7th ed., pp. 199–212). Sudbury, MA: Jones & Bartlett.

Bartlett, D. L., & Steele, J. B. (2004). *Critical condition: How health care in America became big business and bad medicine.* New York: Doubleday.

Bodenheimer, T. S., & Grumbach, K. (2005). *Understanding health policy: A clinical approach* (4th ed.). New York: Lange Medical Books/McGraw-Hill.

DiNitto, D. M. (2000). *Social welfare: Politics and public policy* (5th ed.). Boston: Allyn & Bacon.

Dudley, R. A., & Luft, H. S. (2003). Managed care in transition. In P. R. Lee & C. L. Estes (Eds.), *The nation's health* (7th ed., pp. 379–389). Sudbury, MA: Jones & Bartlett.

Dziegielewski, S. F. (2004). *The changing face of health care social work; Professional practice in managed behavioral healthcare* (2nd ed.). New York: Springer.

Galambos, C. (1999). Resolving ethical conflicts in a managed health care environment. *Health and Social Work, 24*(3), 191–198.

Ginsburg, P. B. (2005). Competition in health care: Its evolution over the past decade. *Health Affairs, 24*(6), 1512–1523.

Gladwell, M. (2005, August 29). The moral-hazard myth: The bad idea behind our failed health-care system. *The New Yorker,* pp. 44–49.

Gorin, S. (1997). Universal health care coverage in the United States: Barriers, prospects, and implications. *Health and Social Work, 22*(3), 223–231.

Health Insurance Portability and Accountability Act [HIPPA] of 1996, P.L. 104-191, 119 Stat. 1936.

Jost, T. S. (2004). Why can't we do what they do? National health reform abroad. *The Journal of Law, Medicine, and Ethics, 32*(3), 433–442.

Kaiser Family Foundation. (2007, January). Key facts: Race, ethnicity and medical care. Retrieved September 4, 2008, from http://www.kff.org/minorityhealth/6069.cfm.

Kuczynski, K., & Gibbs-Wahlberg, P. (2005). HIPPA the health care hippo: Despite the rhetoric, is privacy still an issue? *Social Work, 50*(3), 283–288.

LeBow, R. H. (2004). *Health care meltdown: Confronting the myths and fixing our failing system.* Chambersburg, PA: Hood.

Lee, J. S., & Rock, B. D. (2005). Challenges in the new prospective payment system: Action steps for social work in home health care. *Health and Social Work, 30*(1), 48–55. Retrieved August 31, 2007, from ProQuest Medical Library database. (Document ID: 800172751)

Lee, T. H., & Zapert, K. (2005). Do high-deductible health plans threaten quality of care? *New England Journal of Medicine, 353*(12), 1202–1204.

Lohr, K. N., & Brook, R. H., & Kamberg, C. J. (1986). Use of medical care in the Rand Health Insurance experiment: Diagnosis and service-specific analyses in a randomized controlled trial. *Medical Care, 24,* S1–S87.

Mizrahi, T., & Berger, C. S. (2001). "Effect of a changing health care environment on social work leaders" Obstacles and opportunities in hospital social work. *Social Work, 46*(2), 179–182.

Moniz, C., & Gorin, S. (2007). *Health and health care policy* (2nd ed.). Boston: Allyn & Bacon.

Moon, M. (2003). Medicare. In P. R. Lee & C. L. Estes (Eds.), *The nation's health* (7th ed., pp. 401–408). Sudbury, MA: Jones & Bartlett.

Mongan, J. J., & Lee, T. H. (2005). Do we really want broad access to health care? *New England Journal of Medicine, 352*(12), 1260–1265.

National Association of Social Workers (NASW). (2003). *Social work speaks: National Association of Social Workers policy statements, 2003–2006.* Washington, DC: NASW Press.

Parker, F. R., & Burke, L. (2005). Employers, ethics, and managed care. *Employees Benefit Plan Review, 59*(9), 7–12.

Redmond, H. (2001). The health care crisis in the United States: A call to action. *Health and Social Work, 26*(1), 54–57.

Robinson, J. C. (2005). Health savings accounts: The ownership society in health care. *New England Journal of Medicine, 353*(12), 1199–1202.

Slivinske, L. R., Fitch, V. L., & Wingerson, N. W. (1998). The effect of functional disability on service utilization: Implications for long-term care. *Health and Social Work, 23*(3), 175–186.

Strom-Gottfried, K., & Corcoran, K. (1998). Confronting ethical dilemmas in managed care: Guidelines for students and faculty. *Journal of Social Work Education, 32*(1), 109–119.

Torrens, P. R. (1993). Historical evolution and overview of health services in the United States. In S. J. Williams & P. R. Torrens (Eds.), *Introduction to health services* (4th ed., pp. 3–28). Albany, NY: Delmar.

United States Department of Health and Human Services (HHS). (2008). *Centers of Medicaid and Medicare services.* Retrieved September 3, 2008, from http://www.cms.hhs.gov/

Van Hook, M. P., Berkman, B., & Dunkle, R. (1996). Assessment tools for general health care settings: PRIME-MD, OARS, and SF-36. *Health and Social Work, 21*(3), 230–234.

4

Health Care: A Field of Practice

Teaching and Learning Goals

- Understand the challenges of acute and alternative inpatient care from the client's perspective
- Distinguish between the multiple roles of social workers in health care and how they impact patient care
- Recognize the multiple settings of social workers in health care and the impact on patient health care
- Understand the importance of the social work role in health care

Social work is a very attractive profession for many reasons, but perhaps one of the most appealing aspects of the profession is that social workers are employed in many different types of environments or fields of practice. Health care is considered one field of social work practice, but within health care there exists a variety of settings. Social workers in this field work with individuals, families, groups, communities, and governmental and global systems. Social workers also engage in different roles within the health care system.

In every field of practice social workers must be ready to engage with clients using an integration of professional skills. Social workers provide access to resources and clear communication and documentation for referral. The social worker ensures client and patient systems obtain the necessary support and engages in evaluation and research to improve and revise services. Participation in professional practice leads to critical thinking regarding social work interventions and outcomes, and contributes to the professional literature and the development of evidence-supported practice.

Health care demands interaction and partnership with people who need assistance due to health-related needs. This is potentially complicated and demands social workers practice within a variety of roles and possess a variety of professional skills. The relationship between the social worker and the patient is developed to support the strengths and goals of the patient and designed to maintain the patient's highest quality of living within those goals. The interests of families, groups, and organizations in health care influence an individual's condition so social workers benefit by familiarity with social policies, the financing of social policies, and the resources available to patients. Social workers speak and act as advocates for the patient while maintaining respectful and professional relationships within interdisciplinary teams (Volland, 1996). Social workers strive to keep a balance between the primary commitments to the patient's physical health, like the rest of the staff at a medical setting, and working to ensure health aspects in all areas of patient functioning. The opportunities in health care are growing for social workers. With the aging population growing globally (World Health Organization [WHO], n.d.), the need for more health care services continues to grow.

Social Work and Health Care

Social work is a profession dedicated to a unifying and professional code of ethics and to a common goal to promote social justice. However, because the profession works within multiple environments and fields of practice, and requires interactions with a variety of populations using uncommon professional skills, colleagues are frequently unclear about what social workers do.

Scenario 4:1_____

Life can become complicated very quickly when someone needs health care. The following scenario is about a man named John beginning an interaction with the health care system. As you read about him, think about the issues facing this new patient and his family. Ask yourself the following questions: (1) What does this patient need? Consider the physical, emotional, social, and spiritual resources this situation may require. (2) What does this patient's wife and family need? Consider the physical, emotional, social, and spiritual resources the caregivers may require.

John is an 84-year-old man. He has been healthy his entire life and lives independently and quietly with his wife in a condo; they visit their children, play cards, attend church, and take relaxing vacations. The couple is financially comfortable; they have Medicare and good supplemental health insurance. John and his wife have no chronic illnesses. John takes a multivitamin every morning, but follows no special diet. He feels great, and brags that he has never been hospitalized. His father lived to be 101 years old.

One day John notices some weakness on one side of his body. He meets with his primary care doctor and after a brain scan it is discovered he has a brain tumor. The primary doctor tells John the test results show a brain tumor that resembles cancer and it may mean that John has cancer other places in his body. He is also informed that he can no longer drive because he is at increased risk of having a seizure due to tumor pressure on his brain. John's 85-year-old wife watches on as he hands the car keys to their adult daughter and his role as driver for the couple ends, after 62 years.

John is scheduled the next day for an X-ray and it is discovered that he also has a suspicious mass in his lung. The primary doctor prescribes John steroids to attempt to reduce the swelling around the brain and refers John to a pulmonary doctor for the lung mass. The next day, John meets with the pulmonary physician and learns the mass is an advanced stage of cancer and that John's prognosis in approximately 3–6 months.

The pulmonary physician refers John to a radiologist and 2 days later, John is informed that radiation to the brain tumor could enhance his quality and quantity of life. John meets with the specialist and is fitted for a special mask to protect his head from the beam of radiation scattering to parts of the brain other than the tumor. His wife brings him to his radiation treatment every morning. He must also go to appointments for bloodwork. In addition, blood test results inform the primary doctor that John's blood sugar level has increased to dangerous levels due to the steroids and he must begin to take insulin. John and his wife spend a great deal of time every morning testing John's blood sugar and injecting the correct amount of insulin.

One morning John has trouble standing and his wife calls an ambulance. At the hospital it is discovered that the steroids have interfered with John's immune system and the result is the development of a staff infection around his artificial knee joint. An orthopedic specialist is called in to consult and performs surgery to clean out the infection. The physician begins John on an IV antibiotic through a permanent port in John's arm. When John is discharged he must continue taking an hour of IV antibiotics every day by hooking the medication bag to the port.

John, his wife, and their children and their families are experiencing a radical and frightening change in their lives. The once quiet existence John and his wife enjoyed is gone and the family unit thinks and acts on nothing but John's health crisis. John's life, and the lives of those who support him, becomes a schedule of appointments. He is dependent on his wife for driving and aches as he sees her discomfort negotiating the car across a town that is busy with street repair and detours. He teaches himself how to test his sugar, give himself insulin, and affix his antibiotic to his needle port. John, at 84, must learn all of these tasks, with no medical experience and a sixth-grade education. He must accomplish all of this while dealing with the fact that he has a terminal illness and has limited time to live. Overnight, his wife becomes the primary caretaker of her once healthy husband and has little time to feel the pain of the loss she knows is looming. Every day there is a loss of some sort—loss of energy, loss of appetite, loss of conversation, loss of independence, and other irreversible changes. While working hard to follow directions and live "normally," there is little time or emotional energy to talk about preparing for the end of John's life, despite the daily reminders of the nearness of this event.

These types of stories are difficult for some to comprehend, particularly if experience with illness and disease is limited, but this case is not an unusual account nor is it about a complicated inpatient (hospital) case. This story is about someone who is diagnosed with a chronic illness and remains living independently in his home. This type of scenario is repeated innumerable times throughout the world on a daily basis, and often with families that have less social and financial resources than John and his family.

Reread John's story. He comes and goes from appointments with a minimum of five physicians as well as appointments for blood tests and radiation treatments. No one but John and his wife design the complex schedule or take on the responsibility of putting all of the pieces together, not medically, and certainly not emotionally. There are many points within John's story where a social worker could offer support. Imagine you are the social worker in John's life.

Social Work Roles

During undergraduate and graduate social work education, social work students develop many functional roles, competencies, and related practice skills. Adept at multitasking, social workers rarely practice using a single role; instead, a variety of roles function simultaneously and intersect in a number of ways. Arguably, the common roles for all social workers, regardless of their field of practice, include advocate, communicator, mediator, researcher, educator, evaluator, and recorder.

Each role represents skills for interacting with the patient, family, community, policy, or agency and social workers in health care are academically and professionally trained to practice these roles. The circumstances facing a social worker in health care vary widely and each role involves methods that are necessary in many different kinds of situations. Social workers commonly combine the most useful roles and adjust the priority of roles as conditions demand. All functions intersect and overlap at times and under certain circumstances, but within a patient relationship, a social worker provides continuous quality service, crafted uniquely to the patient's personal needs.

Consider the case study regarding the physical, emotional, and social needs of John and his family; think about how each of these social roles is necessary at different times and with a different priority in the health care experience. Having a social worker respond to patients' needs within these roles offers individuals in crisis ways to improve experience with disease and ultimately improve the quality of life.

Advocate

Sometimes the emotional and social needs of the patient and caregivers get lost in a health care setting. The complex care delivery system of physicians, specialists, and medical environments is often incapable of putting all of the details of care together in a united plan

BOX 4.1 • *Most Common Roles for Social Workers*

Advocate	Communicator
Mediator	Researcher
Evaluator	Recorder
Consultant	Counselor
Educator	Supervisor
Team builder	Assessor
Facilitator	Policymaker
Director	Navigator

that recognizes the individual experiencing the care. Frequently patients are treated in a variety of medical settings and medical specialists practice as experts in a single part of the patient's medical care.

Advocacy occurs when a social worker supports, encourages, and promotes the ideas and goals of the patient, particularly when the goals of the patient are at odds with the routine treatment procedures of the health care system (DuBois & Krogsrud Miley, 2005). Although there are many who follow similar paths of assessment, referral, and treatment for illness and disease, individuals and caregivers may present unique circumstances that call for alterations in care. When the patient or caregivers are unable to speak to people in power in a convincing or authoritative manner to make their needs known, or if they are treated in a dismissive way, social workers promote the need to find a solution (Boyle, Hull, Mather, Smith, & Farley, 2006).

The social worker provides patients with alternative ways to approach the often impersonal bureaucracy of health care and lends resources, connections, and relationships to the patient's attempt to find satisfaction. Advocacy does not always result in the outcome desired by the patient, but the patient is respected when an attempt to be heard is taken seriously and acted upon. Social workers always advocate on behalf of the patient, sometimes because the patient asks them to, but sometimes because the social worker recognizes the patient is lacking an ingredient in care that is necessary to ensure quality.

Social workers remember that they are not the sole advocate for quality patient care. Many individuals, from many disciplines, recognize the need to attend to the individual's needs. The health care team works diligently with colleagues in health care to ensure that working together results in providing the best physical, emotional, and social care possible for every patient and caregiver.

Communicator

If someone has never had a complicated illness requiring treatment or never served as a support person for someone seeing multiple physicians, it may be a surprise to learn that the responsibility for good communication between health providers ultimately rests with the patient. It is common for people to believe that the primary doctor, the one that has the historical relationship with the patient, is the doctor who will build a "complete record" of interoffice care and communication. Unfortunately, this is not the case. Once a patient is referred to a second physician, a new medical record begins. Often the physician's office encourages the patient to sign releases of information so that the new physician specialist can communicate with the referring doctor, but this communication often only takes place when specific information is requested. In other words, the physicians can communicate with each other, but most likely will not unless they believe there is a significant clinical reason.

The training of medical personnel is to treat and, if possible, cure disease and injury. However, in the face of many professionals, each addressing smaller parts of a larger health problem, the patient is at risk of becoming subdivided. Social and emotional tasks enmeshed within the process and progress of chronic illness—such as loss, grief, end-of-life planning, and emotional support—do not fall under the specialty of any of the medical professions. However, attention to social and emotional needs is essential to obtain quality patient health care.

Communication is vital during medical interventions, yet it is so difficult to achieve, particularly because patients vary in skill levels of sophistication to navigate within medical systems. Experienced patients and caregivers may be able to find a way for information regarding health care to flow to and from all health care providers, however, even when this occurs, it is often while the caregivers are attempting to deal with personal, emotional, social, and physical needs.

Many cultures revere physicians as educated leaders within the community and would never disrespect a physician by questioning medical decisions. Unfortunately, many assume all health professionals are working together and communicate regularly. When it becomes obvious this is not occurring, the patient may feel helpless and confused about how to influence the communication in a way that respects the health professionals.

Social workers are in a perfect position to assist in the communication between medical care providers and to ensure all have a complete and accurate picture of patients' health. If a social worker from a primary physician office, hospital, or a home health care agency is assigned to manage the flow of communication between physicians and patient, the patient is assured of not only the flow of medical information, but also attention to the physical, social, and emotional needs of the patient and caregivers.

Mediator

It is quite normal for competent health providers to disagree over the best intervention for effective treatment, but consider how frightening it is when the patient hears criticism about future health providers. When there is disagreement between physicians over medical treatment options, patients are not sure what to do. Indeed, when there is any conflict regarding treatments, it is often alarming and upsetting for a patient and the caregivers because it indicates that even the professional experts do not know the "right" answer. The following case scenario is an example of how a patient, caregivers, and the social worker work together to find a solution.

Scenario 4:2

Frank is a 43-year-old man who drives a food delivery truck across the United States. He is hospitalized with a brain tumor. When he was diagnosed with the tumor 3 days ago, he also learned he has acquired immunodeficiency syndrome (AIDS). The only people who know about his AIDS diagnosis are his two brothers and their wives. Frank is a simple man, unmarried and dependent on his aging parents for a place to call home. His parents still live on the family farm where Frank grew up.

The infectious disease doctor who discovered the AIDS diagnosis informs the family that the brain tumor is a result of Frank's badly damaged immune system. This physician is an expert in the treatment of AIDS and states that Frank has had AIDS for many years and has most likely been exposed to multiple reinfections due to his high-risk sexual behaviors. This physician tells Frank and his family that even with treatment for the tumor, Frank's prognosis is very poor, likely 3–6 months. He recommends palliative care and a referral to hospice.

The oncologist consulted about Frank's brain tumor is well known and is considered aggressive when it comes to cancer treatment. He suggests that Frank undergo surgery and radiation and believes his treatment will successfully eradicate the cancerous tumor and offer some extended quantity of life. Both physicians are insistent that their treatment options are best for Frank, despite radically opposing views.

The caregivers are confused, but reluctant to communicate their frustration to the physicians. Issues that influence treatment decisions are often far more complex for patients than physical survival. Facing serious dilemmas, patient and caregivers need a process to evaluate their goals for a treatment plan they can agree to. The family caregivers ask for someone to talk to and are referred to a social worker. With the help of a social worker, the family plays out the result of each treatment scenario.

In the context of nonpressured and empathetic conversation, a social worker interviews the patient and family for more information about their unique circumstances. If Frank proceeds with the surgery and treatment of the brain tumor, will the likelihood of the revealing AIDS diagnosis to Frank's 85-year-old parents increase? His parents are politically and religiously conservative, and know nothing about Frank's risk behaviors. Frank vigorously wants to protect his parents from the shocking news of an AIDS diagnosis, but Frank's brothers do not want Frank to believe he must make his treatment choices based on protecting their parents.

Will surgery and radiation to his cancerous brain tumor extend Frank's life given the AIDS diagnosis? Is a terminal cancer diagnosis more emotionally and socially tolerable for both Frank and his parents than an AIDS diagnosis? What are your personal values about this patient's circumstances? Do your personal values interfere with the integrity of your relationship with Frank or his family?

As the scenario of Frank indicates, social workers assist patients and caregivers to examine their options and choose one that best meets the patient's health needs. The social worker encourages, teaches, and practices with the family on how they can best inform the physicians of their choice. In addition, the social worker assists the patient and family to come to agreement, empowering them to inform the physicians of their decision (DuBois & Krogsrud Miley, 2005). Through a mediation process, the patient communicates his desire for obtaining what he considers the best quality of life. A social worker helps to amplify the patient's emotional and social needs over stressful discussions about medical treatment decisions.

Researcher

Research in social work is recognized as a major contributor to informing the profession and other professionals about the nature of social work. Research is an ethical, organized, and scientific way of examining the profession and is vital in all areas of social work. Some of the most common areas of research include examination of methods, interventions, the role of diversity, barriers to interventions, and issues of engagement. It is the responsibility of social workers to share professional experiences, observations, and challenges in an objective manner so the profession's knowledge base continues to develop and grow (Wade & Neuman, 2007). Research into the practice of social work in health care includes research that promotes best practice interventions to vulnerable populations (Proctor, 2003). Social workers rely on confirmed ways of meeting patient needs but also develop and use new and creative ways to intervene on behalf of patients. In absence of published reliable research, particularly in the new and developing field of social work and medicine and medical treatments, the results of professional social work and evidence of successful efforts are urgently needed.

It is very difficult, however, for a social worker in health care, after a full day of work, to attend to and participate in research studies. Research is potentially a complicated and time-consuming process. To develop a research study anywhere, but particularly within a hospital, the social worker must receive approval from the hospital's Internal Review Board (IRB). This group of professional health care providers meets to assess all research proposals to ensure the patient is at no risk of harm, is fully informed, and participates voluntarily. Ethical research is demanded in all social work fields of practice and hospitals commonly use an IRB as the formal process for review of each proposal, regardless of discipline. After approval from the IRB, the social worker must collect data and record, analyze, interpret, and write up the results of the data. Research is so time-consuming that many hospitals have research departments and staff who participate in health and medical research full time. It is likely social workers hired in a health care setting will not see research listed as a component of the job description.

An alternative approach to the development of research and evaluation projects is collaboration. Academic settings and other research bodies may have access to resources to assist in writing proposals and grants, and offer assistance in the collection and recording of data. The same creative thinking social workers develop to work with patients must be used to think of creative ways to document and share the results of the work they are doing. The results of research promote knowledge and the use of proven outcomes in social work and health care practice (Wade & Neuman, 2007).

Look for ways to incorporate evaluation and assessment into some of the simple and routine patient interactions that already exist within the health care setting. Perhaps an IRB-approved patient survey becomes part of the patient intake process and the information from the survey collects data. Perhaps a survey is set up in a way to not only collect the necessary data, but it is designed to be easily entered into a computer program that automatically analyzes the data. These simple examples of data collection potentially require little time.

Social workers in health care also contribute to knowledge by the documentation of scenarios from day-to-day experiences and sharing these interactions within social work and with other medical professionals. Social workers know that patients engaged in the health care system experience physical, emotional, and social responses. The profession of social work and patient needs are advanced when these experiences are shared, particularly within a system that frequently subdivides patients into specialty areas. Without professional research, social workers can miss understanding the unique complications associated with the provision of holistic health care.

Rarely is a patient in a health care setting in need of assistance in only one area (Proctor, 2003). Patients experience a variety of complications that Klinkman (1997) calls the phenomenon of "competing demands." Patients frequently experience multiple problems that can be severe and complex and as a result, social workers, working within a variety of professional roles and skills, often deliver far more than one intervention. Research is needed that clarifies the nature, extent, and consequences of competing demands from the perspective of the patient, caregivers, social workers, and the health care setting (Proctor, 2003).

Evaluator

If social workers are truly interested in providing the best possible services to patients and caregivers, they must be certain that what they are doing is really helpful. This is far more than relying on intuition or the positive feedback of one patient. Evaluation allows social workers to examine the interventions used with a discriminating eye. First, evaluation clarifies exactly what is being done. Can the social worker reliably describe an intervention? Do other social workers in the same setting offer the same services under the same conditions? Second, the social worker can examine the consistency of the intervention. Do the social workers in the same setting offer the same services to everyone? How are services the same or different? Why? Answering these kinds of questions help social workers understand the ramifications and quality of interventions. Evaluation is an important step in taking social work from a subjective response to a need, to a deliberate evidence-supported intervention.

It is the responsibility of social workers to maintain quality social work services in the health care setting (Wade & Neuman, 2007). Professional investment in quality social services to patients requires social workers to ask questions about the provision of services and develop continually improving patient care. There are a number of ways to accomplish these goals, but the most basic steps include the evaluation of referral sources, opportunities for patients to complete satisfaction surveys about social work interventions, and requests for interdisciplinary team members to evaluate social work contributions to the team. The evaluation of social work services is best when it is objective, ongoing, and leads to evidence of need for improvement. When a particular evaluation of a service component continues to provide positive results, develop an evaluation process for an alternative area of social work service. Evaluation is vital to the development of the profession, provision of quality patient care, and to providing evidence of professional contributions to compassionate and cost-effective health care.

Recorder

Most social workers would prefer to spend time on tasks other than paperwork, but most would admit there are several very important reasons why social workers need to keep accurate and consistent records. Documentation is important because it is a factual representation of something that has occurred. It serves as evidence and preserves the history of patient needs, process, and progress. When memory fails, or disputes over the facts arise, or when multiple health care providers are involved in the care of the patient, the patient record stands as the formal documentation of events. While these records are important in all day-to-day interactions, they increase in importance when there is an emergency. Records contain patients' information about their wishes regarding treatment and who they want to speak for them in case they cannot speak for themselves. Record keeping facilitates communication between members of the health care team.

Computerized medical records are an incredible luxury in the documentation of patient care and offer access of information to the medical staff involved in patient care. Not all health care settings have this feature of record keeping and retrieval available. Computerization has forever changed documentation and eventually most paper medical records will be replaced. Online records store and share records in ways that are impossible with paper and pen and offer some security and sharing options unavailable to handwritten records. Regardless of the form of record keeping, with any documentation of private matters, there are risks to confidentiality in all record keeping (Nicholas et al., 2007).

It is legally required that patients must agree to and give written consent for their medical records to be shared (Nicholas et al., 2007). Records contain many pieces of personal information and vary on the structure of the record to accommodate the needs of the health setting. Most medical charts, or records, hold demographic information, results of medical or psychosocial tests, copies of official correspondence such as patient-signed release of information forms, and progress notes that document patient and collegial interactions.

Meticulous record keeping is also important for reimbursement. All insurance companies demand records of treatment and will not reimburse without this documentation. If there is no record of service, there is absence of proof that the service took place. In addition, record keeping is one of the safest and most accurate ways to communicate and evaluate service delivery. All accreditation bodies, of both medical and social work services, demand inspection of medical records as a way to assess the timing, type, and quality of services provided to patients.

Educator

Social workers in health care are teachers because education is a primary need for most patients when they are confronted with a new diagnosis. A new diagnosis guarantees many questions as the patient and caregivers attempt to navigate through an unfamiliar and often intimidating health care system. Simple questions include inquiry about hours of operation, where to park, and where the family can wait. Other questions seek to learn about the disease, the side effects of medical treatment, and the possible psychological and social effects of disease. Patiently offering time to answer questions and educate patients is a vital part of the patient empowerment process (DuBois & Krugsrud Miley, 2005).

There are many ways a social worker can assist with patient education. Social workers refer some patients to the many high-quality medical websites available to the public. The helpfulness of these sites cannot be overstated. Most outpatient clinics, physician offices, and hospitals face reductions in the time allotted for personal patient education, so the ability of patients to go online to find out the information they desire is very helpful. One caveat in the use of online education is the fact that not all websites offering medical education are of equal value or reliability. Some sites represent the national experts and organizations that direct medical studies in certain areas, other sites may represent positions of medical supply or drug industries, and some are operated by well-intentioned but misinformed people experiencing the same diagnosis. Regardless of the site, patients are empowered when informed and educated about how to evaluate the sources of information available on medical websites.

Patients benefit by being reminded that they are unique. A single scenario of diagnosis and treatment that is true for one person does not mean it is true for everyone. There are too many variables to consider in the course of health and disease to tell patients exactly what will happen to them. It is important for social workers to remind patients they live with health and disease in a unique and distinct way. This is part of promoting a strengths perspective that recognizes each patient has the physical, psychological, and social strengths that uniquely equip them to deal with life's events.

Social workers also educate colleagues on interdisciplinary teams about the nonmedical needs of the patient (Sheafor & Horejsi, 2006). Social workers, by virtue of not having a medical degree, often become a confidant, someone the patient can trust to provide an unbiased report of future needs and to report the medical situation in understandable nonmedical language. This is an incredible responsibility for the social worker and comes with a word of caution. Social workers must be clear in their communications with patients and never overestimate their knowledge of medical issues. Ethical boundaries demand social workers to be clear with patients and caregivers about the limitations of professional competency. There are many important facts social workers learn about disease, diagnosis, treatment, medications, clinical trials, and outcomes of disease that enhance the care of patients. Social workers grow in competence and confidence in areas of disease-related processes and procedures, but social workers are not free to act as though they are the medical experts.

How can social workers integrate the professional medical knowledge and the supportive educational role with patients without overstepping competency boundaries? Consider ethical issues such as boundaries and patient safety. How can social workers team with experts in medical care to ensure patients receive the most accurate and appropriate information about their medical condition? In some cases the best assistance to patients is to help them locate information from the best person to answer the questions, especially when it is outside the social work area of expertise.

Social workers in health care are a valuable resource for training physicians. This is a very positive addition to medical education and offers an opportunity for social workers to emphasize the complexity of patient care by sharing assessments that include the biopsychosocial perspective. Patient narratives shared by social workers sensitize medical personnel to the complexities of psychological and social patient issues.

Health Care Settings

Social workers are often perceived as "guests" within the health care system because they are not trained to provide biomedical services or treatment, but because patients experience social and emotional needs as well, social workers are a valuable addition to the health care team. The state of health care in the United States promotes the priority goal of health systems controlling costs. Social work, like other health care professions, must be able to justify the need for this professional role in patient care.

There are similarities in roles between social work and other health-related professions that occasionally overlap because all health care professions share a common goal: to provide compassionate and quality health care. But every discipline trains professionals differently and although specific tasks can be accomplished by multiple disciplines, each discipline brings a different philosophy of engagement and interaction to patient care (Dziegielewski, 2004). Social workers are professionally trained to provide services that are based on patient empowerment and the strengths perspective. Professional education, the NASW Code of Ethics, state licensing, and requirements for ongoing continued education give social workers a unique psychosocial perspective that supports holistic patient care. While social workers are clear about the distinctive aspects of their contributions to patient care, the increase in the number of health care profession specialties demands social workers emphasize the practice skills unique to social work that include relationships within the community and referral agencies, mental health and emotional crises assessments, support for patient self-determination, and linking the patient to strength-based systems through case management and caregiver support (Cowles, 2003; Holliman, Dziegielewski, & Teare, 2003; Schneiderman, Waugaman, & Flynn, 2008).

BOX 4.2 • *Social Workers' Skills in Health Care*

1. Take treatment goals and develop the steps or objectives to secure those goals
2. Monitor available patient resources
3. Set up appointments
4. Meet with families
5. Follow up on patients during and after hospitalizations
6. Set up rehabilitation services for patients
7. Assist patients in gathering information
8. Support and encourage patients and their families
9. Organize transport for patients
10. Enhance the patients' opinions of their medical services through personal attention

Health is a universal concern and most of us need health care at some point in our lives. Social workers offer services that help people understand health care options and to live the best quality of life possible given the unique situation, environment, and resources. While health care social workers work within a wide variety of health care settings, all social work roles and accompanying skills are practiced in each setting. In addition, social workers develop specialized knowledge about the health care setting where they are employed. The development of this specialized knowledge is important to better understand the process of health care delivery from both the patient's perspective, the perspective of their caregivers, and from the perspective of the health care setting.

Social workers must adapt to the procedures, forms, and processes that each health setting demands. They will learn the medical jargon and acronyms associated with disease, treatment, tests, and outcomes associated with patient care. This is helpful to the patient and caregivers and necessary to be a vital, respected, and contributing member of the health care team. However, critical thinking about how and why things work or do not work in patient care is always useful in finding ways to advocate for improvements. Social workers assess and evaluate system functioning and are in a good position to develop, support, and improve care through changes that result in enhanced quality for patients and caregivers.

Brief descriptions of social work and health care settings are helpful to understand the vast array of areas that employ social workers. Each setting has unique features, so the role or the combination of roles engaged in by the social worker will vary. Health care settings that employ social workers change as funding, needs, and policy change; however, typically social workers are employed in either inpatient care settings or outpatient care settings.

Inpatient Care

The word *inpatient* is commonly used to describe the location of where a patient receives treatment. Patients who are given care while residing in a health care facility are said to be receiving inpatient care. Frequently this term is used to describe the care given while staying in a hospital, but technically, it is also appropriate to refer to stays in nursing homes, surgical centers, subacute rehabilitation centers, nursing home facilities, hospice centers, and numerous other types of residential health care settings. Inpatient care offers overnight stays to patients who require a form of treatment, monitoring, or support unavailable through outpatient settings.

It is common for people to think that being a social worker in health care is limited to working in a hospital. Although most medium to large hospitals employ educated and licensed social workers on staff (Ginsberg, 2001; Holliman et al., 2003), given the influence of managed care, cost control policies, and the vast changes predicted in the delivery of health care in the future, there are fewer overnight stays in inpatient settings and a growing portion of health care takes place in outpatient settings. Procedures that once demanded a few days' stay in inpatient facilities now require shorter stays. Clinical pathways, the predictable steps of recovery for the average patient, encourage teams to work together to ensure that, as much as possible, patients move quickly and predictably toward less expensive recovery environments such as the patient's home, rehabilitation centers, or other nursing facilities (Schneiderman et al., 2008). The high cost incurred for an overnight stay in a hospital is great incentive for the health industry to seek other ways to provide the patient with appropriate support.

Hospitals are a very expensive form of inpatient care so ways to reduce inpatient time benefit insurance companies employing managed care strategies to pay for a specified and predetermined length of inpatient time. Diagnosis-related groups (DRGs) predetermine the cost reimbursed for inpatient care for Medicare and other insurance providers and hospitals face the choice of absorbing costs or trusting a patient can privately pay for inpatient stays that exceed the limitations set by the DRG designation.

There are times, however, that chronic and acute health events call for inpatient care. The hospital remains an excellent place for health care professionals to observe, test, and treat medical conditions in a coordinated way. Some diseases need medical treatment unavailable in alternative or less expensive inpatient settings. Testing equipment needed for diagnostics—such as computerized axial tomography [CAT] scans, positron emission tomography [PET] scans, and X-rays—is expensive and unlikely to be available through clinics and physician offices. There are many medical reasons why patients may benefit from an overnight stay at a hospital; however, there is immediate and constant pressure for the hospital stay to be as short as possible. Hospitals continue to play an important role in the diagnosis and treatment of disease, but a patient cannot remain in the hospital if they are not receiving active medical care or treatment.

Internal review of medical procedures and efforts to stay within insurance guidelines for hospital stays are constant. Social workers are one of the first of the hospital staff to be alerted to patient stays that risk exceeding the predetermined and medically billable time. In many hospital settings, social workers are employed to ensure timely and well-supported discharge of the patient. This is a multifaceted task because the patient, caregivers, physicians, and the rest of the health care team must all work and communicate with each other on the steps taken to achieve the discharge goal. Ultimately, the physician is responsible to approve the discharge plan that ensures the patient is stable enough to leave the hospital and that appropriate supports are in place. The discharge plan includes the expectations for further care and instructions for the patient to follow as part of recovery. Discharge plans often require instructions to the patient for follow-up appointments, a list of medication prescriptions, a review of the rehabilitation schedule or appointments, instructions for home care support programs, and equipment or transportation options

(DuBois & Krugsrud Miley, 2005). In order to assist in patient discharge, social workers are aware of the best resources available within the community and the resources that are affordable to patients based on their financial resources or insurance coverage.

Hospital social workers access the appropriate parts of the medical record, both paper and electronic versions, to find the information necessary to plan a patient discharge. In addition, social workers record the actions they have taken to facilitate the patient care plan or list questions or barriers that have yet to be resolved. To access medical records, social workers must meet the requirements for "privilege," a standard of professionalism set by the hospital to ensure records are handled by competent and qualified professionals in a confidential manner.

Social workers are an integral part of an interdisciplinary treatment team and together the team communicates changes in the patient's condition, barriers to discharge, and patient strengths and concerns, particularly regarding discharge. Barriers to discharge include safety or mobility concerns, lack of transportation, missing signatures, or scheduling problems for prescribed tests and procedures that are needed before the patient is discharged (DuBois & Krugsrud Miley, 2005).

Some patients do not have a stable home to return to or caregivers ready and willing to make meals, wash laundry, pick up prescriptions, and take them to their appointments. Discharge from inpatient settings for people who are homeless is particularly challenging. The risks of discharge include additional complications of the condition for which the patient was originally hospitalized. Social workers are creative in finding ways to meet the needs of people without visible resources. Patients are often able to assist in developing a care plan that meets their needs for a short time. Social workers identify barriers and advocate for solutions that ensure safe inpatient discharge for all (DuBois & Krugrud Miley, 2005). Someone discharged without resources or adequate insurance coverage is at risk of additional harm; this is an expense to the health care system, and may require community support.

Inpatient settings care for individuals requiring a wide variety of medical services for a variety of conditions. Many hospitals or inpatient settings offer specialty care in areas such as obstetrics, emergencies, heart disease, cancer, orthopedics, pediatrics, renal care, and dialysis. Social workers in inpatient settings may be required to develop expertise within a specialty setting; others may work in all specialty areas throughout the hospital. Specialty inpatient settings may stand alone outside the hospital setting and often represent a residential health facility that offers a less expensive option for care. Alternative inpatient settings include rehabilitation centers, assisted living centers, nursing homes, and inpatient hospice care.

These alternative care sites often offer more than one form of supportive care after acute care discharge from the hospital. Determining the support services that are covered by patients' insurance is very complex and varies from state to state and from insurance provider to insurance provider. For instance, acute care licensing is designated most often to hospitals, but the acute care level may also be a licensed service provided at a rehabilitation center. Subacute licensing is the status of rehabilitation centers, but nursing homes may also designate licensed beds to provide this form of care. Assisted living centers offer varying degrees of support to assist residents in maintaining independent functioning, but may depend on some of the subacute care to be provided by a nursing home. Social workers learn about the resources, insurance providers, and licensing within the community where they are employed and help patients and caregivers navigate this complex system of alternative inpatient care settings.

The best health care after discharge from a hospital requires the social worker to be thoughtfully considered to match the physical needs, but also the emotional and social needs, of the patient. Reflect on the health care needs of the young man in the following scenario.

Scenario 4:3

Ken is a 25-year-old single construction worker who fell through the skylight of a 40-foot building and landed on a concrete floor. His injuries included severe and multiple breaks in both of his arms and a broken hip, pelvis, and leg, three broken ribs, and a punctured lung. Ken also experienced a concussion. After almost 3 weeks in the hospital, Ken is now physically stable but unable to live independently. He requires physical therapy several times a day; he has trouble walking, sitting, standing, getting to the bathroom, and is currently unable to feed himself due to the casts on his arms. He would be in danger if there was any emergency that required him to move. Ken is lucky to be alive, but it will take him a long time to return to independence. For at least a few months, Ken needs to rely on others to feed, clothe, move, and transport him. He is eager to be discharged from the hospital, but his aging parents are unable to provide him with adequate care.

The physician refers Ken to the social worker for discharge planning and there are many needs to integrate into a successful discharge plan. How long will Ken need inpatient care? Is Ken emotionally healthy? What motivation for recovery is he displaying? What is the rehabilitation plan? What are the systems of support in Ken's life? Are there viable options for health support outside the inpatient care options? What will Ken's insurance pay for?

Additional Forms of Inpatient Care

Additional forms of inpatient care services are frequently necessary for people to recover or receive treatment and care when the clinical expertise of a hospital setting are no longer required. When patients experience stability in their acute health needs, but are unable to return to previous levels of independence, forms of inpatient care are frequently necessary to provide some form of rehabilitation or other supportive care. The transition from one health setting to another is not as easy. For instance, if an older adult is stable after hip surgery and ready for hospital discharge, but lives alone at home, discharge back to the home may be impossible. The move from a hospital to an alternative setting, even when it is considered temporary, can increase the likelihood of physical, emotional, and social complications if the discharge plan is not executed in a smooth and thoughtful way (Chaboyer, James, & Kendall, 2005).

The heath care offered by an alternative inpatient option recognizes that the patient is no longer in need of the form of acute care offered in the hospital setting, and so discharge to an alternative residential setting offers limited access to technology, laboratories, and the specialists available at a hospital. It is frequently a far less expensive option. However, it is important to establish a transitional plan of transfer that is seamless and safe each time a patient moves to ensure support for the challenges faced by the patient and caregivers (Chaboyer et al., 2005).

Fear of never returning to their home may deter older adults from seeking medical care in the first place. The greater the age, the greater the fear independence will be lost.

Short-term care may be seen as the worst fear coming true and cause hopelessness and impede recovery (Hong, Morrow-Howell, & Proctor, 2004). Sometimes patients are emotionally and socially prepared to accept their need for continued inpatient care and recognize it as an important step toward returning to their previous environment. However, even under the best of circumstances, referral to a short-term inpatient setting is rarely welcomed. Regardless of the temporary nature of the setting, it is not the first choice for patients; most are eager to return to their own environment. Research suggests an association between minor depression in people over 65 years old and the progress toward the recovery of previous functioning when time must be spent in another inpatient setting after hospital discharge. The increased risk of depression associated with this assignment may interfere with the recovery of the independent living skills necessary for individuals to return home (Allen, Agha, Duthie, & Layde, 2004; Hong et al., 2004).

Some patients in short-term inpatient settings do not recover basic independent living skills and increase the risk of placement into long-term care facilities. The move into long-term residential care can ignite issues of grief associated with the loss of choice, independence, autonomy, and functioning. The grief issues associated with some in long-term care may result in a significantly poorer quality of life and can damage individuals emotionally and socially.

Sometimes, an inpatient setting is viewed with relief by caregivers who worry about their inability to offer the patient the quality and quantity of care (i.e., transportation, diet, IV medication, physical therapy) that is often required after a hospital discharge. Rehabilitation centers, assisted care facilities, short-term care beds in nursing homes, and inpatient hospice care are some of the common forms of nonhospital inpatient health care settings that employ social workers as members of interdisciplinary treatment teams.

Rehabilitation.   Rehabilitation centers are licensed to offer subacute care, an alternative to the acute care licensing of hospitals. When the patient no longer requires the level of medical care provided by a hospital, rehabilitation centers offer short-term stays to people who need the expertise of the facility to recover from injury or health-related conditions. Staff working in rehabilitation settings offer specialized services that prepare individuals to live at the highest level of independence possible, despite an acute or chronic condition (DuBois & Krugsrud Miley, 2005). Many rehabilitation facilities also offer specialized outpatient services to patients who have the option to move back into their homes, but need to continue to rehabilitate.

Rehabilitation centers are often created to meet the needs of specialized populations such as people living with a brain injury or a spinal cord injury. Rehabilitation centers may also offer more general care for people, like a specialty center that addresses an array of orthopedic needs. These centers offer encouragement, support, training, and care to patients and caregivers. In the example of Ken, discussed earlier in the chapter, think about his discharge needs after hospitalization. Ken needs a place to recover and unfortunately it cannot be in his home. Ken is over 6 feet tall and weighs over 200 pounds. It is impossible for untrained individuals to transport him given his many broken bones and casts. He is barely able to use the special-order crutches that attach to his torso with straps.

In a rehabilitation center, staff is trained to provide orthopedic care, treatment, and recovery; however, social workers soon realize a perfect solution to patient discharge needs is not always available. Specialized orthopedic rehabilitation centers are not available in every community so alternative types of facilities are used to meet patient needs. For instance, a nursing home in the community of the patient may admit people recovering from chronic illnesses or acute injuries and offers the residential services needed as well as organizes transportation to rehabilitation services.

When patients are referred to rehabilitation centers, they participate in a biopsychosocial assessment with the social worker. The preliminary assessment, sent from an inpatient setting, is helpful, but the goals of the rehabilitation center are very different than those of other inpatient settings. The patient is now physically stable and there are many other factors that influence the plan of care. The social worker frames the assessment in terms of the strengths perspective. What are the goals the patient must reach to achieve discharge from rehabilitation? Can the patient stand up unassisted? How many steps must the patient be able to take unassisted for safety? How many steps lead into the patient's apartment? These kinds of questions assist the social worker in understanding the environmental barriers and supports of the patient and assist the patient in developing a reasonable course of action. The patient must do the often intense work of rehabilitation and it is vital that the patient and the social worker work together as part of the care team.

Injuries and the complications of chronic disease require physical rehabilitation and often require emotional rehabilitation, too. Will the patient return to his or her previous lifestyle? Does the patient experience depression about the course of recovery? Are there loss and grief issues that interfere with discharge planning? Some are discharged from rehabilitation centers and need to make many adjustments to life that are permanent and powerful. Some people experience injuries that result in paralysis, permanent weakness, and loss of cognitive and emotional strength. The social worker provides support, information, and counseling to the patient, family, and caregivers. They work with the patient throughout the stay and, with the rehabilitation team, help the patient problem-solve about future health care needs and financial issues (DuBois & Krugsrud Miley, 2005). Social workers often advocate for patients to access the specialized care needed but unavailable within the community.

Assisted Living.   Assisted living is a form of inpatient care that offers personalized supportive care. It encompasses a variety of ways to support the patient and family needs for physical support when independent living is no longer possible and when moving into long-term or permanent support settings is not deemed necessary. For instance, as the U.S. population ages, assisted living environments are becoming increasingly important (Spitzer, Neuman, & Holden, 2004). There is an alarming increase in the number of adults diagnosed with a chronic illness or multiple chronic conditions and these conditions can limit the patient's previous activity levels. A variety of supportive care options after discharge from acute inpatient settings are needed to reflect the variation of support needs. It is increasing common for healthy adults to consider retirement options that include on-site assisted living options as a benefit (Sook Park, Zimmerman, Sloane, Gruber-Baldini, & Eckert, 2006; Spitzer et al., 2004).

The intensity and duration of support associated with time spent in assisted living is often viewed as pivotal to future living options. From assisted care, a patient either improves in health and strength, ready to move back to a previous living environment, perhaps with some additional in-home supports, or a patient does not improve to former levels of independence and eventually moves into long-term or more permanent supportive care.

The need for assisted living environments is closely linked to the financial restrictions on other forms of inpatient care associated with managed care. Criteria for inpatient settings is associated with all forms of chronic and acute illness and for every age group. But when the time approaches to be discharged, and the patient is unable to care for him- or herself and is without caregiver support, the services of assisted care offer a bridge to maintain the highest level of independence. Potentially, assisted living provides many supportive services, including medication and health care management, meal preparation, transportation to appointments, and emotional encouragement and support. For those without access to the appropriate level of support needed to recover or maintain health, the variety of assisted living options plays a particularly vital role.

Nursing Homes.   Many nursing homes offer a range of residential and supportive health care services. While nursing homes may specialize and vary in the services offered, many offer the most familiar option: long-term residential care. But nursing homes often present additional types of inpatient care, too, such as short-term care or rooms that are licensed for subacute care. Hospitals or other inpatient settings rely on nursing homes to accept and care for discharged patients who need additional care and support before they return to prior living situations.

Nursing homes play a central role for the timely discharge of patients from an inpatient facility, particularly when home is not an option. Many nursing homes save a portion of beds for patients ready for discharge from the hospital but in need of specialized care. Patients may not require 24-hour care, but special needs such as IV therapy, physical therapy, or other forms of treatment may require some level of skilled care. Admission to a nursing home is often part of a short-term plan to provide time for individuals to regain prior physical strength. Nursing homes, like other alternative inpatient settings, offer patients a safe place to recover and work on health and treatment goals. People with acute injuries such as in the earlier example of Ken, or people experiencing symptoms of chronic illness like cancer and heart disease, recover functional ability with the help of skilled nursing and physician attention and receive the care necessary to return to their highest levels of functioning. The goal for these patients is to return home.

Nursing homes also offer long-term care for individuals. Although long-term care does not mean the end to issues of recovery and efforts toward increased functioning (Schwartz-Cassell, 2004), making decisions about long-term care is often difficult and painful for both the patient and his or her caregivers. Once living in a care facility, patients are often referred to as "residents," the term implying a sense of permanence. Goals may be in place to stabilize and improve residents' health conditions, but caregivers remain challenged to find balance between supporting the wishes of the resident for autonomy and independence and the concerns that the resident will be in danger in an independent setting (Kane, Boston, & Chilvers, 2007).

The social worker employed at a nursing home works with both short-term, perhaps subacute, and long-term residents in achieving goals for the greatest level of independent functioning and recovery. For residents hoping to return to their previous environment, social workers assist them to develop and accomplish the goals necessary to be discharged and encourage and monitor progress. Social workers complete a biopsychosocial assessment based on resident resources and encourage the strengthening of emotional and social strengths (Spitzer et al., 2004).

Consider the following scenario about Louise and the issues related to her health support needs. As the social worker, think about the emotional and social issues involved in making decisions about her care. Many needing care do not have options in where they live, but even when they do, there can be complications.

Scenario 4:4

Louise is a 93-year-old widow with advanced dementia. She also has coronary artery disease, diabetes, and is hard of hearing. She has just been admitted to the dementia unit of a nursing home from the assisted living setting where she lived for 3 years. She had a private room and dined with others in a pleasant atmosphere, but due to her increasing dementia, health care staff determined her care needs had reached a level where she was no longer appropriate for the setting. The transfer was made abruptly because a bed was available. The family approved the move via telephone, but did not visit the nursing home dementia unit prior to the transfer. The assisted living unit was owned and operated by the same company that owns the nursing home and the family trusted that Louise would receive the same quality of care. Upon arrival at the home, the family became very upset. Louise was placed in a four-bed ward. She now eats her meals in bed and sits in a circle with other patients in a large room for the rest of the day. The family thinks the setting is depressing and that the whole unit is drab and colorless. In addition, they discover that because Louise is a "private pay" patient, she is essentially subsidizing other patients by paying a much higher "private pay" rate. The social worker is asked to meet with the family and "calm them down."

What can the social worker do to assist in this situation? Consider the response of the family. What are the social, emotional, and physical issues they are responding to?

Social workers provide biopsychosocial assessments and contribute to the design of a care plan for patients. They investigate access to insurance and the financial resources necessary for the patient to maintain residential care. Social workers build relationships within the nursing home with residents, caregivers, and the interdisciplinary staff. They work to prevent problems, to resolve unmet needs or concerns, and to monitor resident functioning. If changes occur that affect the resident's ability to function, the social worker provides information to the care team and works with the resident and family to stabilize and support the resident in new and appropriate ways. Resources to maintain functioning or build upon strengths are evaluated frequently so the resident can continue to improve the quality of life. The social worker in a nursing home works with the treatment team by informing staff of the mental and social health status of residents and influential environmental issues.

Hospice. Hospice is a specialized health service that offers expertise in support associated with end-of-life care. Individuals referred to hospice understand their health condition has deteriorated, aggressive medical care is no longer required, and recovery to health is not expected. People receiving hospice care understand that treatment of disease is discontinued and that palliative care, or care providing physical comfort, is the priority. Hospice has a long and international history of providing services to people at the end of their lives. While hospice care was first developed in Western Europe, it is commonly used in many countries, including the United States.

Hospice care takes place in many different settings: nursing homes, hospitals, patients' homes, or in a facility operated by the hospice organization. Referrals for hospice care come from many different places. The patient can refer themselves to hospice, or the referral may come from a physician, nurse, social worker, or family member.

Social workers in hospice care are involved in a biopsychosocial assessment. The hospice referral is unlike a medical or health treatment plan, because the goals of care are not designed for recovery or treatment associated with a return to health. Hospice assessments are uniquely focused on the quality of life. Social workers engage with the patient, family, and caregivers at the end of life to help create an environment that results in reduced pain, stress, worry, and trauma (DuBois & Krugsrud Miley, 2005). Hospice is often associated with end of life for older adults, but consider the following scenario.

Scenario 4:5

Mike is a 25-year-old single white male admitted to the Hospice Care Center with terminal cancer. He was transferred from the hospital where the nurses noted that he was a delightful patient, friendly and engaging. He has a rare form of cancer found only in people from the African continent. Mike lived and worked as a missionary for 2 years in Kenya. His parents are not religious and were not in favor of his mission work. They were fearful of his move to Africa and tried to discourage him from going. They visited him in the hospital but are unwilling to take him home and care for him. There are no siblings. Mike has a 26-year-old girlfriend who makes obligatory visits, but it is clear that she is in the process of terminating the relationship. It is the end of the summer and she plans to return to college. She indicates that her visits will be infrequent because the college is quite a distance away. The nurse is requesting social work services to address the lack of support systems and to offer the patient counseling.

What can the social worker do to be of assistance in this situation? How might the personal values of the social worker make this situation challenging? Are there options available to improve Mike's support systems?

Much of hospice care is done within patient homes and social workers make home visits to assess support and patient and family functioning. But not everyone has a support system equipped to help someone with the process of dying and death. When a supportive environment is unavailable to someone who is dying, some communities rely on inpatient beds within a hospice center. These centers offer the patient and caregivers an environment where the patient is physically treated for the pain and discomfort associated with disease and a place where the event of impending death is acknowledged and respected. The ability to acknowledge end-of-life issues is a vital part of the care hospice delivers. In addition, hospice organizations frequently meet many of the psychosocial needs for the patient and caregivers. Conversations with the patient and family about values, goals, and other life events support the patients' path toward reflection and resolve. Impending death may expose many emotions. Dying may result in wishes to comfort and ease the pain for loved ones, reconcile to the approach of death, resolve conflicts, or express unresolved anger. A social worker works to counsel the patient, support the grief work of the patient and caregivers, or refer the patient and caregivers to additional support services (Munn & Zimmerman, 2006).

Outpatient Care

Outpatient or ambulatory care, simply put, is the provision of health care to people who are too healthy for inpatient care or the care required is uncomplicated enough to receive outside an inpatient setting. It is one of the most common ways people receive health care today and is far less expensive than inpatient care. Outpatient care charges are less because typically a person receiving outpatient care does not require items such as food, lodging, and 24-hour medical care required as part of inpatient care. Outpatient care provides a patient with the greatest level of independence and less ability for the health care system to monitor patient health. The need to monitor chronic health conditions from an outpatient setting requires patient education and commitment. Absence of 24-hour support from health care workers adds to the challenge of chronic illness monitoring for the patient. Over the years, particularly since managed care, ambulatory services are created to support the independent attempts of individuals to monitor chronic illness and clinics often specialize in the care of specific chronic health conditions (Schneiderman et al., 2008). Medical treatments or procedures that once demanded a hospital or inpatient stay are now commonly done as an outpatient procedure, with patients recovering at home.

Ambulatory Clinics. Ambulatory care or outpatient clinics are very common today. They are located everywhere and are most common in medium to large communities. Ambulatory clinics, existing in a variety of forms, often serve the acute and chronic health care needs of a majority of the community. Many people today are uninsured or inadequately insured but still need health care. Sometimes federal, state, and local grants fund outpatient clinics and allow the clinic to offer medical services on a sliding scale, based on the patient's ability to pay. Frequently clinics are designed to offer the health services required by specifically designated communities. Clinics are designed to serve communities based on unique features such as (1) level of income (patients living below poverty or considered low income), (2) type of insurance status (veteran or someone who is eligible for Medicaid), (3) type of residence (homeless or in nursing care), (4) type of treatment (e.g., chemotherapy, dialysis, primary care, or obstetrics), or (5) type of chronic illnesses (e.g., heart disease and cancer) (Carpiac-Claver, Guzman, & Castle, 2007; Schneiderman et al., 2008).

In addition to city, state, or federal grants, clinics are frequently affiliated with hospitals. This affiliation exists for a number of reasons. Clinics are a visible way for hospitals to accomplish their mission of equitable health care delivery that is accessible to the community. In addition, ambulatory care clinics are a far less expensive way for hospitals to treat the community members who most commonly use hospital emergency rooms as a primary care entry point. The use of emergency rooms for primary care is an expensive and less effective way to deliver nonemergent health services and best delivered by a primary care clinic physician. Clinics also offer opportunities for health professionals to volunteer professional services and this further reduces the cost of operating the clinic. Community-based clinics offer valuable opportunities for patients to receive health education about disease prevention, and consistent, routine, and affordable health care.

Social workers are indispensable members of outpatient clinic staff. Outpatient health clinics attract people that present with complex biopsychosocial needs due to diagnosis or inadequate resources to establish necessary health care (Schneiderman et al., 2008). Social workers are skilled at interacting in communities that are disenfranchised or without social power. Culturally competent engagement skills are essential to work effectively in the often culturally diverse clinic settings. Informed cultural interactions are invaluable to an ethical and effective interaction with patients experiencing health-related events and unable to access any other health system (Mechanic & Tanner, 2007; Vourlekis & Ell, 2007).

For instance, an ambulatory health clinic for the homeless may require a social worker to participate in case-finding, actually going into the missions and "camping areas" of the population to locate and assess individuals with health problems. A homeless community experiences a high degree of diversity and the population represents people living with a higher than average rate of chronic mental and physical health diagnoses, substance abuse addictions, criminal histories, and developmental disabilities. Social workers represent a nonjudgmental link to health care for a variety of health needs and offer a valuable connection to a variety of community resources (Schneiderman et al., 2008).

Social workers know health problems do not just affect the body so they are beneficial additions on the interdisciplinary team and offer insight into the patient's environment. Social workers help establish the reputation of the clinic by interacting with community resources, leadership, and other linkages that empower the population. The clinic's reputation in the community is absolutely vital if the ambulatory clinic is to be successful. For instance, if the clinic serves people who are infected or affected by HIV, the clinic staff must understand the politics and history of HIV care in the community. The clinic must demonstrate commitment to the community by participation in committees, workgroups, and advocacy. These types of interventions take time to build, but result in a solid foundation for advocacy and positive social change.

The social worker in a clinic that serves disenfranchised populations understands the barriers people experience in the traditional health care setting. It is difficult to follow health instructions to take medication or return for appointments when the priority is to find a place to sleep. It is embarrassing to ask for free services, when, prior to losing a job, there was an ability to pay. Social workers offer nonjudgmental services while freeing medical personnel, like nurses and physicians, to deliver medical interventions. Working as a team, clinic staff develops a rich blend of knowledge and works to complement each other's areas of expertise.

Physician Offices.   Physician offices provide ambulatory care services and this is an area of health care where social work can expand its presence (Hine, Howell, & Yonkers, 2008; Schneiderman et al., 2008). Social workers employed in physician offices work to untangle the insurance issues, support the biopsychosocial needs within medical treatment plans, and provide resources and education to patients and caregivers. Social workers may see patients for "one-on-one" interventions regarding new diagnoses, or work with caregivers to understand the needs and feelings that accompany the progression of chronic illness. Social workers connect and provide assistance for patients to obtain resources for health care in the community (Hine et al., 2008).

Physicians are under fiscal pressure to make the most effective use of time and expertise to maximize income for their office (Hine et al., 2008). Some services for patients are less expensive and best delivered by an alternative staff member. Physician office expenses include rent, utilities, staff salaries, and often staggering malpractice insurance premiums, yet the goal of personnel is to ensure patients have quality care interactions. Physicians understand the importance of establishing therapeutic relationships, but are often unable to develop expertise regarding community health resources. Physician offices that employ social workers offer physicians a clear focus on the medical care needs of the patient and rely on social workers to offer the patient and caregiver ways to address the emotional and social support needs (Hine et al., 2008).

Social workers are trained to take treatment goals and develop the steps or objectives to progress toward those goals. Social workers monitor available patient resources, set up appointments, meet with families, follow up on patients during and after hospitalizations, set up rehabilitation services for patients, assist patients in gathering information and support, and organize transportation. These integrated services enhance the patients' opinion of their medical services and they experience improved quality of care (Hine et al., 2008).

Home Health Care.   Social workers are essential to home health agencies. They offer psychosocial care and environmental assessments and provide treatment teams with an interdisciplinary perspective (Goode, 2000; Lee & Rock, 2005). Home health services, like assisted living options, are increasingly required because they support the need for swift hospital discharge, are a very cost-effective way to provide health care support, offer a level of care that does not require an inpatient stay, and are a respectful and compassionate intervention (Egan & Kadushin, 2004; Goode, 2000). Home health care is a fast-growing service because of the flexibility to design service to meet patients' health needs in their homes at a low cost. They provide individually tailored services for people experiencing a variety, and often multiple, health needs. While home health care organizations are frequently independent from a community hospital, the organizations often work closely with the hospital, and are relied on to accept referrals from hospital social workers for patients that are ready to be discharged but require in-home support.

Consider the following scenario and think about the biopsychosocial needs presented. Often patients and caregivers have health needs but when they are in their homes they are relatively isolated from support. Still, the desire to stay at home is strong (Hong et al., 2004). What does a social worker need to assess the safety and health issues for this family?

Scenario 4:6

Mildred is a 79-year-old married female who was referred for home care services by the emergency department. She lives with her husband who has been her primary caregiver since her stroke 3 years ago. He was able to manage her care until she contracted the flu, which weakened her and caused incontinence. He brought her to the emergency room because he was completely exhausted from taking care of her. Mildred has a daughter who lives in another state and a son who lives nearby. Both her son and his wife work full time and have four young children. They state they are not available to help with Mildred's care. The home care nurse asked the social worker to assess for possible nursing home placement.

What can the social worker do to assist in this situation? What are the possible goals for Mildred? What are the long-term goals of her husband? Are there concerns for the husband's emotional and social health? Why? How can a social worker help the family to evaluate their options for health and safety?

Home health care agencies offer people the support necessary to remain independent at home. Many home health care agencies offer a full range of supportive services: physical therapy, occupational therapy, nursing care, mental health assessment, nutritional care, and medical social work services (Goode, 2000). As part of the treatment team, social workers focus on the psychosocial aspects of illness and recovery and free medical staff to respond to medical issues. The range of needs for people receiving home health care is diverse. Patients include people living with mental illness, developmental disabilities, chronic illness, physical disabilities, and people receiving palliative care.

Social workers in home health care agencies provide consistency of care. The social worker provides a link for patients to the health care system and provides care and interest in their biopsychosocial health. Social workers assess the mental status of patients and because visits are in patients' homes, social workers see the environmental barriers and strengths that influence patients. When a person receives home health care services, the benefits include the support of a social worker, who provides referrals to support services, education, and encouragement to achieve personal goals.

There are many reasons to provide health care within the patient's home. Goode (2000) identifies several common needs for home health care interventions: acute health experiences such as accidents; chronic disabilities; lack of family or other support systems; loss of ability to meet daily living needs; emotional, cognitive and social decline; or a significant reaction to trauma. Despite the provision of low-cost and high-quality care, social work services in home health care are challenged by policies that reduce funding for psychosocial care and threaten the delivery of these services to patients. Social workers' specialty, however, is a strength-based biopsychosocial assessment of needs and advocacy for resources within the systems of community and this role is essential on the health care interdisciplinary team (Lee & Rock, 2005).

Public Health

Throughout history, health has been a public concern (Cule, 1997; Porter, 1999; Rosen, 1958). As communities learn about causes, treatments, and prevention of disease, they learn to work together to reduce individual risk and improve the quality of life for everyone. Public health in the United States is recognized as an important and legitimate service in health care and offers information, education, and prevention of disease within communities. Communities depend on the public health system to offer a variety of health services and to link communities to resources in times of health emergencies. Social workers provide skills that aid in the provision of public health services.

Public health departments provide services that are clearly in the best interests of the community: animal control, community research and data collection, emergency preparedness, families with special needs, food safety, health education and promotion, immunizations, health inspection, the medical examiner, pregnancy and parenting services, vision and hearing testing, well and septic system resources, press releases and publications, and services particularly designed to support women and children. The public health system also represents a place where everyone can assess basic health services. Mothers receive help enrolling for Medicaid and obtain education regarding child care and immunizations for their babies. Public health also offers testing for communicable disease like HIV, sexually transmitted infections, and a variety of communicable diseases, including hepatitis and tuberculosis.

Public health is active in health concerns for individuals, as well as community, national, and global health. Social workers bring skills to the delivery of health education, promotion, and prevention. The growing needs associated with chronic illnesses, HIV, cancer, untreated high cholesterol and blood pressure, poor nutrition and obesity, diabetes, and tobacco and substance addictions damage communities. Social workers engage in the development of programs and interventions to educate and empower individuals and communities to prevent, treat, and reduce disease, and to improve quality and longevity of life.

Social workers are also active in programmatic evaluations. For instance, unhealthy lifestyles influence the development of chronic illnesses. Services are developed for every age to improve the understanding of risk and ways to avoid disease. Public health departments play integral roles in the development and presentation of health education within school systems about topics such as decision making, smoking, and stress. Culturally competent social workers are skilled at engagement, assessment, and communication and provide a respectful way to present health information to populations at risk.

Summary

Social workers are trained to competently engage in professional behaviors that support the diversity of needs experienced by patients and caregivers. Prepared to work with individuals, groups, and larger systems in the field of health care services, social workers provide advocacy, communication, mediation, research, evaluation, and record keeping. Although health systems reassign and restructure tasks due to policy and programmatic changes, social workers are employed in a rich variety of health care settings. Social work remains the best profession to engage and assess patient and caregivers in a manner that respects their medical needs but also attends to the social and emotional needs that accompany acute and chronic health care events. The focus on patient empowerment within the health care system and the recognition of emotional and social strengths and resources of the patient and caregivers is a valuable addition to a health care team and improves the quality and cost effectiveness of treatment planning.

Critical Thinking Questions

1. Despite innovations in outpatient care, what might be lost by reducing hospital stays?

2. Other than cost, what might be the benefits of reduced inpatient stays?

3. Everyone knows someone who has had an unpleasant experience in a hospital. Think of one of those experiences and consider how a social worker may have been helpful, and why.

4. What role or roles do you think a social worker in health care uses the most? Does it depend on where the social worker is employed?

References

Allen, B. P., Agha, Z., Duthie, E. H., & Layde, P. M. (2004). Minor depression and rehabilitation outcome for older adults in subacute care. *Journal of Behavioral Health Services and Research, 32*(2), 189–199.

Boyle, S. W., Hull, Jr., G. H., Mather, J. H., Smith, L. L., & Farley, O. W. (2006). *Direct practice in social work*. Boston: Pearson Education.

Carpiac-Claver, M., Guzman, J. S., & Castle, S. C. (2007). The comprehensive care clinic. *Health and Social Work, 32*(3), 219–223.

Chaboyer, W., James, H., & Kendall, M. (2005). Transitional care after the intensive care unit: Current trends and future directions. *Critical Care Nurse, 25*(3), 16–27.

Cowles, L. A. (2003). *Social work in the health field: A care perspective* (2nd ed.). New York: Hayworth Social Work Practice Press.

Cule, J. (1997). The history of medicine. In R. Porter (Ed.), *Medicine: A history of Healing* (pp. 12–41). Thailand: The Ivy Press Limited.

DuBois, B., & Krugsrud Miley, L. (2005). *Social work: An empowering profession* (5th ed.). Boston: Pearson Education.

Dziegielewski, S. F. (2004). *The changing face of health care social work: Professional practice in managed behavioral health care* (2nd ed.). New York: Springer.

Egan, M., & Kadushin, G. (2004). Job satisfaction of home health social workers in the environment of cost containment. *Health and Social Work, 29*(4), 287–296.

Ginsberg, L. H. (2001). *Careers in social work* (2nd ed.) Boston: Allyn & Bacon.

Goode, R. A. (2000). *Social work practice in home health care.* New York: Hayworth Press.

Hine, C. E., Howell, H. B., & Yonkers, K. A. (2008). Integration of medical and psychological treatment within the primary health care setting. *Social Work in Health Care, 47*(2), 122–134.

Holliman, D., Dziegielewski, S. F., & Teare, R. (2003). Differences and similarities between social work and nurse discharge planners. *Health & Social Work, 28*(3), 224–231.

Hong, L., Morrow-Howell, N., & Proctor, E. K. (2004). Post-acute home care and hospital readmission of elderly patients with congestive heart failure. *Health & Social Work, 29*(4), 275–285.

Kane, R. L., Boston, K., & Chilvers, M. (2007). Helping people make better long-term care decisions. *The Gerontologist, 47*(2), 244–247.

Klinkman, M. S. (1997). Competing demands in psychosocial care: A model for the identification and treatment for depressive disorder in primary care. *General Hospital Psychiatry, 19,* 989–1011.

Lee, J. S., & Rock, B. D. (2005). Challenges in the new prospective payment system: Action steps for social work in home health care. *Health and Social Work, 30*(1), 48–55. Retrieved August 31, 2007, from ProQuest Medical Library database. (Document ID: 800172751).

Mechanic, D., & Tanner, J. (2007). Vulnerable people, groups, and populations: Societal view. *Health Affairs, 26*(5), 1220–1230.

Munn, J. C., & Zimmerman, S. (2006). A good death for of long-term care: family members speak. *Journal of Social Work in End-of-Life and Palliative Care, 2*(3), 45–59.

Nicholas, D. B., Darch, J., McNeill, T., Brister, L., O'Leary, K., Berlin, D., et al. (2007). Perceptions of online support for hospitalized children and adolescents. *Social Work in Health Care, 44*(3), 205–223.

Porter, D. (1999). *Health, civilization, and the state: A history of public health from ancient to modern times.* London: Routledge.

Proctor, E. K. (2003). Research to inform the development of social work interventions. *Social Work Research, 27*(1), 3–6.

Rosen, G. (1958). *A history of public health.* New York: MD Publications.

Schneiderman, J. U., Waugaman, W. R., & Flynn, M. S. (2008). Nurse social work practitioner: A new professional for health care settings. *Health and Social Work, 33*(2), 149–155.

Schwartz-Cassell, T. (2004). Wellness for the subacute patient. *Nursing Homes, 53*(10), 104–108.

Sheafor, B. W., & Horejsi, C. R. (2006). *Techniques and guidelines for social work practice* (7th ed.). Boston: Pearson Education.

Spitzer, W. J., Neuman, K., & Holden, G. (2004). The coming of age for assisted living care: New options for senior housing and social work practice. *Social Work in Health Care, 38*(3), 21–45.

Sook Park, N., Zimmerman, S., Sloane, P. D., Gruber-Baldini, A. L., & Eckert, J. K. (2006). An empirical typology of residential care/assisted living based on a four state study. *The Gerontologist, 46*(2), 238–248.

Volland, P. J. (1996). Social work practice in health care: Looking to the future with a different lens. In M.D. Mailick & P. Caroff (Eds.), *Professional social work education and health care: Challenges for the future* (pp. 35–51). New York: Hayworth Press.

Vourlekis, B., & Ell, K. (2007). Best practice case management for improved medical adherence. *Social Work in Health Care, 44*(3), 161–177.

Wade, K., & Neuman, K. (2007). Practice-based research: Changing the professional culture and language of social work. *Social Work in Health Care, 44*(4), 49–64.

World Health Organization (WHO). (n.d.). *Commission of Social Determinants of Health.* Retrieved August 31, 2007, from http://www.who.int/social_determinants/en/

Part II

Social Work, Health Care, and Practice

Sarah completed her BSW field placement in a health care clinic when she was a student in her accredited BSW program. When she graduated, she interviewed for a case management position at the clinic and was hired. The clinic is a federally funded ambulatory care clinic and offers a sliding scale to patients who are economically challenged. Sarah's job is to assess and set goals with pregnant women for ongoing health care and prenatal education. The age range of the women she sees varies from 15 to 37, they are single and married, and represent a wide range of educational, economic, racial, and ethnic cultures. Sarah must establish relationships with the women, encourage them as they work on their goals, and advocate for the resources they need.

Social work practice combines the basic professional skills necessary for all interactions yet the application is unique to each situation. Social workers are taught the "basics" in their educational experiences, but through the application of theoretical concepts, they continue to refine their skills to meet the needs of each environment or individual. The engagement techniques necessary to develop a working relationship with one woman are not necessarily effective in developing a relationship with another. Social workers soon learn the subtle cues that help shape the best choices for relationship building. As with the practice of any skills taught, the more someone practices the more confident and competent they become. When social workers understand the reasons why interactions are successful or unsuccessful, they use their professional skills to elaborate, adjust, or refine their interactions.

Social workers, who build their practice skills based on the systems theory, the strengths perspective, and the promotion of the empowerment and self-determination of the patient, understand that accurate assessment of need can only be attained through culturally competent practice. Personal goals and objectives are not necessarily the goals for the patient. It is essential to understand that the cultures that influence the options and choices for others are not necessarily our own. A social worker must constantly assess the fit between the choices of the patient with the options the health system presents.

Understanding personal values is essential when working as a social worker. Without awareness of personal characteristics and values, social workers risk not hearing or supporting the goals of the patient. Social work is not using a personal interpretation of "good judgment" or "common sense" to give the "right" advice to others. Social work is based on professional methods, skills, and knowledge and is taught through accredited educational programs and supported by professional research. Social workers benefit from the work and supervision of mature and experienced practitioners and over time are frequently asked to supervise others.

Health systems benefit from social work input because of the clear prioritization of the biological, social, and psychological needs of the patient. The biopsychosocial perspective supports the maintenance of the whole patient and recognizes that health, healing, and illness are more than physical conditions. Social workers contribute to interdisciplinary teams and are a vital link between the patient, the caregivers, and the medical team. While roles on teams occasionally blur, a professionally trained social worker brings expertise in cultural competence, assessment, systems, engagement, and resource development. Social work practice is a cost-effective way to add quality and efficiency to patient care in all areas of health care. In addition, social workers contribute to the advocacy, planning, implementation, and evaluation of health-related programs.

5

The Foundation
of Social Work

Teaching and Learning Goals

- Demonstrate knowledge of various social work models and perspectives
- Recognize the basic theoretical concepts underlying social work in health care
- Demonstrate knowledge regarding social work models of practice
- Recognize the role of professional social work language

It is common to hear new social work students state that the profession of social work is appealing because they want to "help people." This is a popular reason to consider the profession of social work, but social work is far more than offering assistance to others. Beyond the emotional motivation to help others, it is important to recognize that social work is a profession and professional social workers are trained to communicate in a professional language, schooled in theories, models, and perspectives that shape social work interactions with patients, caregivers, and support systems. In addition, all practice interventions are based on a professional code of ethics.

An examination of the professional practice of social work gives evidence that social work is far more than the use of "common sense" or "doing the right thing." Social work interventions in health care are shaped by planned steps based on social theories, models, and perspectives. These assessment, planning, and intervention models have many things in common because they shape and mold interactions with patients, caregivers, organizations, and a variety of health care professions. Theoretical frameworks also provide the social work practitioner a way to assess, analyze, and synthesize information that leads to quality social work services.

Social workers in health care are skilled to accomplish many tasks based on a variety of social models and theories, but frequently interventions in the health care setting are based on the biomedical or disease model alone. The biomedical model shapes patient assessment by looking for the presence or absence of disease. In addition, the health system continues to practice forms of the patriarchal and paternalistic model called the "medical model." This is a model that supports the idea that the physician is at the very top of the health system's hierarchy of power. Physicians carry incredible responsibility for disease assessment, diagnosis, and treatment, but the model that values the physician as the sole designer of all treatment plans is at risk of missing the rights of patients to determine their future. For instance, if a physician believes there is a medical treatment that provides a patient a good option for treatment of disease, the patient must still be given adequate treatment information, be allowed to ask questions, and be given the opportunity to accept or decline treatment. Social workers support patient self-determination and can be perceived as being at odds with medical colleagues. Patients have choices and their care is perceived as best when this partnership is recognized.

In contrast to the medical and biomedical models, the "biopsychosocial model" and the "determinants of health model" offer distinctly different assessment models. Both theories offer holistic frameworks of examining the interactions between patients and their environments and shed light on the relationships between the person and the environment—a systems perspective.

All models, theories, and perspectives propose certain ways of collecting information. Social workers using a biopsychosocial model, assess the patient's physical, emotional, and social health and learn about an individual's culture, home, neighborhood, family, experiences, resources, and emotional status. This kind of assessment results in a much richer and integrated collection of information when compared to biomedical assessments that primarily seek evidence to support the presence or absence of disease.

Professional social workers are taught to assess patients based on a code of ethics that promotes the empowerment of the patient, cultural competence, a strengths-based perspective, and evidence-based interventions. Through social work education, frameworks such as the advanced generalist and generalist perspectives and other models promote the multiple system approach. Social workers are encouraged to build on their liberal education and to apply critical thinking to the assessment and care planning needed to ultimately assist patients, caregivers, and communities.

Social Work Language

The system of health care in the United States is very complex and obtaining health care often involves interactions with many professionals of varying academic degrees, certifications, experiences, occupations, and expertise. Although the staffing of health care organizations is complex and interdisciplinary, it remains dominated primarily by the medical professions. All nonmedical professions are colleagues and collaborators and when cost-effectiveness of services is evaluated, the nonmedical professions particularly, including social work, must defend the legitimacy of contributions to quality care, improved patient health, and cost savings within the system.

Social workers in health care frequently collaborate with health professionals who are unclear about what social workers do. Even though health care teams know social workers play a valuable role in the quality of patient care, they may be unable to articulate exactly what it is social workers actually do. Frequently social workers are typecast as the staff that work with insurance providers and make referrals to obtain insurance coverage for the uninsured. For some social workers in health care, performance of these tasks is a valid part of the job; however, there are many other tasks social workers complete within the health care system and the responsibilities are as unique as the individual patients who need health care. Clearly social workers must do a better job in promoting their professional abilities because social work is the vital lubricant that makes the complex machine of health care respond better to both patients and caregivers. When positive interactions and relationships are experienced anywhere in the system, all health professionals are in an improved position to deliver treatment, care, and support in a compassionate and humane manner.

To better understand how social workers function in the health care system, it is important to understand how social workers accomplish tasks and become familiar with some of the professional concepts that shape the profession. Social work is a profession that is taught in accredited universities and colleges and results in professionals who are licensed or certified by state regulatory groups. In addition to professional training in the United States, the profession of social work is also taught globally within colleges and universities and is practiced throughout the world.

Like most professions, social work uses a professional technical language that clearly and effectively communicates resources, plans, and ideas. Frequently, trained professionals, including social workers, use acronyms, words, and terms to communicate, at times forgetting this language is not familiar to everyone. This is true in each field of practice, including the field of health care.

The Foundational Concepts of Social Work

Social workers in all fields of practice share the fundamental concepts of social work practice and build additional expertise by the application of theoretical models. The most common professional concepts that offer the foundation for social work practice in health care include the National Association of Social Workers Code of Ethics, cultural competence, evidence-based practice, the strengths perspective, liberal education, critical thinking, the systems perspective, and the generalist perspective. These concepts represent the professional building blocks of social work and when these concepts are solidly in place, the social worker in health care is better prepared to respond to patient needs.

The National Association of Social Workers Code of Ethics

Many professional organizations expect members to adhere to a professional code of ethics; this is also true for social workers. The code of ethics was developed and is practiced by social workers as published by the National Association of Social Workers (NASW, 1999).

A preliminary review of the code demonstrates that social workers are committed to work that serves the needs of people who are hurting and disenfranchised from healthy functioning in the community. The Code summarizes that commitment by establishing that social workers strive "to enhance human well-being and help meet the basic human needs and empowerment of people who are vulnerable, oppressed, and living in poverty" (NASW, 1999, p. 381). The Code of Ethics also identifies social workers' core values, ethical principles, professional obligations, and ethical standards. By featuring the social work mission, values, principles, obligations, and standards, the Code socializes new social workers to the profession and is used to assess unethical conduct within the profession.

In social work health care, social workers rely on the NASW Code of Ethics (1999) to guide decision making through many complex situations. For instance, the health care system in the United States is challenged to provide equitable access to health care, but the millions who are uninsured remain in need. Social workers are guided by the ethical code of conduct to advocate for changes in policy and to find ways to meet the needs of people without resources for adequate health care (Galambos, 2003).

Every day social workers in health care are ethically challenged as they witness the inequity of choices people experience based on socioeconomic status or insurance coverage. It is challenging to know that despite the benefits of medical technology, many technologies and medical interventions are not available to everyone. From the medical needs of premature infants to the health crises for the medically frail, many with health problems would benefit from available interventions. Health systems face decisions between offering life support or ending medical treatment. Social workers rely on the Code of Ethics (1999) to help guide the formation of ideas and options that result in advocacy for the rights of individuals to determine their health care options.

Cultural Competence

A commitment to cultural competence is arguably one of the most important features of social work and the Code of Ethics (NASW, 1999) and challenges social workers to develop and practice skills, knowledge, experience, and education about the diversity of culture. Culturally competent practice is absolutely essential to social work interventions in health care. The concept of competence is not the same concept as cultural sensitivity. While cultural sensitivity suggests that differences are noticed and perhaps tolerated, tolerance is not the goal of a professional social worker (Abrums & Leppa, 2001). Culturally competent social workers are expected to provide a level of cultural expertise.

Cultural competence goes beyond the simple recognition that all people are unique. For social workers cultural competency is the continual development of the ability—based on social work knowledge, skills, and values—to acknowledge the unique interactions between a person's race, ethnicity, health, age, gender, sexual preference, religion, politics, and socioeconomic status. Once the features that make a person unique are recognized, the social worker seeks to learn how these factors influence the person's worldview. Learning to support the path of patient choice is only accomplished if the health team understands how culture interprets the patients' perception of the world, including their view of health care choices. Sometimes the choice others make is different from the choice the social worker would make for themselves. In fact, sometimes the decision patients make may not be the selection we think is "best" for them. The recognition that people have the right to decide health care treatment based on personal values is one reason why cultural competence is so vital.

Obtaining skills in cultural competence is a neverending process (Galambos, 2003) that attempts to combine two somewhat opposing ideas. It makes generalizations about the cultures of groups of people while recognizing and treating every individual as unique. As is true in the attempts to diagnose mental illness, the use of a diagnostic manual may lend insight and direction to our attempts to clarify a behavior, but the manual generalizes symptoms and is only helpful when the information is applied to the specific circumstances of an individual. The same strategy is true with cultural competence. For example, if a white, middle-class, female social work student attempts to makes sweeping declarations about the cultural experience for all white, middle-class, female social work students, her declaration will only be partially correct. White, middle-class, female social work students may have many things in common, but they vary by sexual preference, religiosity, family of origin, and a host of other factors. People vary by innumerable variables and social workers add to their cultural competence every time they recognize this fact (Abrums & Leppa, 2001).

In addition, cultural competence demands social workers learn as much as they can about the circumstances of various communities of people so patients are not burdened to completely educate the social worker about their culture (Galambos, 2003). Social workers learn about culture in a couple of different ways. First, social workers must read about other cultures. Access to information about cultures has never been easier. University libraries often have many professional journals available online and offer peer-reviewed articles about cultures and the unique features of culturally based and health-related interventions. Information is also available through cultural presentations such as plays, movies, festivals, and cultural meetings. Professional social workers need to look for opportunities to join other social workers in learning about cultures through conventions, training, and professional organizations.

One of the most effective ways to learn about cultures is through the development of a relationship with someone from an unfamiliar culture and by spending time with them; they become a personal cultural guide. For instance, if someone wants to learn something about living with human immunodeficiency virus (HIV), it is best to talk to someone who is HIV-positive. This experience gives insight and depth to a culture in a way that is difficult to gain from other mediums. Beyond personal insights, social workers acquire genuine respect by developing relationships with people who live lives that are different from their own. The social worker must integrate the generalized facts about various groups of people and apply them lightly to an individual with the knowledge that individuals are unique. For instance, no one can speak with authority on all issues for all people who live with HIV, but as social workers add to their repertoire of knowledge, the picture of cultural diversity becomes clearer (Taylor-Brown, Garcia, & Kingson, 2001).

Often relationships between the health care social worker and the patient are brief. It makes cultural competence all the more important. The short period of time spent with a patient at the beginning of a relationship (the engagement period) must be as seamless as possible based on accurate knowledge of cultural diversity. Cultural competence enables the social worker to see and hear the unique issues of the individual. Lack of cultural competence is a significant barrier in establishing relationships and wastes the patient's valuable time (Galambos, 2003).

In the culture of health, professionals recognize the diversity of cultural experiences related to the human response to disease, illness, pain, and treatment. For instance, women that experience childbirth are a perfect example. Some women talk about the terrible pain they experienced during childbirth, and others describe childbirth much differently, with less emphasis on pain. But even if the pain experience could be scientifically measured and two women experienced exactly the same degree of pain, they would still respond to the experience of pain differently. Some people report and want medical attention for all physical conditions whereas others believe that avoiding the medical establishment keeps health problems away. Social workers in health care must be careful not to rely on generalizations about how people experience health, illness, and healing (Taylor-Brown et al., 2001).

Evidence-Based Practice

Social workers in health care settings are under increased pressure to identify and practice social work interventions that are proven to demonstrate effectiveness (Jenson, 2005; Witkin & Harrison, 2001). Evidence-based practice is the strategic consideration of professional evidence when selecting social work practice techniques (Gossett & Weinmann, 2007). In the competitive and fast-paced health care industry, social workers must be able to demonstrate that the interventions selected are both cost-effective and of high quality. The phrase "evidence-based practice" is a relatively new term in social work practice, but the idea of limiting payment to settings unless evidence-based interventions are used is increasing common in many social work environments. Using evidence-supported interventions is viewed as a way to stem health care costs (Strite & Stuart, 2005).

Historically social workers in academic settings published qualitative and quantitative research findings based on social work practice, but social workers in practice settings are continually challenged to deliberately apply evidence-supported concepts in practice and often experience barriers to contribute to the social work evidence-based practice literature.

Social workers may find it difficult to contribute to evidence-based research based on professional clinical work experiences for many good reasons. Health care settings rarely assign social workers the task of contributing to research as part of the job description. The day-to-day tasks of patient care are expected to take precedent and implementation of a research project takes time. In addition, there is little financial incentive, time allowance, or professional recognition for research projects and many social workers feel inadequate or unqualified to design and develop studies. Once social workers leave academic institutions, most find few opportunities to experience a role in professional research and development and over time believe they are no longer capable of contributing to this area.

Unfortunately, the most likely contributors to social work research are often found in academic settings, in clearly designated research roles and often removed from social work practice. The distance from practice can challenge some academic researchers to make research relevant to the social work practitioners (Hall et al., 1996).

A possible answer to this problem is found in forms of collaboration. Social work researchers, possibly from academic settings, and social work practitioners in the health care field mutually benefit by working together and these collaborative research efforts add depth and reliability to the social work knowledge base. The process of developing an evidence-based practice calls for the ethical collection of data about a social work intervention. This is most commonly done by social work practitioners with access to the social work practice environment. Once the data is collected, it is synthesized and analyzed. Often, social work practitioners are disadvantaged by time and support issues in this part of the process. Social work researchers and practitioners benefit most when full partnerships exist through the entire process. Practitioners experience the reality of organizational and operational issues in the field and the authentic application of practice methods adds quality to the research results (Hall et al., 1996).

Social work interventions based on empirical evidence are expected, to some degree, if not demanded for insurance reimbursement in most social work settings. Health care settings rely on critical pathways, the average expected care continuum, and the progress of an uncomplicated care plan. In addition, health care settings respond to predetermined insurance rates that offer health systems incentive to use the best practice techniques from every health profession.

Social workers recognize that the work environment is a rich system to study and document for the most effective interventions and thus contribute to the collection of evidence-based practice research. Working together with other health professions to participate in writing proposals for research, approaching the hospital's internal review board for consent to implement research projects, and publishing the results of the research in professional journals are valuable contributions to the profession and to patient care. Evidence-based practice requires practitioners to accept the possibility that some interventions may not result in the expected outcomes. Patients and caregivers benefit and deserve to have access to the most effective treatment possible, both in behavioral and physical health care, and social workers know using the best interventions possible provides ethically sound, quality care.

Strengths Perspective

The strengths-based perspective supports social workers to locate the strengths and resources of patients in an effort to remind them of their personal assets and social capital. In addition, social workers assist patients in recognizing their assets as both useful and powerful means to achieve goals and realize dreams. The process of empowerment assists patients to recognize their personal power. Health care environments frequently challenge an individual's sense of power and patients and caregivers are likely to feel helpless or powerless when diagnosed with a disease or feel threatened with incredible life changes. A strengths-based assessment reveals the many resources and opportunities available to patients that enhance their ability to self-determine and design their future (Early & GlenMaye, 2000; Saleebey, 1997).

The strengths perspective is far more than the recognition of strengths in a patient. The perspective suggests that the relationship between the social worker and the client be collaborative and creative. The social worker turns the focus of the conversations to possibilities instead of problems (Saleebey, 2007). Encouraged by recognition of resources, patients develop hope, strength, and mobility. They believe in their personal capacity to make change and to take effective leadership in their lives (Early & GlenMaye, 2000).

Patients in a health care system are frequently surrounded with documentation and conversations based on disease treatment models—models that assess and treat deficits. Words like *diagnosis, prognosis, disease, abnormality,* and *pathology* are based on a health care system that is problem focused. Patients often have little opportunity to be involved in conversations about how their personal strengths will allow them to succeed in achieving their goals to live with short-term or long-term health issues (Saleebey, 1997).

Scenario 5:1

Paul is a 63-year-old obese white male. He has been smoking for 45 years. He has been treated for high blood pressure and diabetes for the past 20 years and is experiencing increased pressure in his chest. Paul's physician informed him that his recent test results show he has obstructed arteries and that his kidney functioning is very poor. The physician is planning to call in a renal specialist and perhaps begin dialysis. He is currently hospitalized for heart monitoring and is referred to the social worker to evaluate his insurance coverage issues before changing the course of treatment.

What does your assessment for patient strengths reveal? What are some ways to make strengths recognizable to the patient and caregiver? What can you do if the patient is already aware of his strengths?

For a hospital social worker, this brief paragraph about Paul might easily be the brief introduction you are given as a referral to this new patient. Plainly, there are not many strengths noted in this case referral; however, during the visit to Paul, the goal is to look for his strengths. Everything in the interaction with Paul will be an attempt to highlight his talents, knowledge, capacities, and resources (Early & GlenMaye, 2000; Saleebey, 1997). Entering Paul's room, the social worker notices many "get-well" cards and balloons. He greets you warmly and interjects a humorous remark. His wife, quietly sitting and reading near his bed, smiles and stands up to shake hands. It becomes obvious that Paul is a man with resources, both emotional and environmental. He will need all of his strengths to cope with the physical changes and new treatments that await him. The process of empowerment begins when Paul and his wife recognize the strengths of his emotions and environment.

Unfortunately, in a disease treatment model, a physical disorder is often assumed to have a remedy. In the case of Paul, there will most likely be no physical remedy for his current state of health, particularly given the progression of his serious and multiple health concerns. Paul's health situation and absence of a cure is frequently the scenario for many patients in a hospital setting because much of disease today is chronic and systemic in nature. In order to find ways of coping with the results of chronic illness, problems need to be constructed in a way that allow the patient to recognize the choices and actions that lead the patient to a position of power, although these choices may not lead to a medical solution.

The strengths and resources of patients are not the same as solutions. Saleebey (1997) is a great proponent of the strengths perspective and asserts that strengths can be found using many strategies. Clearly, one of the most important ways to communicate about strengths is through words; however, because the medical system is based on the disease model, the language focuses on the description of problems. Social workers are tempted to communicate using words that focus only on the "problem." When social workers complete an assessment, we frequently ask the patient, "What is the problem?" or some other question that attempts to elicit the same response. Words are powerful and social workers must be aware of the choices made while addressing the patient. In addition, given the multiple service providers in health care, and the fact that many complete unique assessments based on a problem-focused model, patients repeat their "problem" and what is "wrong" with them many times. Through repetition, patients are often convinced they are the "problem." Rarely is this balanced with the message that they also have strengths and can contribute to their health and have power over their future (Early & GlenMaye, 2000).

One way to assist in creating opportunities for patients is through the promotion of empowerment (Early & GlenMaye, 2000; Saleebey, 1997). The role of social workers in the empowerment process begins with an evaluation of personal beliefs and values. Social workers believe in the strengths of individuals, families, and communities to take power and responsibility. They resist paternalistic ways of interacting with patients and instead provide opportunities for patients to pursue their agenda, as they define it. The process of empowerment includes relying on patients' decisions and intuitions as it pertains to their lives. Although professional status is one form of power, social workers choose to honor the power of the patient. Advocating for the patient to make decisions can put a social worker in an awkward position with others on a medical team, especially when the team has an alternative opinion about the best way to proceed. Even when the patient is unable to represent themselves, it is vital that the wishes of the patient be brought to the attention of the health care team.

The strengths perspective is built on several assumptions and when practiced develops into a strengths-based practice (Early & GlenMaye, 2000; Salebeey, 1997). First, social workers must recognize that every individual, group, family, and community has strengths (Chadiha, Adams, Biegel, Auslander, & Gutierrez, 2004; Early & GlenMaye, 2000; Redko, Rapp, Elms, Synder, & Carlson, 2007; Salebeey, 1997). Social workers know little more than the illness, disease, or injury when they first meet the patient. At this point the strengths of the patient are not very obvious, yet the patient and the caregivers have the assets, wisdom, experiences, and intuition that will lead them to make decisions (Chadiha et al., 2004; Early & GlenMaye, 2000; Redko et al., 2007; Salebeey, 1997). By expressing genuine concern about their welfare and confidence that they can succeed in their goals, the social workers partner with patients to detect resources.

Second, while illness can be harmful, it can also be a source of challenge and opportunity (Salebeey, 1997). Throughout life people learn through adversity and challenges can produce skills and emotional assets that enable people to survive through the hardships (Redko et al., 2007). Patients access the same strengths they rely on for other challenges in life. Social workers support patients by offering complete and accurate information about their options and by supporting their plan (Chadiha et al., 2004; Early & GlenMaye, 2000).

Third, social workers should expect to be surprised by how much people can change and grow (Saleebey, 1997). Frequently, social workers begin to align with the medical perspective and allow the disease or diagnosis model to set the standard for patient success. Saleebey (1997) suggests that too often health care personnel recognize the diagnosis as "the verdict" for the patient. Social workers support patients by keeping high expectations of their abilities and by aligning with their hopes, visions, and values (Redko et al., 2007). Where other professionals see defeat, social workers continue to expect that the patient will find a way to solve the problem (Early & GlenMaye, 2000). For instance, when the diagnosis for a disease to be cured is bleak and the prognosis is poor, the patient may find the emotional resources to accept that the time that remains will allow them to meet certain goals. Patients finding strengths in the face of a fatal illness is played out over and over in the health care system. The resilience of the human spirit is inspiring, but sometimes we never see the resolution of the pain and conflict of the patient. Patients have a right to have the power to decide and ultimately, their decision will be the right one (Chadiha et al., 2004; Early & GlenMaye, 2000; Redko et al., 2007; Salebeey, 1997).

Next, patients do best when they are included in their care (Redko et al., 2007; Saleebey, 1997). Social workers, along with other health care professionals, have power in the health care system. Credentials, training, and roles place health care personnel in a role that makes the official power system unequal, and patients experience this inequity. Social workers have the power to move through the hospital system, speak to the medical staff, and read and write in medical charts. If social workers attempt to interact with patients only from a position of power, they will completely miss the opportunity to collaborate with them and to recognize their strengths and assets. For instance, many people live successfully, every day, with significant limitations due to chronic illness. The ability to manage life despite frequent challenges allows people to develop expertise in self-care. Listening to patients' stories helps a social worker truly appreciate their knowledge, proficiency, and capabilities.

Finally, every environment is full of resources (Early & GlenMaye, 2000; Saleebey, 1997). Sometimes it is difficult to believe that rough and impoverished environments are rich with opportunities, but with vision and creativity, social workers recognize these resources. Although the encouragement offered patients to recognize resources in a bleak environment is important, it is also essential to continue to work for social and economic justice. Advocating for community resources to provide equitable opportunities is an important part of a social worker's job and helps patients recognize our support of and belief in their ability to meet their goals (Chadiha et al., 2004; Saleebey, 1997).

Liberal Education

Social work education is carefully constructed with the goal of producing social workers capable of skillful and ethical social work practice in a global community. To ensure that the quality of social education is consistent in all social work education, universities and colleges participate in an accreditation process monitored by a national governing body. The process of accreditation is not unique to social work; many organizations and professional schools, including hospitals, require accreditation. Many funding sources in health care demand that participating organizations or institutions be accredited and social work jobs in health care demand that social work employees be graduates of an accredited school of social work.

Social work education is accredited by the Council of Social Work Education (CSWE). Every accredited school of social work in the United States is accountable to and

BOX 5.1 • *Standards of Professional Social Work Practice*

1. Identify with the social work profession and behave professionally
2. Apply ethical principles to guide professional practice
3. Apply critical thinking to inform and communicate professional judgments
4. Engage diversity and difference in practice
5. Promote human rights and social justice
6. Engage in research-informed practice and practice-informed research
7. Apply knowledge of the human condition
8. Engage in policy practice to deliver effective social work services
9. Respond to and shape an ever-changing professional context
10. Engage, assess, intervene, and evaluate with individuals, families, groups, communities, and organizations

Source: Council on Social Work Education (2003).

evaluated by CSWE on compliance to high standards of preparation and education of social work students, both in undergraduate and graduate programs. Social work students can begin evaluation of social work programs by confirming their accreditation status.

Part of the educational preparation for social workers is built on the expectation that students, both beginners and advanced, start their education in social work based on a platform of liberal education. The CSWE (2008) accreditation standards give social work programs the responsibility of ensuring their students have a liberal education. Based on a variety of ways to think, ask questions, and develop opinions, liberally educated students are taught to think critically about individuals, their history and culture, through art, literature, science, history, and philosophy. Liberal education can result in student development of a holistic perspective of human beings and respect for the diversity of culture, social conditions, and environments.

Liberal education is the foundation of the social work profession and promotes critical thinking and lifelong learning. Social workers must integrate knowledge across disciplines and cultures and be prepared to make contributions to their community. Although the goals of liberal education are mandated by CSWE, the objectives of liberal education are complimentary to standards necessary to be an effective social worker.

Grounded in liberal education, the accreditation body for social work education (CSWE) expects social work practitioners to be prepared to exhibit the core competencies of professional practice (Box5.1).

Critical Thinking

Critical thinking is only one of the goals of liberal education, but the concept is so important to good social work practice that it calls for additional attention. This form of thinking is the ability to analyze and synthesize information. It is the ability to evaluate information based on facts, experiences, and other forms of input. A social worker must have this skill, and it is particularly vital in the field of health care. Critical thinking is essential for social workers because without it, faulty assumptions and ineffective solutions are more likely to occur. Paul and Elder (2006) describe uncritical thinking as being prone to bias, distortion, and prejudice, while critical thinking raises questions, assesses relevant information, develops reasonable conclusions, is open to alternate explanations, and communicates effectively with others.

During each working day, social workers in health care are expected to integrate information from multiple sources: medical records; physician, nurse, and family input; and the patient assessment. Social workers analyze and synthesize the information quickly, accurately, and concisely. Every health-related situation is unique, so there are always new or different details to take into consideration; health is not a constant and the details continue to change. Social workers learn to think "outside the box" and develop creative and effective strategies based on the circumstances of the moment.

Ecological Systems Theory

During the 1950s, two models of psychological intervention emerged: the systems theory and a subtheme of this model, the ecological perspective. Both are ways of looking at the human condition and are rooted in a biological approach. Biologist Ludwig von Bertalanffy named this approach the general systems theory in 1945 (Boyle, Hull, Mather, Smith, & Farley, 2009). Over time, the theory evolved into a "conceptual framework for interdisciplinary applications" (Mikesell, Lusterman, & McDaniel, 1996, p. xiv). The systems theory promotes the idea that there are vital connections between individuals, groups, and environments.

The ecological systems theory examines the individual as part of a larger system, and recognizes every system is made up of smaller systems, or subsystems (Boyle et al., 2009). This framework continues as a major influence in the development of research and social work with families. The theory shapes the way social workers recognize the primary influence of larger systems on the behavior of individuals and families. It encourages social workers to recognize the integration of subsets so instead of looking at the individual and the family alone, it exposes the effect of inter-related systems, such as schools, religious institutions, neighborhoods, and economics, on individuals. Assessment tools such as ecomaps show clients and social workers the relationships between systems.

The systems theory, like the biopsychosocial model, looks beyond the scientific and linear approaches of assessment. Social workers in health care search for strengths within patient and community interactions and resource connections. Interventions are more likely to fail if patients' systems are not considered. No one lives in complete isolation and even the most avoidant or socially disabled person is still part of a system (Mikesell et al., 1996).

Interventions that use the systems theory for assessment result in care plans that include the promotion of quality of life through client relationships with family, caregivers, medical staff, friends, school or work, and church, mosque, or synagogue. A systems perspective assumes the influence of the social, emotional, spiritual, and physical factors in all aspects of health and illness. It endorses the use of community resources, minimizing the impact of disease on the physical, emotional, and functional development of the patient and the caregivers. Interventions based on the systems theory shape a dynamic balance between disease management and quality of life for the patient and caregivers by encouraging the whole system to integrate the functioning of the patient into the environment (Mikesell et al., 1996). Consider the following scenario and consider the possible relationships the patient has with the systems in her life.

Scenario 5:2

Mary was recently told she has multiple sclerosis. The social worker must assist Mary in developing a care plan and in examining her needs and resources for support. She shares that she lives in the city alone and that all of her family members live in a nearby state. Mary left home when she was 17 to pursue her education and employment goals. When Mary talks about how upset her family was when she moved out of the home, telling her they wanted nothing more to do with her. Mary states she has trouble making friends and despite 10 years of independent living, she still feels guilty about leaving home and fears telling her family about her diagnosis.

What role does the family system appear to have in Mary's life? What can a social worker do to help the patient see the benefits of some systems? Is it important for Mary's family to be involved? How could the social worker's values affect an intervention?

Mary's family has a powerful influence in her life. Her family relationships clearly affect her lifestyle and her feelings about herself and others, and the family system will also influence how Mary is able to respond to her chronic illness diagnosis. Mary might gain insight into her relationship with her family, but Mary knows her family best, so regardless of the family dynamics, Mary will use her strengths to guide her response to her health care needs. There are many ways to aid patients toward balanced and healthy interactions using a systems approach and these include open channels of communication, providing education regarding the illness, emphasizing the importance of balance between medical management of the disease and quality of life, and initiating conversations about appropriate self-care (Mikesell et al., 1996).

Caregivers represent a system influenced by disease. Challenges to caregiver well-being can result in family members or others seeming remote or uninvolved in the life of the patient. Economic stress, extended family issues, blended families, losses, changes, and fear about the future can also be significant barriers for caregivers and keep them from stepping into supportive roles. Social workers understand the role of culture and recognize the unique functioning of patients and their supporters.

Systems can have a fixed quality that is resistant to change (Boyle et al., 2009). For instance, if the father is always the strong problem-solver in the family, when the father is sick he may need to remain strong and not reveal that disease has weakened him or that he is ready to die. Families are eager to encourage and to hear good news and frequently fear the news that reveals the progression of disease. It is common to witness a family member communicating with the patient with phrases like, "You feel better, right Dad?" It is important to watch a patient trying to comfort family by reassuring or minimizing the medical condition. The patient is often more willing to reveal the truth about feelings to a social worker than family members. When this occurs, it is a chance to assist the patient to bring the family into more authentic interactions. A change in one member of a supportive unit, as with a new diagnosis of chronic illness, changes the rest of the family system (Dewees, 2006).

Health care systems also respond systemically to the changes that occur within an organization. When a new administrative policy is enacted in one area of a system, it sends a ripple of change through the entire structure. Organizational change has consequences for patients as they negotiate not only their personal experience of disease or illness, but also their experience of the health care system. Acknowledging the influence of multiple and interacting systems ensures social work advocacy is effective for patients, caregivers, and the health care system.

Generalist Perspective

The generalist perspective is the model used to organize undergraduate social work curriculum nationally. The generalist perspective is a philosophy of social work education based on the belief that social workers must gain knowledge, skills, and values that enable them to be capable professionals regardless of the method, system of intervention, client, or field of social work practice. Generalist social work education emphasizes basic techniques such as engagement, crisis intervention, and program planning and social workers apply these skills specifically within their special areas of practice (Christ, 1996; CSWE, 2008).

The CSWE (2008) accreditation body promotes schools of social work to prepare students by using the generalist perspective. Introductory texts in social work clarify the main features of this model: 1) use a human behavior in social environment perspective as a theoretical guide for assessment and intervention; (2) practice social work in multiple levels of intervention that include interactions with client systems such as the individual (micro), groups (mezzo), and large systems or organizations (macro); (3) assume diverse roles as necessary, such as direct service provider, case manager, educator, program developer, advocate, and researcher; (4) practice the integration of direct practice, policy, and research; and (5) conceptualize practice as consisting of five stages: engagement, assessment, planning, implementation, and evaluation of interventions (Kirst-Ashman & Hull, 1999; Miley, O'Melia, & DuBois, 2001; Poulin, 2000).

The generalist perspective trains social workers to assess each unique situation in context of the environment and intervene with the appropriate system, individual, family, community, or organization. Trained to assume a variety of roles and skills, generalist-trained social workers are not limited to use a particular method or model of intervention, such as individual counseling or group counseling. They have the skills to intervene based on a careful assessment of client needs and appropriateness of the intervention to the clients' environment. This process, based on the tenets of the generalist perspective, allow social workers to think broadly, flexibly, and creatively about practice.

Scenario 5:3

Susan is a social worker and works in an HIV clinic. She takes issues of confidentiality very seriously, so it is particularly frustrating that the lab work requested from the hospital arrives at the clinic with personal client information listed next to the lab results. Most people would not recognize the lab work as related to the treatment of an HIV diagnosis, but many staff are aware of the HIV specialty area of the clinic. Susan immediately calls the lab to report this infraction and completes the paperwork needed to formally report the incident to the administration to make sure it does not happen again.

What are the ramifications of policy in an organization? How do patients and workers experience policies? What more can Susan do to ensure this form of breech of confidentiality does not occur again?

Susan understands the systemic movement of information through the hospital. She knows her concern about confidentiality must be communicated beyond the lab technician for improvements to take place. Susan also knows about the stigma experienced by people living with HIV and how this breech of confidentiality might hurt an individual and his or her caregivers. Generalist practice training allows the social worker to interact with the vast array of individuals, groups, and organizations involved in the production of health care interventions for the patient.

Practice Models

Practice models frame an approach to health care delivery and there are distinct differences between the models. The practice model selected determines the type of assessment, intervention, and treatment the patient is offered. One form of practice model treats the disease exclusively, and another model features several areas of assessment and intervention. This is an oversimplification of the differences between practice models, but it reinforces the idea that social workers frequently have a unique perspective in the health care setting because of their attention to the social effects of the illness, not the just the medical condition (Volland, 1996). Treatment plans developed by social workers rely on a clear understanding of the social environment and the interplay between biological, social, emotional, spiritual, and psychological forces. The medical and biomedical models of health care are very different from the biopsychosocial model and the determinants of health models used by social workers and a growing number of other health care professionals.

The Medical Model

When social workers begin to work in health care, they will notice a distinct way of interacting with patients, which is significantly different than experienced in social service agencies. Sometimes the difference is subtle; subtle differences are more common in intimate health care environments such as medical offices or clinics where familiar and respectful professional relationships exist between the medical care providers and patients (Gregorian, 2005). Sometimes the difference in interactions between medical personnel and patients is very obvious and oppressive.

The medical model refers to the structural hierarchy of power that exists in the health care profession. The medical model is a regimented and hierarchal system that recognizes the physician to be the ultimate authority and in sole control of all aspects of care. This way of providing patient care is stifling and unnatural to social workers and other professionals who recognize the worth of interdisciplinary teamwork. A social worker may be caught off guard by this control of patient care, especially if they are prepared instead to "partner" with the other professionals delivering health care (Gregorian, 2005).

The hierarchal roles of patient and physician are deeply rooted in the traditional medical model. The physician is the trained expert and authority, in charge of diagnosis and treatment of disease. The role of the patient is to unquestioningly accept the judgment of the physician and cooperate and comply with the prescribed treatment. The difference between this model and other interdisciplinary alliances is impossible to ignore, particularly for "nonmedical" health care providers. When the medical model is practiced, the patient and other health care professionals are "ordered" by the physician, perhaps in a manner that is condescending, authoritarian, or dictatorial (Gregorian, 2005; Marlatt, 1998).

Recently, I spoke with a past colleague. She is a nurse and the two of us worked side by side during several health-related crises. I asked her about her career. She informed me she is now supervising social workers and stated how incompetent she believed the social workers are and how they did not seem to focus or know how to do simple things, like make referrals, she expected of them. In a small but significant way, this is an example of the medical model at work. This new supervisor is trained to look at health care and at social workers through a medical lens that limits her understanding of what a social worker does. The social workers who work "with her" see their role of intervention as one of listening, assessing, educating, or informing caregivers, and connecting them with medical information and resources for the patient. From a medical model, the clear linear intervention responsibility for social workers appears to be "make the referral." It is common for health care providers trained in the medical model to misunderstand the role of a social worker in the health care field.

Strict practice of the medical model moves patients away from their right to self-determine because health professionals simply follow the orders of the physician. Fortunately, practice of the medical model is on the decline. It is now common for physicians to be taught about the social aspects of disease, cultural competency, and the role of patients in determining their health care. Physicians are also trained to recognize the strengths other disciplines bring to patient health care. Still, the physician has the dominant role in approving the care plan. Social workers are wise to develop and maintain good working relationships with all medical personnel and invite them to witness the care skills they bring to the treatment team (Gregorian, 2005).

The Biomedical Model

Medicine practiced in the West, and particularly in the United States, is based on a model related to the medical model, the biomedical model. The medical model is based on the traditional hierarchy of medical personnel and the linear relationships between doctors, nurses, and patients, but also includes a linear relationship between biology and health. The biomedical model is based on the assumption that health care is based solely on the diagnosis and treatment of disease (Moniz & Gorin, 2007). This model fails to incorporate assessment of human behavior in the social environment and relies on a biological and scientific "cause and effect" method. An assessment of health based on this model needs very little input from the patient, caregivers, or nonmedical disciplines. The value of an assessment using this model is the scientific testing and lab results indicating the disposition of the disease, but when practiced in the purest form, neglects the emotions and social conditions of the individual and promotes a linear understanding of disease (Marlatt, 1998; Moniz & Gorin, 2007; Weick, 1986).

Engel (1977), a physician who challenged the efficacy of the biomedical model, asserted that the biomedical model reduces the assessment, diagnosis, and treatment of illness to the biological. He stated, "It [the biomedical model] assumes disease to be fully accounted for by deviations from the norm of measurable biological variables" (p. 130).

While the biomedical model fits the concept of disease, it ignores the role of health, sickness, and healing and provides little attention to understanding what makes life worth living or what enhances quality of life (Engel, 1977; Greaves, 2002).

Research shows (Cousins, 1979; Engel, 1977; Hubbard, 1995) that traditional medical training shapes physicians and other medical personnel to think of disease and treatment within a biomedical framework before they begin to interact with patients and caregivers. This form of training results in many health care providers that practice the separation of the physical condition from the rest of the patient, including social, emotional, and spiritual conditions. Biomedical health care treatment coupled with the impersonal attention of managed care ignites public discontent with the health care system and often results in the health care system being perceived as impersonal, uncaring, inflexible, and rushed (Engel, 1977).

The Biopsychosocial Model

Radical modifications are occurring in medical training and health professions are emerging from the practice of treatment based on biology alone to more holistic models of care, models that weave together the biological, the psychological, and the social aspects of life (Hine, Howell, & Yonkers, 2008; Zittel, Lawerence, & Wodarski, 2002). As the term suggests, the biopsychosocial theory incorporates the biological, the psychological, and the social determinants of life, and claims assessment in all spheres is necessary in consideration of health and illness (Engel, 1977; Moniz & Gorin, 2007). The model is inclusive and resists the attempt to separate spheres of functioning. The biopsychosocial theory identifies and supports the priority of quality life and incorporates this measure as an important ingredient in understanding and respecting how individuals experience illness and disease (Claiborne & Vandenburgh, 2001; Weick, 1986; Zittel et al., 2002). The biopsychosocial theory embraces the idea that although disease is diagnosed, the individual may feel healthy, and conversely, an individual may feel ill but have no biological evidence of disease (Engel, 1977; Gilbert, 2002; Moniz & Gorin, 2007).

The infusion of the biopsychosocial theory into health care is a significant step in the delivery of care (Moniz & Gorin, 2007). Recent scholarly literature reflects the increased use of the biopsychosocial theory of intervention (Claiborne & Vandenburgh, 2001; Gilbar, 1996; Gilbert, 2002; Hoffman, 2000; Hubbard, 1995; Moniz & Gorin, 2007; van der Walde, Urgenson, Weltz, & Hanna, 2002; Zittel et al., 2002). The biopsychosocial theory is implemented in the treatment of many physical, social, and emotional illnesses (Gilbar, 1996; Ross & Alexander, 2000; Sestini & Pakenham, 2000). There are many advantages to use of the biopsychosocial theory. First, the diagnosis of diseases in minority populations are recognized as being treated more effectively using the biopsychosocial framework (van der Walde et al., 2002). The theory encourages the inclusion of the many unique circumstances of oppression and stigmatization experienced by minority populations in society as well as within the health care system (Moniz & Gorin, 2007). Second, the biopsychosocial theory is incorporated into successful treatment of diseases with particularly challenging interventions such as treatment planning for alcoholism (van der Walde et al., 2002). For example, women who are addicted to alcohol experience biopsychosocial realities that are significant contributors to addiction and different from those of men. Women experience gender-based circumstances such as "social stigma, double standards, differing expectations for men and women, and the fact that women are an oppressed group in numerous cultures" (van der Walde et al., 2002, p. 148). Understanding and incorporating strategies to address these differences is an important step in the design of an accurate and beneficial treatment plan. The biopsychosocial model also assists in understanding the connections between the biological, psychological, and social components in suicide (Hoffman, 2000) and ways to account for the neurological, psychological, and person-in-environment links for people living with Alzheimer's disease (Carson & Goetz, 1998).

Finally, Morantz-Sanchez (2000) suggests that the biopsychosocial theory offers insight into emotional and social incremental inclusion of women in medical care and attributes the model for recent feminist scholarship and the progress made in treating women. Medical systems are making progress in attempts to assess, treat, and receive patient-specific input into all aspects of care, from the initial assessment to the treatment plan. The biopsychosocial theory offers an opportunity to fuse emotional health with physical health for patients, and presents ways to understand the changes in feelings and physical conditions in the overall experience of quality of life (Claiborne & Vandenburgh, 2001).

Every disease has unique psychosocial and developmental challenges and characteristics, whether episodic, chronic, progressive, or life-threatening. However, despite the differences between diseases, there are features that diagnosis of disease has in common, such as fear, helplessness, change, and a sense of isolation. The inclusivity of the biopsychosocial approach assumes that the well-being of the patient depends on the continual adjustment of balance between many spheres of human functioning. Maintaining a sense of balance is vital for patients of all ages and balance is challenged if the only concern is about the receipt of the best possible medical care and ignores quality of life issues.

Social Determinants of Health Model

The people of the world share one common ecological system, the earth. The systems theory is an appropriate framework for assessment of global health because it is clear that the health issues in one country affect the health issues in other countries. Global health is best understood using a model of assessment called the determinants of health model.

An examination of global health quickly reveals the significant inequalities in health, illness, and healing and this gap is widening, particularly between the rich and the poor (Kass, 2004; Marmot, 2005; Saunders, 2006; WHO, 2006). As some countries enjoy the benefits of advanced technology, new medical treatments, and knowledge about the spread of infectious disease, other parts of the world suffer with poor health and remain vulnerable to even the most preventable of health-related conditions. Health is often measured by the longevity of life within a population and when this standard is applied to the state of health throughout the world, the results are staggering. Marmot (2005) reports that inequalities in health based on longevity are radically diverse both between countries, but also within countries. For instance, in Sierra Leone, the longevity rate is 34 years, while in Japan the rate is 81.9 years. In Australia the longevity rate varies by 20 years between the most disenfranchised populations to the most privileged populations (WHO, 2006).

Poverty is certainly the chief contributor to the health status of people and countries, but this is not the complete answer. There are many social causes, or determinants of health, that influence the health and longevity of people. The social determinants that influence health include socioeconomic status, geographic environment, employment status or type of work, violence, and social status. Adequate food or clean water affect the health of an individual, but access to those necessities is often based on social standing and thus are socially determined (Marmot, 2005; WHO, 2006).

The World Health Organization (WHO) established the Commission on Social Determinants of Health with the mission of linking the knowledge of social causes of health and disease and acting to change those social conditions. One obvious way to change social causes is through social solutions, but this relies on change in national and global policies and few prioritize and address global health inequalities (WHO, n.d.).

The Social Determinants of Health model in understanding health promotes the philosophy that health is not purely biological in nature, but that the issues of living in society—psychological, social, cultural, economic, and geographic—also influence health (Frank, Moore, & Ames, 2000; Marmot, 2005; WHO, n.d.). This framework informs social workers that health within a community is related to the social circumstances within the environment. If a community lives in violence, with no access to clean water and limited housing permeated with lead paint, the health conditions for the community are affected. Biological sciences explain the biological process within individuals, and anthropological, historical, and sociological analyses offer the framework to understand the effect of the social environment on health (Kass, 2004; WHO, n.d.).

Application of Theory

Social work students face an enormous challenge when they tackle the complex realities of a professional practice in health care because people collaborating with the health care system as patients are frequently engaged in a form of health crisis. The crisis is associated with disease and affects the quality and longevity of life. Many patients experience an alteration in their understanding of life and may experience profound epistemological struggles as they experience the harsh realities of diagnosis, prognosis, and treatment. There in no way to remain invulnerable to the news of significant health changes and how those changes influence the future.

It is under these circumstances that social workers in health care most often intervene. Few would argue about the need for a social work intervention, but it is important that beyond offering engagement and empathy, social workers strategically apply theoretically based practice. Social theories offer ways to assess, predict outcomes, recognize patterns and relationships, and explain, compare, and evaluate interventions. Theory helps explain, understand, and recognize the unexpected relationships or circumstances that arise. "Theory helps us to bring some order to our practice by providing a filter, screen, or framework with which to put into perspective that mass of knowledge, facts, impressions, and suppositions we develop in the process of therapeutic contact with an individual, family, group, or community" (Turner, 1986, 12).

Social workers are familiar with a range of theories and apply them appropriately to a variety of settings. Social work programs teach many theories, including cognitive-behavioral, developmental, crisis, systems, feminist, and other empowerment theories. These theoretical concepts and methods are applied to complex and demanding settings of professional practice. To do this demands clear and informed critical thinking (Cox, 2001; Petrovich, 2004).

Beyond mastery of diverse theories and applied skills, social workers are also expected to use professional knowledge, skills, and behaviors to promote social justice, empower the disenfranchised, protect confidentiality, and advocate for political change. Social workers enhance competence through partnerships with diverse populations, effective collaboration with all systems, and by encouraging empowerment through recognition of strengths within all systems (Dziegielewski & Green, 2004). The assignment is daunting, particularly when patients and caregivers frequently feel disempowered, disenfranchised, and are resource challenged. The vulnerability of individuals experiencing a health care crisis underscores the need for social work interventions to be organized around solid theories with evidence of success.

Once exposed to the work of social work health care, the reality of the assignment can challenge the most optimistic and idealistic of social workers (Gregorian, 2005). Many experience a crisis of confidence due to the unending human suffering faced on a daily basis. Through private and personal interactions, patients become real people with names, personalities, and families and social workers stand alongside them at some of the most intimate of moments. The complex social network of inequities and forms of discrimination are exposed in the workplace as well as the broader community and present additional challenges (Petrovich, 2004). Social workers personally experience the frustration of nonresponsive systems and seemingly uncaring political structures and may move from excitement about a job in health care to experiencing cynicism, frustration, or anger. The benefit, however, of working in this field remains the knowledge that the unique professional perspective of social workers truly enhances the respect and empowerment of vulnerable individuals in crisis. This field of practice requires professional supervision and support to address the challenges associated with loss, pain, social inequities, and ethical dilemmas.

Summary

Integration of a theoretical approach that both empowers patients and at the same time challenges the traditional biomedical approach to health care is a necessity (Cox, 2001). Theoretical application based on a strengths-based, culturally competent assessment and collection of accurate data recognizes the best resources available to the patient. These resources are best when recognized through the strengths perspective because without this prism there is the risk of missing the strong cultural and social relationships many rely on in crisis. As social workers gain experience, they find answers and understand the real-life situations of the people they partner with. The goal is to work collaboratively with patients, to help them find a sense of ownership of their lives and the strength to determine their course. This is a challenge when the stimuli of the medical environment results in stress, fear, and vulnerability. While the medical model brings focus to the problems and pathology of the disease, social workers encourage colleagues to attend to the whole patient and identify patient strengths.

It is helpful to remember that vulnerable populations are resilient (Saleebey, 1997). People live in dire situations and survive. Patients, too, find ways to go forward and survive despite challenging circumstances. Partnership with a social worker improves the journey. The combination of the strength's perspective and the view of individuals living as part of a complex environment assist the social worker to create a biopsychosocial assessment that reflects the complexities and the opportunities for change for the patient, health care system, and the policies that govern national and global health.

Critical Thinking Questions

1. What kinds of reactions to a disease diagnosis are common to all individuals?

2. How do people in the United States experience the issues of health, illness, and disease that exist in other countries?

3. Do you believe your interactions with health professionals are different with medical personnel than the interactions of your grandparents or elders? Give examples and consider why the differences may exist.

4. How do social workers select the right skills, roles, and theories for providing effective interventions?

5. How can you, as a social worker, advocate and help medical professionals to better understand the social work role with patients?

References

Abrums, M. E., & Leppa, C. (2001). Beyond cultural competence: Teaching about race, gender, class, and sexual orientation. *Journal of Nursing Education, 40*(6), 270–276.

Boyle, S. W., Hull Jr., G. H., Mather, J. H., Smith, L. L., & Farley, O. W. (2009). *Direct practice in social work* (2nd ed.). Boston: Pearson Education.

Carson, W., & Goetz, D. (1998). A biopsychosocial perspective on behavior problems in Alzheimer's disease. *Geriatrics, 53*(1), 56–60.

Chadiha, L. A., Adams, P., Biegel, D. E., Auslander, W., & Gutierrez, L. (2004). Empowering African American women informal caregivers: A literature synthesis and practice strategies. *Social Work, 49*(1), 97–108.

Christ, G. H. (1996). School and agency collaboration in a cost conscious health care environment. In M. D. Mailick & P. Caroff (Eds.), *Professional social work education and health care: Challenges for the future* (pp. 53–72). New York: Hayworth Press.

Clairborne, N. & Vandenburgh, H. (2001). Social workers' role in disease management. *Health & Social Work, 26*(4), 217–225.

Council of Social Work Education. (2008). *Educational policy and accreditation standards.* Alexandria, VA: CSWE Press.

Cousins, N. (1979). *Anatomy of an illness: As perceived by the patient.* Toronto: Norton.

Cox, A. L. (2001). BSW students favor strengths/empowerment-based generalist practice. *Families in Society, 82*(3), 305–313.

Dewees, M. (2006). *Contemporary social work practice.* New York; McGraw-Hill.

Dziegielewski, S. F., & Green, C. E. (2004). Concepts essential to clinical practice. In S. F. Dziegielewski (Ed.), *The challenging face of health care social work: Professional practice in managed behavioral health care* (2nd ed., pp. 107–132). New York: Springer Publishing Company.

Early, T. J., & GlenMaye, L. F. (2000). Valuing families: Social work practice with families from a strengths perspective. *Social Work, 45*(2), 118–130.

Engel, G. (1977). The need for a new medical model: A challenge for biomedicine. *Science, 196,* 129–136.

Frank, J. W., Moore, R. S., & Ames, G. M. (2000). Historical and cultural roots of drinking problems among American Indians. *American Journal of Public Health, 90*(3), 344–351.

Galambos, C. (2003). Moving cultural diversity toward cultural competence in health care. *Health and Social Work, 28*(1), 3–7.

Gilbar, O. (1996). Introducing a biopsychosocial approach in an oncology institute: A case study. *International Social Work, 39*(4), 163–176.

Gilbert, P. (2002). Understanding the biopsychosocial approach: Conceptualization. *Clinical Psychology, 14,* 13–17.

Gossett, M., & Weinmann, M. L. (2007). Evidence-based practice and social work: An illustration of the steps involved. *Health and Social Work, 32*(2), 147–151.

Greaves, D. (2002). Reflections on a new medical cosmology. *Journal of Medical Ethics, 28*(2), 81–85.

Gregorian, C. (2005). A career in hospital social work: Do you have what it takes? *Social Work in Health Care, 40*(3), 1–14.

Hall, J. A., Jensen, G. V., Fortney, M. A., Sutter, J., Locher, J., & Cayner, J. J. (1996). Education of staff and students in health care settings: Integrating practice and research. In M. D. Mailick & P. Caroff (Eds.), *Professional social work education and health care: Challenges for the future* (pp. 91–113). New York: Hayworth Press.

Hine, C. E., Howell, H. B., & Yonkers, K. A. (2008). Integration of medical and psychological treatment within the primary health care setting. *Social Work in Health Care, 47*(2), 122–134.

Hoffman, M. A. (2000). Suicide and hastened death: A biopsychosocial perspective. *Counseling Psychologist, 28*(4), 561–572.

Hubbard, R. (1995). *Profitable promises: Essays on women, science and health.* Monroe, MA: Common Courage Press.

Jenson, J. M. (2005). Connecting science to intervention: Advances, challenges, and the promise of evidence-based practice. *Social Work Research, 29*(3), 131–136.

Kass, N. E. (2004). Public health ethics: From foundations and frameworks to justice and global public health. *Journal of Law, Medicine, and Ethics, 32*(2), 232–242.

Kirst-Ashman, K., & Hull, G. (1999). *Understanding generalist practice* (2nd ed.). Chicago: Nelson-Hall.

Marlatt, G. A. (1998). Highlights of harm reduction: A personal report from the first national harm reduction conference in the United States. In G.A. Marlatt (Ed.), *Harm reduction: Pragmatic strategies for managing high-risk behaviors* (pp. 3–29). New York: Guilford Press.

Marmot, M. (2005). Social determinants of health inequalities. *The Lancet, 365,* 1099–1104.

Mikesell, R. H., Lusterman, D. D., & McDaniel, S. H. (1996). *Integrating family therapy: Handbook of family psychology and systems theory.* Washington, DC: American Psychological Association.

Miley, K. K., O'Melia, M., & DuBois, B. (2001). *Generalist social work practice: An empowering approach.* Boston: Allyn & Bacon.

Moniz, C., & Gorin, S. (2007). *Health and health care policy* (2nd ed.). Boston: Allyn & Bacon.

Morantz-Sanchez, R. (2000). Negotiating power at the bedside: Historical perspectives on nineteenth-century patients and their gynecologists. *Feminist Studies, 26*(2), 287–309.

National Association of Social Workers (NASW). (1999). *Code of Ethics.* Washington, DC: Author.

Paul, R., & Elder, L. (2006). *The miniature guide to critical thinking: Concepts and tools.* Dillion Beach, CA: Foundation for Critical Thinking

Petrovich, A. (2004). Using self-efficacy theory in social work teaching. *Journal of Social Work Education 40*(3), 429–440.

Poulin, J. (2000). *Collaborative social work: Strengths-based generalist practice.* Itasca, IL: Peacock.

Redko, C., Rapp, R. C., Elms, C., Synder, M., & Carlson, R. G. (2007). Understanding the working alliance between persons with substance abuse problem and strengths-based case managers. *Journal of Psychoactive Drugs, 39*(3), 241–250.

Ross, D. D., & Alexander, C. S. (2000). Management of common symptoms in terminally ill patients: Part I. Fatigue, anorexia, cachexia, nausea, and vomiting. *American Family Physician, 64*(5), 807–815.

Saleebey, D. (1997). Introduction: Power in the people. In D. Saleebey (Ed.), *The strengths perspective in social work practice* (2nd ed., pp. 1–18). White Plains, NY: Longman.

Saunders, D. (2006). A global perspective on health promotion and the social determinants of health: Widening gap in health experiences between rich and poor. *Health Promotion Journal of Australia, 17*(3), 165–166.

Sestini, A. J., & Pakenham, K. I. (2000). Cancer of the prostate: A biopsychosocial review. *Journal of Psychosocial Oncology, 18*(1), 17–38.

Strite, S., & Stuart, M. E. (2005). What is an evidence-based, value-based health care system? *Physician Executive, 31*(1), 50–55.

Taylor-Brown, S., Garcia, A., & Kingson, E. (2001). Cultural competence versus cultural chauvinism: Implications for social work. *Health and Social Work, 26*(3), 185–187.

Turner, F. J. (1986). *Social work treatment: Interlocking theoretical approaches* (3rd ed.). New York: Free Press.

van der Walde, H., Urgenson, F., Weltz, S., & Hanna, F. (2002). Women and alcoholism: A biopsychosocial perspective and treatment approaches. *Journal of Counseling and Development, 80*(2), 145–153.

Volland, P. J. (1996). Social work practice in health care: Looking to the future with a different lens. In M. D. Mailick & P. Caroff (Eds.), *Professional social work education and health care: Challenges for the future* (pp. 35–51). New York: Hayworth Press.

Weick, A. (1986). The philosophical context of a health model of social work. *Social Casework: The Journal of Contemporary Social Work, 67*(9), 551–559.

Witkin, S. L., & Harrison, W. D. (2001). Editorial: Whose evidence and for what purpose? *Social Work, 46*(4), 293–297.

World Health Organization (WHO). (2006). *About WHO.* Retrieved September 10, 2008, from http://www.who.int/about/en/

World Health Organization (WHO). (n.d.). *Commission of Social Determinants of Health.* Retrieved September 10, 2008, from http://www.who.int/social_determinants/en/

Zittel, K. M., Lawrence, S., & Wodarski, J. S. (2002). Biopsychosocial model of health and healing: Implications for health social work practice. *Journal of Human Behavior in the Social Environment, 5*(1), 9.

6

Cultural Competence

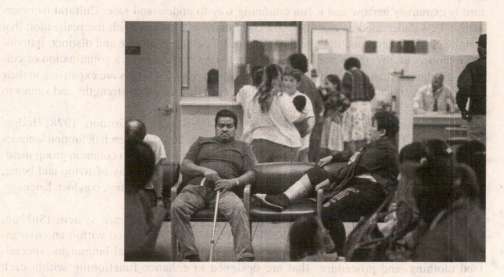

Teaching and Learning Goals

- Recognize the various elements that are important in cultural competence
- Understand that people are members of a variety of cultures
- Recognize ways society responds to cultures
- Discover strategies to enhance cultural competency skills

Cultural memberships influence all aspects of life and are vital to how individuals identify themselves and how they see the world. The influence of cultures is powerful, especially in issues regarding health, illness, and healing. Cultures affect how people experience the health care system, and the support, resources, and choices selected to treat and care for disease-related conditions. When culture is misunderstood or ignored, and when the power of culture is underestimated, conflicts arise. Social workers in the health care system

117

cannot afford to be culturally ignorant because culturally ill-informed health care providers put patients at risk of health complications, unnecessary and recurrent hospitalizations, and early or avoidable death. Health care providers interact with others in ways that value the diversity within cultures, encourage and earn genuine trust and respect. A trusting relationship results in the delivery of quality services to individuals seeking care (Simon & Kodish, 2005).

The Concept of Culture

Social workers are often invited to participate in discussions or trainings on "cultural competence" that are limited to discussions of race. This restricted way of teaching culture is extremely narrow and it is a confining way to understand race. Cultural membership is best understood as existing on a continuum of diversity with the realization that despite cultural commonalities, each member of a culture is unique and distinct. Individual members of any group are unique in many ways. Everyone is a combination of cultures that intersect and together create an individual. Social workers are expansive in their understanding of culture and recognize cultures provide essential strengths and values to individuals.

Culture is defined in a variety of ways by scholars (e.g., Gordon, 1978; Hodge, Struckman, & Trost, 1975; Lum, 1999; Simon & Kodish, 2005), and each definition includes many similarities. Culture is viewed as a group of people who due to common group membership share similar beliefs, values, and behaviors. Culture is a way of living and being, learned and passed on by ancestors, and based on history, beliefs, values, conduct, language, art, and social and personal relationships and experiences.

Cultures also exist in organizations such as the health care system (Subban, Terwoord, & Schuster, 2009). The health care system is organized within an environmental culture that assigns employees unique roles, professional languages, specialized clothing, and procedures that are designed to enhance functioning within each unique health setting. There are systemic values, policies, skills, and knowledge that pass from the elder or experienced professionals to members who are new to the culture. In addition to the system's complex culture, each employee is a complex combination of personal and professional cultures. Every professional in the health culture is influenced and informed by their personal cultures, professional cultures, and by the location, environment, community, and goals of the specific setting. Patients and caregivers rely on individuals, groups, and communities—the micro, mezzo, and macro cultures of health systems—to deliver health care and support and every interaction is a cross-cultural experience (Brody & Hunt, 2005; Lum, 1999; Miley, O'Melia, & Dubois, 1998).

When people associate with the health care culture as patients, they risk experiencing the same fear, ignorance, racism, and stigmatization that exists within other systems in society. Social workers are confident that despite the vast diversity within health care environments, all systems are capable of making positive and incremental changes toward improved cultural competence. The improved cultural competence of individuals and within systems results in respectful and equitable treatment of others. The ways individuals respond to culture is related to both personal and community cultures.

Personal Culture

Culture is personal and although it is often defined based on some form of consensus within cultural groups, there is a vast variety of identity among members. Predicting the values and beliefs of patients by categorizing them into cultural stereotypes is a faulty system, just as categorizing all health care professionals into a specific culture is flawed (Brody & Hunt, 2005; Simon & Kodish, 2005). As social workers gain experience, they witness great diversity within groups. All individuals have needs, wants, beliefs, personalities, knowledge, experiences, and so on, and this personal package of attributes is what makes an individual unique, even within their cultural memberships.

Simon and Kodish (2005) suggest approaching culture in a balanced way that includes the individuals' sense of identity within a culture but values the individuals' personal preference, beliefs, and attitudes. The authors state, "Culture is a more accessible, far less abstract entity if its effects are explored and determined at the individual level" (p. S137). The cultural meaning of health and health treatment varies within cultures, but differences in preferred health interventions are even more obvious between individuals.

Cultural experiences of individuals shape their perceptions of health and health care. Globally, family environments represent the first place family members learn about health. Children are taught about maneuvering through their community and are taught how to avoid danger. In addition, when dependent family members feel ill, the family unit is frequently the first place approached for supportive care. Dependent family members such as older adults, the very young, and those with disabilities or chronic illnesses rely on family to support them and provide care. Outside Westernized and traditional biomedical health care systems, families fill an important role in health care. For instance, primary health treatments for fever, discomfort, pain, bleeding, and other conditions are frequently routines and rituals taught and practiced by families, through many generations. When families recognize they are no longer effective using cultural health care strategies, many approach the health care system or use other alternative health care strategies.

As the generations pass, the adult children may continue to practice some of the remedies they learned within family units, but they are also influenced by their exposure to information, experiences, and environments and this may result in the introduction of new forms of health care. For instance, young adults, newly independent from their families, may realize detrimental health effects of some culturally traditional foods and make personal changes in diet to improve their health. Others protest the traditional safe sex practices taught within families, such as abstinence, and so choose to use alternative birth control or safe sex measures.

Community Culture

Culture is also identified within community and at a macro level culture is influenced by regional and global changes, cross-cultural contacts, globalization, urbanization, technological change, violence, and poverty (Simon & Kodish, 2005). Community cultures are further influenced by inexpensive access to the Internet and the immediate and massive amount of information offered through this medium. Cultures are constantly changing because they are dynamic and respond to environmental alterations. Many examples of changing cultures exist, such as the changes that occur when isolated community cultures are introduced to the effects of incremental changes due to globalization or the dramatic shifts in national economies.

Many countries within the European Union experienced an influx of money and people when they attained membership. For instance, people who grew up in the largely homogenous Irish culture of 50 years ago recognize the extraordinary changes and witness accompanying cultural alterations. Social workers are in danger of making inaccurate generalizations about groups of people if they rely solely on their knowledge of a population and culture and fail to consider the influence of changes that are continually occurring (Schultz, 2004).

Traditional ways to provide health care and healing within minority communities are a valid substitute for those excluded from the biomedical health system. Many cultures continue to practice forms of traditional health care and this influences the interactions with biomedical strategies. For instance, members of the female culture share information about subjects like menopause, pregnancy, menstruation, and other health-related subjects within families and other informal community settings. Women share experiences, beliefs, and observations about pregnancy and childbirth that influence the perceptions of other women. In addition, some ethnic cultures habitually practice herbal and dietary routines and remedies that are respected and effective in treating disease or illness or maintaining health.

Cultures and Health Care

The cultures of individuals inform their worldview. Cultures are alive and are passed to generations through narratives, songs, and traditions that recall, grieve, and celebrate experiences of the past. Cultural competence is necessary to provide respectful and accurate health care and without it, health providers are likely to minimize or misunderstand the emotional, social, or physical reactions of patients and caregivers to social situations. Historically, many cultures have experienced mistreatment related to health that results in cultural suspicion and distrust of the current medical system (Subban, et al., 2008). Some cultures may teach community members to avoid formal medical systems due to past mistreatment and abuse directed toward their community (Subban, et al., 2008).

There are many examples in history that expose the abuse and inequality of health care delivery due to patients' cultural membership. The evidence includes scandalous treatment toward minority cultures such as delays in treatment, withholding treatment, and inadequate, inferior, or dangerous treatment. For instance, the Tuskegee Study (see Chapter 2) serves as an extraordinary reminder of racism within the health care system and may still support cultural fears about issues of safety and quality (Subban, et al., 2008).

Despite the similarities shared, differences are frequently used as an excuse to discriminate. The most common way to understand culture is based on ethnic or racial identities, but it is only part of the picture. Additional variables that influence discrimination include race, gender, sexuality, spirituality, religiosity, age, ethnicity, and economics. Tragically, society uses stereotypes and generalizations to define and compartmentalize cultures and often misses that these broad definitions are only minimally accurate when applied to individuals. Generalizations about groups or communities never account for the unique characteristics of an individual.

The demographics of the United States are constant dynamic and dramatic shifts in populations that support the urgency for the practice of culturally competent social work (Galambos, 2003; NASW, 2003a). The remarkable growth in cultural interactions between countries is also reliant on cultural competency. Many nations are strongly affected by increased exposure to global markets and international news and as a result experience radical changes in the once predictable cultural makeup of their countries (Reynolds, 2004). Once homogenous, many nations are now familiar with the immigration of refugees, asylum seekers, and workers from all over the world seeking employment, safety, or new opportunities. The diversity of cultures requires different methods of health care delivery and requires the provision of effective, high-quality, and culturally appropriate services. This task is both complex and challenging (Leishman, 2004). Frequently, the health needs of new immigrants are complicated due to the extraordinary losses associated with environmental changes and require culturally respectful physical, social, psychological, and spiritual interventions.

Globally, professionals no longer rely on a simple or fixed way to define culture (Moxley, Mahendra, & Vega-Barachowitz, 2004). The traditional definitions and stereotypes of culture are quickly outdated and are no longer accurate ways to understand individuals. This increases the need to professionally critique professional research for legitimate information. For instance, the professional literature describing the cultural experiences of individuals living with HIV or the cultures of Middle Eastern women from 10 years ago are no longer a valid description of those cultures because of radical social changes. Many cultures integrate social changes, although other cultures experience little change. It is unwise to rely on one definition or way of knowing to understand cultural complexities.

Understanding culture helps social workers understand how individuals experience health care and why conflicts can exist between professionals, patients, and caregivers (Brody & Hunt, 2005; Galambos, 2003). Stereotypes of any culture are a poor foundation for culturally competent practice unless validated as accurate by the individual patient. Issues of time and space, extended family participation, verbal and emotional expression, the hierarchy of socioeconomic status, and alternative healing systems vary greatly within cultures and between individuals (Moxley et al., 2004). Each individual is a unique combination of cultures and it includes identification within race, ethnicity, gender, sexuality, religiosity, age, and economics; these variables ensure each individual is more complex than any cultural generalization.

Race

Race is often assigned using visible physical features such as skin color or other distinguishing features and then dividing them into a minimum of three categories: African American, Asian American, and white or Caucasian. There is no simple way to define race. The ramifications and consequences of racial membership are socially determined and socially assigned to explain, justify, support, and practice inequity. In health care, as in society, racial identity can result in the refusal of treatment or inferior care (Malik, 1996; Subban, et al., 2008; Witzig, 1996).

Although there are many different races in the world, the United States often minimizes the significance of these rich and unique cultures into a "black" and "white" issue.

This crude demarcation of race reveals how ineffective it is to use race as a useful descriptor (Witzig, 1996). Racial culture is socially exploited to designate some races as inferior and others as superior. All members of minority cultures experience discrimination, oppression, and inequities in the United States to varying degrees, but individuals of African ancestry predictably suffer race-related social, emotional, and physical assaults in every part of life.

The rich contributions of African Americans are apparent in all areas of society, despite unimaginable and innumerable experiences of suffering, pain, and abuse at the hands of the majority cultures. Despite the legislative progress made due to the Civil Rights Movement of the 1960s, U.S. citizens continue to practice forms of legalized and value-based discrimination that results in cultural distrust, fear, and hatred between the races. Racism is arguably the most challenging social dilemma in the United States. Inequities experienced due to racial membership influence power and access to societal resources, and individual values regarding race continue to affect relationships and can result in defensiveness and suspicion between races.

All racial minorities, but particularly the very poor, experience a lower level of access to quality health care than whites and those who are economically secure. As a result, chronic illness and other life-threatening diseases are statistically and consistently greatest in African American communities. When a racial minority member has access to health care, the experience of racism and discrimination remain (Subban, et al., 2008).

Often the U.S. health care system continues to represent the power of white culture. One way this is evident is in the European American values and traditions of care, but it is also apparent in the fact that an overwhelming majority of health care practitioners are white (Subban, et al., 2008). Providing culturally competent and quality health care, including improved access to care, will continue to be a significant social problem until the health system enfolds individuals, values, and customs into the management of health care (Subban, et al., 2008).

Social workers understand the prevalence of racism, both the intentional and unintentional actions that result in inequitable treatment based on race (Keating & Fox Wetle, 2008). They also know that respectful, genuine, clear, complete, and culturally competent communication is essential with all patients and caregivers. This form of communication, both verbal and nonverbal, is an essential skill for professional practice. The National Association of Social Workers (NASW) Code of Ethics (1999) promotes the principles of service, social justice, dignity and worth of the person, importance of human relationships, integrity, and competence (1999). These principles require social workers to demonstrate empathy, offer access to information, follow through with details in support of health care, and develop trusting relationships with all patients, particularly with individuals who are rightfully concerned about receiving inferior medical treatment.

Ethnicity

Everyone has some form of ethnic identity. While racial cultures are often determined based on skin color, ethnicity is based on the physical characteristics, name, or some other feature thought to identify the national origin of individuals or their ancestors. Sometimes individuals of European descent, particularly those who are generations away from the immigration of their ancestors' experience, express some difficulty identifying with their ethnic culture. The decades or more of acculturation seem to erase or minimize a connection with their ancestors' culture or country of origin. Particularly in the early 1900s, immigrants attempted to quickly blend into predominant United States culture to show their patriotism. This form of acculturation continues to occur today but there is also a growing awareness of the rich legacy inherent in membership within ethnic cultures. More ethnic minority communities work to preserve language, celebrations, history, and other unique characteristics relating to their cultural heritage.

In addition, as second- and third-generation immigrants increasingly identify themselves as a citizen within the country where they reside, the effects of blending and blurring of ethnic cultural traditions occur. However, many are challenged to recognize the specific characteristics of the national culture associated with being a U.S. citizen.

In an effort to educate visitors to the United States, Althen (1988) describes "American ways" and suggests that the U.S. culture has general social traits. The national characteristics of the U.S. national culture are helpful as a way to understand the accuracy of the characteristics assigned to other national cultures. Althen suggests the U.S. culture possesses several predictable, although generalized values: (1) Individualism is a prevalent value that promotes the ideas that individuals need to be responsible for their own life and the consequences of their choices. (2) Equality, although violated regularly, is part of the national culture and proposes that people are born equal and have equal protection under law. (3) Informality is prevalent in U.S. culture and is often evident in an informal manner of speech, dress, and behavior regardless of circumstances. (4) Interest in the future, change, and progress is preferred in U.S. society and is often less concerned about history. There is more interest in working together for change. (5) Commitment to achievement, action, work, and materialism results in admiring people who are driven to work hard. (6) Directness and assertiveness is seen in forthright, frank, and direct discussions and actions. These strategies are perceived as the best ways to communicate and resolve conflict. (7) Time is seen as a resource that can be wasted or used to get things done. Although many might disagree with these statements as U.S. traits, it is a good example of how commonalities within ethnic cultures can be over-simplified or generalized, yet still act to help individuals from other cultures understand unfamiliar experiences.

People subscribe to ethnic values in varying degrees within social situations. The identification and depth of an individual's relationship with ethnic culture is influenced by

---

BOX 6.1 • *Generalized and Predictable Values of U.S. Culture*

1. Individualism
2. Equality
3. Informality
4. Interest in the future, change, and progress
5. Commitment to achievement, action, work, and materialism
6. Directness and assertiveness
7. A concern about time

Source: Althen (1988).

many factors: the length of time living in the United States, socioeconomic status, and societal resources. The connections to ethnic culture contribute to personal values regarding health, illness, and healing. Recognizing the diversity within ethnic cultures is vital. Issues of health, illness prevention, suitable options for treatment, coping, support systems, and the basic beliefs about the value and end of life are part of all cultures. Ethnicity is best understood based on the individuality of each patient (Lassiter, 1995).

There are traditional health treatments in ethnic cultures, including highly developed societies. Often traditional ways to treat disease and injury remain part of an individual's response to a health crisis because ethnic cultures teach about how to relate to life, disease, and death. Patients benefit when their medical assessment and treatment is conducted within their worldview. If generalizations about ethnic cultures are liberally applied to an individual, they miss the unique experience of the individual.

Gender

When a child is born, gender is assigned. If the child is not obviously male or female, a physician decides. Gender identification is significant and determines many social roles including profession, socioeconomic status, and social power. All ethnic cultures use gender identification as a way to organize culture and to assign tasks (Stockard & Johnson, 1992). For instance, regardless of economic or racial privilege, all women experience forms of sexism.

Women who live in the United States are often viewed and treated in discriminatory ways. The dominance of the male gender, regardless of ethnicity or race, is evident in most ways society functions. However, when the female culture intersects with race, poverty, age, sexual identity, or marital status, women experience increased oppression (DuBois & Miley, 2008).

The health care system reflects national sexism. Institutionally, the chief administrative roles in health care systems are primarily held by men. Most of the highest paying and most powerful companies that support the health care industry are run by men. Men determine insurance reimbursement and represent an overwhelming majority of the U.S. legislature and will determine the future of health care policy. Within the profession of social work, despite a clear majority of female professionals, men commonly hold positions of authority and power.

When women seek health care, they risk treatment based on models of care proved beneficial for men, but not necessarily for women (Millner & Widerman, 1994). Women risk experiencing condescending interactions based on stereotypes of women as less intelligent, weaker, emotional, and less capable to handle bad news. Women may experience heightened physical vulnerability in an environment where they are disrobed and physically examined by a male physician. Women may also be reluctant to ask gender-related questions.

Social workers understand that women experience a less powerful position and take concerns or complaints about sexist treatment seriously. Social workers advocate for female patients to access the same information and treatment offered to male patients. In addition, social workers advocate for institutional change when discrepancies in treatment or issues of vulnerability based on gender are apparent, or when promotions and hiring practices fail to consider the capabilities of women candidates.

Sexual Orientation

The culture of sexuality includes a wide range of behaviors, beliefs, and values. For the purpose of this discussion, the topic of sexuality is limited to consensual sexual activity between adults.

Everyone, with very few exceptions, experiences sexual relationships during their lives; however, while some choose to be sexually active, others may abstain from sexual activity. Some are attracted to and may engage in sexual activity with people who are of the other gender, and this is socially labeled as *heterosexual* behavior. This sexual orientation is considered the majority culture of sexual orientation in the United States and male–female relationships experience the privileges associated with this cultural membership.

Some are attracted to or may engage in sexual behavior with people of the same gender and this is socially labeled as *homosexual* behavior. Others are attracted to and may engage in relationships with either gender and this is called *bisexual* behavior. *Transgender* is an overarching term applied to a variety of individuals who do not self-identify with the gender they were assigned at birth or the role society traditionally expects. Transgendered individuals self-identify as a male, female, male/female, female/male, or with some other identity on a gender continuum (DuBois & Miley, 2008). The acronym "LGBT" (lesbian, gay, bisexual, and transgender) is used to unite these cultural minorities. As is true within the sexual relationships of the heterosexual culture, some members of the LGBT culture remain in one committed relationship for decades, whereas others are involved in multiple sexual relationships. The LGBT culture(s) represent sexual identities that result in discrimination and oppression similar to that of other minority cultures.

Research suggests LGBT cultures exist within all social and cultural groups (van Wormer, Wells, & Boes, 2000). In some cultures, members of the LGBT culture are respected and included as important members of the community; however, in other cultures participation in same-gender relationships is prosecuted and punished both formally and informally. Evidence of this oppression is historic, global, and exists today (van Wormer et. al., 2000).

The predominant U.S. culture values heterosexual norms and recognizes heterosexual activity as "normal" and agrees to sanction marriage when the partners are a man and a woman. This gives the heterosexual culture the social power to identify all other forms of sexuality as morally wrong, deviant, illegal, or pathological. Many in society respond with hatred and hostility to people who practice forms of sexual activity other than heterosexuality (van Wormer et. al., 2000). The practice of irrational fear and hatred toward gay and lesbian people is called *homophobia*. Homophobia is a fear of people who practice same-gender sexual relationships and results in physical, social, and emotional rejection by community, family, and religious institutions (DuBois & Miley, 2008). Identifying oneself as gay or lesbian is a potential barrier in many social interactions such as adoption, marriage, hiring, promotion, and housing.

Homophobia exists within the health care system, too (Steele, Tinmouth, & Lu, 2006). Because the LGBT community is stigmatized, men and women may experience delays or avoid getting health care. Barriers to health care and discriminatory practices based on the culture of sexual identification are systemic within all health organizations. For instance, health systems may present barriers to members of the LGBT community that discriminate based on the unique differences in family membership such as restrictions barring partner visitation policies or absence of health insurance coverage to same-sex partners. Identified LGBT health care providers may not have the same opportunities for being hired or promoted. Individuals seeking health care may experience barriers to identify health professionals with expertise in assessment and treatment, and in medical knowledge that supports the LGBT community (Barton, 2003; Lewis, Gladstone, Schmal, & Darbes, 2006; Mravcak, 2006; Preston, D'Augelli, Kassab, & Starks, 2007; Thayer, 2004).

Similar to other minority cultures, members of the LGBT community are at an increased risk of chronic illnesses including risk factors that lead to depression (Silenzio, Pena, Duberstein, Cerel, & Knox, 2007). For instance, gay men continue to experience stigma in health care that aligns homosexual behavior with HIV-positive status. When HIV first came to the public's attention, national political leadership attributed the cause and risk related to the virus as unique to gay men, despite overwhelming evidence to the contrary. The U.S. president and the national administrative team responded to the decimation of the gay community with silence and cut funding for HIV-related research. The national inaction to the health needs of gay men infected with HIV remains a powerful example of the homophobia and hatred within the powerful systems that influence health care policy and medical treatment. The virus became the "gay disease" and all other forms of chronic illness in gay men were minimized.

Women also face barriers to health care that interfere with quality care. Mravcak (2006) states women are often reluctant to ask physicians about their sexual orientation. This leads to a reluctance of the patient to disclose her sexual orientation, and may result in women that lack good information about health issues specific to their sexual orientation (Steele, et al., 2006).

The health care issues for the LGBT community remain understudied (Heck, Sell, & Sheinfeld Gorin, 2006; Steele, et al., 2006). As the LGBT population continues to age, the issues of caregiving and interdependence will influence management of chronic illness, and ultimately determine issues such as quality and quantity of life (Lewis et al., 2006).

Religion

Religion is a propelling force in society and the influence of religious culture is evident everywhere: in individual values, family structure, national policies, and global wars. Organized religion is powerful in society and the members of religious cultures, both traditional and sectarian groups, frequently take the stance that a supreme being supports their beliefs and activities. Religion and spirituality are not synonymous (DuBois & Miley, 2008). Religion is an organized group, while spirituality is a personal way of understanding.

The Judeo-Christian culture is socially accepted as the powerful majority religious culture in the United States (DuBois & Miley, 2008). All other religious cultures are at best tolerated and some cultures are proclaimed evil or viewed as false. Identification with a religious culture often plays an integral role in the life of an individual. It provides a framework for coping with crisis and "it provides roots, a sense of identity and a sense of belonging" (Mindell, 2007, 227).

Social workers understand some patients rely on a religious outline that may be unknown or misunderstood by the majority culture. When a person or caregivers are in crisis, reliance on the language, behaviors, and beliefs associated with a religion are important and help the patient and caregivers make sense of misfortunes and catastrophes (Jacobs, 2008). It is vital that social workers in health care acquire knowledge about the cultures of religion and learn how patients understand the world (DuBois & Miley, 2008). Missing the importance of knowing about a patient's religious culture causes misunderstandings and unnecessary miscommunications between health care providers and the patient.

Religious cultures may share similarities, but there may be vast differences within cultures. There are personally unique beliefs and values about life and death within cultures that are shaped by individuals' experiences. As with all cultures, it is dangerous to assume that membership in a specific form of religion predicts the nature and practice of an individual. Minority religions in the United States are particularly at risk of being viewed with suspicion, ignored, or misunderstood and can result in inappropriate treatment, voidance, or substandard care.

Age

All human beings age; it is one of life's great equalizers. Regardless of race, gender, or socioeconomic status, members of the same generation share personal, national, political, and global experiences that result in a culture that shares language, values, and memories (Hooyman & Kiyak, 2008). Observe individuals who are younger and older and consider how age influences all aspects of life. A culture of age can influence the worldview about music, art, religion, values, beliefs, and actions but is unique to each individual based on their unique combination of cultural memberships.

In a health care system, it is important for social workers to understand that the U.S. culture values youth (DuBois & Miley, 2008). Although some ethnic cultures practice values that show respect for older adults, this is not the case in all cultures. Marketing is often geared toward younger cultures and society values looking, thinking, and acting young.

Within health care systems, older adults are at risk of being treated in a condescending or infantile way. Older adults may experience communication that is simplified and edited as though the content is too difficult for them to understand. Incomplete information about medical choices can lead to care and treatment decisions that are made without regard to their questions or preferences (Diwan & Balaswamy, 2006). Members of the aging culture may value quality of life over longevity and in some situations may choose to discontinue treatment. Quality over longevity is a value conflict in a medical system designed to extend life for as long as possible. Older adults may experience disrespect in a system that promotes strength and vigor as goals. Older patients can be perceived and treated as hypochondriacs, complaining about all kinds of insignificant physical discomforts.

Social workers know many older adults in the United States are on fixed incomes and experience severe financial challenges. Changes to the modern nuclear family often increases geographic distances between family members, resulting in older adults that experience less social, emotional, and physical support from their children. Elders may no longer have children or grandchildren living near them who are available to help them care for their health needs (Bergeron & Gray, 2003; Berkman, Gardner, Zodikoff, & Harootyan, 2005; Diwan & Balaswamy, 2006). Social workers treat older patients with respect. Older adults may initially require education about the radical changes within the health care system, the new treatment options, and the best ways to navigate through an often impersonal health system. Paperwork and insurance claims are overwhelming for most, including older adults. Small print and the demanding and legalistic language of insurance forms can lead to frustration and despair. Social workers understand that the alterations to the system have created barriers for aging patients that are vastly different from the past (Diwan & Balaswamy, 2006). Older adults, particularly those who have been healthy and are not familiar with the current system, may experience feeling overwhelmed and hopeless and benefit from respectful and culturally competent interventions (Berkman et al., 2005).

Socioeconomic Status

Economic culture is arguably the most influential culture in the world when it pertains to the examination of inequity of access to health care (Becker & Tsui, 2008; Ponce, Cochran, Mays, Chia, & Brown, 2008; Reynolds, 2004). The health care individuals receive is often directly linked with their access to goods, money, and other forms of power. The culture of poverty and the accompanying language, beliefs, values, and skills create a unique worldview and acts as a way to translate reality (DuBois & Miley, 2008; Payne, 2001). Worldviews are influenced by personal economics; for those living in poverty, the middle class, and the very rich. The values associated with economic cultures operate to interpret experiences in the health care system. Payne offers several points regarding economic cultures that are transferable to social workers within a health care system: (1) Poverty is relative to environment. Definitions of poverty and wealth are created based on relationships to quantities of money or other resources within the environment. (2) Poverty occurs in all cultures and in all environments. (3) Economic culture is not easily defined, despite attempts to impose criterion and guidelines. (4) Generational poverty, or inherited poverty over generations, is different from situational poverty. Situational poverty is often time-limited and based on current circumstances. (5) There are always exceptions to every stereotype of a culture. (6) All individuals bring an understanding of the rules that operate within their economic culture, such as borrowing, lending, gifts, and support. (7) Health care systems operate from a middle-class to upper-middle-class economic culture and operate using often unclear and hidden rules. (8) Social workers need to understand the economic rules within the health system and teach them to patients so they can improve their success in obtaining services. (9) Patients are often unaware of the economic culture of the health care system because it differs from their own cultures. (10) To utilize the health care system, people cannot rely on their own economic culture. Regardless of economic poverty or wealth, the cultural rules in health care are unique (Payne, 2001).

Social workers recognize the strengths of the patient and are aware finances are not the sole indicator of resources or ways of coping. It is essential to model how the health care system can assess, interpret, and interact with patients in a manner that respects all biopsychosocial resources. To effectively meet the economic expectations of the health system, patients benefit by knowing how charges and bills for services are created, how the resources are utilized, ways to lessen costs, and the options for financial support that are available to them.

BOX 6.2 • *Economic Culture Applied to Health Care*

1. Poverty is relative to environment.
2. Poverty occurs in all cultures and in all environments.
3. Economic culture is not easily defined.
4. Generational poverty, or inherited poverty over generations, is different from situational poverty.
5. There are always exceptions to every stereotype of a culture.
6. All individuals bring an understanding of the rules that operate within their personal economic culture.
7. Health care systems operate from a middle-class to upper-middle-class economic culture and operate using often unclear and hidden rules.
8. Social workers must understand the economic rules within the health care system and educate others about the rules to obtain services.
9. Patients are often unfamiliar with the economic culture of health care.
10. To utilize the health care system, people cannot rely on the rules of their personal economic culture.

Source: Payne (2001).

Poverty is stigmatized in the United States culture (Becker & Tsui, 2008; Payne, 2001; Ponce, et al., 2008) and patients who are poor are at risk for being treated as second-class citizens. Many living in poverty are without insurance and may use emergency rooms as a primary access point to health care for both acute health events and chronic illnesses.

All patients are members of a variety of cultures. The cultural memberships, with all of the rich and unique combinations of multiple cultures, are significant factors in how individuals experience health and the health system designed to care for them. Although cultural values in the United States indicate all should have equal access to affordable, accessible, and culturally competent health care, the privileges associated with majority status within a variety of cultures results in the best health care.

Privilege

Not all cultures are treated equally. Some cultures, particularly members of the "majority" cultures, live with access to power, resources, and money because of the privilege associated with these favored groups (DuBois & Miley, 2008). Acknowledging privilege is important because it is so easy to ignore how this inequity shapes perceptions of the groups that live without privilege. Without privilege in society, people are often suspected as being broken and dysfunctional (Swigonski, 1999).

Many people experience some form of privilege or status within a cultural group. Education, leadership, charisma, talent, wealth, and social status all influence the achievement of privilege. If individuals belong to a socially marginalized group, it is frequently difficult for the privilege they experience within their culture to transfer to another social setting and their status may be lost. For instance, if a female Mexican immigrant creates a successful business and creates jobs and economic growth within the community, she is viewed as a leader in her community. However, her skills and success may be overlooked by the business community of the city where she lives and works. European Americans, however, may experience their privilege extended over many cultural groups by virtue of social power imbedded in the Caucasian culture. Unfortunately, this privilege can result in neglecting the need to understand the values and worldviews of others. Swignoski (1999) challenges European Americans to consider how different life would be without privilege and emphasizes the need to understand privilege from the perspective of marginalized cultures.

Social workers and other health care professionals are members of a privileged culture. Most have access to information, connections, and resources that make their experience with the health care system far different than the patients they are employed to serve. Professional cultures give health care workers power in all of their interactions. Health care providers are often unaware of this privilege or perhaps take it for granted, but it is wise to continually examine the role of professional privilege in cultural competency. Health care workers are often white, educated, and economically secure and would benefit by serious efforts to learn the beliefs, behaviors, and values of other cultural groups (Germain, 1992).

Diversity

Understanding the benefits of diversity and developing an appreciation for the similarities and differences that exist between cultures is the first step toward a lifelong journey of building cultural competence. The human experience is unpredictable so it is impossible to organize individuals into categories. Individuals within cultures exist on a continuum of values, skills, knowledge, and experiences. Attempts to simplify the features of cultures by using generalizations will miss the complexity inherent in all groups. The realities of most cultures challenge the simplistic categories used to organize understanding (Galambos, 2003; Simon & Kodish, 2005).

Consider the following scenario. Think about meeting Moses in an inpatient or outpatient setting. What do his cultural memberships tell you about him?

Scenario 6:1

Moses is a 57-year-old male. He lives in the Midwest and is doing research at a university in Iowa. Moses is in the hospital because he has been experiencing chest pain. He has dark skin, but he is not African American. His parents married in France during World War II. His mother is from Jordan and his father is from Egypt. Moses was raised in Great Britain until he was 20 years old and then moved to the Netherlands to attend a university. He has been living in the United States for the past 15 years. He is not married, but is close to his family who lives in a variety of locations throughout Western Europe, the Middle East, and the United States.

The description of Moses is not unique in today's health care system. Who is Moses? What cultural membership does he claim? How much can social workers depend on professional research alone to understand his interactions with health care?

Social workers approach patients with preconceived ideas regarding the customs of various cultures and confidence about how individuals from many diverse cultures experience health care. However, until the patient is asked, professionals are ignorant of the unique relationship an individual has toward health, illness, and healing.

There are many similarities in the way people live as individuals, in communities, and in countries. Despite striking global differences, there are uniting human themes in the reasons people seek health care for themselves or their families (DuBois & Miley, 2008). People seeking health care want respect, attention, and many feel anxious or fearful. Social workers are of benefit to individuals when they pause to consider how they might feel if they were the patient and interacting with a health care system under similar circumstances. Empathy for the patient and caregivers help social workers to best consider the ways the experience is unique.

Stereotypes and Stigma

Developing stereotypes is part of how humans organize and categorize information about others. Stereotypes are used to explain, predict, or interact with cultures that are different (DuBois & Miley, 2008). Formation of a stereotype often occurs based on an experience with an unfamiliar person or group; and the experiences result in positive, neutral, or negative perceptions. At times, a single event or relationship is associated with and influences future relationships with everyone who shares similar cultural qualities. Negative stereotypes can be dispelled by positive experiences and positive experiences can change negative perceptions.

Realistically, not all people have the same access to experiences with individuals from different cultures. For instance, the United States is made up of many communities developed around ethnic immigrant groups that are homogeneous and experience little contact with people from other racial, ethnic, and religious cultures. In big cities like New York, there are communities where a person can comfortably survive never speaking English. There are also communities throughout the United States where immigrant groups maintain traditional values and relationships and rarely venture out beyond the cultural environment. Bakeries, stores, and churches may all speak the same language and observe similar cultural values, and this offers individuals an opportunity to live in an environment that supports a worldview that is rarely challenged by new and authentic cultural differences.

If individuals do not experience exposure or relationships with the unfamiliar, they develop stereotypes based on artificial and incomplete knowledge. Often stereotypes are based on some form of media coverage. For instance, if someone believes they do not know anyone who is gay, the absence of that kind of relationship significantly limits perceptions of the gay community. The result may be a stereotype that reduces a rich culture of individuals to qualities portrayed through the media. Stereotypes change when knowledge and experiences are acquired and generalizations are challenged by knowledge of a real person. Relationships with individuals from other cultures uncover the diversity that exists between and within cultures.

When stereotypes are unchallenged, they become the groundwork for dangerous stigmatization of groups. This occurs in all social systems, including health care. Stigmatization occurs when fear of certain behaviors, relationships, symptoms, or diagnoses in others leads to discriminatory practices (DuBois & Miley, 2008). HIV is a perfect example of this practice. Decades after the initial cases of HIV came to the nation's attention, it is still considered a gay man's disease (DuBois & Miley, 2008). People continue to wonder if a thin gay man might be HIV-positive. Stigmatization encourages society to avoid advocacy for certain groups and to agree to cultural rules or policies that leave stigmatized people out of mainstream support networks. Society often steps away from groups that are perceived as being outside the mainstream and certain diseases and addictions are regarded as closely associated with disenfranchised groups and often results in overt and subtle incidences of discrimination.

There are many benefits to learning about the basic values and beliefs associated with cultures, but it is important to understand people beyond the group culture definitions (Simon & Kodish, 2005). For instance, many cultures rely on a variety of alternative therapies and practices for their health care, but the practice of alternative treatments varies by each individual. Allow opportunities for patients and caregivers that practice alternative health care to educate, inform, and lead the health team in the development of mutually acceptable treatment options. Taking opportunities to listen and learn from patients takes time, but is of great value to the patient, the social worker, and, ultimately, the health care system (Brody & Hunt, 2005).

Ways to Understand

The health care system in the United States is primarily based on the dominant culture, in a Judeo-Christian, European American male tradition (Galambos, 2003; Reynolds, 2004; Swigonski, 1999). Historically, research, knowledge, and treatment of disease were based solely on the experience of a white male. Provision of health care for European American women was often restricted to issues of pregnancy and childbirth. All ethnic and racial minorities, male and female, were expected to receive their health care "elsewhere."

Today, the traditional model developed for the European American male is understood to be inappropriate to treat all, particularly because of the vast diversity of cultures and the accompanying assortment of biopsychosocial needs. While this fact is understood, frequently health care systems continue to follow traditional patterns of care. The cultural diversity within the U.S. has changed faster than the cultural competence within the health care system. Reynolds (2004) states that the experience of being separated from the security of the culture of origin leads to significant misunderstandings and barriers that interfere with access to culturally matched quality care. The tension that results from the routine application of health-related interventions and a disinterest in patients' cultural connections can eventually lead to struggles and conflicts for both the health care provider and patients. When cultures are misunderstood or ignored, individuals seeking health care and health care professionals collide, resulting in interactions that leave both feeling dissatisfied. Cultural detachment between patients and health care providers can lead to the delivery of substandard care. Some cultures underutilize health services due to the discomfort or pain associated with the cultural insensitivity they experience within the health care system (Galambos, 2003).

Improved competency in interactions with unfamiliar cultures requires social workers to engage in active learning and skill acquisition. In addition, cultural competence calls for a "heightened consciousness and analytical grasp of racism, sexism, ethnocentrism, class conflict, and cross-cultural and intra-cultural diversity" (NASW, 2003b, p. 71). Using an ecological systems approach that recognizes the micro, mezzo, and macro effects of culture in the development of an individual's worldview, social workers recognize the presence of culture as part of every interaction between people (DuBois & Miley, 2008).

There are endless research studies available that examine the combinations of cultures, such as HIV prevention among Hispanic communities; childcare challenges for poor, single-parent families; sexual orientation issues for African American males; depression for gay white males; economic challenges for people living with physical disabilities; and so on. The lists of possible variables that come together for cultural examination highlight the diversity that exists both within and between cultures.

There are some predictable ways for social workers to improve their cultural competence. Two primary ways to learn about the ever-changing nature of culture include (1) examining the generalizations about cultures in the professional research, and (2) by asking the patient.

Generalizations

One way to learn about culture is through knowing and understanding the generalizations that exist regarding cultures. While relying on generalized information about cultures seems dangerously like stereotyping, it is recommended that this information not be the sole source of cultural input. The study of the cultures that exist in society as represented within professional research can illuminate health workers about how cultures may treat and manage disease. Knowledge regarding research studies and experiences with others can create a broad foundation for understanding. Knowing how specific cultures are perceived as interacting with health, illness, and healing frequently informs social workers of how to proceed to assess and treat individuals and how to gather more patient information in a respectful manner (Abrums & Leppa, 2001; Galambos, 2003; Simon & Kodish, 2005).

Social workers recognize that everyone is a composite of many cultures and that reliance on one source of information about individuals' cultures is potentially dangerous. For instance, consider the cultural combinations in the new patient, Marta. She is a young, first-generation Bolivian immigrant. She is a single mother and a full-time professional. Each of her cultures—age, ethnicity, gender, parent, and professional—influence her worldview. To reduce her to a membership in one culture misses vital components that shape her way of functioning and reduces the accuracy and strength of any form of assessment. Regardless of the quality of the research regarding Bolivian immigrants and health care, the qualities that make Marta unique will not emerge. Each of Marta's cultures is rich with language and meaning and together intersect to create the lens she uses to interpret the meaning of her world. Marta's combination of cultures and her personal strengths influence her interactions with her health and the health care system.

Asking the Patient

Another way to understand culture is to ask the patient questions. Genuine and respectful communication with patients is the most accurate way to acquire information about their goals for health. Until social workers ask patients about their needs and expectations, the opportunity to provide culturally competent care is missed. Predictably, individuals do not fit into a generalization, so asking questions, listening, and observing is the best way to understand (DuBois & Miley, 2008; Simon & Kodish, 2005).

Social workers with humility, curiosity, flexibility, and understanding allow the patient to be the teacher and this results in the development of improved cultural competency. It also results in the social workers' ability to respect and advocate for the patient to be treated as they request, within legal and institutional policies. Sometimes the application of cultural values is challenging within institutions. For instance, in some cultures it is not appropriate for a family member to be told about a serious health condition. Perhaps it is considered inappropriate in some cultures to consult with a sick family member about end-of-life care planning or advance directives without additional or specific family members involved or making the decisions. Disrespect of traditions regarding health can damage or sever the opportunity to support the positive efforts to improve the patients' and caregivers' quality of life. Cultures may determine appropriate behaviors (DuBois & Miley, 2008). For instance, in some cultures it is not appropriate for women, like a female social worker, to talk to men about safe sexual behaviors or it may be inappropriate for a male social worker to be alone with a woman. Individuals, with few exceptions, appreciate being asked about their personal beliefs and values and are willing to teach health care providers if they are asked in a respectful and sincere way (Brody & Hunt, 2005; DuBois & Miley, 2008).

To improve understanding of diverse cultures and norms, listen carefully to people that represent all combinations of cultures and allow new information to challenge preconceived ideas. Social workers continue to improve interviewing skills and this results in a respectful and genuine patient relationship that improves the health system's ability to provide quality care.

Cultural guides, professionals and leaders within cultures, are invaluable consultants and can serve as great navigators through sensitive issues or when the social worker is uncertain of how culture is influencing a process. This form of cultural consultation is beneficial and can prevent insulting or hurtful situations and language. For instance, speaking about death varies from culture to culture. A cultural guide can teach ways to talk about end of life that meets the standard of cultural respect and supports conversations regarding grief and loss.

Professional cultural competence is never fully acquired, because the possible blends of cultures and the uniqueness of individuals are overwhelming. However, progress and improvement toward meeting the goal of cultural competence is possible through a commitment to building values, knowledge, and skills through personal and professional development (DuBois & Miley, 2008).

Building Competence

Building cultural competence is a life journey, but progress toward the ultimate goal is essential (Galambos, 2003). Cultural competence is essential to the social work helping process. There are important tools that social workers can use to increase their levels of cultural competence, including self-awareness, a focus on cultural awareness, knowledge acquisition, and skill development (DuBois & Miley, 2008; Lum, 1999; McPhatter, 1997; Moxley et al., 2004; NASW, 2003a; Schultz, 2004; Weaver, 2004).

Self-Awareness

The NASW Code of Ethics (1999) and policy statements (NASW, 2003b) support the critical nature of cultural competence. The NASW Standards for Cultural Competence in Social Work Practice (2001) states that cultural competence includes the principle that behaviors, attitudes, and expectations of professionals, agencies, and systems are harmonious in efforts to deliver services respectful of culture. To support this principle, the profession (DuBois & Miley, 2008; NASW, 2001) promotes the importance of social workers participating in ongoing self-awareness and evaluation of their personal behaviors, attitudes, and expectations.

Self-awareness promotes recognition of personal barriers to professionalism: racism, discrimination, stigmatization, and stereotyping. Authentic examination of self includes recognizing personal participation in these types of prejudice and the realization that these behaviors, attitudes, and values undermine respectful and successful relationships with individuals from other cultures (Heydt & Sherman, 2005). Recognition of personal and biased perceptions of others is the preliminary step toward positive change. Without examination of personal bias, a faulty system of cultural exchange continues to mold interactions with others. Confrontation of stereotypical beliefs, attitudes, and behaviors regarding people from other cultures is a vital step toward achieving self-awareness. As an advocate for patients, developing an understanding of their experiences of discrimination and oppression is critical. Personal or systemic interactions based on cultural incompetence contribute to a variety of barriers and results in unsuccessful attempts to build relationships (Abrums & Leppa, 2001; DuBois & Miley, 2008).

Development of cultural awareness occurs when social workers acknowledge their own cultural identity and the influence this identity has on their understanding of others (Lum, 1999; NASW, 2003a; Schultz, 2004). Schultz (2004) suggests that self-evaluation include (1) a professionals' growing awareness of personal prejudices, (2) understanding their limitations in knowledge and skills, and (3) insight into the effect of their culture on interactions with patients. Authentic self-evaluation is challenging, but if it is truly achieved, it is life-altering and can lead to profound insight into one's personal worldview. Self-evaluation requires complete honesty about issues of discrimination, stereotypes, and racism and is frequently painful. The self-examination includes recognizing personal privilege or coming to terms with experiences of discrimination that resulted in feelings of denial, accusation, guilt, and confession (Abrums & Leppa, 2001; DuBois & Miley, 2008). Although the evaluation process can lead to personal pain, the enhanced level of awareness is essential.

Self-awareness can move social workers toward recognition of similarities between cultures. Commonalities between individuals from a variety of cultures are powerful and reach beyond the ignorance and devaluation of others. Admittedly, the self-awareness process is only the beginning, but social workers who recognize the common elements people share are more likely to experience empathy for others. This is a healthy place to start a professional relationship. Empathy influences all interactions with a patient because it shapes relationships in both personal and professional ways that consider the situation from the patient's point of view (DuBois & Miley, 2008; Sheafor & Horejsi, 2008).

Part of self-awareness is the ability to see oneself as both an individual and as a member of various cultures. Cultural connections that offer societal privilege require frequent examination of how those advantages affect the social worker's worldview and relationships with others. Self-awareness leads to self-examination in personal and professional roles.

Social workers work toward honest reflection about their barriers to culturally competent care. By facing personal and professional contributions to discrimination, social workers move toward seeing individuals from unfamiliar cultures with empathy. Learning to listen and honor the behaviors, needs, and desires of the patient, social workers promote the development of a cultural bridge (DuBois & Miley, 2008; Reynolds, 2004; Schultz, 2004; Sheafor & Horejsi, 2008; Taylor-Brown, Garcia, & Kingson, 2001).

Cultural Awareness

The effects of racism, sexism, ageism, and homophobia are damaging in the lives of individuals. The damage occurs when the dominant and privileged cultural values, defined as the norm for society, result in situations of oppression for others (Abrums & Leppa, 2001). Social workers benefit by interacting with people who are different from themselves because it develops understanding and empathy in personal ways that influence professional practice (DuBois & Miley, 2008; Sheafor & Horejsi, 2008).

Because the cultures of patients influence their experiences, social workers interact with cultures to learn how best to meet the needs of patients, caregivers, and communities in the most appropriate ways possible. Understanding the needs of patients contributes to how care provision contributes to overall problem solving and matches the strengths of culture to the appropriate health interventions (Williams, 2006).

Despite the growing diversity of cultures represented by health care professionals, the cultural norms of a health care system are powerful and are frequently limited in offering culturally sensitive services (Schultz, 2004). Many who enter a health care system experience the frightening nature of the unknown. The sounds, sights, smells, and procedures are foreign to most, and often add to a sense of helplessness.

The practice of cultural competence is fundamental to the provision of health care because patients are vulnerable to misunderstandings and mistakes when the environment is unknown. Reynolds (2004) suggests several underlying themes that pose significant challenges to health professionals acquiring cultural competence: (1) a lack of basic cultural knowledge, (2) a lack of appreciation and respect for culture, (3) a lack of translation and interpretive services, and (4) a hierarchal approach to health care. Health systems frequently possess these characteristics and this can result in the obstruction of quality care. To make advancements toward cultural competence, some health care systems incorporate trainings at all levels of service delivery and are vigilant about the maintenance of this training.

Health care environments possess opportunities to send strong messages regarding the value of cultural competence. Hospitals, physician offices, and clinics can employ professionals from a variety of racial and ethnic groups. Intercultural workforces increase the likelihood patients from minority cultures will feel safe and understood and may offer accommodations of other languages. Hiring people from a variety of cultures also strengthens cultural competency of staff from privileged cultures and is a powerful way for people to share professional cultures, as well as to cross-teach ethnic, racial, and other cultural norms (Subban, et al., 2008). Health care environments that provide information in a variety of languages and furnish offices in culturally thoughtful ways show respect for a variety of cultures and enhance satisfaction with care delivery. Social workers assess and monitor health care environments and advocate for ways to break down cultural barriers.

Knowledge Acquisition

Individuals receiving care for health conditions soon learn the language and culture associated with the symptoms, diagnosis, testing, and treatment of their medical condition. Social workers, too, soon learn the language of the health care system. In addition, when social workers interact with individuals from unfamiliar cultures, they learn about new worldviews, languages, beliefs, values, and behaviors. Personal interactions with individuals are the best way to learn about cultures, but it is also very important to apply other forms of knowledge about culture in interactions with others (NASW, 2003a).

A broad understanding of cultures assists social workers to consider the cultural specificity of interventions. For instance, social workers know culture influences the way individuals interact with their family and community. Knowing this can shape the questions asked at intake and during assessment (Sheafor & Horejsi, 2008). The social worker understands that all interactions with patients, caregivers, and other professionals are culturally influenced so knowledge of cultural history, experiences, and values can help guide the process to result in competent interactions and support.

Social workers know that ways of behaving, thinking, and feeling within a health system are based on many types of cultures (Schultz, 2004). The cultures of gender, age, economics, and sexual identity also influence the selection of interventions in health settings. Women do not have the same symptoms of distress prior to a heart attack that men have. Children and older adults do not take the same medications or dosages that adults do. African American men have higher rates of some diseases than European American men and people living in industrialized countries are more prone to obesity, diabetes, and heart-related illness. While these facts are generalized to populations, the generalizations can serve an important role foundation for professional relationships with individuals. Facts about how an individual experiences health is specific to individuals, but may begin with the knowledge acquired through reading and studying of professional research before engagement with an individual.

Skill Development

The development of professional skills results in social workers applying their professional knowledge of other cultures in practice (DuBois & Miley, 2008; Lum, 1999; Sheafor & Horejsi, 2008). Relying on the skills of empathy are not enough, and this is what makes social workers unique within the health care system. The creation of productive relationships between racially and ethnically diverse patients depends on good communication, cultural competence, and respect of differences (Reynolds, 2004).

Social workers in health care must learn to quickly be comfortable with the unpredictable. This is challenging because hospitals and clinics work with all kinds of people, some experiencing very disturbing situations. People using the health care system include individuals from a wide variety of cultures. Some individuals enter health care intoxicated, psychotic, or desperate. Others are severely sick or hurt, and still others are worried and in crisis about someone they love. The cultures of mental illness, poverty, and addiction overwhelm health care systems designed to work with people who are competent, compliant, and capable, and when one of these components is missing, frequently staff, intentionally or unintentionally, communicate discomfort, if not disgust (Nelson & Merighi, 2003; Weaver, 2004).

Social workers are skilled in interview techniques and rely on the ability to communicate and empathize with the patient and build trust and respect. They are trained to ask patients open-ended questions, educate about health options, guard patients' dignity and confidentiality, attend to patients' priorities, and create ways to support caregivers (Weaver, 2004).

Social workers in health care quickly learn how to help patients from a different culture become more comfortable. The damage from stigma, prejudice, intolerance, stereotypical generalizations, and continued discrimination can leave little trust. Professional social workers attempt to use their privileged culture to work for justice, and this is evident within culturally informed interactions with patients.

The steps of self-awareness, cultural awareness, knowledge acquisition, and skill development are helpful steps toward cultural competence. Social workers apply critical thought to process, analyze, and evaluate information and events with the goal of refinement and improvement in cross-cultural understanding (Lum, 1999; Paul & Elder, 2006; Sheafor & Horejsi, 2008). This process leads to improved reasoning and results in acknowledging and respecting a patient's values and decision-making power regarding health.

An individual's culture is their strength (Lum, 1999). Identification with culture gives everyone a way to negotiate the unknown and offers a source of strength. Instead of interpreting differences as "wrong," social workers look for the cultural characteristics to emerge as strengths in the patient's life. Patients survived prior to their interaction with the health care system and the same source of resilience that supported them through other issues in their lives is the foundation of strengths used to survive in all situations. The NASW Code of Ethics directs social workers to respond to diversity factors in practice by recognizing strengths and empowering patients to shape self-determined interventions (DuBois & Miley, 2008; Galambos, 2003; Sheafor & Horejsi, 2008).

Summary

The changing demographics in the United States, and throughout the globe, demand social workers continue to develop their cultural competency skills and recognize the rich and complex issues related to cultures (Abrums & Leppa, 2001; DuBois & Miley, 2008). Quality care relies on systems at all levels—personally, organizationally, nationally, and globally—to communicate and understand that cultural factors affect health behavior. Social workers prioritize the practice of cultural competence within the health system and encourage and support health care management to achieve improved equity and care for all patients. Positioned to be leaders in promoting systemic change (Reynolds, 2004), social workers need to continually add to develop, practice, provide, and teach culturally competent care.

Critical Thinking Questions

1. What health-related strategies and knowledge did you learn within your culture?

2. What kinds of cultural experiences influence your interactions with the health care system?

3. How many cultures influence your identity? Does one of those memberships influence you more than others? Why?

4. What are some of the subtle or overt ways your ethnicity influences your perception of health or your interactions in the health care system?

5. Watch the movie *Philadelphia* with Tom Hanks and Denzel Washington. How do both of the characters they play challenge social stereotypes?

6. What are some of the cultural features of the health care environment?

References

Abrums, M. E., & Leppa, C. (2001). Beyond cultural competence: Teaching about race, gender, class, and sexual orientation. *Journal of Nursing Education 40*(6), 270–276.

Althen, G. (1988). *American ways: A guide for foreigners in the United States.* Yarmouth, MA: Intercultural Press.

Barton, M. A. (2003). Who should reap the benefits? Cities and counties debate whether to extend benefits to domestic partners. *American City and County, 118*(13), 64–66.

Becker, D., & Tsui, A. O. (2008). Reproductive health service preferences and perceptions of quality among low-income women: Racial, ethnic and language group differences. *Perspectives on Sexual and Reproductive Health, 40*(4), 202–211.

Bergeron, L. R., & Gray, B. (2003). Ethical dilemmas of reporting suspected elder abuse. *Social Work, 48*(1), 96–106.

Berkman, B. J., Gardner, D., Zodikoff, B. D., & Harootyan, L. K. (2005). Social work in health care with older adults: Future challenges. *Families in Society, 86*(3), 329–338.

Brody, H., & Hunt, L. M. (2005). Moving beyond cultural stereotypes in end-of-life decision making. *American Family Physician, 71*(3), 429–431.

Diwan, S., & Balaswamy, S. (2006). Social work with older adults in health-care settings. In S. Gehlert & T. A. Browne (Eds.), *Handbook of health social work* (pp. 417–447). Hoboken, NJ: Wiley.

DuBois, B., & Miley, K. K. (2008). *Social work: An empowering profession* (6th ed.). Boston: Allyn & Bacon.

Galambos, C. M. (2003). Moving cultural diversity toward cultural competence in health care. *Health and Social Work, 28*(1), 3–6.

Germain, C. (1992). Cultural care: A bridge between sickness, illness, and disease. *Holistic Nursing Practitioner, 6*(3), 1–9.

Gordon, M. M. (1978). *Human nature, class, and ethnicity.* New York: Oxford University Press.

Heck, J. E., Sell, R. L., & Sheinfeld Gorin, S. (2006). Health care access among individuals involved in same-sex relationships. *American Journal of Public Health, 96*(6), 1111–1118.

Heydt, M. J., & Sherman, N. E. (2005). Conscious use of self: Tuning the instrument of social work practice with cultural competence. *Journal of Baccalaureate Social Work, 10*(2), 25–40.

Hodge, J. L., Struckman, D. K., & Trost, L. D. (1975). *Cultural basis of racism and group oppression.* Berkeley, CA: Two Riders Press.

Hooyman, N. R., & Kiyak, H. A. (2008). *Social gerontology: A multidisciplinary perspective* (8th ed.). Boston: Allyn & Bacon.

Jacobs, M. R. (2008). What are we doing here? Chaplains in contemporary health care. *The Hasting Center Report, 38*(6), 15–20.

Keating, N., & Fox Wetle, T. (2008). Longevity, health and well-being: Issues in aging North America. *The Journal of Nutrition, Health & Aging, 12*(2), 2.

Lassiter, S. M. (1995). *Multicultural clients: A professional handbook for health care providers and social workers.* Westport, CT: Greenwood Press.

Leishman, J. (2004). Perspective of cultural competence in health care. *Nursing Standard, 19*(11), 33–39.

Lewis, M. A., Gladstone, E., Schmal, S., & Darbes, L. A. (2006). Health-related social control and relationship interdependence among gay couples. *Health Education Research Theory and Practice, 21*(4), 488–500.

Lum, D. (1999). *Culturally competent practice.* New York: Brooks/Cole.

Malik, K. (1996). *The meaning of race: Race, history & culture in western society.* New York: New York University Press.

McPhatter, A. R. (1997). Cultural competence in child welfare: What is it? How do we achieve it? What happens without it? *Child Welfare, 76,* 255–278.

Miley, K. K., O'Melia, M., & Dubois, B. I. (1998). *Generalist social work practice: An empowering approach.* Boston: Allyn & Bacon.

Millner, L., & Widerman, E. (1994). Women's health issues: A review of the current literature in the social work journals, 1985–1992. *Social Work in Health Care, 19*(3/4), 145–172.

Mindell, C. L. (2007). Religious bigotry and religious minorities. In G. A. Appleby, E. Colon, & J. Hamilton (Eds.), *Diversity, oppression, and social functioning: Person-in-environment assessment and intervention* (pp. 236–246). Boston: Allyn & Bacon.

Moxley, A., Mahendra, N., & Vega-Barachowitz, C. (2004). Cultural competence in health care. *ASHA Leader, 9*(7), 6–11.

Mravcak, S. A. (2006). *Primary care for lesbians and bisexual women.* Shawnee Mission, KS: American Academy of Family Physicians. Retrieved September 10, 2008, from http://www.aafp.org/afp

National Association of Social Workers (NASW). (1999). *Code of ethics.* Washington, DC: NASW Press.

National Association of Social Workers (NASW). (2001). *National Association of Social Workers standards for cultural competence in social work practice.* Washington, DC: NASW Press.

National Association of Social Workers (NASW). (2003a). Cultural competence in the social work profession. In *Social work speaks: National Association of Social Workers policy statements, 2003–2006* (pp. 50–62). Washington, DC: NASW Press.

National Association of Social Workers (NASW). (2003b). *Social work speaks: National association of social workers policy statements, 2003–2006.* Washington, DC: NASW Press.

Nelson, K. R., & Merighi, J. R. (2003). Emotional dissonance in medical social work practice. *Social Work and Health Care, 36*(3), 63–79.

Paul, R., & Elder, L. (2006). *The miniature guide to critical thinking; Concepts and tools.* Dillon Beach, CA: Foundation for Critical Thinking.

Payne, R. K. (2001). *A framework for understanding poverty.* Highlands, TX: aha! Process, Inc.

Ponce, N. A., Cochran, S. D., Mays, V. M., Cia, J., & Brown, E. R. (2008). Health coverage of low-income citizen and noncitizen wage earners: Source and disparities. *Journal of Immigrant Minority Health, 10,* 167–176.

Preston, D. B., D'Augelli, A. R., Kassab, C. D., & Starks, M. T. (2007). The relationship of stigma to the sexual risk behavior of rural men who have sex with men. *AIDS Education and Prevention, 19*(3), 218–230.

Reynolds, D. (2004). Improving care and interactions with racially and ethnically diverse populations in healthcare organizations. *Journal of Healthcare Management, 49*(4), 237–250.

Schultz, D. (2004). Cultural competence in psychosocial and psychiatric care: A critical perspective with reference to research and clinical experiences in California, US and in Germany. *Increasing Cultural Competence in Services: Managing Diversity, 39*(3/4), 231–247.

Sheafor, B. W., & Horejsi, C. R. (2008). *Techniques and guidelines for social work practice* (8th ed.). Boston: Allyn & Bacon.

Silenzio, V., M., Pena, J. B., Duberstein, P., R., Cerel, J., & Knox, K. L. (2007). Sexual orientation and risk factors for suicidal ideation and suicide attempts among adolescents and young adults. *American Journal of Public Health, 97*(11), 2017–2019.

Simon, C. M., & Kodish, E. D. (2005). "Step into my zapatos, doc": Understanding and reducing communication disparities in the multicultural informed consent setting. *Perspectives in Biology and Medicine, 48*(1), 123–139.

Steele, L. S., Tinmouth, J. M., & Lu, A. (2006). Regular health care use by lesbians: A path analysis of predictive factors. *Family Practice – an international journal, 23,* 631–636.

Stockard, J., & Johnson, M. M. (1992). *Sex and gender in society* (2nd ed.). New York: Simon & Schuster.

Subban, J. E., Terwood, N. A., & Schuster, R. J. (2008). With or without intent: How racial disparities prevent effective implementation of care. *The Journal of Nutrition, Health & Aging, 12*(10), 770S–775S.

Swigonski, M. E. (1999). Challenging privilege through Africentric social work. In P.L. Ewalt, E. M. Freeman, A. E. Fortune, D. L. Poole, & S. L. Witkin (Eds.), *Multicultural issues in social work: Practice and research* (pp. 50–61). Washington, DC: NASW Press.

Taylor-Brown, S., Garcia, A., & Kingson, E. (2001). Cultural competence versus cultural chauvinism: Implications for social work. *Health and Social Work, 26*(3), 185–187.

Thayer, L. (2004). For better lesbian health, fewer barriers to care. *The Women's Health Activist, 29*(3), 6–8.

van Wormer, K., Wells, J., & Boes, M. (2000). *Social work with lesbians, gays, and bisexuals: A strengths perspective.* Boston: Allyn & Bacon.

Weaver, H. N. (2004). The elements of cultural competence: Applications with Native American clients. *Journal of Ethnic and Cultural Diversity in Social Work, 13*(1), 19–35.

Williams, C. C. (2006). The epistemology of cultural competence. *Families in Society: The Journal of Contemporary Social Services, 87*(2), 209–220.

Witzig, R. (1996). The medicalization of race: Scientific legitimization of a flawed social construct. *Annals of Internal Medicine, 125*(8), 675–679.

7

Engagement and Assessment

Teaching and Learning Goals

- Recognize the importance of the beginning of the patient/social worker relationship
- Understand the significance of an initial assessment
- Understand the traits that impact engagement
- Recognize the types of assessment and how to use them
- Understand the elements that influence individuals in crisis

Engagement is the process of establishing a professional relationship and it is an essential part of working with everyone in every field of social work practice. The success of engagement depends on several key factors: the personalities of the professional social worker and the patient, the skills of the social worker, and the circumstances leading to the initial meeting (Gearing, Saini, & McNeill, 2007). The social worker develops relationships grounded in authenticity, personal warmth, and displays of respect. A skillful social worker is purposeful in beginning and sustaining relationships. An important element in sustaining a professional relationship is the ability to attend to both physical communications and the emotional meaning beyond the actual words. The circumstances leading to the beginning of the relationship shape the engagement process (Sheafor & Horejsi, 2008). For instance, if someone is seeking routine health care, the process of relationship building will demand the same skills as meeting someone who is recently referred to hospice; however, the unique circumstances inherent in these different situations molds how the patient, family, and social worker proceed (Clairborne & Vandenburgh, 2001; Murphy & Dillon, 2003; Sheafor & Horejsi, 2008).

Process of Engagement

Engagement is typically the word used to describe relationship building, particularly the first meeting with an individual, group, or community, but the engagement process continues after the first meeting. Beyond the initial meeting, the social worker and patient (or group) continues to build on past interactions. These interactions form the relationship necessary to work together on the patient's goals. Goals are formed through an assessment process and are frequently addressed through a series of steps that take place in one or more meetings or interactions with the patient or his or her caregivers. From the first moment of engagement, assessment begins and the steps follow a rather predictable path: introductions, questioning, and reflection. Although assessment remains ongoing throughout the relationship, it is the entire process that forms and revises the goals and objectives of the patient, and assists the care team to support the patient (Clairborne & Vandenburgh, 2001; Sheafor & Horejsi, 2008).

There are many ways to complete an assessment; the most common way is an interview. Health care settings rarely offer social workers opportunities to meet with patients for lengthy appointments to discuss the psychosocial needs of the patient, so assessment is done through questioning the patient, reading the patient record, and through other assessment tools such as a genogram or ecomap. The type of assessment completed depends on the characteristics of the people involved, the situation, the environment, and the culture. In health care settings, assessment is frequently completed during a time of crisis so immediate and concrete actions of support are particularly helpful ways to begin the engagement process. Social workers have limited time to display empathy and support to patients and caregivers and help them understand their choices so it is vital that the time spent meeting and working with the patient is productive. The success of engagement is not accidental but depends on professional skills and deliberation. Read the following scenario and consider the challenges and opportunities to engagement and the development of a professional relationship.

Scenario 7:1

A social worker from a HIV clinic never works on the weekends, but this weekend she receives a call at home from one of the clinic's infectious disease physicians. He asks if she would please go to one of the city hospitals and meet Molly, the wife of a man named George. George is newly diagnosed with acquired immunodeficiency syndrome (AIDS). The couple has two children, ages

12 and 14. Two days ago, George presented to the emergency room with a serious and resistant pneumonia that did not respond to routine medical treatment. Given his marital status, the primary doctor never considered ordering a HIV test. After the consultation with the infectious disease physician, and a HIV test, it is confirmed that George has pnemocystis pneumonia, a form of pneumonia that is a relatively common opportunistic disease for people with late-stage AIDS. George is sedated and on a ventilator to assist with breathing and Molly is in shock. The physician is waiting for Molly to absorb all of the news—her husband's critical condition, his diagnosis, and his risk factors. The physician wants Molly to be tested for HIV as soon as possible, but is reluctant to discuss this with her given all of the shocking news she is experiencing. The physician wants the social worker to speak with Molly about taking a HIV test.

What can you assess about the situation based on the physician phone call? What facts do you still need to know to begin engagement with Molly? Do you have any personal values that influence your plan of action?

When two people meet, there are many ways to respond. Sometimes both parties experience a genuine and warm interaction almost immediately and a professional relationship is quickly formed. Other forms of relationships are more utilitarian. The stress of meeting new people, sharing personal information, and perhaps engaging in several interviews by many different kinds of professionals can often leave a person experiencing a health concern emotionally altered and vulnerable. People respond to stressors in many different ways, including hostility, fear, numbness, confusion, and denial (Clairborne & Vandenburgh, 2001; Gearing et al., 2007). Some patients try hard to be the "perfect" patient, hoping to be liked by staff and treated well. For a social worker in health care the moment of meeting a person in crisis is best recognized as a privilege. It may be the worst day in the life of this person, but there is an opportunity to support them. The social worker joins with the patient and support systems at a point that is uniquely personal and private and interactions call for the social worker to respond with personal and professional strength (Gregorian, 2005).

Personal Strength

The social worker must display personality strength in the engagement process. There are many skills that are essential to bring to interventions, but social workers must also rely on their innate ability to express genuine and authentic concern for others. It is impossible to falsify genuine concern for very long. Social workers must genuinely believe in the strength of people and respect the uniqueness of each individual. It also means stepping away from critical and judgmental attitudes and opinions about people who act and react to situations in unfamiliar ways (Gregorian, 2005). For instance, when approaching Molly, paralyzed with shock beside the bed of her husband, empathy can be expressed in actions, facial expressions, and words. In addition, the moment requires evidence of genuine concern about the biopsychosocial needs of both George and Molly despite any potential conflicts between them.

One way social workers express their authenticity is through personal warmth and regard for patients and their support systems. Authenticity, approachability, expressions of care, acceptability, ability to listen, confidentiality, and predictable follow-through are all ways social workers express their personal warmth and regard for others (Sheafor & Horejsi, 2008). Showing authentic respect for Molly may mean being silent with her, or using a soft voice. Perhaps saying her name in a gentle manner will bring her back into the moment. A genuinely caring social worker will be in touch with the moment and express empathy in the unique way necessary for this individual, Molly, in her situation, in this environment, and with respect for her culture.

Showing respect for patients includes embracing their right to self-determination. Sometimes it is challenging to support the decisions of others, particularly when those decisions do not match the choice the social worker would make under the same circumstances. Self-determination does not mean standing back to watch patients make decisions based on incorrect or inadequate information, but it does mean that after all of the options of health treatment, including the choice of no treatment, are presented, the patient is the one who decides. Working with Molly, and George, if he recovers enough to be taken off the ventilator, means review of information they already heard from the medical staff. Social workers communicate clearly with patients and resist language that is too technical. They assess if the patient and family really hear the information and understand the content and implications. The social worker for Molly and George communicates concerns about their coping skills and other concerns to the rest of the health team so that the entire health team has an opportunity to consistently and accurately meet their biopsychosocial needs (Clairborne & Vandenburgh, 2001).

The personal right to make a decision about one's health treatment seems so obvious, but there are many barriers in place to interfere with this right, including well-intentioned health care teams (Luptak, 2004). It is the role of the social worker to clearly help the patient maintain control over the treatment agenda within the medical team. When health care teams ignore or minimize the patient's decision, it is rarely done with deliberate disrespect. Instead, the health care team may be so prepared to provide an effective form of treatment, they fail to consider the biological, psychological, and social circumstances that might lead the patient to make a different treatment choice.

Professional Skills

The social worker also practices professional skills in the engagement process. The process requires thoughtful and deliberate choices to engage with Molly; an assessment of the situation begins before meeting her. What is known about the person? What is known about the situation? Are there additional supportive resources in place? What emotions might be experienced in this situation? Social workers proceed by setting personal issues aside and begin the move into the moment. Often there is little time to facilitate professionally approaching a new situation, so social workers learn to adjust to new situations quickly (Gregorian, 2005).

Meeting Molly while she is experiencing emotional shock may mean that Molly will not think and process in her routine fashion. Molly has just absorbed several shocking and confusing pieces of news and her strength may be depleted. It is helpful to prepare to meet Molly by reviewing the information she has just absorbed. First, her husband is so sick he cannot breathe on his own and there is a serious chance he could die. Second, her husband has AIDS. Molly, like many others, may be ill-informed about the disease and unaware that it could have anything to do with her "no-risk" lifestyle; that George is diagnosed with this disease is truly unbelievable. Third, her husband is currently unable to speak for himself, but she may wish he could answer her many questions, including how he contracted the virus. She may be trying to remember all she can about AIDS, but if she is overwhelmed, the goal is daunting. Finally, Molly may be concerned about the risks to her children. Has living with George put them at risk for contracting AIDS? She may feel panic, anger, or pain as she tries to think of ways the children could have been exposed to the virus. Are the children HIV-positive? Perhaps, after all of these concerns, she may consider the idea that she could have AIDS herself, but if she is completely overwhelmed, she may be truly unable to grasp more at this particular point in time (Livneh, 2000).

While medical personnel can continue to speak to Molly and give her information, it is important to realize that people experiencing a crisis are limited in the ability to process and retrieve new information (Clairborne & Vandenburgh, 2001; Cox, 1996; Livneh, 2000). Even though Molly might ask questions, the social worker assesses the questions to determine if the questions are simply rhetorical or if Molly is functioning well enough to hear the answers. If Molly is able to hear the answers to her questions, her memory may be at least somewhat unreliable. In these kinds of situations, a social worker may consider the pros and cons of written information. It is easy to hand people information to read and this is appropriate, especially if they ask for it. But it is not always appropriate to give information in written form, especially when the information is delicate, overwhelming, or confidential. For instance, this may not be the time for Molly to be given materials about HIV/AIDS, particularly if she is unclear about how, when, why, and to whom to disclose her husband's diagnosis.

In addition to the challenges of taking in all of the news about George's health status, Molly's main support person—her husband, George—is currently unable to partner with her. George, who has always been her confidant and a reliable companion , cannot communicate. Currently he cannot add his problem-solving strengths to hers to develop a plan of action, a coping strategy they have used throughout their 20 years of marriage. Both George and Molly have family members living out of state, but they are not currently aware of the critical nature of George's health. They have many friends in the community, from church, and from work, but Molly is barely able to think about what to do next. How will she tell people about George's diagnosis? Who will she tell? How can she tell her friends and family that George has AIDS when she is unable to comprehend it herself?

The social worker learns to quickly and accurately assess and respond to the messages of the patient, both verbal and nonverbal, and begins to identify strengths (Gregorian, 2005; Livneh, 2000; Sheafor & Horejsi, 2008). When the social worker enters the hospital room where George is lying connected to the ventilator, she sees Molly standing near the bed, staring at her husband. The social worker may consider, what is Molly thinking or feeling? Although social workers consider the personal thoughts and feelings they might experience in that moment, they stay open to the full array of responses that are possible. For instance, if a social worker believes he or she would be worried about his or her spouse and eager for him or her to physically improve, it's important to remember that this is not necessarily how Molly is feeling. Perhaps the social worker believes she could be enraged at deception within their marriage, or filled with grief at the potential loss of their marriage. Certainly any of these reactions is appropriate under the circumstances, but the professional goal is to discover where Molly is in this process and how she is coping. It is helpful to thoughtfully approach Molly. Perhaps physically joining her at the bedside and quietly making an introduction to her would offer her support. Consider telling her that you are going to stand by her and help her problem-solve when she is ready. A variety of approaches may be effective in giving Molly a chance to move into the phase of thinking about what to do next. The professional choices about the delivery of the words said to Molly will serve as a platform for the rest of the relationship; it is the beginning of the engagement stage between the social worker and the patient.

Molly can communicate in a number of ways: A silent stance, staring into space, drooping shoulders, and her tear-stained face all serve to communicate before any words are said. While social workers need to check for further clarification, the assessment has begun. The same is true for the social worker. Before speaking, the communication with the patient and caregiver begins. There is frequently powerful nonverbal communication in interactions that is very powerful. Consider the following scenario.

Scenario 7:2

Clarice drives to her mother's home to accompany her mother to a physician appointment. She is very worried about the appointment and believes the physician will confirm the presence of cancer. Clarice believes this because her mother is convinced this is the case. Although her mother has been feeling ill all week, when Clarice arrives at her mother's home, she is waiting by the door. Her mother is dressed beautifully, her hair is well groomed, her clothing has been carefully selected and she has chosen to wear some pretty pieces of jewelry. Her mother looks as though she is going out to a nice restaurant with friends.

What is the nonverbal communication coming from Clarice's mother telling you? What does it mean that she is dressed up and ready to go? Why would she make the decision to look her best?

The mother could have chosen to go to the oncologist office in her robe and slippers, but she made a different decision. Think about how the clothing and jewelry choices influence how she feels, or perhaps how her choices will influence her introduction to a physician who may share potentially frightening news. Does how she looks align with how she feels emotionally? Regardless of our interpretation, Clarice's mother is participating in nonverbal communication and offers social workers preliminary clues about how she is thinking and feeling.

Engagement is influenced by the health-related event that brings the lives of social workers and patients together (Gregorian, 2005; Livneh, 2000). Consider the variety of circumstances that bring people into the health care system. Being in the health care system is frequently associated with, at minimum, additional stress. Sometimes a social worker interacts with individuals in the most distress they have ever experienced. Whether the patient just found out she is pregnant or a patient is in the end stages of cancer, they experience an increase in adrenalin, a primitive reaction to the news about perceived threats to the body. Even good health news is emotionally altering. In addition to the very personal emotional reactions, the patient is also expected to interact and communicate with health care staff. Given the many different places social workers interact with people in the health care field, there is no one way of engagement that fits every scenario. Working in an ambulatory clinic with individuals who are homeless may lead to patient circumstances that are totally unfamiliar to you. So engagement with a patient must take into account many factors: the uniqueness of the person, the environment, the unique combinations of cultures, and the diagnosis and prognosis of the health event (Sheafor & Horejsi, 2008).

Reconsider the assessment of Molly and George; the social worker begins to integrate the information learned about Molly's health care experience. What did the patient just experience? What does Molly know now and what will she need to know soon? What does her culture teach her that influences her ability to cope? These are only a few of the questions that Molly will answer as she begins to disclose her personal experience. Rather than prioritizing the full completion of a written assessment, it is important that nothing stand in the way of Molly freely speaking about her thoughts in this moment. Molly can choose to begin anywhere in time; for instance, she may start telling her story since the moment the AIDS diagnosis was given. She may start the story when George started complaining about painful breathing, or she may even begin by telling you how she and George first met. All are appropriate and necessary thoughts and expressions for Molly to disclose and reveal information about Molly's strengths and goals to a thoughtful social worker. Engaging with Molly in her crisis—treating her with empathy, integrity, patience, and skill—will lead to an accurate assessment and the development of a therapeutic relationship.

Assessment

For social workers, the word *assessment* is used both as a verb and as a noun. The way a social worker completes an assessment (the verb) is based on several factors: the theoretical process implemented by the social worker, the setting where the social worker is employed, and the age, gender, culture, and circumstances of the patient. A social worker assesses a patient using the strengths perspective, the systems perspective, and the biopsychosocial model (Gearing et al., 2007; Sheafor & Horejsi, 2008). The combination of these three models reveals how the patient is part of a network that includes the environment, society, and self (systems). It is a reminder that individuals are more complex than their physical presentation and it assists the social worker to recognize the resources available within patients and their environments (De Jong & Miller, 1995; Kivnick, & Murray, 2001; Saleebey, 1992; Sheafor & Horejsi, 2008).

An assessment is also a piece of paper or more likely a form of several pages (the noun). Most importantly, an assessment form is frequently part of the initial introduction to the patient. An assessment is a requirement in most health care settings, but if it were not a requirement, it would still be an important way to create a verbal picture of the circumstances the patient is experiencing. The picture or "snapshot" of the patient at the initial meeting is an important part of monitoring progress and can serve as a memory for both the social worker and the patient (Sheafor & Horejsi, 2008). Assessments are frequently stored within a patient file, both paper and digital.

If not at the first meeting, the first assessment is completed at the very beginning of a service or program. The process of assessment is a way to organize interactions with a patient. In other words, it is the beginning of bringing attention and focus to the patient and asking them to take a step toward trusting. The first impression is important and the relationship benefits from a good start. Whether the patient is visited as part of an inpatient (hospital) or outpatient (clinics) service, a poor first meeting can make following meetings a struggle. The patient may refuse to see or speak with the social worker again, or in the case of an outpatient experience, the patient may not return for services. Sometimes assessment takes place in one meeting, but in some settings, assessments may take several meetings to complete, or remain in constant revision as the health issues of the patient change (Clairborne & Vandenburgh, 2001; Sheafor & Horejsi, 2008).

Using an assessment form as a guide, the social worker elicits information that offers the health care team a realistic and accurate picture of patients and their ecological system. The primary goal of an assessment is not necessarily to fill in the answer to every question on a printed form in the order they appear on the form. The goals of an assessment include: documentation of a moment in time, gathering critical information, engaging and listening to the patient, communicating effectively and accurately with other professionals, and establishing the patient's goals and objectives (Sheafor & Horejsi, 2008; Sparks, Travis, & Thompson, 2005).

The act of assessment varies with each patient. Often a patient is able to communicate verbally or in some nonverbal way, but sometimes the patient is unable to communicate due to disability, language barriers, treatments, or the severity of illness or disease. Completing an assessment is unique based on the environment where the social worker is employed, but despite the environment, many health care settings ask similar questions on assessment forms. Depending on the site, assessments call for the social worker to ask some unique and perhaps uncomfortable questions. If the clinic serves people who are infected or affected by HIV, the questions asked include conversations about high risk behaviors associated with the transmission of the virus. If the health care setting is for pregnant teens, the assessment is geared toward education and empowerment.

It is helpful to remember that the patient owns the medical record, and so owns the assessment. There is no need to complete the assessment in a way that magnifies the difference in power between patient and social worker. In the case of Molly, perhaps the less visible role of the health care professional is best with an emphasis on attempts to support her multiple challenges. In addition, because patients own their medical records, it is important to consider the words used to describe events, issues, or circumstances in a way that respects patients, their support systems, and professional colleagues. At some point Molly may need or want access to George's medical record. Perhaps she will need copies of notes or assessments for insurance purposes or some judicial proceedings. She will read the notes about the first meeting with the social worker and the social worker's perceptions. If a social worker always writes an assessment from the standpoint that the patient and caregivers will read it, the assessment will be written in an appropriate and ethical manner (Sheafor & Horejsi, 2008).

Forms of Assessment

Assessment is accomplished in different ways. Interviewing a client in a confidential environment is the most common way to gather information for many fields of social work practice. In health care, social workers are also required to assess patients while they are in their hospital beds, in emergency rooms, or gather patient information in alternative ways. Particularly in an inpatient setting, the patient may not feel well or may be medicated and unable to fully participate in an interview. In these cases the family or designated caregivers may, with the patient's permission, be able to offer the information needed. In other cases, social workers must rely, in great part, on the assessments that are available within patients' charts, such as those completed by other social workers or perhaps a health professional from another discipline.

Interviews: Lessons Learned

Regardless of the differences of each interview, there are some things that hold true for all. The most important similarity is the need for social workers to conduct interviews within the guidelines of the NASW Code of Ethics (1999). Patients have a right to self-determination and deserve to be treated with dignity, respect and with genuineness; this sets the stage for a professionally healthy and functional relationship (De Jong & Miller, 1995; Gearing et al., 2007; Kotria, 2005; NASW, 1999).

Interviewing is a combination of both learned skills and innate skills. Interviews have a beginning and an end and result in a product. The unique nature of an interview is a result of differences in personalities because interviews call for the creative incorporation of the self. Two interviews are never the same. The relationships that develop between the social worker and the person interviewed results in a distinctive description of the experience. While social workers are responsible to collect similar information from all patients, the time it takes to collect the information, the style of collecting the information, and the information actually collected is very different for each interview and depends on many factors.

Individuals, place, circumstances, and cultures involved in the interview process require social workers to be thoughtful and strategic. Although social workers will learn many lessons about interviewing through their professional experiences, it may be helpful to review some examples of how to best achieve successful engagement and helpful interviews with patients, caregivers, and colleagues.

Cultural Guides. If unaware of the patient's relationships within cultures, ask questions. Learning to ask respectful questions of cultural guides is an invaluable aid to learn the philosophy and psychology of a culture. Again, this does not address the unique experience of an individual, but it gives a much sharper focus on how life is experienced within a certain culture and how it might influence individuals. For instance, death is a predictable human experience and it is experienced in certain ways in all cultures, but how it is talked about or understood varies dramatically from one group to another. To understand and avoid erecting barriers, speak with a respected member of the community; this will be of great assistance.

The Power Differential. There is a power difference between patients and those who work for the health care establishment, and the difference is significant (Mason, 2005). When a social worker asks questions or seeks information, it can be intimidating for the patient. Health care personnel can forget that their role in the system gives them power. Patients wishing to fully cooperate may be willing to respond to every question asked so social workers need to evaluate interviews and assessment forms to ensure the information requested is really necessary. This is important because the information collected is entered into permanent reports and accessible to many through computerized medical records. It is important to only ask for the information necessary to assist patients to make the best decisions for their health. Another reason to avoid asking more questions than necessary is because of the often heightened sense of paranoia that patients may feel. The level of vulnerability is already high for the patient, and excessive personal questions can cause further anxiety.

Vulnerability.   Some vulnerable and disenfranchised populations are particularly suspicious and nervous about giving information (Mason, 2005). For instance, for social workers at a big urban hospital, a homeless clinic, a HIV clinic, or perhaps in a mental health clinic, the patients using these facilities may have experienced significant penalties in their lives because of the information they shared with professionals. For instance, some lose benefits, services, or opportunities because the information they gave resulted in ineligibility. Many people experience inequities in care based on forms of stigma and racism (DuBois & Miley, 2008). Health care systems are often obligated to forms of criteria and patients desperate for care may sometimes try to find the word or condition that makes them eligible for care. For instance, a homeless clinic funded by a source that insists that all patients be "homeless" to receive free health care gives individuals who are homeless a distinct advantage. Some people live in a house with many people and do not pay rent and would be living outside or at a mission if not for people taking them in. Is this considered homelessness? This is an ethical dilemma for many social workers working with at-risk populations. While gathering information, it is important to understand the criteria of the system and try to meet the intention of the funding. There are many good reasons why people alter personal information, especially when asked multiple times by multiple health care providers.

One way to reduce a patient's anxiety is to include them in the assessment process and show them the assessment form as it is being completed. Attempt to place the form used within clear view of the patient. Consider reviewing the form with the patient before beginning the interview and ask for assurance that the information collected is an accurate account. A social worker can also inform the patient about why the information is needed and who will have access to the patient's chart. The patient is reassured when they understand that information in the medical record is private and requires the patient's permission to be shared with others.

Environment.   The location where the interview takes place influences the style used to complete an interview (Browne, 2006). For instance, an interview in an emergency room with the parent of a child just brought in after a car accident may be accomplished standing outside the treatment room with multiple family members offering assistance and support. This is an interview that clearly comes with a heightened sense of urgency and seriousness. An emergency room social worker does not expect the family to focus on the paperwork, but does everything possible to ensure that the best and most immediate care and support for the child is underway.

In a pediatric health office, a mother may be more likely to concentrate, complete the necessary paperwork, and offer health information if her child is content and monitored, playing with toys in the room. In a neighborhood where there are homeless people, a health care social worker may complete an interview outside while sitting on a street curb or on the steps of an abandoned building. An interview is a process that adjusts to multiple settings and health care social workers adapt to the circumstances of the moment, because an interview is not about filling out a form, it is about gathering information.

Taking Notes.   If the social worker is not working in a traditional setting with an office and a desk, but is reluctant to rely solely on memory to later write assessment notes, it is helpful to develop a technique to take simple notes. Instead of writing the permanent, official notes immediately, jot down key words to help recall important points. To minimize wariness between the social worker and the patient, explain the technique, show the patient the written words, or make it easy for the patient to see the notes. For instance, if a patient talks to the social worker about his family and shares that his oldest brother is a barrier to his getting the medication he needs for his diabetes, perhaps writing "older brother" will be enough to recall his statement and not feel threatening to the patient. Remove as many barriers to engagement as possible to encourage the partnership for future interactions.

Listening. Social workers know that when they are talking, patients are not talking. The ability to listen and be quiet results in the social worker learning the information necessary to be a valuable resource to patients (Sparks et al., 2005). Sometimes it is difficult to allow for silence in a conversation. A minute of silence can be very uncomfortable for many, but there are good reasons why it is worth waiting for a reply instead of filling quiet moments with words. Patients may have trouble finding the words they want because of disease, treatment, or emotional trauma. Allow them a moment to collect their thoughts; it is respectful and it results in the most accurate responses. In addition, some questions may be very personal and is the first time patients are asked to put their answers into words. Be tolerant of the time needed and allow for the exchange to be mutual. Sometimes a question results in an unpredictably long answer, but the path to the answer may inform about health issues in an important way.

Confidentiality. Social workers try to promote privacy and confidentiality as much as possible when speaking with or in consultation about the patient. This can be challenging because sometimes interviews are necessary in emergency waiting areas, or in hospital wards with multiple beds. Trying to use a softer tone of voice, movable curtains, or alternative spots to ask patients for private information is respectful. Asking if they are comfortable providing the answers in the current environment is another way to show the patient their privacy is valued. Social workers are committed to providing patients with the highest level of confidentiality possible, but it can be very challenging to find privacy in hospitals, nursing homes, and busy health clinics.

Consider the challenges to confidentiality in the following scenario. An old down-town office space was donated to establish a homeless health clinic. Although remodeled to some extent, all of the exam rooms are directly off the waiting area. There are doors on the exam rooms, but anyone in the waiting room sees the patient traffic to and from the rooms. Patients can talk to their friends and others in the waiting room while they wait in the exam room with the door open. The clinic provides excellent services, but the issues of privacy and confidentiality are challenged due to the physical environment. The staff at the clinic place all waiting room chairs facing a solid wall with the exam rooms behind them in an attempt to minimize visual access. Over time the patients that regularly use the clinic often ignore the traffic to the exam rooms and the lack of privacy issues. Unfortunately, these kinds of environments are not uncommon, but social workers continually seek ways to problem-solve and keep individuals' information private.

Another common confidentiality issue is the personal conversations between professionals. In the course of the work day, staff members often discuss their work, frustrations, or perhaps funny situations they were involved in. When these discussions are done within hearing range of patients, the conversations may sound demeaning to them, out of context, and unprofessional. There is also a risk that even when a patient name is not used, the patient is identified by the listener. It is important to always be aware of what is said to colleagues and remain aware of who is listening.

Empowerment. Show empathy to patients, not pity. Many are suffering through hopelessness or helplessness and it may be difficult to hear the personal details. It becomes even more difficult when the social worker and the patient have had a long-term relationship. Frequently, social workers in health care work with patients long enough to eventually meet their spouse, partner, family members, and caregivers, adding to the personal and professional knowledge of patients' situations.

When engagement occurs, a partnership to create solutions to identified barriers to care begins. Empathy is appropriate, but pity is a weaker and more disabling emotion and fails to empower and help patients recognize their strengths. Put yourself in the patient's role, step closer to understanding what is happening in their life and consider how it would be to live with the same circumstances.

Thoughtfulness. Consider paying attention to small concerns. Helping patients develop a discharge plan is important, but so is taking a moment to fluff the pillow in his or her hospital bed. Sometimes the workload at hospitals, nursing homes, and other inpatient facilities is so unending social workers focus only on the professional assignment given by hospital administration. While this assignment is important, so is displaying respect and dignity to the person who finds him- or herself in a patient role. The few minutes it takes to assist patients with personal needs makes a difference in their comfort and ultimately in building relationships. A family standing outside a hospital room trying to make decisions about where the patient can recover may be deeply moved by the social worker offering to find a private room so the family has a comfortable space to talk. If the patient is worried and distracted because some expected medical test result has not arrived, take the concern seriously. Perhaps a quick check with the nurse or physician relieves their worry and supports the social worker–patient relationship. Outpatient settings are also good environments to ask patients about their continuum of health needs. Are the patients getting adequate food, sleep, and support? Are they staying warm in the winter and cool in the summer? Do they need a drink of water? Looking beyond the professional assignment and expressing care for the whole person is the role of social worker.

Social workers can offer resources to patients that improve quality of life in ways that are not necessarily in the social work job description including bringing coffee, a drink of water, or a warm blanket; starting a conversation; getting a wheelchair; looking for different magazines for the patient to read; calling the chaplain; or getting in touch with the financial office to answer a question about a bill. Procurement of resources that assist the patient in coping, in any way, improves the patient's overall quality of life. These kinds of tasks may be listed in the "nonprofessional" category by some, but it is the very essence of social work. In a frequently emotionally cold environment inhabited by changing physician teams and shifts of changing nurses, the expression of care through immediate and concrete action can make a significant difference in the patient's perception of care (Gregorian, 2005).

Treatment of Colleagues. It is inappropriate to disparage medical care, services, or personnel in front of the patient, despite the validity of concerns. Sometimes social workers develop relationships with patients that are so unique from that with other medical personnel; patients may feel comfortable sharing their personal and sometimes critical views of colleagues. Despite personal opinions, it is never appropriate to disrespect colleagues to patients and caregivers. There are many ways to support the concerns of patients and at the same time show support of the rest of the health care team. For instance, if an oncologist rarely makes medical rounds when patients are awake or families available, they may believe the doctor is avoiding them, unwilling to speak to them, or reluctant to answer their questions. If patients complain about this, acknowledge their concerns and promise to pass their request to the doctor for an appointment to meet with them. It is not appropriate to say, "This doctor never talks to the patients. The reason he comes in so early is because he does not want to be bothered or spend the time in conversation with the patients and their families." Agreeing with the patient is not supportive, but instead damages the relationship between the patient and the physician. This relationship is very important, and while not always perfect, the social worker must seek to strengthen it, when possible. Patients rely on physicians to give them the information they need to make very important decisions about their health. If patients feel insecure or distrust the physician, the ability to make good decisions is damaged (Gregorian, 2005).

Social workers practice wisdom in making decisions about how to respond to the complaints patients express regarding their colleagues. Social workers are frequently seen as a "guest" in the medical system and if their role becomes one of joining patient criticism and undermining important collegial relationships, it will soon be impossible to be seen as having any credibility (Gregorian, 2005). If there are concerns about patients' care, it is important to discuss these issues with a supervisor and get advice about how to proceed. All health care providers are unique individuals and all contribute to patient care in their own way. Remember, the social worker's role is to support patients so they can make the best decisions for themselves given the circumstances (Gregorian, 2005).

Unspoken Cues. Without an accurate assessment, future planning may develop based on a flawed framework, potentially harmful to the patient (Mason, 2005; Sheafor & Horejsi, 2008). It is important to listen carefully when preparing to receive information from a patient. Listen to patients and gather meaning beyond the words they say. Be sensitive to how things are said and try to feel what they are feeling when they talk about their goals and concerns. Using social work skills during an interview is vital. Remember, the person speaking is vulnerable and may attempt to show more strength than is actually felt (Sparks et al., 2005). Some patients attempt to be the "perfect" patient and may unconsciously hope this behavior benefits them, increases staff interest, and improves care. Maybe being friendly and good-natured helps patients feel healthier and more in control. Still others show the staff just exactly how irritated they feel or how frustrated they are. These patients rely on the professionalism of the staff to look past their pain and continue to treat them professionally even though they act in an offensive manner. Be sensitive to the fact that although patients act certain ways, they are not necessarily feeling the same way. Social workers know there is valuable information to be found in the incongruence of the action and feeling (Sheafor & Horejsi, 2008).

Home Visits.   Occasionally home visits are necessary to create an accurate assessment. Inpatient health care settings offer social workers little information to develop an accurate picture of how the patient lives. In some circumstances a home visit quickly resolves any questions regarding health care options. An assessment done within the patient's own environment gives the social worker a clear picture of not only the physical environment, but it also reveals potential support or strengths (Goode, 2000). A home visit to an older adult who lives alone will quickly reveal if the setting is safe, clean, and healthy. Is there a way for him or her to ambulate, or safely move, from room to room? Is there a functioning refrigerator? Is the environment sanitary and ventilated? Is there any evidence of support systems being available in case of an emergency? Be aware that personal standards of clean or safe do not influence the assessment. If dishes are always washed in your home, do not assume this is the standard for others. If your home is in the suburbs, do not assume living in the city is unsafe.

Rarely do patients voluntarily state that home environments are inadequate to live in during their rehabilitation, especially if they want to go home. Most people want to go home rather than stay in a dependent setting such as a nursing home or rehab facility or in a hospital. However, the pressure to move patients from inpatient to subacute care or to their homes means patients are discharged under more physically vulnerable circumstances than in the past. Assess to ensure a patient is discharged to a physically safe environment. In some cases it is important to ask caregivers to verify their plans to be available to assist the patient, or confirm that the patient is indeed able to manage the more independent environment. In some hospital settings, the patient is expected to show evidence of ambulation before discharge.

Safety.   Examine the safety issues involved in making home visits. Always let someone know where you are going and when you plan to be back. When possible, have someone accompany you. Be alert in unfamiliar surroundings and cognizant that a social worker visit is not always perceived as a positive thing. In other words, in some environments, social workers are not welcomed. Cellular phones are helpful and offer a fast way to request assistance. If you approach an environment that feels unsafe, respect intuition and leave; safety is a priority.

Teamwork.   A reliable assessment and the development of a healthy professional relationship with the patient promote the reputation of the entire health care team (Gearing et al., 2007). The link with the patient offers an important contribution to the patient planning discussion. It is worth the time and energy used in the beginning of the relationship, particularly through the first assessment, to solidify connections with patients and their caregivers. The relationship influences the decisions and results of all the health team members and enhances patients' sense of quality care; patients are the ones who truly benefit (Sheafor & Horejsi, 2008). Realistically, not all patients are interested in a professional relationship with social workers for a number of reasons. Not all patients need assistance; patients may have all support issues resolved and the social work role is limited to a confirmation of their plans (Browne, 2006). Perhaps a patient believes a social worker is totally unnecessary to the health care plan and chooses to not participate in a meeting. This is valid and is not a mark of success or failure. The social worker must be available for the times a working relationship is necessary and must treat the brief encounters with as much professionalism as the longer and more complicated relationships.

Appearing Unhurried. Resist acting hurried or inconvenienced (Gregorian, 2005). Many patients spend hours in their hospital rooms, assisted living spaces, or isolated in their homes. Someone coming to talk with them can be a welcome intrusion. When patients are welcoming, try to keep thoughts of other pressing assignments in check and focus on the moment. If possible, take time to listen to a patient story, admire the photos of their children or grandchildren, or listen to how annoying the traffic is in their hometown. These acts are all forms of engagement and give professional relationships a personal touch and increase comfort and meaning for the patient.

Follow-Through. When social workers offer patients a timeline of getting back to them with information, it is important to respond as promised. Patients depend on this. Social workers are often the most reliable connection to the health care system. Despite the many legitimate reasons why the information for patients is late or did not get done, patients rely on the timely completion of tasks. Constant mismanagement of time, failure to prioritize, promising unreasonable results, or forgetting the details of what was promised hurts the reputation of social workers. Informal word travels quickly through communities. A good deed by a social worker is hailed by all as evidence of competence, but the same is true for the times a social worker fails to deliver. Someone might not get the help promised and perceive social workers as untrustworthy, unprofessional, or inept.

Flexibility. Some patients and caregivers assertively and independently problem-solve and plan around the issues of health care. Families may quickly assemble physical, emotional, and social resources to deal with chronic illness diagnoses or other forms of crisis. If the social worker wants to assist families and caregivers, they must express their desire to help to patients and enable them to achieve their goals. Take the time to see patients, caregivers, and colleagues as people doing the best they can under the circumstances.

While every person using the health care system is unique, most individuals share a desire to live a life free from biological, psychological, and emotional pain. Social workers can contribute to this common goal.

Alternative Forms of Assessment. Not everyone benefits by the same form of inter-action or assessment. There are many styles of communication and many ways to collect the information needed from patients (Kuehl, 1995). How many times do patients participate in interviews or assessments related to their health? The number varies, but often the questions repeatedly asked are remarkably the same. Consider options other than a traditional interview to collect patient information and assess if completing a pictorial assessment is appropriate. Genograms and ecomaps are two illustrative ways to complete an assessment and in the right circumstances add another level of patient participation to the assessment process (DuBois & Miley, 2008; Sheafor & Horejsi, 2008).

Genograms. The genogram is a way to collect assessment information from a patient. The genogram is a pictorial representation of a family, and as necessary, illustrates several generations of a family (Kuehl, 1995; Sheafor & Horejsi, 2008). Using a genogram gives patients an opportunity to furnish information about their families in a creative and comprehensive way and allows patients to physically participate in a project that contributes to their care. The act of taking paper and pencil and drawing a figure is an activity and offers patients a physical contribution to their health care. Family genograms offer a complete and easy-to-read record of a patients' family and is especially helpful if there is a need to track the presence of genetic links to disease (Kuehl, 1995). Genograms are helpful in recording the members of the family and familial relationships. This form of assessment concisely presents complicated family relationships over generations and may inform the social worker about potential strengths or barriers to discharge by revealing the presence or absence of resources (McGoldrick & Gerson, 1985). The genogram centers on family information such as marriages, births, deaths, divorces, separations, causes of deaths, names, ages, and sibling order. A genogram can also clarify other familial patterns or historical events.

There is no "right" way to do a genogram (McGoldrick & Gerson, 1985). As with a more traditional interview, the skill of social workers and the unique factors of patients, including the environment and health status of patients, influence the results. One way to introduce a genogram assignment is to explain to patients how the picture is developed and offer them a chance to participate. If working with a female patient, draw a circle and indicate that this circle represents a female. Assist the patient to arrange the circles (female) and squares (males) that represent members of the family. This form of assessment can be very powerful and often difficult to complete in one meeting. Some patients draw a symbol and then stop to share information about the personality, role, or relationship of this symbolic family member.

Development of a genogram relies on the ease of drawing simple symbols to represent relationships and events within a family. Like all assessments, genograms are only useful if culturally appropriate. Recently, when teaching the use of genograms to social work students in Moscow, students were required to create a genogram showing their family over the past three generations. The next day a student inquired about the symbol for abduction and stated that during the Stalin era two of his great uncles were abducted. He believed his uncles were dead, but no one ever knew their final fate. The genogram literature does not teach symbols for abduction and in the United States the need for this symbol is less than in other cultures. The Russian student was encouraged to design his own symbol to represent abduction.

Ecomaps. The ecomap is another pictorial assessment tool. Developed by Hartman (1979), it is a dramatic way to illustrate the relationships of the patient within an environment. The ecomap is a graphic display of the patient's ecological system and includes the patient's relationship with family members, professionals, organizations, institutions, social groups, and friends. It shows patterns of emotional support, conflict, and stress and helps identify ways for the patient to find needed support and strengths in the community. An ecomap assists social workers in the discovery of patients' resources, those that benefit patients and those that do not (Boyle, Hull, Mather, Smith, & Farley, 2006; Sheafor & Horejsi, 2008).

As with the genogram, the invitation of the patient to participate in the creation of an ecomap enhances the partnership between the social worker and the patient. Particularly in health care settings, patients can feel isolated and helpless, as though they are not included in treatment and care decisions. They are also aware that there is information in charts about them that they never see and have relatively little control over. Genograms and ecomaps are forms of assessment that result in a useful picture of the patient's environment. These assessments include the patient and give the patient a creative and concrete opportunity to contribute to the documentation within the medical record. Patients frequently enjoy the process of drawing their lives because they can be seen as a relief from the frequent verbal assessments done within the health care system. The process can result in unidentified patient resources coming to the surface.

People in Crisis

People define crisis in life in different ways. Some experience crisis at the possibility or diagnosis of an acute or chronic disease. Some patients respond to catastrophic change slowly and are less likely to seek assistance or use resources promptly. Patients that do not ask for help are not necessarily without a need for assistance. There are several reasons why some patients do not seek help: (1) They are content with present recovery or treatment plans, (2) they have a calm genetic disposition, (3) they are experienced with their own or others' health care, or perhaps (4) possess a dogma, spirituality, or worldview that sustains them. Everyone is different so treating everyone the same, even when the health event seems similar to that of others, is bound to fail.

As with the unique perceptions of crisis, people cope with crisis in different ways (Gearing et al., 2007; Mechanic & Tanner, 2007). Some are isolative with their news, seeking to protect their families or finding strength in keeping things inside where they experience more control over handling the health event. Some patients immediately rally family and friends and take charge of the support available to them. They act as organizers of their care and are empowered to make treatment and support decisions for themselves. Others display signs of surrender to the biological course and allow for what they see as a natural process to occur. Reacting in a personal way to crisis allows patients to continue to respect and be invested in life, but some responses significantly impair a connection to quality of life. Social workers are aware that it is natural for people to respond to crisis in a variety of ways, many functional and some potentially problematic.

The existence of a support person, family, or caregiver makes a huge difference in facing the future. Maybe someone is confident about the support of friends and family during emergencies, but this is not the case for everyone. Although it is uncomfortable to witness, there are many who have no one to call in case of emergency. For instance, on an assessment form at a health clinic for the homeless, there is a tough question that social workers who are employed there are encouraged to complete, despite the challenges to obtain the answer. This question on the assessment asks the patient to name a "next of kin" should the patient be unable to speak for themselves. It gives the health care system someone to consult or inform if some medical emergency happens in the life of the patient. Time after time, patients shrug their shoulders and say there is no one to list. Despite tenacious efforts to gain a name, patients still are unable to list someone in their lives that would care enough to want a call or to offer them help in a life-threatening situation.

Support systems of friends and family are frequently a strong support for people coping with new diagnosis of chronic or acute illness, especially for individuals depending on help with the chores of daily living. But support systems can also influence patients to minimize their condition in an effort to not be a problem for family and friends. When asked how they are doing, a patient may continue to state they feel improved health because they know this is what the family wants to hear. Social workers must develop a keen sense of the influence of patient supporters and watch the interactions of the patient when they are with others and compare it to times when the patient is alone (Sparks et al., 2005).

Social workers practice a balanced reaction to patient and caregiver crisis. A social worker must acknowledge the crisis and take it seriously; never minimize the anxiety and stress the patient and support system reveal. But the social worker must also exude a sense of calm and steadiness. This allows the patient a strong resource for reassurance and assures the patient that there are strengths to draw on health-related circumstances.

Immediate and Concrete Action

Most likely, social workers will not be able to offer the patient a solution to any medical problem. Despite all of your wishes, the health of the patient is not in your control, and it is not in the control of the physicians or nurses; the result of treatment for disease is not predictable, despite the very best care. Patients may not recover or live as long or as well as hoped. The prognosis of "3–6 months" of life may result in 6 weeks, or perhaps 6 years. Patient health depends on many factors, including strength, genetics, spirituality, environment, medication, and the type, tenacity, and stage of the disease. The social work role is to support the patient in obtaining the best quality of life for as long as possible in keeping with the patient's goals.

Understand the limitations. There are many roles represented on a health care team, and each profession has something important to contribute to the care of the patient. Social workers are not physicians, nurses, or pharmacists and do patients a disfavor by acting as though they are. It is unethical, unsafe, and illegal to attempt to treat patients in areas if not qualified to practice in those areas. Despite years of working alongside doctors and despite the ability to seemingly predict what they would say or do in regard to patient care, social workers must limit their practice to the profession in which they are trained.

Offering a solution to the health crisis is not the only way to help patients and their families. There are many things to do beyond the details of disease treatment that make the situation better for everyone. Never underestimate the importance of being present with someone as they experience a health care crisis. Know that while the medical focus is important, the social worker–patient relationship gives the patient a nonmedical resource, someone who verifies feelings and gives attention to the social, cultural, and environmental circumstances of the disease. This relationship is vital for the patient and to the medical team because it brings a perspective to the patient that is frequently not the priority in a health care setting. Medical personnel are frequently not in a position to accommodate the family and caregiver regarding psychological or environmental details. In addition, cultural issues are at risk of being undetected unless the social worker highlights the issues to the health care team.

Limited Time

It is amazing how brief a time most social workers spend in a professional relationship with a patient, particularly in an inpatient setting. Depending on where the social worker is employed, the relationship can vary from a few minutes to possibly a few years. If the relationship is part of a hospital stay, it is perhaps a day or a few days, although in the case of chronic illness, a patient may return for additional hospital stays. If a patient is in a nursing home, the relationship is significantly longer, perhaps lasting for years. Compared to the life most people live prior to moving into nursing home settings, the relationship with the social worker is a brief one. But despite the short time, the social workers' influence in the patient's quality of life is notable (Kotria, 2005). The importance of the interactions is heightened because patients rely on the social worker to access resources they need and are otherwise challenged to do alone. The health crisis places the patient in a highly vulnerable situation and so the social worker and patient relationship develops in intensity faster than it would under normal circumstances. This is true in other forms of crisis as well—in battle or in teams that face extraordinary competition, individuals rely on each other and work together quickly and without pretense to achieve the common good. Although this varies by culture, many, when they are threatened by disease experiences, need reinforcements. Social workers are commonly part of this support.

Many outpatient or ambulatory care sites offer patients social work services on an as-needed basis. The social work appointment is scheduled for less than an hour, maybe only minutes, but the meeting offers opportunities to connect. The social worker and patient develop, monitor, and maintain a care plan that assigns each of them tasks: phone calls, completing applications, or obtaining information about resources. Things can change very quickly in all areas of health: biologically, psychologically, and socially. Not all patients access health care easily, so make the best possible use of time to make the appointment worth the patient's time, effort, and sometimes cost. If patients must sign a form and it is difficult for them to come in, is there another way to expedite the signature? Ambulatory clinics treat patients who are more likely to have no or little insurance. They see more people with economic challenges as well. Social workers who work at ambulatory sites need to work toward the development of resources. For instance, group services are a cost-effective way to offer services and offer patients an opportunity to be part of support and educational groups, when information and support would not be available to them on an individual basis.

Empathy

Empathy is important in all areas of social work; in fact, there is no way to effectively practice social work services in health care without the ability to put yourself in the situation the patient is experiencing (Sheafor & Horejsi, 2008). That does not mean you can assume the patient feels like you would feel under the same circumstances. Empathy means you attempt to experience how the situation feels from the patients' perspective. Resist interpreting emotions through a personal prism and try to join patients in how they are experiencing the event. This involves understanding how culture influences the meaning attached to events and it means individualizing responses to the specific issues of patients (Gregorian, 2005). The study of history and culture informs the ability to be empathetic, but it does not fully inform about the unique experience of each individual.

Education

Frequently social workers are involved in dispensing information and in teaching the physical, social, and emotional aspects associated with health and illness. It involves teaching a patient about how to proceed through the health care system to access support services and what to do if things do not go well. It means educating patients, as individuals or groups, about the things they can do to maintain or improve their health or perhaps informing caregivers how they can protect against exhaustion and isolation while being a support.

Social workers are responsible for different forms of education. Verbal communication can be overwhelming, especially during a crisis. Social workers look for creative ways to provide information in effective ways, stay informed, and develop resources such as updated websites to share with patients, brochures or information sheets to dispense at health settings, or DVD libraries about health maintenance.

Not all patients read, and some may not read English, so social workers need a variety of resources. Translation of brochures by bilingual resource groups in the community is a big help for patients and caregivers. For people who can't read, diagrams and other pictorial forms assist patients in getting important messages, particularly when given with some verbal instruction and review. Pay attention if the patient asks to have someone present with him or her when they get new information. It may be a clue that the patient is not able to read or it may also be that they cannot rely on his or her memory. It is often helpful to have a caregiver or family member present if the patient agrees. A second person is a great resource for the patient who needs to recall what was said later, after health staff is gone. Always ask if the explanation was understood or if there are any questions and offer paper and pen to aid in taking notes.

Families

All social workers need to understand the definition of family as patients define it and realize the days of family being defined as male and female married adults with children and grandparents is no longer the only definition of family. Regardless of the politics involved in defining family, the reality is people are loved and supported by people who are not necessarily connected through blood ties or legal means. These people are sometimes identified as friends and sometimes they are identified as family. The concept of family is expanded to include many relationships and this is true because of changes of meaning in cultures and social structures. The definition of concepts such as marriage, adoption, single, gay, blended, and nuclear family have all been radically reinvented to adapt to the changing world (DuBois & Miley, 2008). Some areas of the United States experience the new definitions of family more slowly due to smaller populations and more social isolation. Cities particularly have greater diversity in the composition of families. It is far more common for rural communities, once rather isolated from family breakups, to experience divorce and blended families.

When a health-related episode occurs to an individual, it is common for the individual to pull in family for support. The ecological systems perspective supports the concept that when someone in the family is affected by a health problem, it influences the interactions within the entire family (DuBois & Miley, 2008). Social workers keep the interplay between family members in mind when they are called in to work with a patient (Gregorian, 2005).

Listen carefully to the patient or, if the patient is unable to communicate, to the individuals who identify themselves as having an important relationship in the patient's life. Health care settings will have policies about who is legally included in communication regarding the patient, but many health care settings include ways to interact with people important to the patient, regardless of their legal or emotional links. The most common way for the patient to include significant others in the communication is by signing a "release of information."

The reason it is important to correctly identify the family is because the family needs to be assessed through an empathetic lens as well. Again, it is important not to minimize the stress and concerns experienced by a person caring for someone with medical needs. Try to understand the wide range of emotions that threaten to overwhelm caregivers, including hopelessness, helplessness, fear, anger, and loneliness (Holland & Lewis, 2000).

Social workers understand that it is difficult for some family members to talk about their emotions because they believe their feelings are meaningless compared to those of the patient. Families may express some of their feelings to health care personnel through their advocacy for the patient with comments like "I don't feel as though anybody is telling my Dad what is going on," but it is more difficult for a family member to say, "I feel like everything is out of control," or "I am worried that no one understands how important this person is to me." Each family member has unique connections to the health process and each will raise unique issues (Holland & Lewis, 2000).

Understand that family issues are further complicated when the assessment takes the family's ethnic origin, cultural values, religion, and attitudes toward illness into consideration. This level of assessment requires careful and sensitive attention to details. When illness occurs within a family, it is a serious event and it is important to remember that not everyone has a neatly packaged family to identify and rely on for support (Holland & Lewis, 2000).

Summary

Solid engagement with patients, families, and caregivers is essential to develop an accurate assessment (Gregorian, 2005). Without an assessment based on reliable facts, the goals, objectives, and interventions will fail (Sheafor & Horejsi, 2008). Engagement relies on both the learned skills of social work and the innate personal abilities and intrapersonal skills of the social worker. The little time patients and social workers spend together in health care settings is very productive when it results in patient and caregivers finding support for their goals and objectives. Social workers assist the patient to move toward the achievement of those goals through a relationship built on solid engagement and skillful assessment.

Critical Thinking Questions

1. What personal strengths do you possess that will be beneficial to your patients?

2. Aside from education, what are the ways we can develop professional skills?

3. Create your own three-generation genogram and describe the relationships that stand out in your family.

4. How might your approach to an interview influence a patient's goals?

5. How is engagement with others affected by your personal skills? How is engagement with others affected by your culture?

References

Boyle, S. W., Hull, G. H., Mather, J. H., Smith, L. L., & Farley, O. W. (2006). *Direct practice in social work.* Boston: Pearson, Allyn & Bacon.

Browne, T. A. (2006). Social work roles and health-care settings. In S. Gehlert & T. A. Browne (Eds.), *Handbook of health social work* (pp. 23–42), Hoboken, NJ: Wiley.

Claiborne, N., & Vandenburgh, H. (2001). Social workers' role in disease management. *Health and Social Work, 26*(4), 217–225.

Cox, C. B. (1996). Discharge planning for dementia patients: Factors influencing caregiver decisions and satisfaction. *Health and Social Work, 21*(2), 97–105.

De Jong, P., & Miller, S. D. (1995). How to interview for client strengths. *Social Work, 40*(6), 729–736.

DuBois, B., & Miley, K. K. (2008). *Social work: An empowering profession.* Boston: Allyn & Bacon.

Gearing, R. E., Saini, M., & McNeill, T. (2007). Experiences and implications of social workers practicing in a pediatric hospital environment affected by SARS. *Health and Social Work, 32*(1), 17–27.

Goode, R. A, (2000). *Social work practice in home health care.* New York: Hayworth Press.

Gregorian, C. (2005). A career in hospital social work: Do you have what it takes? *Social Work in Health Care, 40*(3), 1–14.

Hartman, A. (1979). The extended family as a resource for change: An ecological approach to family-centered practice In C. B. Germain (Ed.), *Social work practice: People and environments* (pp. 239–266). New York: Columbia University Press.

Holland, J. C., & Lewis, S. (2000). *The human side of cancer: Living with hope, coping with uncertainty.* New York: HarperCollins.

Kivnick, H. Q., & Murray, S.V. (2001). Life strengths interview guide: Assessing elder clients' strengths. *Journal of Gerontological Social Work, 34*(4), 7–32.

Kotria, K. (2005). Social work practice in health care: The need to use brief interventions. *Health and Social Work, 30*(4), 336–339.

Kuehl, B. P. (1995). The solution-oriented genogram: A collaborative approach. *Journal of Marital and Family Therapy, 21*(3), 239–246.

Livneh, H. (2000, April/May/June). Psychosocial adaptation to cancer: The role of coping strategies. *Journal of Rehabilitation,* pp. 40–49.

Luptak, M. (2004). Social work and end-of-life care for older people: A historical perspective. *Health and Social Work, 29*(1), 7–16.

Mason, T. C. (2005). Cross-cultural instrument translation: Assessment, translation, and statistical applications. *American Annals of the Deaf, 140*(1), 67–72.

McGoldrick, M., & Gerson, R. (1985). *Genograms in family assessment.* New York: Norton.

Mechanic, D., & Tanner, J. (2007). Vulnerable people, groups, and populations: Societal view. *Health Affairs, 26*(5), 1220–1230.

Murphy, B. C., & Dillon, C. (2003). *Interviewing in action: Relationship, process, and change.* Pacific Grove, CA: Brooks/Cole.

National Association of Social Workers (NASW). (1999). *Code of ethics.* Washington, DC: NASW Press.

Saleebey, D. (1992). Introduction: Power in the people. In D. Saleebey (Ed.), *The strengths perspective in social work practice* (2nd ed., pp. 3–19). New York: Longman.

Sheafor, B. W., Horejsi, C. R. (2008). *Techniques and guidelines for social work practice.* Boston: Allyn & Bacon.

Sparks, L., Travis, S. S., & Thompson, S. R. (2005). Listening for the communicative signals of humor, narratives, and self-disclosure in the family caregiver interview. *Health and Social Work, 30*(4), 340–343.

8

Chronic Illness: Grief, Loss, and Coping

Teaching and Learning Goals

- Understand chronic illness and its physical, social, spiritual, and psychological effect on patients
- Recognize the effects of chronic illness
- Understand the issues of loss and grief in relationship to chronic illness
- Understand the biopsychosocial forms of loss

The epidemic of chronic illness in society completely changes how the United States delivers health care and this has significant implications for social workers (Auslander & Freedenthal, 2006). Social workers in health care spend much of their time interacting with patients and caregivers who are dealing with the effects of chronic illness, grief, and loss.

The implications for social work education include the need to teach and learn about chronic illness. Familiarity with the psychosocial issues related to chronic illnesses and preparation to interact with patients, families, caregivers, and the health care team is necessary to practice in a knowledgeable and effective manner. Being informed about chronic illness means that social workers need to know as much about a chronic condition as the well-informed patient living with the illness and recognize how biological changes influence psychological and social changes.

Social workers are involved in a variety of roles in patient care (Auslander & Freedenthal, 2006). They teach and encourage patients and caregivers to adhere to treatment plans and help patients problem-solve as they attempt to adapt to their diagnosis. In addition, social workers need to recognize and support individuals affected by chronic illness and experience the psychosocial symptoms of distress. Adaptive coping strategies offer patients opportunities to maximize both longevity and quality of life.

Social workers need skills in the area of loss, particularly as it pertains to the losses experienced with chronic illness. Despite effective treatments for chronic illnesses and the results of an extended life span for many people living with chronic illness, the grief and bereavement experienced due to loss remains a predictable result of disease. Everyone who is diagnosed with a chronic illness experiences losses. Loss of good health, loss due to advancing disease, and the losses experienced with the preparation for death result in people experiencing sadness and grief.

The Advent of Chronic Illness

Most of human history traces the role of health, illness, and healing and the attempts by societies to control or treat sudden, accidental, and fatal conditions (Porter, 1999). Historically, people did not develop and live with the chronic illnesses that are prevalent today. Contagious diseases, infections, malnutrition, wars, and natural disasters killed large communities of people in single events (Porter, 1999). Individuals worked in unsafe conditions, had no sanitary processes, and no antibiotics. Infection was common with most injuries and complicated and compromised recovery. The lack of medications (particularly antibiotics) and a shortage of expertise and personnel in health care all contributed to the likelihood that events related to accident or a change in physical health would be life-threatening. Diseases such as tuberculosis, pneumonia, influenza, and diphtheria were the leading causes of death at the beginning of the 20th century (Porter, 1999; Tarlov, 1996). Newborns and infants were likely to die and the longevity of adults was limited to what is now considered early middle age.

The emergence of chronic illness is relatively new in U.S. society and has resulted in two societal changes. First, the development of medicine, medications, understanding of environmental effects on health, access to immunizations, and quality food has increased life expectancy (Auslander & Freedenthal, 2006; Sidell, 1997). Today, people are living longer. Second, due to poor nutritional choices and inactivity, both clearly symptoms of the

Westernization of culture, people are very likely to develop a chronic illness, and often live with more than one disease.

Today, U.S. citizens are likely to die of chronic long-term conditions and diseases such as Alzheimer's, cancer, acquired immunodeficiency syndrome (AIDS), heart disease, or diabetes. These diagnoses are considered chronic, progressive, and noncurable. Chronic illness influences all aspects of a person's life—the biological, the psychological, and the social. These three areas of functioning are pivotal to consider in attaining "quality of life" for people living with chronic illness, despite dramatic variations in experiences between and among different diagnoses (Auslander & Freedenthal, 2006). Fortunately, there are many treatments that successfully manage the biological symptoms of disease and successfully manage, temporarily stop, or delay the advancement of disease. Longer life gives many individuals a chance to adapt to chronic illness (de Ridder, Geenen, Kuijer, & van Middendorp, 2008). In addition, there is more information about risk factors, ways to control risks, prevent chronic illness diagnosis, and advances in technology and pharmacology that will reduce the effects of chronic illness in patients.

Chronic Illness

Chronic illness is a disease that interferes with the healthy functioning of the body, is not curable, and is frequently and progressively more symptomatic (de Ridder, et al., 2008). Living with a chronic illness can interfere in physical functioning and over time is likely to influence the emotional and social functioning of the individual (Auslander & Freedenthal, 2006; de Ridder, et al., 2008; Kelly & Field, 1996). There is wide variation in symptoms and severity between chronic illnesses and within diagnostic categories of chronic disease. People diagnosed with chronic illness typically require some form of treatment to control the symptoms or delay the progress of the disease. Some individuals require a level of medical treatment, care, and support over the rest of their life. Depending on the unique health factors of the patient, the diagnosis, and the stage of the disease, people can live productively with chronic illness for days, weeks, months, or years (Rothman & Wagner, 2003). The trajectory of the disease influences the demands for changes in lifestyle and the challenges it may present to social functioning, quality of life, and symptom control. Quality of life is often related to variables such as economic factors, race, ethnicity, gender, age, and level of fitness (Auslander & Freedenthal, 2006).

Chronic illness, as the term implies, is a persistent condition that is often successfully treated or controlled for varying periods of time. Despite successful treatment, the presence of chronic illness stills affects people personally, even under the best of circumstances. Caregivers and family members also experience the effects of chronic illness (Auslander & Freedenthal, 2006). The systems theory supports the understanding that family members living with a diagnosis change the rest of the family system.

Historically, medical needs were primarily associated with acute disease or experiences related to accidents and injury (Porter, 1999). The entire health care system was fundamentally developed around the diagnosis and treatment of these kinds of events. When an illness or injury was diagnosed or assessed, the health care team developed goals to cure or promote healing through effective medical treatments. There was little attention to the psychological or social needs of patients. This approach to health care is still evident when comparing the patient rooms in new hospital wings with the patient rooms in the outdated portions of a hospital. Past hospital rooms were often wards with many beds or small, private rooms. Old rooms are impersonal, and primarily designed to efficiently support the diagnosis, treatments, and discharge of the patient. The "new rooms" in hospitals frequently include many patient comfort features: pullout couches for family members to stay the night, refrigerators, DVD players, and wireless computer access. Today, rooms are designed to meet the needs of chronic illness and long-term treatments that affect the body, emotions, and social elements of life.

With a growing number of people requiring treatments for chronic illness, the model of care requires significant modifications for the health care system and changes are already occurring in health professions (Auslander & Freedenthal, 2006). Even though chronic illness is not considered curable, health care providers must supply health services and this presents considerable changes in treatment planning. It is tempting to treat chronic illness with a treatment model that includes curative goals, but treatment plans that fail to acknowledge the chronic nature of a patient's diagnosis miss a vital opportunity to educate and empower patients to improve health and prevent an increase in health care needs (de Ridder, et al., 2008).

Health providers specializing in chronic illness understand the need to encourage and support people to modify lifestyles and to accommodate the necessary alterations caused by the disease. Some diagnoses call for a radical modification, but success with achieving healthy goals can lead to many benefits. It produces a sense of well-being, creativity, and productivity and it may slow down the progression of the disease, or control pain. Some forms of chronic illness benefit less, if at all, from lifestyle modification, but health providers are still an important link for patients as they partner to control symptoms and pain through encouragement and support (Auslander & Freedenthal, 2006; Curtin & Lubkin, 1990).

Social workers know patients with chronic illness are more than people with a biomedical problem. It is essential to know that people require support in all areas of life, including the emotional and social aspects. Without this perspective, successful health care attempts are limited and opportunities to provide the essential elements of support and quality assistance are missed (Curtin & Lubkin, 1990; de Ridder, et al., 2008).

If health care providers recognize the biopsychosocial factors affecting patients, and looks beyond the biological changes, it enhances their understanding of the patient's relationship with their diagnosis. For instance, consider the circumstances of a 33-year-old woman who is diagnosed with breast cancer. If no one in the health system knows or understands she has three small children and is terrified that she will die and leave them without a mother, chances to educate her about the positive outcomes of treatment may be missed. This young mother, isolated from good education about breast cancer, may be so paralyzed by fear that she experiences fitful sleep, poor nutrition, and depression, jeopardizing her chances for a healthy life and increasing her symptoms.

Chronic illness diagnosis can include a major assault to a person's identity. Failing to recognize the significance of this event may interfere with attempts to build a therapeutic relationship. Individuals respond to the news of a diagnosis in a number of ways, but predictably cope with their diagnosis in the same way they have coped with other crises in their lives, by relying on their strengths (Curtin & Lubkin, 1990). Social workers help patients experiencing a form of crisis to consider the strengths patients have and assist them to move toward those strengths. Families and caregivers are often viewed as a significant strength when coping with chronic illness.

Types of Chronic Illness

There are many kinds of chronic illness, but a list of some of the most common types include Alzheimer's disease, cancer, AIDS, diabetes, and heart disease. Each disease is associated with extensive resources available to patients through national and professional disease education and advocacy and support groups. In addition, many larger communities offer resources for support and information through resource centers and health organizations. It is vital for a social worker to keep an updated list of the reputable disease-related resources available to patients and their families. In fact, brochures about all resources are valuable and a great resource to place in a new patient information folder.

An overview of the epidemiology of a chronic illness shared today, even by the most reputable resources, may change tomorrow. New clinical trials, research, and breakthroughs occur in disease-related studies and quickly replace outdated responses to illness. If social workers are complacent and lean on old information, they risk giving patients inaccurate information. Social workers benefit patients by staying aware of the progress being made in the treatment of disease. Basic knowledge about chronic illness is important for social workers to know as they establish patient relationships. It is essential to speak knowledgably in conversations, recognize myths regarding diseases, and refer patients to the appropriate resources with questions and concerns.

Social workers encounter people living with chronic illness in every health care setting: emergency rooms, hospitals, outpatient clinics, community centers, hospices, nursing homes, and rehabilitation centers. When social workers develop expertise in physical and behavioral health issues, they provide an important role in the support of patients and families attempting to maintain quality of life and adherence to their medical treatments (Auslander & Freedenthal, 2006; de Ridder, et al., 2008). In addition, basic information about the epidemiology of chronic illnesses improves the social worker's understanding of the journey for individuals and caregivers managing chronic illness. Knowledge about the prevalence of the disease, the populations at risk, and the trajectory of chronic illness and possible treatment assist the social worker and health care team to understand patients, caregivers, families, and community challenges.

Quality of Life

Quality of life is uniquely perceived by individuals and is influenced by more than living with a disease (de Ridder, et al., 2008). The choices to achieve quality living are influenced by many variables: the stage or severity of the illness, age and gender of the individual, prediagnosis health, and the support needed to live within the community. Healthy people often take personal independence for granted, yet, in the face of illness, this condition becomes of ultimate value. In the United States, we value and admire independence and it is taught, expected, and craved. So when people living with a chronic illness are challenged to care for themselves, it is frequently difficult for many to ask for help. In some cultures, dependence due to illness is a severe assault to one's integrity and quality of life, while other cultures support and honor the concept of dependence on social networks. In other words, the cultural view of chronic illness plays an important role in the individuals' attitude toward the concept of independence. There are striking differences in attitudes regarding issues of chronic illness and the role of family and community support (Curtin & Lubkin, 1990; Hooyman & Kiyak, 2008).

Unfortunately, many forms of chronic illness are undetectable until symptomatic and so many do not benefit from treatment opportunities available early in the disease. When the condition is symptomatic or problematic, the patient and the family seek help from the health care system and it is then that the disease diagnosis is made. If diagnosis occurs in later stages, the patient may immediately require increased levels of treatment or support and sometimes advanced disease leads to dependence on the support of caregivers and health care professionals. Advanced disease may also lead to the need for additional medical care, appointments, and medications. As the needs increase, the need to manage care increases, and individuals are more likely to consider alterations in their life and reflect on the changes in their quality of life (Hooyman & Kiyak, 2008). Reactions vary depending on the personality of the individual, issues of pain, presence of support, and the economic and environmental resources available to live with the disease.

Spirituality

For many years, research regarding patient spirituality was avoided in the professional literature. While this is changing due to the publication of new articles and texts addressing the role of spirituality issues present in patient health and coping, the subject is still viewed suspiciously. Perhaps the recognition of spirituality issues for patients are minimized because of the nonscientific nature of the concept or because spirituality is perceived as the same as religiosity. Social workers understand religions are social institutions and unfortunately can be used to discriminate against people who do not hold the same religious views (DuBois & Miley, 2008). The power of religious institutions can sometimes result in social, emotional, and physical pain for disenfranchised individuals living outside the norms of their religious affiliations. It is with appropriate thoughtfulness that social workers engage in conversations with patients about their religious practices. However, the definition of spirituality is uniquely personal and has evolved to include multidimensional and existential perspectives that are often vital to the well-being of those that are chronically ill and their caregivers (Chu-Hui-Lin Chi, 2007; DuBois & Miley, 2008; O'Neill & Kenny, 1998).

The definition of spirituality defies a full description, but is not the same thing as religiosity. Spirituality does not refer to a type of religion, but rather to the fundamental issues addressed by every religion, including view of life, ethical values, emotional preparation for dealing with pain and tragedy, and how to make meaning of experiences (Leifer, 1996). Burkhardt (1993) identifies characteristics of spirituality as belief in a higher power, prayer, a sense of inner strength, and relationships with others and nature. Spirituality is defined as the force that gives meaning to one's existence, pervades all aspects of being, and is experienced in caring connections with self, others, nature, and God or Higher Power (O'Neill & Kenny, 1998). Clearly spirituality is a way to better understand the way someone experiences life and loss.

Spirituality is commonly identified as an important factor in maintaining health and well-being and in coping with illness. It is commonly identified as a key element in hope (Chu-Hui-Lin Chi, 2007; O'Neill & Kenny, 1998) for people experiencing the diagnosis and advancement of chronic illness and for people who are dying or bereaved. But patients and caregivers also rely on spirituality as a coping mechanism that improves the ability to cope with stress. Some studies describe the experience of spiritual well-being as a sense of harmonious interconnectedness, with self, others, and the infinite (O'Neill & Kenny, 1998).

Diagnosis of a chronic illness is a major life event and often causes individuals to question themselves, their purpose, and their meaning in life (Pulchalski & Sandoval, 2003). These are existential and spiritual questions. Illness disrupts a life journey by disrupting careers, relationships, and future plans. In addition, a diagnosis affects how a person experiences joy; these issues are the fundamentals of life. The work of Viktor Frankel (1984) is crucial to understanding the role of spirituality in adverse situations. Frankel drew upon his experiences as a prisoner in a Nazi concentration camp during World War II to develop an existential theory identifying people as spiritual beings. Frankel proposed that the spiritual task of finding meaning in life through self-transcendence and relationships with others are the core elements of existence.

There is far more to the medical treatment of a person than the treatment of the body. Individuals with a diseased body cannot separate the experience of disease from their emotions, social relationships, or spiritual perspectives. The biopsychosocial theory, credited to Engel (1977), recognizes the existence and interaction of the unique domains of human functioning. Furthermore, this theory suggests the biological, psychological, emotional, and spiritual spheres affect an individual's quality of life and influences his or her ability to interact with the disease process.

A social worker in health care can anticipate potential and actual growth in patients and will witness these changes (de Ridder, et al., 2008). Social workers are ready to learn from and facilitate growth in patients' integration of spiritual meaning with living and the end of life (Dunbar, Mueller, Medina, & Wolf, 1998). Willingness to discuss spirituality, the meaning of life, and suffering can act as an opportunity for patients to change, to see things differently, and to perhaps find peace and support for life goals. Many patients with chronic illness share how interactions about life and the meaning of life enriched them or caused them to stop and see events in a richer and fuller way. People rely on the medical system for cure from a disease, but may look to spirituality for meaning, purpose, and understanding (Chu-Hui-Lin Chi, 2007). Medical care and spiritual care are a valuable combination for many in the health, symptoms, and healing associated with all diseases, at any stage.

Family and Caregivers

The diagnosis of a chronic illness affects the patient's family and caregivers in many ways, too. The family, a system, changes whenever a member of the system is altered. When family members respond to the physical, psychological, and social changes associated with disease, it changes the routine of day-to-day living, even if the changes are minor, or positive (Hooyman & Kiyak, 2008; Waldrop, 2007).

Physical strength may be altered by disease and the family may notice differences in how the individual looks, acts, or interacts. Some individuals living with chronic illness experience rather dramatic differences in living such as an inability to negotiate stairs or drive a car. Individuals may experience the loss of strength to physically pick up a grandchild or independently prepare meals. Environmental changes can be as subtle as a shelf in the home newly dedicated to prescriptions or medical treatment supplies. Families adjust to these changes, but it means the ways of interacting are different than before the diagnosis. Family members may also experience physical symptoms: changes in appetite, sleep, or interests, and nausea, weakness, or pain (Waldorp, 2007).

Changes result in a new sense of family vulnerability and may result in families also experiencing a change in psychological or emotional well-being (Hooyman & Kiyak, 2008). Families and caregivers may witness a progression of disease they are helpless to stop or reverse. Social workers know individual family members experience a variety of feelings including guilt, shame, grief, helplessness, anger, and resentment (Waldorp, 2007).

Some forms of social change are associated with a new or increased level of vulnerability. If a family is financially challenged, it is often devastated by the additional costs a chronic diagnosis of a family member presents. Some services and treatments are covered for the insured, but benefits never cover every cost associated with chronic disease. For instance, some disease treatment requires frequent appointments, so transportation to the physician office, pharmacy, and other treatment centers are costly and perhaps unaffordable. If the patient depends on family members or caregivers, the transportation can require they take time off from work. Families pay for parking, childcare, and an increase in the payment of co-payments. It is common for families to rely on two incomes to meet the obligations of the family budget and perhaps the patient contributed to the family income prior to the disease diagnosis. When a family member is no longer able to work, despite disability plans, families experience a reduction in income. Families experiencing chronic illness are economically vulnerable.

To adapt to chronic illness, the patient, family, and caregivers must commit to the work necessary to maintain the best possible conditions for improved longevity and quality of life. Unfortunately, individual responses to chronic illness are seldom predictable. Not everybody experiences chronic illness in the same way, so a condition that is tolerable for one person may be totally overwhelming or intolerable for another.

The significant differences patients experience in their physical, emotional, and social experience with chronic disease is similar to the significantly different ways families and caregivers respond to the disease (Waldorp, 2007). Each person and each family member or support person experiences a unique health care experience and must be treated with respect and attention.

Roles for Social Work in Chronic Illness Care

One of the most significant changes in health care is the common occurrence, diagnosis, and treatment for chronic illnesses in the United States. This escalation has changed the kinds of roles social workers perform in health care. Chronic illness changes the relationship between a patient and the health care system because now it is long term. Potentially, the relationships are more personal due to increased contacts. The primary role for social workers within hospitals continues to revolve around safe, effective, and efficient discharge planning, but the considerations of discharge also reflect the conditions associated with chronic illness (Waldorp, 2007). In addition to communication with the team regarding the biological, social, and psychological needs of patients and families, social workers also consider the longer term and ongoing coordination and treatment needs of the patient. Social workers are also more active in the assessment and support of caregivers.

For many individuals, there are significant barriers to obtaining consistent chronic illness care. Sometimes people are uninsured or underinsured. Frequently even the routine needs for a patient's personal care are challenging, such as the requirements for a specialized diet, medication, exercise, rehabilitation, transportation, or caregiving. When these needs go unmet, patients are more likely to appear in the health care system due to a health-related emergency. Untreated and unmonitored chronic illness care is dangerous for patients, a crisis for families, and challenging for physicians and others on the health care team. Patients come to emergency rooms with symptoms of chronic disease that are out of control and physicians, who are unfamiliar with the patient, attempt to treat them. This quality of health care is a grim reality for people with no insurance coverage. Patients with chronic illness receive the most expensive form of care, despite the poor quality. Physicians and health care teams work to avoid these kinds of health emergencies because no one benefits from this form of treatment.

The best treatment for chronic illness is supported by adequate insurance. This allows the patient and health care provider to establish a relationship created around illness management and improves the chances that the patient is periodically examined and tested for new or altering symptoms. It improves assessment of patients, revision of medications, opportunities for participation in clinical trials, or other forms of progressive disease maintenance and treatment techniques. Ambulatory and specialty clinics attempt to assist patients in dealing with the challenges of living with a chronic illness and offer opportunities and referrals to receive forms of medical, psychological, or social support. The most common responsibilities for health care social workers in chronic illness treatment include those listed in Box 8.1.

Prevention

Health care social workers may work with chronic illness solely through prevention efforts. Prevention is the best method to treat the effects of chronic illness for a minimum of two reasons. First, prevention is far less expensive than treatment of disease. The cost of chronic illness management for private and public insurers is overwhelming. Second, poor access to health care is common. Access is less necessary when there is absence of disease. Prevention of chronic illness supports people to live without the health risks associated with chronic illness, encourages the best quality of living, and increases opportunities for long life.

BOX 8.1 • *Common Roles for Health Care Social Workers Treating Chronic Illness*

1. Work toward prevention.
2. Support for adherence to treatment.
3. Assist to identify strengths and potential barriers.
4. Provide psychosocial care by offering support to patients and caregivers.
5. Offer effective techniques to help patients and caregivers utilize effective coping skills.

Prevention is one of the most sensible methods to use to control chronic illness. Many types of chronic disease are developed due to lifestyle habits and behaviors that put people at risk. Not all individuals participate in prevention programs, learn about the risks of disease, and actually change their behaviors, but for those who do, there is a real chance that long-term disease is delayed or avoided. Prevention of chronic disease may require behavioral changes that are difficult to maintain (Auslander & Freedenthal, 2006). However, prevention is still a far better solution than the development of a disease that was at one point preventable.

Social workers in health care clinics, health departments, and other forms of outpatient social work are frequently involved in prevention services to the community. There are different forms of prevention: primary, secondary, and tertiary (Wheeler, 2000). Primary prevention emphasizes stopping something before it happens. For instance, it means educating people about the risk behaviors associated with forms of chronic illness so that behaviors change and disease diagnosis is averted. Secondary prevention is slowing down the advancement of disease or stopping the disease from inflicting further damage. An example is support for the lifestyle changes associated with heart disease such as weight loss, exercise, and medication. Tertiary prevention is the treatment of disease in a way that improves quality and quantity of life. This is done through medical treatments or case management roles. Most social workers in health care are involved in some or all forms of disease prevention (Wheeler, 2000).

Adherence to Treatment

Individuals with a diagnosis of chronic illness can plan on changes in many areas of life (Auslander & Freedenthal, 2006; de Ridder, et al., 2008). But two very common areas include alteration in daily living habits, and a new relationship with the health care system. Social workers are instrumental in assisting individuals in adjusting to these changes.

Patients with a new diagnosis are often assigned new and important health care tasks and must rely significantly on self-motivation. Unfortunately, despite real desire and sincere efforts, changes in daily habits are difficult to achieve. However, because many forms of chronic illness benefit by some types of change in behaviors such as losing weight, starting an exercise program, abstaining from alcohol and drugs, and improving levels of stress, sleep, and nutrition, it is worthwhile for patients to attempt these changes. Making successful changes to daily habits varies from person to person and is frequently associated with patients' belief that the effort will help them reduce their chance of more advanced disease. Individuals must also take new personal responsibility for taking medications or following through on the requests for tests and appointments. Often forms of emotional and physical fatigue accompany the commitment to the demands of the medical system and the new responsibilities are often long term. They require additional time for scheduling, preparing for, driving to, and waiting for appointments, transportation, poor parking, and interruptions in a work day.

Social workers teach and support patients to adhere to programs and treatment plans that alter the life of patients and families (Auslander & Freedenthal, 2006; de Ridder, et al., 2008). These changes are often accompanied by feelings of significant grief and loss as they recall days before the diagnosis, when perhaps life seemed simpler. Patients miss the days when they took no medication and often grieve the loss of living without chronic illness. Social workers assist patients to identify their goals and encourage and promote steps toward accommodating and eventually achieving positive change. This role of encouragement recognizes positive attempts and helps to identify resources for support. Personal discipline is an important factor for change, but having someone from outside the family or support system be honest and share defeats and frustrations offers a fresh perspective.

Strengths and Barriers

Living with chronic illness is stressful and although many forms are controlled with medications and result in a longer and better life, the new relationship with chronic illness is long term (de Ridder, et al., 2008). The medical aspects of the disease are only a part of a relationship with chronic illness and patients are also challenged to find ways to survive and thrive with all aspects of the disease. The health care system is designed to focus on the medical course and treatment of the disease, but the social worker understands the emotional and social needs as well. The course of chronic illness is uncertain and unpredictable.

It is common for patients to ask questions regarding a chronic illness that seeks to commit disease advancement to a predictable route, yet frequently health providers must respond with uncertainty. This can be maddening because it interferes with any sense of control the patient attempts to experience in the management of his or her life. The symptoms, course, length of time, pain, and other variables are unique for every chronic illness and vary for every person (Sidell, 1997). One of the universal responses to chronic illness is a feeling of powerlessness. Each step of disease management is filled with some level of ambiguity.

From the moment individuals are diagnosed with a chronic disease, they develop ways of coping with the news, changes, treatments, and the idea that life is now redefined to include a disease (de Ridder, 2008). Chronic illness is progressive, but not everyone hears this message when diagnosed. They hear they have a condition calling for some lifestyle changes, or they need to take medication, or schedule regular lab or examination appointments. This is a good place to start. Some patients immediately research the diagnosis and soon realize that the condition demands their serious attention because it is long term and calls for strategic planning.

Pollin and Golant (1994) suggest that a person diagnosed with a chronic illness is likely to experience "a wide range of powerful and painful emotions such as anxiety, terror, denial, anger, depression, helplessness, frustration, and even shame" (p. 8). These emotions are normal and expected, but can camouflage the personal strengths of the patient. There are many moments when patients with a chronic illness feel particularly vulnerable: at the time of diagnosis, during significant changes in the illness, and after hospitalization (Pollin, 1994). It is the role of the social worker to remind patients and their support systems that everyone experiences crises differently, and most reactions are normal and valid. This is also the time to remind individuals or their family and friends that they have successfully responded to overwhelming issues in the past and are capable of doing so again.

For instance, the diagnosis of human immunodeficiency virus (HIV) is likely to present a significant crisis. When a person is diagnosed, the words sound like a death sentence; the patient may experience emotional paralysis and an inability to think. This coping mechanism happens automatically and is normal. It is as if the mind numbs and one cannot feel emotional pain. After receiving the initial news, changes in reaction occur as the patient begins to cope, and the strengths used to survive emerge. An increased sense of balance and a return to personal strategies of problem solving begin to take shape. Perhaps the patient returns home, locates social and emotional support, reads brochures and online information about the disease, or gets feedback from someone who is personally affected by the disease. As the disease progresses, sometimes over many years, the patient may experience other times of impaired coping. For individuals living with HIV, perhaps a crisis occurs when they learn that they need new and more powerful medications. Similar to the reaction to the diagnosis, the patient may experience an emotional assault. However, as patients receive external support and reassurance from family, caregivers, and the social worker on the health care team, they progress in their adjustment to the news.

There are many areas of strength that help people cope with crisis. This may be difficult to remember when the diagnosis and treatment aspects are tied to a "disease concept" model (Rapp, 1997). The strengths model—a model that supports social work engagement, assessment, and interventions—is persistent in guiding social workers to help an individual "recognize past situations when they made good decisions, demonstrated competence, or displayed skills" (Rapp, p. 87). This is not to minimize the idea that the person and the caregivers are not facing some tough barriers or problems. It does, however, promote the belief that problems are not the sole element of life. Weick and Chamberlain (1997) summarize this support by suggesting that despite the condition or disease, social workers acknowledge that "a person is always more than his or her problem" (p. 45). Each step of living with chronic illness is uniquely personal and despite attempts of support the journey can be frightening and lonely.

Adaptation Skills

When chronic illness limits and changes routine functioning for patients it is accompanied by a sense of loss and grief (Sidell, 1997; Walsh-Burke, 2006). The patient begins to understand the impossibility of returning to a prediagnosis state. The sense of loss follows the patient during the course of the illness, but patients describe the process as similar to a "roller-coaster ride." U.S. culture promotes pride in being independent and successful. Individuals plan and organize everything including the hours in a day, development of 5- and 10-year plans for the future, career advancement, and vacations. The ability to plan the future is taken for granted, but people with chronic illness experience a radical alteration in this form of thinking. As chronic illness symptoms increase, some wonder if they will see their children get married, if they will be able to walk during an upcoming vacation, or to spend hours without needing treatments like injections or other medications. In the moment of diagnosis, the patient is often overwhelmed by the potential power of the disease and his or her unpredictable future. For some, the future becomes frightening.

There are many potential feelings experienced when diagnosis of disease occurs. Pollin and Golant (1994) say fear is a common reaction and suggest eight unique forms of fear associated with the diagnosis of chronic illness, listed in Box 8.2. People react to overwhelming news with denial, acceptance, anger, grief, and many other emotions, but all reactions are normal and unique to the individual.

BOX 8.2 • *Common Fears in Reaction to the Diagnosis of a Chronic Illness*

1. Loss of control
2. Loss of self-image
3. Dependency
4. Stigma
5. Abandonment
6. Expression of anger
7. Isolation
8. Death

Source: Pollin & Golant (1994).

Most feel overwhelmed with the sense that nothing is the same, because chronic illness diagnosis interferes with the ability for people to recognize themselves as the same person they were. Perhaps no one knows or notices the incredible change that has occurred, yet the individual with the new diagnosis is radically altered. Chronic illnesses potentially develop symptoms that result in increased dependence (Walsh-Burke, 2006). Even the possibility that at some point others will feed, bathe, clothe, or care for us is shaming and terrifying. For many the most terrifying thought is that someone will need to assist us with our bodily waste.

Society uses labels to identify the strengths and weaknesses in people and the presence of disease is perceived as a weakness and leads to stigmatization (DuBois & Miley, 2008). A person altered or different because of disease frequently experiences reactions in others because of the disease. Friends may be reluctant or uncertain about someone's health condition and individuals living with chronic illness may be unsure of how or when to mention their experiences. Being treated differently, or stigmatized, is powerful and is displayed in both obvious and covert ways (DuBois & Miley, 2008) When physical changes occur and the ability to hide the disease progress disappears, societal reactions can be emotionally draining (Walsh-Burke, 2006). For instance, the loss of hair from chemotherapy or weight loss due to AIDS are both socially recognizable effects of disease or disease treatment.

Social workers employed in areas of chronic illness services offer patients an opportunity to prepare for the variety of reactions they may experience due to their disease. Empathy and identification of patients' coping methods offers improved support to the patient and his or her family. Every stage of coming to terms with a diagnosis is accompanied by emotional steps for patients and their support system. Social workers teach patients and health care teams that reactions are normal, common, and expected and encourage the use of adaptive coping skills to enhance a patient's ability to deal with their future. When a social worker discusses fears and reactions to diagnosis and disease with a patient, colleagues on the health team benefit and come to view the continuum of emotional reactions as part of a normal process, not a maladaptive way of functioning.

Social workers in health care practice in many areas and the relationships social workers develop with patients depend on the health care setting. It is not common, however, for social workers in health care to engage in long-term psychological patient therapy. It is vital for social workers to know counselors in the community who have expertise in working with individuals and families experiencing chronic illness so referrals for longer-term emotional needs can continue to be addressed. But there are important and helpful steps a social worker in every health care setting can do to assist patient and caregivers to adapt to disease.

Understanding the clients' needs and their perceptions of change during the course of illness and treatment provides social workers critical information about how to best support the psychosocial needs of patients and their families (Walsh-Burke, 2006). Knowledge of the patients' psychosocial needs, obtained through careful and thoughtful assessments that ask open-ended questions and allow patients to reveal their honest experiences (Sidell, 1997; Walsh-Burke, 2006), are good reminders that how individuals identify crisis and how they cope are unique and continue to change.

Psychosocial Coping

Coping with chronic illness relies on the patient developing a wide range of strategies (de Ridder, et al., 2008; Walsh-Burke, 2006). Livneh (2000) suggests that most recognized ways of coping are frequently targeted at three dimensions: emotion-focused, problem-focused, and avoidance or minimizing. Individuals rely on a variety of emotional strategies to minimize or avoid emotional pain because loss and change vary by stage and experiences with the disease. The role of psychological defense mechanisms reduces emotional distress and assists patients to manage fears of pain, change, weakness, and loss. Coping methods help individuals function and attain some level of problem-solving behaviors and psychological adaptation to disease. Problem solving helps the patient limit experiences with avoidance, passivity, submission, self-blame, and other maladaptive coping styles that contribute to emotional distress. When functional changes occur and concrete evidence of chronic illness is evident due to medical intrusions, radical changes in daily routines occur, strengths emerge, and resilience can develop (de Ridder, et al., 2008; Livneh, 2000; Walsh-Burke, 2006).

Individuals cope with personal crises based on their personal strengths and choice of strategies. But coping is also related to family of origin, ethnicity, and many other cultural components. Some patients are interested in learning new and effective coping measures, particularly if they remain distressed and unable to experience an ability to function or to maintain an adequate quality of life. Consistently unresolved symptoms of stress are destructive to health maintenance and health providers recommend patients find ways to decrease the emotional symptoms of disease to better treat physical symptoms. Social workers benefit from recognition of the reactions to disease and to the various coping techniques. By understanding the ways patients cope, social workers help create and enhance ways to integrate strengths. Social workers encourage a positive supportive network, and challenge and reframe negative thoughts and experiences (Livneh, 2000).

Finding ways to cope is essential for patients living with chronic illness and these strategies become essential skills that help patients maintain the greatest level of functioning (de Ridder, et al., 2008). Social workers are helpful when they educate the patient and family regarding functional coping strategies that allow the patient to emotionally move forward in a way that supports their unique physical and social circumstances (Walsh-Burke, 2006). The social worker offers a safe place for the patient to vent feelings and learn alternative ways to cope. This is difficult for some patients to do, especially when they believe they must protect their families from the emotional pain. Sometimes patients benefit from a social work referral to psychosocial groups where they interact with others experiencing some of the same health care crises. There are benefits to understanding and teaching coping skills to patients. It improves problem identification, solution strategies, and positive goal-directed living (Livneh, 2000).

Loss Due to Illness

Loss is defined in several ways, but advancing chronic illness often means patients or families no longer have something they once had. The emotion most commonly linked with loss is grief, the experience of intense sadness or great sorrow.

The losses experienced because of changes due to chronic illness, dying and death are all part of the human journey and are frequently recognized within the health care system. It is rare if individuals do not experience the emotions associated with loss in their lives. Grief is a common life experience because it is often experienced when things change. Grief due to loss accompanies positive changes in our lives as well as negative changes (Walsh-Burke, 2006). When we graduate from school, leave the family of origin, or start a new job, the past is often missed, if only because of the change it causes to a familiar routine. But when the changes experienced are perceived as negative and unwelcome, particularly the loss due to chronic illness, change is particularly challenging.

Chronic illness is a progressive condition even though people live longer and better with a chronic illness diagnosis than ever before. Advanced chronic illness occurs when the symptoms of the disease increase in frequency and intensity and signal that the body is under additional stress. Progression of advanced disease may look and act differently for each chronic illness, varies within the diagnosis of chronic illness, and by the unique biopsychosocial responses of each individual (Walsh-Burke, 2006). For instance, two people diagnosed with diabetes may have the same diagnosis but often experience a very different reaction, perhaps in how their bodies adjust to medication, exercise, or weight loss. The same is true with two women diagnosed with the same type and stage of breast cancer. The side effects of treatments and the individual's ability to tolerate treatments are often unique to each individual. How the cancer responds to treatment and the time and consistency of remission varies for each woman.

Changes experienced due to advancing disease are often first experienced when some event occurs and the loss is recognized (Walsh-Burke, 2006). The moment individuals experience these feelings of loss is not always predictable to the patient, the caregiver, or the health care team. Patients may experience overwhelming sadness at what appears to be a rather common or benign everyday experience, yet the individual meaning of the event and the loss it represents acts to accentuate the event as a loss, leading to significant feelings of grief. The first time the patient needs help getting up from a chair, drops a cup while washing dishes, or cannot get to the top of the bleachers to watch his or her grandson's basketball game may be experienced as a moment of significant loss. A specific event breaks through some thin layer of denial and in that moment, the patient is face-to-face with the truth of the physical changes that are occurring. These are personal and private moments and others may not always recognize when these moments occur. The same is true for family members; their moments of loss are often associated with common events that are now changed forever due to the significance of disease. The grief experienced by families and caregivers is also personal and private (Waldorp, 2007).

Bodies change and often follow developmental processes. Physical development is combined with environmental experiences such as socioeconomic status, gender, age, race, ethnicity, geography, and exposure to pollution. Change also occurs due to genetic composition, or inherited physical and emotional traits. But when change occurs due to chronic illness, people frequently acknowledge feeling scared, helpless, panic, or depressed (Walsh-Burke, 2006). If the illness results in changes that are moderate in effect and the consequences are relatively insignificant in the normal routine of life, individuals tend to adapt quite easily to the change. In contemporary U.S. society, individuals take medications for all kinds of ailments, and early chronic illness detection is frequently interpreted as just another condition requiring a pill. It is often easy to take medications, but the process of treatment, particularly in absence of disease symptoms, can often disguise the seriousness of a chronic condition. Sometimes patients attempt to joke about the number of medications they must take or the changes in their sleep and appetite. However, when the symptoms of disease are no longer easy to ignore, changes are experienced as traumatic and individuals more vividly experience the loss of health and feel grief.

Advancing disease commands change. It may interfere in the physical and functional abilities of the individual, in emotional stamina and ability to cope, and may alter the patient and caregiver environment and interactions with society (de Ridder, et al., 2008; Waldorp, 2007). These forms of radical change are best supported by interventions based on the holistic biopsychosocial model. The biopsychosocial model of health care assumes the integration of the biological, psychological, and social (including environmental issues) of patients in the health care system. Changes that occur in patients' physical health or biological systems are damaging to the psychological and the social systems as well.

Physical Losses

When chronic illness is first diagnosed, frequently it may have few symptoms the patient notices. Life goes on relatively the same as it did before the diagnosis. If it is early heart disease, there is an introduction of medications or routine testing and medical advice for lifestyle changes. Sometimes an HIV diagnosis calls for medications and occasional blood tests to determine viral activity. In these two examples, the changes demanded are seemingly rather simple. Some diagnoses, like breast cancer, may require treatments to be immediate and radical. There may be recommendations for swift action and invasive treatment methods. Breast cancer in very early stages is treated with forms of chemotherapy that might cause hair loss; with some breast cancer diagnoses, health care providers urge a form of surgical treatment as soon as possible. Regardless of the timing or the presence or absence of the physical alterations, eventually patients realize disease has an influence on their bodies. When those changes become noticeable to the patient, family, or caregivers, emotional responses are common (Waldorp, 2007).

For individuals who are "feeling healthy" there may be a strong sense of denial. Denial is an effective coping strategy for many people, for at least some period of time. Denial allows people to continue to live life without experiencing full emotional pain. It allows individuals with chronic illness to emotionally distance themselves from reality (Galambos, 1989). Eventually evidence of reality interferes with denial and individuals are required to take another step toward coping with the reality of circumstances. Coping is incremental.

Looking ahead and recognizing the possibilities of physical challenges allows individuals to consider alternative scenarios such as the possibility of changes in independence, or possibly the issues related to the end of life. It is important for social workers in the health care system to be aware of the power of denial and to respect denial as a strategy that helps individuals cope (Galambos, 1989).

Emotional Losses

No one totally understands the experience of an individual living with chronic illness. Even if individuals have the same diagnosis, the best they can offer is informed empathy. Social workers empathize and can imagine the reality of patients, often because the social worker has interactions with many who share similar experiences. However, because of the subjectivity of feelings, it is difficult to understand exactly how the experience feels to the patient. This is part of the loneliness people experience when they live with chronic illness. People respond to this sense of aloneness in a variety of ways. Some may attempt to share how they feel, and maybe it makes them feel better. Others state how they feel, but after recognizing no one understands, they avoid talking about their emotions. This is particularly true when they tell people who love them, perhaps a spouse, parent, or child, how they feel and it results in a negative reaction such as pain, sadness, or minimization from the family member.

All family members play a role and offer vital contributions to the strength of a family. Patients may hold many social roles in life such as the care provider, wage earner, or symbol of family unity. When they are diagnosed with chronic illness, families experience their own sense of denial and the patient is sometimes unwilling to let the family see them as weak or unwilling to fight for health. This is truly an emotional battle, especially as patients experience advancing disease. They may attempt to protect the family by not communicating about their reality. Patients spend their time reassuring the family that they are doing fine and they try to protect them from feelings of grief and loss. Unfortunately, time spent supporting the unrealistic goals of the family takes time from the opportunities to process and support changes. If social workers are observant, they will see this form of caregiving by the patient happen frequently; it is observed in the family dynamics when health concerns are discussed. For instance, the patient may be reluctant to speak about symptoms in front of the physician and allows the family to tell the physician how well things are going.

Chronic illness can exact great energy from patients due to a combination of medications, treatments, and appointments, less strength due to the disease, and perhaps little exercise or good nutrition. When the body is fighting disease the exhaustion taxes emotional strength and powerful feelings of hopelessness, helplessness, entrapment, and frustration can lead to changes in personality. Social workers assist patients to maintain hope, not necessarily for the cure or arrest of the disease, but hope for other positive conditions. Patients benefit by having hope for pain control, family attention, and the ability to maintain relationships. Research supports the idea that hope is an important emotion for quality of life when living with advanced chronic illness (Aronoff, 2000; Back, Arnold, & Quill, 2003; Chu-Hui-Lin Chi, 2007; Clark, 2002; Galambos, 1989; Rushton, Spencer, & Johanson, 2004). Galambos (1989) suggests hope is critical for many in their efforts to maintain a positive emotional balance in their lives. Aronoff (2000) suggests hope actually improves a person's ability to cope with the losses due to chronic illness.

Social Losses

As individuals become increasingly affected by the advancement of illness, changes occur in their environment. There are many ways environments are redefined but minimally the concept includes the patient's personal, social, and community space.

Personal Space. Personal space includes places such as patients' rooms and their homes. As a disease progresses, patients experience changes in physical functioning that can impair using space the way they did in the past. This means several things. For instance, it may mean using stairs is challenging or impossible or perhaps there is a need for a special bed or a commode. If a patient requires oxygen support, there is a need for adequate room for the equipment to go from room to room. Showers and bathtubs are frequently challenging for people with reduced physical strength so perhaps handrails are installed or the patient requires equipment to assist someone to bathe them.

Frequently there is room needed for the array of medications the patient may be prescribed. Directions for treatments and doctors' appointments may now cover a desk or fill a calendar. If patients are unable to sit at a table, they are now fed while in bed or while sitting on a couch. Trays and dishes are brought to different places within the house. Personal space also changes if other forms of support equipment, such as canes, walkers, and wheelchairs, are introduced.

Socialization. Social space changes as chronic illness intensifies. How people with advanced illness interact with others inevitably changes due to weakness, pain, discomfort, and energy. When someone feels sick, they are less likely to enjoy the company of others, or at least be less likely to display that pleasure. Friends and family, once part of the patient's social group, make adjustments to the biopsychosocial changes by engaging in shorter visits. Patients spend more time in their homes or make social contact with others less often. Everyone makes social accommodation efforts to increase or maintain the comfort of the patient. Social change occurs in subtle and obvious ways and old patterns of socialization, for patients and their social circles, take on a new look. Patients are well aware of their loss of the desire or ability to socialize with spontaneity and outwardly directed interactions.

Social change occurs within intimate relationships, too. Chronic illness can influence sexual intimacy and perhaps impair sexual functioning (Claiborne & Rizzo, 2006; Nusbaum, Hamilton, & Lenahan, 2003). Sexual functioning is altered by many things in life, including physical, social, and emotional health. People living with chronic illness experience physical changes due to disease, various medications, and other treatments and the physical changes influence reactions to the social and emotional attention of loved ones, influencing the patient's potential to experience sexual desire and arousal (Nusbaum et al., 2003). Disinterest or an inability to participate in intimate relationships at a time when closeness to others could benefit them, adds to their sense of grief and loss.

Community Mobility. Community space changes for individuals with advanced chronic illness. People, who were once independent, driving, and walking to any place they desired, experience limited mobility. There are some limitations because of changes in strength and endurance while other limitations restrict concrete tasks like walking or driving an automobile. In some cases, people with advanced disease are unable to change physical positions without assistance or need help to change from being seated to standing. When significant limitations exist in mobility, the constraints affect where people go and how they physically get there. It also interferes with a sense of autonomy and as changes occur in social spaces, both environmental and in relationships, chronic illness deteriorates levels of independence.

Change in the level of independence leads to other significant losses for both patients and caregivers. For instance, for older couples and those who are single, functional decline may raise questions about continued independent living. Caregivers are not always able to accommodate the increase in care needs and sometimes the support system must look at alternative residential care options. If the family can afford this luxury monetarily or through various forms of public assistance like Medicare, there are other significant changes to life. The emotional losses surrounding the decision to use residential care facilities are many. Both families and patients frequently deny need for patients to lose their personal residence and even under the best of circumstances, families experience guilt for moving patients. Family members are frequently challenged as they face decisions about the relocation of family members to nursing homes or other care facilities. For some patients, the decision to relocate is not their own and the final choice of residence is not their choice (Kao, Travis, & Acton, 2004).

All forms of relocation are stressful for patients and caregivers. The effect of the change to another location alters patients' physical and emotional health. Sometimes a person experiences relief that assistance is nearby 24 hours a day and relief they are not intruding on the time of family caregivers. In a residence that is organized and communicates respect and information to the patient and family, health coordination can improve. In some instances, patients' perception of hope declines and they suffer a sense of abandonment or depression. All forms of loss influence the experience of quality of life. Social workers treat individuals and caregivers with respect for their individual strengths and recognize coping with loss is complicated. People living with chronic illness are resilient and most adjust as necessary to the circumstances associated with advanced disease.

Palliative Care

Palliative care refers to the active medical treatment provided when recovery and cure are no longer the expectation. The symptoms of the disease are treated, particularly pain, but palliative care is much different than the assertive measures used to treat and cure disease (Davis, 2005). Treatment continues, but the goal is to minimize the negative effects of the symptoms produced by the disease.

The movement toward palliative care and hospice is a response to the medicalization of death. Due to the advancements in health technology after World War II, death became the foe. All treatments are designed to destroy and treat diseases for as long as possible. But over time, physicians, families, and patients often realize that longer life is not necessarily the way to measure successful health care. Instead, focus begins to shift to measuring the patient's ability to interact with others in meaningful ways and quality of life. For instance, although some chemotherapies temporarily extend life, the symptoms of the treatment may outweigh the benefits and offer little or no hope of improved health. While continued treatment is one way the patient continues to fight disease, the result of the treatment does not necessarily add to quality life (Ballard & Elston, 2005; Davis, 2005).

Palliative care is an attempt to merge the common end-of-life struggle between two strong feelings; hope and acceptance (Clark, 2002). Palliative care changes the goal of health care from continued medical treatment to facing the inevitability of death. Acceptance of death, however, does not mean there is no room for hope. This is essential for social workers to understand. When palliative care begins, the goals of patients and caregivers change. Instead of treating the disease and hoping for a cure, the hope moves toward providing comfort from pain. Palliative care is a great example of the biopsychosocial model at work because the method treats the biological needs of the patient, but also treats psychological and social needs.

Summary

Chronic illnesses are the leading cause of health problems in the United States. There are many types of chronic illness and the variations of disease progression are as unique as the individual with the diagnosis. Social workers perform vital services to people affected by chronic illness by partnering with patients and caregivers as they speak knowledgably about chronic disease, assist them to recognize their strengths, reassure them about their reactions to change, and encourage healthy coping techniques. Social workers diligently try to find effective ways to prevent chronic illness and help others to experience improved quality of life.

Critical Thinking Questions

1. What are some ways that social workers can stay informed about medical advancements? What are some of the barriers?

2. Think of a time when you, or someone you know, received overwhelming news. How did you cope? What emotions were involved?

3. Think of all the things you do in a day. How would your day be affected if you lost the ability to drive or walk? How would you adapt? How would it feel?

4. How would your spirituality be impacted, or impact you, if you were diagnosed with HIV?

5. There were several forms of loss mentioned in association with chronic illness. What form of loss would be the most difficult for you? Why?

References

Aronoff, G. M. (2000). Pain medicine: Hope is a powerful analgesic. *Geriatrics, 55*(9), 38–39.

Auslander, W., & Freedenthal, S. (2006). Social work and chronic disease: Diabetes, heart disease and HIV/AIDS. In S. Gehlert & T. A. Browne (Eds.), *Handbook of health social work* (pp. 532–567). Hoboken, NJ: Wiley.

Back, A. L., Arnold, R. M., & Quill, T. E. (2003). Hope for the best, and prepare for the worst. *Annals of Internal Medicine, 138*(5), 439–443.

Ballard, K., & Elston, M. S. (2005). Medicalization: A multi-dimensional concept. *Social Theory and Health, 3*(3), 228.

Burkhardt, M. A. (1993). Characteristics of spirituality in the lives of women in a rural Appalachian community. *Journal of Transcultural Nursing, 4*(2), 12–18.

Chu-Hui-Lin Chi, G. (2007). The role of hope in patients with cancer. *Oncology Nursing Forum, 32*(2), 415–421.

Clairborne, N., & Rizzo, V. M. (2006). Addressing sexual issues in individuals with chronic health conditions. *Health & Social Work, 31*(3), 221–225.

Clark, D. (2002). Between hope and acceptance: The medicalisation of dying. *British Medical Journal, 324,* 905–907.

Curtin, M., & Lubkin, I. (1990). What is chronicity? In I. M. Lubkin (Ed.). *Chronic illness: Impact and interventions* (2nd ed., pp. 2–20). Boston: Jones & Bartlett.

Davis, M. P. (2005). Integrating palliative medicine into an oncology practice. *American Journal of Hospice and Palliative Medicine, 22*(6), 447–456.

de Ridder, D., Geenen, R., Kuijer, R., & van Middendorp (2008). Psychological adjustment to chronic disease. *The Lancet, 372*(9634), 246–255.

DuBois, B., & Miley, K. K. (2008). *Social work: An empowering profession* (6th ed.). Boston: Allyn & Bacon.

Dunbar, H. T., Mueller, C. W., Medina, C., & Wolf, T. (1998). Psychological and spiritual growth in women living with HIV. *Social Work, 43*(2), 144–155.

Engel, G. (1977). The need for a new medical model: A challenge for biomedicine. *Science, 196,* 129–136.

Frankel, V. E. (1984). *Man's search for meaning.* Boston: Beacon Press.

Galambos, C. (1989). Living wills: A choice for the elderly. *Social Work 34*(2), 182–185.

Hooyman, N. R., & Kiyak, H. A. (2008). *Social gerontology: A multidisciplinary perpective.* Boston: Allyn & Bacon.

Kao, H., Travis, S. S., & Acton, G. J. (2004). Relocation to a long-term care facility: Working with patients and families before, during and after. *Journal of Pyschosocial Nurising and Mental Health Services, 42*(3), 10–16.

Kelly, M. P., & Field, D. (1996). Medical sociology: Chronic illness and the body. *Sociology of Health & Illness, 18*(2), 241–257.

Leifer, R. (1996). Psychological and spiritual factors in chronic illness. *American Behavioral Scientist, 39*(6), 752–767.

Livneh, H. (2000). Psychosocial adaptation to cancer: The role of coping strategies, *Journal of Rehabilitation, 66*(2), 40–49.

Nusbaum, M. R. H., Hamilton, C., & Lenahan, P. (2003). Chronic illness and sexual functioning. *American Family Physician, 67*(2), 347–354.

O'Neill, D. P., & Kenny, E. K. (1998). Spirituality and chronic illness. *Image: The Journal of Nursing Scholarship, 30*(3), 275–281.

Pollin, I., & Golant, S. K. (1994). *Taking charge: Overcoming the challenges of long-term illness.* New York: Random House.

Porter, D. (1999). *Health, civilization, and the state: A history of public health from ancient to modern times.* London: Routledge.

Puchalski, C. M., & Sandoval, C. (2003). Spiritual care. In J. F. O'Neill, P. A. Selvyn, & H. Schietinger (Eds.), *A clinical guide to supportive and palliative care for HIV/AIDS* (pp. 1–10). Rockville, MD: U.S. Department of Health and Human Services, Health Resources and Services Administration, HIV/AIDS Bureau.

Rapp, R. C. (1997). The strengths perspective: Proving "My Strengths" and "It Works". *Social Work, 52*(2), 185–186.

Rothman, A. A., & Wagner, E. H. (2003). Chronic illness management: What is the role of primary care. *Annals of Internal Medicine, 138*(3), 256–261.

Rushton, C. H., Spencer, K. L., & Johanson, W. (2004). Bringing end-of-life care out of the shadows. *Nursing Management, 35*(3), 34–40.

Sidell, N. L. (1997). Adult adjustment to chronic illness: A review of the literature. *Health & Social Work, 22*(1), 5–12.

Tarlov, A. R. (1996). Social determinants of health: The sociobiological translation. In D.Blane, E. Brunner, & R. Wilkinson (Eds.), *Health and social organization: towards a health plan for the 21st century* (pp. 71–93). London: Routledge.

Waldorp, D. P. (2007). Caregiver grief in terminal illness and bereavement: A mixed-methods study. *Health & Social Work, 32*(3), 197–206.

Walsh-Burke, K. (2006). *Grief and loss: Theories and skills for helping professionals.* Boston: Allyn & Bacon.

Weick, A., & Chamberlain, B. R. (1997). Putting problems in their place: Further explorations in the strengths perspective. In D. Saleebey (Ed.), *The strengths perspective in social work practice* (2nd ed., pp. 00). New York: Longman.

Wheeler, D. P. (2000). HIV/AIDS prevention. In V. J. Lynch (Ed.), *HIV/AIDS at year 2000* (pp.188–196). Boston: Allyn & Bacon.

9

The Health Care Team

Teaching and Learning Goals

- Understand the roles of social work on a health care team
- Recognize the contributions of social workers to the health care team
- Recognize the different forms of health care teams

Social workers in every field of practice are expected to work effectively with teams of professionals from a wide variety of specialty areas. Given the current trends in health care, collaboration with a variety of professionals is recognized as a very effective way to deliver to patients the best quality, most cost-effective, and most holistic form of care (Bronstein, 2003; Redman, 2006). Social workers and other health care professionals are expected to be productive in patient and organizational interactions and are evaluated for contributions to the cost-effectiveness within the health care system. Quality services are essential for patients, but in addition, health care systems want to know how social workers contribute to cost savings.

All social workers in health care settings work as part of teams. At minimum, every social worker teams with the patient, but must also partner with the patient's support system, other social workers, and multidisciplinary or interdisciplinary teams that operate within and outside the health care setting.

Social workers are at risk of being stereotyped into a professional role that limits their skills to the resolution of insurance problems or making referrals to agencies, but a professional education prepares social workers to contribute in additional valuable ways. Trained in a variety of skills, values, and theories the participation of social workers in the health care team is vital. Services that are determined as necessary and then delivered to the patient through the lens of the biopsychosocial perspective add depth to a more limited biomedical intervention. Use of a holistic assessment of the patient supplies information and a viewpoint that strengthens the health care team when they consider appropriate interventions. A holistic assessment can be developed in a number of ways when a variety of professional disciplines work together for the best patient care. In addition, social workers are committed to work with populations that are disenfranchised from mainstream society and bring recognition and respect for cultural differences.

It is often difficult to measure the financial savings a specific profession brings to an employer. Managing health care systems based exclusively on biomedical interventions are frequently at risk of missing the measure of quality social workers contribute. However, social workers offer more than a dimension of quality to health care. When the treatment measures examined are limited to only the biomedical interventions, health systems fail to recognize the strengths of addressing the additional psychosocial components that affect the financial bottom line. When health care teams attempt to function with only knowledge and expertise in the treatment of the patient's biological condition, the risk of health complications, more frequent hospitalizations, or earlier rehospitalizations occurs. Social workers contribute psychosocial information to health care teams that improves patients' quality of care and assists the system in preventing predictable spending by arranging for cost-saving supports (Bronstein, 2003).

Social workers have a rich history of working on health care teams. For over a century health care teams have contributed to patient care in inpatient settings. Teams are now commonly recognized as an essential way to deliver assertive, complete, and respectful services to patients experiencing health needs that require forms of outpatient care. As social workers continue to make contributions to health care teams, they bring depth and richness to all points of care through an empathetic commitment to populations at risk, application of social theories, cultural competence, and advocacy for patient self-determination.

History of Social Workers on Health Teams

The high-risk patient populations of the 1900s were not all that different from the high-risk patient populations of today: those living in poverty, minorities, immigrants, people without any kind of medical insurance, people unable to read or speak English, and individuals unable to provide for the basics that contribute to health such as food, shelter, and medicine. At Massachusetts General Hospital in the early 1900s, a physician took strong steps to change the delivery of health care based solely on the biomedical treatment model. Dr. Richard Cabot was aware that during medical treatment, there was little attention focused on the social needs of the patients (Gehlert, 2006b). Cabot, familiar with the profession of social work, recognized that when social work and medicine cooperated, each contributed skills the other profession needed. Cabot acknowledged that medicine relied too much on the scientific knowledge and ignored the realities of patients' social issues and social workers relied too much on doing good and paid too little attention to ensuring scientific and systematic methods were used. Cabot used his own money to employ social workers at the hospital to ensure that attention and support was provided to the psychosocial needs of patients. In the early 1900s, Garnet Pelto and later, Ida Cannon, became the first health care social workers employed at Massachusetts General and were recognized as contributing members of an interdisciplinary health care team (Gehlert, 2006b; Gregorian, 2005).

The same types of patients' needs exist today and often extend beyond purely medical interventions. Public health concerns remain, such as the prominence of chronic illness, and require an approach to health care that assesses and partners with patients to meet their biological, emotional, and social needs. Social workers, physicians, and other health professionals unite to form a network of communication that produces improved quality and holistic health care to the patient (Bronstein, 2003; Gehlert, 2006a; Gregorian, 2005).

Social workers have been practicing social work on interdisciplinary teams since the earliest days of the profession, but the work was often without a clear theory (Bronstein, 2003). The biopsychosocial theory, one of many health models, creates opportunities for individuals to intervene in a holistic manner and supports the multiple dimensions and needs of patients. Social workers contribute a vital role in revealing the individuality of a patient by contributing a broad and more accurate assessment to the health care team (Gehlert, 2006b; Parker-Oliver, Bronstein, & Kurzejeski, 2005).

Role of the Social Worker on the Health Care Team

A health care team is a group of two or more people, often professionals, who work together to accomplish a goal (Redman, 2006). The team concept promotes the idea that treatment success is enhanced by the efforts of all health care providers and relies on all members to accomplish specific roles. Experienced members of health care teams also know that it takes the integration of distinctly different skills and experiences from all professionals to contribute to attainment of the shared goal: provision of skillful and quality health care. A team is as strong as the variety and skills of its members, and when professionals collaborate, the team becomes a vehicle that overcomes barriers, works smoothly and collectively, and ultimately respects and supports patients' decisions regarding their health. There is no other discipline that contributes the unique values, skills and perspectives delivered by social workers and health care teams are weakened when social workers are not involved (Bronstein, 2003).

Managed care policies, with little exception, dictate how health care is provided. This form of cost management controls expenditures by designating who, how, why, where, and when patients receive insurance-covered interventions. Third-party treatment and cost controls were a radical philosophical shift in health care and now demand physicians, nurses, social workers, and other health care professionals work within managed care criterion and guidelines. For instance, due to the exorbitant cost of inpatient care, overnight hospital stays are avoided or significantly shorter in duration (Bronstein, 2003). All but the most significant and high-risk surgeries, procedures, and treatments are delivered in outpatient clinics. So social workers, members of inpatient teams, experience the complicated discharge needs of patients after medically significant events. The goal of the health care team is to medically treat patients and this is best accomplished when treatment includes attention to the social and emotional stressors that accompany significant health challenges. The social and emotional circumstances of the patient and their caregivers influence the success of medical treatment and recovery (Bronstein, 2003).

The world of health care is intimidating to visitors. Like an unfamiliar country, the language, environment, policies, uniforms, food, and routines often contribute to patient and caregiver stress and anxiety. The serious circumstances related to disease or injury are often communicated during times of emotional crisis. Frequently the overwhelming nature of diagnoses, prognosis, or treatment options regarding the medical concern add to the chaos. Social workers encourage patients and caregivers by acting as an interpreter or guide by explaining directions and policies and ensuring patients and caregivers understand the steps necessary to attain the necessary services (Bronstein, 2003; Gehlert, 2006).

Utilizing multidisciplinary, interdisciplinary, or transdisciplinary teams are effective ways to connect patients to the full array of health services. Research shows that health care teams, with members from many professions, are successful with a variety of health concerns: children with potentially life-limiting illnesses, delivery of mobile services to older adults in rural communities, and patients and families receiving hospice services (Hayward, Kochniuk, Powell, & Patterson, 2005; Jennings, 2005; Oliver, Porock, Demiris, & Courtney, 2005). When a team approach works well, it results in an overall increase in patient and caregiver satisfaction with care, a decrease in the number of hospital visits and stays, and an increase in patient sense of empowerment and self-determination (Bronstein, 2003; Jennings, 2005).

Although all health care teams presumably share the goal of providing excellent health management, the achievement of this goal is accomplished through strategic steps. Teams establish the design and implementation of the standards of care for patients, propose a biopsychosocial assessment and evaluation of patient needs, create an intervention plan that include patients' and caregivers' input, and evaluate the team process based on patients' input. Social workers add a unique patient-centered dimension by contributing the values, theories, and perspectives of their professional discipline (Bronstein, 2003; Gregorian, 2005).

Values

Professional social work values influence the patient information obtained and the interpretation of patients' and caregivers' needs. Social work values, combined with personal and professional strengths and skills, contribute to their effectiveness as members of the health team. Personal characteristics such as honesty, respect, understanding, critical thinking, and communication are particularly valued by members of a health team (Bronstein, 2003). It is easy to underestimate the importance of being trustworthy, approachable, flexible, and supportive to fellow team members. Relationship building between colleagues from a variety of disciplines helps minimize the threat of one profession encroaching on the roles of another profession, or "turfism." Team members who know and respect each other as individuals and professionals improve their ability to expect and value the best in their colleagues. Social workers must understand and respect the professional cultural differences represented on the team, recognize the benefits of alternative perspectives, value the ideas of others, and trust and respect team members (Bronstein, 2003; Gregorian, 2005; Reese & Sontag, 2001).

Theories

Professional social workers are educated to apply a variety of theoretical perspectives that remain unique to the discipline of social work (Reese & Sontag, 2001). After an assessment of patients' situations and with knowledge about the continuum of care offered by the health care setting, social workers intervene within the unique conditions of patients and their support systems. In addition to the practice of the biopsychosocial theory, two of the most commonly used and influential theories in the social work profession are the ecological systems perspective and the strengths perspective; these two theories guide assessments and shape patient interactions. The recognition of patients' strengths and the role of systems in patients' health, illness, and healing contribute to planning and discussions within the health team (Gregorian, 2005).

Ecological Systems.   Social workers frame interactions with patients by recognizing the influence of their environment. A predominant guide for the organization of patient resources, social workers understand that the patient's connections to systems is essential in treatment planning and this knowledge enriches the team's understanding of the patient's strengths and resources. The systems perspective is an important way to understand how individuals and groups of individuals rely on the formal and informal relationships within their physical and social environments to provide a framework for support and survival.

The theory offers insight into how human systems operate but also how they interact with one another. Systems theory relies on biological terminology like ecosystem, adaptation, and evolution to explain the life and characteristics of humans living with others. Patients live in environments that influence their existence and although this is a simple concept, failure to recognize the characteristics of these unique relationships often results in significant mistakes with treatment planning. Ignorance of the conditions of the patient environment, where they find personal and social meaning, and the supports they need to survive increases the risk that discharge and treatment planning will miss opportunities for the patient to succeed. Understanding the patient's environment is a key to helping equip the patient for success in living with acute or chronic health conditions. All changes that occur in the patient will result in changes to their environment. When the health care team is committed to patients' success it assesses how they will transition back into the home environment. The systems theory offers an invaluable perspective that exposes how patients interact within multiple social and physical relationships (Anderson, Carter, & Lowe, 1999; DuBois & Miley, 2005; Germain & Gitterman, 1995).

Systems are everywhere and are part of all human interactions. Families, cultures, teams, employees, gangs, neighborhoods, clubs, organizations, agencies, and politics are all unique systems yet all may interact as part of the patient's system. Systems possess characteristics that distinguish one from another and exhibit predictable patterns in achieving goals and participating in interactions. Members within a system share commonalities that ensure function. The systems perspective maintains that the smallest of systems, perhaps two individuals, is part of a larger system that is part of a still larger system, and so forth. Members of one system may be highly dependent on each other, as evident in some families, while other systems seem less dependent on each other, such as neighborhoods. All systems, however, exist to accomplish goals as a whole that would not be possible to accomplish independently. Some systems are open and interact and exchange resources with other systems, while others have boundaries that are closed and are nonreceptive to outside exchange or transactions (DuBois & Miley, 2005).

The ecological systems perspective is an expansive way to recognize patients because systems contribute to, or fail to contribute to, an individual's health-related needs. The patient, a member of a system, lives within the boundaries of the systems, open or closed, that influence assessment, treatment, health interventions, and discharge and aftercare plans. Systems evolve and change and a social worker will look for ways to support system strengths and enhance the quality of life for the patient (Taylor, 1997). Teams benefit by the social worker's knowledge of system barriers and strengths and the expertise offers opportunities to openly problem-solve and discover the best ways to meet patient needs. The skills of connecting the micro, mezzo, and macro levels of system support add to the success of care planning (DuBois & Miley, 2005).

Strengths Perspective.   There are few social work settings that challenge teams to think about patient strengths more than health care settings. Typically, individuals do not enter the health care system at their strongest moment, in fact, quite the contrary. Many who seek health care are concerned about or in crisis regarding a health condition and experience an increased sense of vulnerability. A health event such as a broken bone or a heart attack creates a sense of helplessness and causes individuals to rely on health professionals and results in a relationship of dependency. People are frequently intimidated by health settings and are unfamiliar with the process, jargon, and structure of the environment. Regardless of friendly and efficient professionals, the exam rooms, supplies, uniforms, and charts all contribute to the lack of control patients experience when receiving medical treatment.

The health care environment, still dominated by a biologically centered model of care, frequently interacts with patients using the steps of problem assessment, diagnosis, disease treatment, and cure. Health care settings do not always respond to the patient in a way that is reassuring, informing, and empowering. Instead, patients may experience treatments that imply they are "broken" and need to be "fixed." Although physical symptoms respond to medical interventions, ultimately the survival of patients depends on a successful discharge that is designed around their strengths and the strengths of their environment, "because every environment is full of resources" (Saleebey, 1997, p. 15). The biological strengths of the patient are a vital part of the biological exam, but the emotional and social strengths are essential to patients' maintenance and recovery of health.

Social workers often adopt the language of the health care system because it is the most common form of communication in health settings. It is used verbally and in writing and sharing the same language with other professionals ensures communication is as clear as possible. It is tempting to use the language of pathology because the collection of information for the health care system, the biomedical system, and insurance companies are all designed around this language. Social workers must be competent in this language to effectively communicate with a variety of professional systems, but ultimately, the introduction of strengths-based language and concepts within a health team is vital (Holmes, 1997; Saleebey, 1997). Social workers frequently lead teams in the assessment for strengths in patients and their support systems.

Strengths-based practice brings a language of power (Saleebey, 1997). Words useful in assessment of strengths include *competency, wellness,* and *effectiveness.* Consider the difference between strengths-based language and the vocabulary of the pathology model with words such as *defect, disease,* and *diagnosis.* Sometimes social workers witness patients adapting to the pathology model when hospitalized as they start to describe themselves and their illness in these biomedical terms. Saleebey (1997) states that both the language of pathology and strengths language are at best useful metaphors that attempt to communicate facts. Since the majority of patient information is communicated to the health care team through the biomedical lens, it is important that social workers advance the strengths of patients and their environments in strengths-based language. Often patients clearly communicate the strengths and barriers within their environment that are not necessarily a part of the medical assessment, but offer valuable clues to their personal and environmental strengths. Social workers are trained to listen and bring the words or ideas of the patient to team treatment planning.

Cultural Competence

Another way social workers contribute to the health care team is through shared insight regarding families and high-risk patient populations. Imbedded in this expertise is the value of respect for patients' right to self-determination and their entitlement to health services delivered in a culturally competent manner.

Social workers constantly add to their understanding of other cultures to ensure effective and respectful practice. Often cultural competence is simply understood as generalized knowledge about patient populations, but cultural competence must also incorporate the application of generalized knowledge to the unique circumstances of individuals.

The skill of applying knowledge of culture is also a great skill for social workers to better understand the professional cultures represented on a health team. Developing competence in the cultures of professionals relies on many of the same strategies used to improve expertise in any culture. Competence in cultures serves to treat others in a respectful and valued way. A culturally competent social worker approaches differences between and within professional cultures with the goal of understanding how individual professionals see reality and knows that it influences values, beliefs, experiences, knowledge, and relationships. Professional social workers practice cultural competence in their relationships with both colleagues and noncolleagues.

Patient Cultures.   Language, environment, history, and experiences shape worldviews in all cultures (Hobbs, 2005). Cultural competence is best improved through a variety of ways. One form of cultural competence available to health organizations is based on personnel with shared membership within a culture. Health care organizations committed to cultural diversity of staff are often challenged to find and keep trained professionals that represent the ever-growing representation of cultures within the health system. When professionals are members of a culture that represents patient populations that utilize the services of the health care setting, communities may feel respected. Attempts to hire professionals who are familiar with or members of specific cultures and perhaps speak a shared language show the organization's commitment to cultural competence. An improved ability to understand and communicate can improve treatment planning and ensure interactions between the patient, physician, and the rest of team is culturally accurate.

When there is a language barrier, sometimes the patient locates a family member, a caregiver, or a member of his or her community to translate during assessment or when the health teams discuss health issues. Health care providers and patients benefit by knowing if the frequently complex technical language of medicine and treatment options are understood accurately. For instance, if an adult male patient asks his 10-year-old daughter to translate for him, the information will be given to the child and translated to the patient in ways that accommodate the relationship, age, and gender of the child. Although using the child as translator for a parent is inappropriate, under desperate situations, this scenario may occur. A health care provider who is proficient in the language and culture of the patient is the best resource for translation and in giving input for treatment planning. It is important to know enough about the patients' culture to relate to patients in ways that are familiar and comfortable to them. If patients are comforted or directed by religious or spiritual guides or prefer certain kinds of foods or rely on spiritual or social customs that are important to them, referrals for these services show cultural respect and add to quality of care (Gregorian, 2005).

Beyond language, the ability to comprehend and to be understood is vital. Teams must share a commitment to develop the best interventions possible and when all members recognize patient cultures as valid and different than their own, it may result in interventions that are creative and unique. Cultural competence is not knowledge that, once learned, is true in all situations, but it becomes a set of skills that must constantly be applied to interactions with individuals to better understand their worldviews (Reynolds, 2004). There is a wide variety of ways members of a culture act, think, and believe and when assessed, all patients will identify their own specific cultural traits and beliefs (Hobbs, 2005; Reese & Sontag, 2001).

Even if teams practice methods associated with cultural competence, barriers can remain, particularly between patients and their health care providers and can ultimately affect treatment (Reese & Sontag, 2001; Reynolds, 2004). Sometimes medical providers are frustrated at their lack of ability to help and the patient is labeled a problem. Labeling of a patient can quickly turn into "a fact," become part of a patient's identification, and affect quality of care. Discussion of patients must always be respectful and free of judgmental comments. Patients living with significant and co-occurring challenges such as mental illness or addiction are particularly difficult individuals for teams to understand. Sometimes the patient's behaviors are unfamiliar, bizarre, or frightening, and trigger fear and panic in team members. Social workers can teach the team about how to assess, interact, and respect the cultures of unfamiliar populations (Reese & Sontag, 2001).

Professional Cultures. Social work education teaches the strength of groups, but professional cultures are not always recognized as a diverse and powerful force in the development of teams. All members of professional cultures are academically acculturated into a language, environment, history, and experiences that shape the unique worldviews they bring to health care. The differences in professional cultures are sometimes radical and can lead to passionate disagreements between colleagues.

Health care teams are created to benefit patients and their support systems. To enhance the functioning of the team, social workers learn the skills and strengths of each health-related profession. Within each profession there are a variety of specialized skills that improve patient care, and each professional also has their own unique personal characteristics. Members of the team believe the values of their profession represents the optimum standard of professional care and like social workers, they are committed to the delivery of ethical quality care. Professionals may negotiate and advocate for care decisions in conflict with other professionals and sometimes passionate disagreements occur within the team. Social workers recognize and respect the differences in values and theoretical perspectives of team members and respect and appreciate colleagues for their commitment and expertise (Bronstein, 2003; Gregorian, 2005).

It is challenging, however, to respect other professional disciplines on the team if members of those professions consistently show disrespect to the culture of social work (Reese & Sontag, 2001). If the social worker models professional respect for others, team members may recognize the benefits of mutual respect and witness the results as evidenced by improved team planning, less team stress, healthy debate with eventual consensus, good working relationships outside team meetings, and ultimately the delivery of a quality care plan. Respect and patience with each other's point of view leads to a team that functions better and improves progress toward the primary purpose of every team member: to provide the best possible service to the patient (Gregorian, 2005; Reese & Sontag, 2001).

Teams work best when the power and responsibility among the team members is equal. When all unite together equally respected and recognized as valuable and contributing members, the team is stronger (Gregorian, 2005; Jessup, 2007; Reese & Sontag, 2001). The goal of the team is to work as one unit, not to work as a split and segmented group, unable to come to agreement. To become one unit, team members need to share the process of assessment and planning with the patient from the earliest developments. Self-determination requires patients are offered an opportunity to have input into the design of the plan created to achieve their goals. When team members take responsibility for their share of the plan, as well as supporting the other team members in accomplishing their goals, the team becomes a single, strong working entity.

Team ownership of the planning process strengthens the collaboration. Team members do not always agree on the same course of action, but as with disagreements between individuals, a healthy team makes the effort to address conflicts openly and civilly and look for ways to reflect common team goals. Partnering professionals have an opportunity to create benefits to patients that do not exist if they work independently of each other. For individuals to successfully work together, it demands all professionals be flexible and find ways to resolve disputes (Bronstein, 2003; Gregorian, 2005).

Bronstein (2003) suggests that the collaboration of a health care team is influenced by the professional cultures, environmental characteristics, personalities, and history of the team. Many different professionals come together from different cultures, perhaps with guardedness about potential interference into their part of patient care. But when unity for common goals overrides the differences, the team's work is outstanding. Social workers engage with all collegial and patient cultures; learn the language; respect differences; understand the unique beliefs, values, and theories; and work with individuals in a respectful manner.

Professional Social Work Expertise

There are many roles for social workers in health care teams. The roles include facilitation of communication, the contribution of professional beliefs and values to group decision making, identification of system barriers to patient health through a biopsychosocial perspective, contributions of insight on how to work with caregivers and high-risk patients, and support of patients' right to self-determination.

Facilitate Interdisciplinary Communication

Unfortunately, there are many factors that potentially interfere in the smooth process of team members working together. Flawed communication and decision making can introduce uncertainty and skepticism about other professions or specific team members (Gearing, Saini, & McNeill, 2007). Professionals are capable of sabotaging the effective use of patient-related information in a way that interferes with the ability of other professionals to contribute their expertise (Bronstein, 2003). Perhaps assessment information about a patient is missing, incomplete, lacks direct observation, or is without key pieces of evidence. Reports may be unintentionally incomplete, or sometimes purposefully unreliable, contradictory, or misleading (Benbenishty & Chen, 2003). Ethically, information brought to the team must be the best and most accurate possible because based on this information, the team makes decisions about allocation of resources. It affects decisions about admission of the patient for treatment, authorization of services, hospitalization, discharge, or commitment to involuntary care. When professionals attempt to control the team process and the involvement of other team members in the delivery of patient care, this undermines the team process and puts the patient and the health organization at risk (Benbenishty & Chen, 2003; Jessup, 2007).

Social workers maintain the goal of high-quality patient care. The issues of recognition or the pressures associated with evaluations to produce cost-effective measures are not an excuse to engage in forms of competition with other professions, not when the decisions and actions made influence the health of an individual. It is important to model professional and ethical care and know professional contributions vary based on the needs of the patient (Gregorian, 2005).

Contribute Professional Social Work Culture

Teams are a combination of health professionals: nurses, social workers, case managers, dietary counselors, spiritual care providers, physicians, and developmental or disease specialists (Bronstein, 2003; Jennings, 2005). Health care professionals are not immune to biases and shortcomings. In addition, some actions may be based on the theories, values, and cultures of their profession that conflict with those of their colleagues. But this can be an incredible strength for the team and for the patient, or it can become a serious problem. Decisions made by the team are of immeasurable significance, so despite conflictual opinions about the best course for optimal health, the team must practice collaboration (Benbenishty & Chen, 2003).

The systems perspective supports the idea that a professional team provides improved coordinated health care service. All parts of the team influence the decisions of the whole through a process of discussion, compromise, and additional information sharing. The partnerships between the professionals aid the patient, the support systems, the community, and all invested in the health of the patient. The best efforts of the treatment team often result in the best results for the patient (Gearing et al., 2007; Hayward et al., 2005).

When socioeconomic challenges affect an industry such as health care, systems develop creative measures to improve budget issues: changing job descriptions, hiring freezes, increased workloads and responsibilities, and evaluations of professions based on cost–benefit analyses (Auerbach, Mason, & LaPorte, 2007). Health care professionals are not immune to guarding their areas of expertise from other professionals perceived as able to perform similar tasks. Unprofessional responses to the fear of job changes can result in professionals misrepresenting their work, the needs of the patient, or the professional role in intervention. The decision to bring inaccurate information to the team has many negative ramifications and poses a real health risk to the patient, professional and ethical risks to individual licensure, loss of credibility with the team and perhaps loss of credibility or employment within the health system.

Members of the team participate in altering roles with respect to leadership and the skills all professionals bring to patient care. Recognition of colleagues' strengths encourages continued collaboration. The care of the patient is multifaceted and depends on the expertise of a wide range of professional skills. No single profession or professional can offer the same quality of care to a patient as an entire team of professionals working toward the same objective. As the care needs of the patient become increasingly complicated, physically, emotionally, or socially, the benefits of teamwork increase. Team members unite and share empathy toward the patient's circumstances and explore and create patient-focused interventions and support to caregivers. Sometimes the difference in professional values, approaches, and power creates the best result for the patient (Oliver et al., 2005).

Social workers who remain silent on a team lose an important opportunity to share their professional values with the team. Social workers benefit by preparation to actively participate in team discussions and contribute to decision making. Contributions based on the values, traditions, and training of the social work profession assist the team in development of a biopsychosocial treatment plan that takes a holistic perspective, and considers and encourages the participation of the patient in the effort (Hobbs, 2005).

Identify Adjustment Barriers

Social workers have beneficial skills for assessment. They are capable of providing the most complete assessment for several reasons: application of professional interview techniques and skills, recognition of the need for cultural competence, employment of a strengths-based perspective, and the search for strengths within patients' environments. Assessment based on strengths offers a vital balance to the often multiple challenges interfering with patient health. A plan of care develops and activates a supportive response from multiple patient systems including caregivers, family, supporters, agencies, and other connections within the environment (Gearing et al., 2007).

The social worker uses the language and concepts of the strengths perspective and assists the patient and the team to identify the emotional, social, or environmental barriers to healthy functioning. Once medical needs are identified, the social worker determines with the patient the issues or obstacles that may interfere with treatment and works with them to find solutions. For instance, Mary is ready for discharge and the physician writes an order for oxygen. In order to ensure that necessary and accurate services are in place for discharge, the social worker needs to ask several questions: Will insurance pay for this service? Does the managed care plan identify certain oxygen suppliers as participating members? Are there monthly or annual copays for the patient? Will the supplier deliver the oxygen to the home? How often? Do the suppliers train the patient and caregivers? Who will monitor the patient's condition related to this treatment?

Environmental barriers may interfere with the ability of the patient to experience health improvement (Coleman & Newton, 2005). Consider the scenario of Lenny.

Scenario 9:1

Lenny is 66 years old and after treatment for a chronic condition, he is being discharged in 2 days. His daughter tells his social worker, Salvador, that Lenny was living with them until his hospitalization, but she has four children and three of them are preschool age. She cries and states she is overwhelmed and is unable to take on the additional responsibilities of Lenny's growing care needs. She does not know where her father will live when he leaves the hospital. Salvador tells Lenny's daughter that he will investigate further and attempt to find possible options for Lenny's discharge.

Will the daughter take her father if there is payment for her services? Is Lenny eligible for caregiver reimbursement? Are there home health services that will meet Lenny's additional health needs? Does Lenny need a form of subacute care? Does his insurance plan provide reimbursement for outpatient support services? Is there a caregiver group or family member that can meet with Salvador and Lenny to talk about options? What other questions would help Salvador discover options for Lenny?

Lenny's scenario describes some of the potential barriers in environments that interfere with patient health. Individuals may have multiple challenges in their environment. The social worker partners with the patient and the health team to find ways to make recuperation or maintenance of health progress smoothly.

Supply Expertise Regarding High-Risk Groups

The social worker is prepared to contribute to the treatment needs of populations at high risk for complications. These populations include people who live with absence of health care insurance, with disabilities, addictions, mental illness, chronic physical illnesses, and social stigma. Older adults, members of racial and ethnic minorities, and people living in poverty may also require intervention by social workers because of their ability to successfully assess biopsychosocial needs. Social workers find opportunities to improve care for patients with environmental challenges and advocate to improve or expand organizational or community support (Gearing et al., 2007).

Sometimes social workers can identify high-risk characteristics at an intake assessment. Perhaps the patient exhibits symptoms of extreme stress, "hears voices," or appears incoherent. Some hospitals practice policies that automatically refer patients to social workers for psychosocial assessment and interventions. Social workers are common in emergency rooms because individuals and families experience emotional and social trauma associated with physical emergencies. In crisis, individuals may need to connect with specialized resources in the community. Appropriate referrals can prevent rehospitalizations and is a significant way social workers contribute to cost reductions in the health care system. Referral policies that utilize the skills of social work increase the likelihood of appropriate treatment (Reese & Raymer, 2004).

There is a significant movement to educate physicians regarding the importance of effective communication skills, but not all professionals are equally skillful. Social workers may witness the discomfort of physicians and other health care professionals in the delivery of diagnosis, prognosis, and other kinds of painful or unwanted medical information to patients or caregivers. Admittedly, it is difficult to deliver dismal and life-altering news and some physicians may attempt to avoid its delivery. Patients and caregivers are aware of staff avoidance and misinterpret the evasion as the physician not caring about them. Social workers are helpful and support the mediation between the patient and the physician by helping each respond to one other in positive and respectful ways (Abramson & Mizrahi, 1996).

Support Patient Self-Determination

One of the pillars of social work's Code of Ethics is the recognition that patients have a right to self-determination (National Association of Social Work [NASW], 1999). Every competent adult has a right to accept or reject medical care and the right to approve the medical course of action. At times, patients' right to determine their care can prove very frustrating to health care professionals, including social workers. An experienced team agrees that a certain course of treatment or rehabilitation is the best, most cost-effective, and the least invasive plan of action, but the patient may say "no." While frustrating, the social worker's role is to advocate for the patient's right to self-determination.

Social work practice is designed to improve interactions between people and their environments, and this includes the modification and support of the patient's situation. Teams work together to create a care plan and to strengthen patient resources; however, patients do not always feel included in the team. If the patient is being treated in a hospital, perhaps it is impossible to physically meet with the team. Sometimes patients do not realize they have a health care team. But the best and most experienced teams develop options to facilitate accepting the patient's input into the treatment process.

The easiest way to ensure patients' input is to inform them about the team, the goals of the team, and the patient's role as a leading member of the team. If patients are not ambulatory or responsive, the social worker must find the legal representatives of the patient or, with patient permission, consult with caregivers. Patients must be informed of their health needs and choices and asked about their goals. It is respectful to consult privately with patients so they are free to speak without undue influence from family members and caregivers. As an additional option, the team may send a small delegation of team members to the patient's room for a briefing. When possible, this ensures patients of their power and strength over the process, because literally, the team is listening directly to them (Reese & Raymer, 2004).

In some ways, it is easier to include patients treated in outpatient care settings in the team process. However, even in outpatient settings there are challenges to ensuring the patient's presence; homelessness, poverty, lack of transportation, and work or family responsibilities can interfere with the patient's ability to attend a health team meeting. Regardless of the inpatient or outpatient environment, patients who participate in team meetings improve the level of honest dialogue among the team members and bring a valuable personal connection to the care plan that is lost when the patient is absent. Patients experience a sense of respect and personal attention when they are included; respect and attention can increase levels of care and satisfaction with health care interactions.

Families and caregivers of the patient may feel ignored in the process of the health team. The role of patients and caregivers depends on the organization of the team. In some forms of health teams, the caregiver is viewed as a team member and contributes expertise about the patient (Oliver et al., 2005). Team functioning is influenced by family and caregiver involvement, especially during assessment, planning, and implementation of plans. When teams fail to include input from the patient's support system when problem solving or making care decisions, it results in an ineffective plan, created based on assumptions.

Teams benefit by the input from patients, families, and caregivers. Caregivers and family members may offer the team valuable feedback about how the team intervention is perceived by the patient. When this feedback is formalized, it offers an effective way to evaluate the teams' work. Teams can be totally unaware of how intimidating or unresponsive they are until they receive feedback. Patients and families offer the team their vital perspectives on how biopsychosocial challenges were resolved (Oliver et al., 2005). When patients' and families' involvement in the team is the standard practice, the patient's wishes are known, their options are communicated and the team receives feedback about their process and develops ways to improve their role in patient care. Oliver et al. (2005) suggests that teams consider less traditional ways of teaming with the patient, including dividing into smaller units, establishing a standard way of reporting patient/team communication, and the inclusion of family members or caregivers in the team.

Learning the Language

Professions have their own language. When social workers attend the first meeting of a health care team meeting and listen to the conversations and the discussions of a variety of disciplines, they may be unclear about what they are hearing. The communication is often peppered with acronyms of organizations and companies, and may include references to unfamiliar technical procedures and policies. The content can seem indecipherable. Social work students may also experience this sensation when they go to the first team meeting at their field placement site. Even social work terminology can seem unfamiliar at these meetings because within social work, some of the professional language used varies between fields of practice. Professional language is specialized to communicate specific information in the most precise way.

Social workers in the field of health care use a professional language that blends social work language with the language more common to the health environment. As part of a health team, they cannot rely solely on social work terminology. Knowing only the professional language of social work will result in ineffective communication (Gregorian, 2005). Social workers must learn the health language of the medical setting and professional culture because a shared terminology improves communication within the team, improves accuracy of communication with referral resources, adds credibility to the social work role on the team, presents social work participation in professional care to the patient and caregivers, and improves the ability to advocate for the patient across professional cultures.

Learning the language of any culture shows respect for that culture. It is beneficial to respect the cultures of colleagues by learning to communicate effectively with each team member despite the differences in professional language and is vital to the delivery of care (Gearing et al., 2007; Gregorian, 2005; Hayward et al., 2005; Oliver et al., 2005). When communication works well, it enhances professional sharing, group decision making, and, ultimately, the patient's quality of life.

Improved Communication

In health care, the language is often specific to the environment where the care is being practiced. For instance, if the team specializes in working with people who are homeless or people living with AIDS, or heart disease, the language used will vary to respond to the vocabulary of the specialty area. If the team is part of a health clinic with a wide variety of health-related functions, the language reflects the variety of patient needs, including the names of blood tests, treatments, symptoms, medications, and complications. Communication improves collaboration within the team and people on the team keep each other better informed about the changing needs of the patient (Bronstein, 2003; Soler & Shauffer, 2003). They improve accurate transmission of information to each other about current patient conditions and changes in treatment plans.

Community Referrals

Social workers are always involved in connecting the patient and caregivers with resources, agencies, and organizations that offer the best possible support services to meet patient needs. Agencies that accept health-related referrals require social workers to communicate clearly and precisely by using the professional language associated with their services. Communication with an agency is usually done first through a phone call, but the details discussed verbally are also delivered to the referral source in writing to ensure no mistakes are made. Social workers setting up a discharge plan know when a discharge plan does not fit the norm. This expertise serves as an additional level of quality assurance. Unusual orders for equipment or for medications not typically associated with the patient's health condition are questioned and rechecked with other team members to ensure accuracy. Communicating accurately with the professionals that provide medical and supportive services ensures patients get the care they need. There is an increased risk of serious error if health conditions and services are misunderstood.

Credibility with Patients and the Team

There are times when professional roles overlap. For instance, when a social worker is part of a HIV case management team, they may have the responsibility to meet with patients that recently learned of their positive HIV status. The patients' interaction covers many things but includes ways patients can obtain support for their health through good nutrition and a reduction in alcohol and drug use. Education regarding nutrition is not necessarily an area of expertise for social workers, but given the overlap of roles on the team, the social worker is prepared to contribute this information and refer patients to the team when specific questions are beyond their knowledge. A nurse on the same team asks patients, "How are you doing?" and hears about their sadness or anger, or develops concerns about patients' emotions or behaviors. While nurses are not trained to do emotional counseling, they team with the social worker and patients benefit from the team's overlapping roles. Team members listen empathetically to patients but when concerns about emotional or social situations are shared, the team refers patients to the social worker for assistance.

Cultural Advocate

When patients discover they have a chronic illness diagnosis, they frequently spend time talking to others with similar diagnoses, reading information about the condition or going online to research their new diagnosis. Patients have access to all kinds of information about medical conditions due to the Internet. It is not uncommon for patients and families to arrive for a health care appointment with a good understanding of some of the treatments available for their medical condition and perhaps an understanding of the trajectory of the illness. It benefits patients when all health team members learn all they can about the health conditions treated in their setting. In the early days of HIV treatment, the populations at risk were so disenfranchised from society they were forced to be their own advocates and to know all they could about the virus and possible treatments.

Patients from a health clinic might know the most recent clinical trials and the medications poised for FDA approval. Social workers in chronic illness health settings attempt to learn as much as the best informed patient at the clinic. To build professional credibility with patients, it is important for social workers to know the latest information about the systems that affect the health of the patient. The patient looks to the health care team for expertise and should not be expected to teach team members the basic disease and health information. Patients do, however, always teach social workers about their unique experience with the disease. A social worker knows the names of common tests, the language of the results of these tests, and predicts what the results might mean to the patient. They know the kinds of treatment, what the treatment is like, side effects, and the time it takes to receive the treatment. Social workers should visit the chemotherapy and radiation treatment rooms, meet the staff, visit the surgical floor, listen carefully to the patients' stories, and try to understand how the patient experiences these components of the disease. This firsthand knowledge builds a strong position for advocacy and empathy.

Social workers do not have the training or licensure to interpret medical tests, to diagnose medical conditions, or to recommend treatments. It is essential to stop educating the patient when the medical information the patient requires is not within the social worker's area of expertise. Social workers need to know the biomedical language because it opens up opportunities to join patients in their experience, but resist giving medical advice. Patients take professionals' feedback seriously, so uninformed or unprofessional opinions about health care or health care providers are both unethical and dangerous. The "medical advice" from a social worker must always be a recommendation for patients to discuss their medical questions with their physicians. The social worker can role-play with patients and assist them to prepare their questions and concerns for discussion with the most appropriate professional or offer to accompany them to find the answer to their questions.

All patients are on a personal journey with their health experience, often filled with emotions, events, and challenges that are helpful to remember when interacting with other patients. The experiences of one patient can potentially influence or inform the path of another patient who is experiencing similar events or circumstances. It is honoring to inform patients that when they share their private experiences related to health, their triumphs and grief help you to better understand the experiences and reactions of others. Patients benefit by knowing that their experiences with disease or injury make a positive contribution to the life of another.

Patients are relieved when social workers help them communicate and translate the new language associated with their diagnosis. Often this language is new to them. However, remember that the communication is not just a medical language; it is important information about the patients' condition; they receive the facts but also experience emotions. The language of the illness is not the center of their lives, but the changes caused by the diagnosis expose them to environments where this language becomes a common way for them to communicate. Perhaps family and caregivers do not know or understand the medical language or understand the stresses of the patient's treatments. Social workers can stand with patients and caregivers by recognizing the trauma of entering the new culture of health care.

Types of Teams

There are at least three different kinds of teams used to provide services to patients in the health care system. How a team is established and developed contributes to the function of the team and depends on the setting and the structure of the organization. Some of the most common types of teams are multidisciplinary, transdisciplinary, and interdisciplinary (Benbenishty & Chen, 2003; Gehlert, 2006b; Hobbs, 2005; Jessup, 2007). Regardless of the kind of team, all rely on the strengths of individual team members to accomplish goals and advocate for patients to receive quality care.

A common form of teaming is through the multidisciplinary team. One of the greatest advantages of a multidisciplinary team is that members represent great diversity in knowledge, observations, values, and cultures. The primary contribution of this form of team is the broad range of professional disciplines represented. Each discipline, within group meetings or if consulted as individuals, approaches the patient care plan with assessments, interventions, skills, and experiences unique to their professional expertise. Case conferences to discuss patients' progress are commonly done in the absence of the patient. The variety of professional perspectives are reviewed through a collegial exchange and integrated to form patient health plans that result from a broad range of viewpoints. The multidisciplinary team members partner in patient care, but maintain their own professional language and processes (Gehlert, 2006b; Jessup, 2007; Redman, 2006).

Hobbs (2005) suggests that the transdisciplinary team is also a viable option for health care planning. The approach builds on an approach used by business team models and adapted for use in health care settings. The approach is unique because of the cross-teaching between the professional disciplines. Cross-teaming depends on professionals acknowledging and respecting their differences in expertise and trusting each other to communicate, coordinate, and share information relevant to patients and their care (Gehlert, 2006b). The goal of the team is to improve all professional treatments by enriching each perspective. For instance, when the physician can assess or predict social issues regarding the disease, and when the social worker can predict the possibility of medication reactions, professional judgment improves and patients benefit (Hobbs, 2005).

Social workers may also be part of an interdisciplinary team. This team approach integrates separate disciplinary approaches into a single consultation. All team members share a single patient assessment, diagnosis, intervention, and treatment goals. The language used in common across every discipline is represented on the team. The result of the interdisciplinary team is a common understanding and holistic view of all aspects of patient care (Jessup, 2007; Redman, 2006). In addition, the patient is encouraged to contribute or question the team. As with other kinds of team efforts, success depends on cooperation, communication, coordination, and partnership as vital ingredients. Although merging professional expertise and language through a common funnel, as opposed to relying on many discipline-related contributions, the interdisciplinary team strongly relies on team members sharing equal power within the group. The team effort can be threatened if one personality, representing a specific discipline, emerges as a dominant force and suppresses contributions from other team members (Bronstein, 2003; Gehlert, 2006b; Jessup, 2007).

All health teams rely on a variety of professional disciplines to provide avenues for communication within professions, greater ease with technical and professional language related to the patient, and most importantly, consistent communication with the patient and their family (Benbenishty & Chen, 2003; Redman, 2006). Each team member represents a perspective of the patient's health or environment that shapes the care plan. Social workers recognize teams representing multiple disciplines as also bridging the gaps between multiple systems: micro, mezzo, and macro. Social workers contribute a biopsychosocial multisystem assessment to clarify the interactions between the physical disease process, the emotional responses, and social behaviors, but also assess the experience of the patient, the caregivers, and the patient environment. The social worker brings the patient's history of services and outcomes to the team and contributes a culturally competent perspective. In addition, social workers supply creative ways to locate services, reduce the need for inappropriate medical interventions, and increase patient and caregiver satisfaction (Benbenishty & Chen, 2003; Gehlert, 2006b; Reese & Raymer, 2004).

Regardless of team membership, collaboration must be intentional. Members share professional perspectives and integrate the perspectives of other disciplines, adding depth and richness to the process. The team must intentionally develop professional relationships that cross professional cultures and enhance the best professional practice of each member (Hayward et al., 2005). An interdisciplinary approach is one of the most effective ways to provide holistic and coordinated services to patients.

While social work is perhaps the most experienced and educated to practice teamwork, it is challenging. Social workers are empowered to advocate for the patient, and are uncomfortable when introduced to the hierarchy of power that exists within the professionals in the biomedical system of health care (Bronstein, 2003; Gregorian, 2005; Reese & Montag, 2001). Social workers may assume all disciplines are equally respected because they know each system is influenced by other systems and understand that collaboration, not isolation, is the key to success. This value is influential in assessment and treatment

BOX 9.1 • *Social Work Responsibilities on a Health Care Team*

1. Complete a biopsychosocial assessment
2. Support family and caregiver(s)
3. Engage with the patient regarding their emotional needs and stresses
4. Link patient to support with referrals for services within the community
5. Ensure patient's social, psychological, and cultural needs are addressed by the team

Source: Hobbs (2005).

planning with the patient and guides the social workers' relationship to the health team (Hobbs, 2005). Social workers have legitimate responsibilities on a health team that improve the outcome of patient health interventions (see Box 9.1).

Team Settings

Teams are everywhere in health care because they are cost-effective and improve quality of care to the patient. They are effective in providing quality care to the patient in both inpatient and outpatient settings. Teamwork is growing in a number of settings and is in demand as health systems seek to reduce costs by transitioning services into outpatient settings as much as possible.

Inpatient Settings

Teams that function within hospitals and other inpatient settings rely on social work to detect environmental strengths and barriers that influence problems with patient discharge. Many inpatient teams of health professionals typically work together in high-risk medical situations with vulnerable populations. Inpatient teams consist of social workers, physicians, nurses, and other professionals who are consulted on specific assessment issues.

Teams of various professions, working together, are very visible in inpatient settings. For instance, in an inpatient setting, social workers rely on the information and medical assessment of the patient completed by medical professionals to establish a relationship with the patient to inform appropriate referrals for support needs as a part of discharge planning. Social workers join other disciplines in communicating with team members through the medical record, and contribute to the process of quality patient planning through the integration of professional expertise (Bronstein, 2003).

Outpatient Settings

Teams composed of many professional disciplines are effective in the treatment and support of patients in outpatient settings, too. The effectiveness is particularly clear in the outpatient care of chronic illness. When chronic illness is diagnosed, the goal to maintain optimum health is common. The support of professionals from a variety of disciplines is an effective way to ensure the assessment of patient strengths and needs are adequately and accurately communicated. A patient who lives with a chronic illness benefits greatly from the expertise of multiple professionals working together to develop care strategies, understand barriers, and offer ongoing support. Sang (2006) suggests that outpatient settings need to work toward fully integrated services in the community, especially for individuals at risk of hospitalization and before the hospitalization occurs.

Prevention or reduction in hospitalization is a chief goal in the treatment plan for an outpatient team. When team health care is introduced early in the process of chronic illness, it contributes to quality of care, but it also saves money. Professionals work as teams to delay the need for hospitalization and reduce the days of hospitalization when the patient is admitted. The growing number of people living with chronic illness promises a generation of aging individuals with needs for health care. The team is potentially a continuous and seamless approach to individual care and offers exciting incentives, including the treatment of chronic illness in an outpatient setting with consistent and personal attention. Resources used in the care of people living with chronic illness, both private and public, are in high demand and the need for additional resources continues to grow. The goal of health systems is the reduction of hospitalization and improved quality of care so health professionals will continue to work together and develop seamless, creative, and consistent ways to care for patients in the community and within the health care system (Sang, 2006).

Challenges of a Health Care Team

An ongoing challenge for professional social workers is the hiring of non-social work professions to provide psychosocial assessment and interventions in health care. All states require professional licensing or certification, but health care organizations are singularly motivated to save money. If health systems remain unknowledgeable about the advantages of hiring a skilled professional social worker, unprepared to provide the expertise necessary to contribute to the health team, the system will hire nonprofessionals. Social workers need to be active in their roles on the team and prove their contribution adds to quality patient care and give evidence of how the results of their interventions are cost-effective. Social work is cost-effective but social workers must continue to collect the data necessary to show this is true, just as professional colleagues evaluate and share the value of their work to the health care system (Dziegielewski, 2004).

Managed care changed the role of social work and offers less reimbursement for the costs of emotional and psychological patient support. This is a common conflict for social workers as they observe their jobs reduced to discharge planning. It is particularly difficult when social workers witness professionals less qualified in psychosocial interventions attempt to fulfill this role. Well-meaning professionals offer patients personal opinions about what the patient should do without attention to the patient's personal or cultural goals. This form of patient interaction is destructive and leads to the breakdown of patient self-determination, decreases empowerment, and fails to recognize the patient's strengths or barriers. Social workers are in the difficult position of informing the team of the inadequacy of psychosocial care while continuing to contribute to and support the team. It increases professional vulnerability when a social worker advocates for interventions that are not traditionally supported by the team (Sulman, Savage, Vrooman, & McGillivray, 2004).

BOX 9.2 • *Barriers to Optimum Functioning of Teams*

1. Lack of knowledge of the expertise of the other professions
2. Role-blurring
3. Conflicts arising from differences in professional values and theoretical practice
4. Theoretical differences
5. Negative team norms
6. Lack of commitment to the team process
7. Lack of willingness to share equally in the work of the team
8. Blaming specific team members when there is a problem
9. Power differences between team members
10. Patient stereotyping

Source: Reese & Sontag (2001).

The challenge for all team members is to practice collaborating in a healthy and responsible manner and to participate effectively and contribute to team unification. Social workers benefit from group projects during their social work education, and learn that working with others is the best way to complete a big task, that communication and partnership are essential. Social work education must encourage students to learn about work on teams and how to respect the skills and values of others, collaborate, and understand how collaboration benefits the patient (Hayward et al., 2005; Sulman et al., 2004).

Professional competence and autonomy within and across professions is required to maintain professional identity despite the integration of multiple disciplines. When teams respect the expertise of all professional disciplines, the result is delivery of services that are coordinated and comprehensive. Collaboration supports cooperation and provides an opportunity to share knowledge, information, and resources, supporting problem-solving and decision-making skills necessary to effect change (Hayward et al., 2005; Reese & Sontag, 2001).

Reese and Sontag (2001) extensively describe the barriers to optimum functioning of teams within hospice care, but are potentially barriers to the healthy functioning of all health care teams (see Box 9.2).

Summary

There is no denying that a team has the potential to improve holistic care for all patient populations, increase mutual respect between professional colleagues, and decrease health care costs while improving quality of care for the patient. Integrated health care benefits the patient and caregivers, but the results of integrated care also benefit the wider community. Social workers benefit teamwork by bringing their knowledge of policy, practice, and professionalism with underserved populations and people who are disenfranchised by society's dominant cultures (Csikai, 2004; Rose, Lyons, Miller, & Comman-Levy, 2003).

The goals for each patient vary because despite a similar diagnosis, patients bring their unique cultures and strengths. The team aids the patient to maintain or improve his or her health and designs a safe and smooth discharge to home or placement into a subacute setting, helps determine and provide support services, and finds ways to resolve psychosocial problem situations (Csikai, 2004).

Despite all of the benefits to teamwork in health care, the social worker will also encounter several challenges. Working in an environment of medically trained professionals, the social worker is the guest. Social workers may experience dismissive responses to their treatment recommendations, or experience stereotypical limitations to their professional roles. Despite ethical challenges regarding issues of confidentiality, privacy, cultural incompetence, and stigmatization of populations, social workers must continue to guard the patient's right to self-determination in an often paternalistic system of health care that focuses primarily on biological concerns and the healing of disease (Csikai, 2004). The health care team is a great fit for the skills of the professional social worker.

Critical Thinking Questions

1. How might the values and ethics of different professionals intersect during their work on health care teams?

2. Why is it important to learn the health care language and how does that impact services?

3. What would a social worker do differently in an inpatient setting than in an outpatient setting?

4. What are the positives and negatives of social work representation on a health care team?

References

Anderson, R. E., Carter, I., & Lowe, G. (1999). *Human behavior in the social environment: A social systems approach* (5th ed.). New York: Aldine DeGruyter.

Auerbach, C., Mason, S. E., & LaPorte, H. H. (2007). Evidence that supports the value of social work in hospitals. *Social Work in Health Care, 44*(4), 17–32.

Benbenishty, R., & Chen, W. (2003). Decision making by the child protection team of a medical center. *Health and Social Work, 28*(4), 284.

Bronstein, L. R. (2003). A model for interdisciplinary collaboration. *Social Work, 48*(3), 297–306.

Coleman, M. T., & Newton, K. S. (2005). Supporting self-management in patients with chronic illness. *American Family Physician, 72*(8), 1503–1510.

Csikai, E. L. (2004). Social workers' participation in the resolution of ethical dilemmas in hospice care. *Health and Social Work, 29*(1), 67–77.

DuBois, B., & Miley, K. K. (2005). *Social work: An empowering profession* (5th ed.). Boston: Allyn & Bacon.

Dziegielewski, S. F. (2004). *The changing face of health care social work: Professional practice in managed behavioral health care* (2nd ed.). New York: Springer.

Gearing, R. E., Saini, M., & McNeill, T. (2007). Experiences and implications of social workers practicing in a pediatric hospital environment affected by SARS. *Health & Social Work, 32*(1), 17–27.

Gehlert, S. (2006a). Communication in health care. In S. Gehlert & T. A. Browne (Eds.), *Handbook of health social work* (pp. 252–281). Hoboken, NJ: Wiley.

Gehlert, S. (2006b). The conceptual underpinnings of social work in health care. In S. Gehlert and T. A. Browne (Eds.), *Handbook of health social work* (pp. 3–22) Hoboken, NJ: Wiley.

Germain, C., & Gitterman, A. (1995). Ecological perspective. In R.L. Edwards (Ed.), *Encyclopedia of social work* (19th ed., Vol. 1, pp. 816–824). Washington, DC: NASW Press.

Gregorian, C. (2005). A career in hospital social work: Do you have what it takes? *Social Work in Health Care, 40*(3), 1–14.

Hayward, K. S., Kochniuk, L., Powell, L., & Paterson, T. (2005). Changes in student's perceptions of interdisciplinary practice reaching the older adult through mobile service delivery. *Journal of Allied Health, 34*(4), 192–199.

Hobbs, M. D. (2005). The social worker on the medical transdisciplinary team. *Journal of Health Care for the Poor and Underserved, 16*(2), 186–192.

Holmes, G. E. (1997). The strengths perspective and the politics of clienthood. In D. Saleebey (Ed.), *The strengths perspective in social work practice* (2nd ed., pp. 151–164). New York: Longman.

Jennings, P. D. (2005). Providing pediatric palliative care through a pediatric supportive care team. *Pediatric Nursing, 31*(3), 195–201.

Jessup, R. L. (2007). Interdisciplinary versus multidisciplinary care teams: Do we understand the difference? *Australian Health Review, 31*(3), 330–331.

National Association of Social Workers (NASW). (1999). *Code of ethics.* Washington, DC: Author

Oliver, D. P., Porock, D. Demiris, G., & Courtney, K. (2005). Patient and family involvement in hospice interdisciplinary teams. *Journal of Palliative Care, 21*(4), 270–277.

Parker-Oliver, D., Bronstein, L. R., & Kurzejeski, L. (2005). Examining variables related to successful collaboration on the hospice team. *Health and Social Work, 30*(4), 279–287.

Redman, R. W. (2006). The challenge of interdisciplinary teams. *Research and Theory for Nursing Practice, 20*(2), 105–108.

Reese, D. J., & Raymer, M. (2004). Relationships between social work involvement and hospice outcomes: Results of the national hospice social work survey. *Social Work, 49*(3), 415–423.

Reese, D. J., & Sontag, M. (2001). Successful interprofessional collaboration on the hospice team. *Health and Social Work, 26*(3), 167–176.

Reynolds, D. (2004). Improving care interactions with racially and ethnically diverse populations in healthcare organizations. *Journal of Healthcare Management, 49*(4), 237–250.

Rose, M. A., Lyons, K. J., Miller, K. S., & Comman-Levy, D. (2003). The effect of an interdisciplinary community health project on student attitudes toward community health, people who are indigent and homeless, and team leadership skill development. *Journal of Allied Health, 32*(2), 122–125.

Saleebey, D. (1997). *The strengths perspective in social work practice* (2nd ed.). New York: Longman.

Sang, B. (2006). Continuity and connectivity: Who will stabilize the systems that support health care outside hospital? *Journal of Integrated Care, 14*(1), 38–44.

Soler, M., & Shauffer, C. (2003). Fighting fragmentation: Coordination of services for children and families. *Education and Urban Society, 25,* 129–140.

Sulman, J., Savage, D., Vrooman, P., & McGillivray, M. (2004). Building a professional collection of hospital social workers. *Social Work in Health Care, 39*(3/4), 288–307.

Taylor, J. B. (1997). Niches and practice: Extending the ecological perspective. In D. Saleebey (Ed.), *The strengths perspective in social work practice* (2nd ed., pp. 217–228). New York: Longman.

10

Caregivers, Family, and Friends

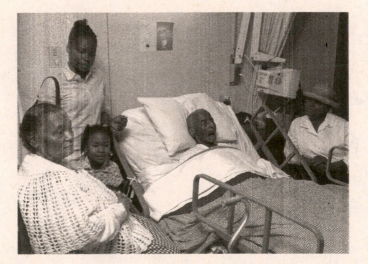

Teaching and Learning Goals

- Understand the issues surrounding support and caregivers
- Understand the personal responses to caregiving
- Recognize the biological, psychosocial, and social ways caregiving influences individuals
- Recognize the social workers' role in supporting caregivers

It is a challenge to capture the many kinds of supportive relationships that develop when an individual faces the losses associated with increased dependence due to advanced chronic illness. After possibly years of managing chronic illness independently, individuals must now turn to their support systems to find assistance. Supporters often step up in a variety of ways to offer care to the patient. Caregivers attempt to assist the patient to face the challenges of additional care needs and in some cases, the end of life.

Caregivers are frequently the unsung heroes in the provision of health care to individuals living with chronic health conditions. Often caregivers are identified as the family and friends of the patient, but, more specifically are connected to the patient through a variety of relationships: family, friend, partner, spouse, sibling, neighbor, coworker, volunteer, and child. If someone provides biological, emotional, or social care for someone, they are a caregiver (Family Caregiver Alliance, 2006a, 2006b). The "family" system used in this chapter is best identified broadly to include all forms of emotional ties that result in caregiving relationships.

Within the relationship of caregiver and patient, the caregiver offers support to the person in the patient role but the tasks performed potentially affect the caregiver emotionally, physically, and socially. Caregivers often face tremendous challenges and a sense of being overwhelmed and unprepared to adequately care for all the patient's care needs. In addition, caregivers experience their own losses due to the changes that occur in their own lives, in their family system, and in the life of the person they care for (Rabow, Hauser, & Adams, 2004).

There are many important contributions that social workers offer to alleviate some of the stress associated with advancing chronic illness and ease the burden and worry for caregivers and patients. However, there are also difficult moments when acknowledgment of end of life is recognized and discussed or avoided. This is a complex and often difficult time in the life of the caregiver and their family member. The social worker in health care offers assistance to caregivers by presenting emotional, physical, and social supports. Adequate and empathetic support increases the sense of success for caregivers and helps improve their lives and the life of the patient (Rabow et al., 2004).

The Support System

When a personal assault occurs in life, individuals often seek assistance from their network of friends and family. Frequently the primary members of the group that offer aid are from two populations: those who are biologically related and those who are emotionally connected. The diagnosis of chronic illness is frequently perceived as a personal assault yet rarely is the individual with the diagnosis the only person affected by the news. The entire support system of the person with the "new" disease is influenced, concerned, or altered by the diagnosis. The change in health for one person represents a change for everyone connected and the system responds to the change in a variety of ways.

The systems theory supports the existence of an interface between environments and individuals (Rodway, 1986). For instance, when change occurs in one part of the system, it results in changes to other parts of the system. Members of a system form a network and lives are intertwined long before the needs associated with the onset of chronic illness or caregiving needs arise. The family system bonds develop through many shared events and experiences that connect and shape individuals into a supportive group, including the commitment of two or more people to form a family, the birth or adoption of children, shared goals and life plans, and relationships with a parent(s) or elders. The connections that form often exist prior to the emergent needs of a family member for support due to a health crisis (Aneshensel, Botticello, & Yamamoto-Mitani, 2004).

The traditional family system (biologically or legally related) is one of the most consistent and principal resources for the nurturing and support of human beings. It is where most people find some form of shelter from the demands, challenges, and assaults experienced living in society. While certainly not true in all cases, for many the biological family unit is a resource that represents some level of safety. The family, identified in this traditional way, is historically acknowledged as the location in society where its members are acculturated. Within the family, members learn values, skills, and beliefs that result in a lens used to see and interpret the world. The family is the most influential interpersonal system in the life of an individual (Mitrani et al., 2006).

The nuclear family is perceived as the primary unit where people go to seek the assistance or care they cannot receive elsewhere. Without the caregiving of family members to individuals with advanced chronic illness, many are challenged to receive the support and treatment they need to survive (Gopalan & Brannon, 2006; Hudson, Hayman-White, Arand, & Kristjanson, 2006). Although families often make attempts to provide types of care to sick members, this is frequently a difficult task and many families are tested to provide care for a variety of reasons (Grbich, Parker, & Maddocks, 2001).

Not all families are designed in ways that prepare them to offer assistance to each other, but many families, despite less than perfect circumstances, make attempts to provide at least some form of support. Working in health care, social workers witness a variety of unique family units form to offer what they can to support a loved one who is ill. Families vary in their structure and membership and there are many combinations of relationships, both formal and informal, that define a family. Although biological families are often the first place to seek support when in crisis, through the course of a lifetime, nonbiological family members also offer support to individuals in a variety of ways.

Regardless of the legalistic definition of family as based on biological relationships, caregivers are more broadly defined as members of an intimate group of people invested in the health and safety of the person who is sick. They are neighbors, longtime friends, or coworkers. They are also partners, lovers, and relatives from outside the primary family unit. They may live with the person in need of care or reside outside the patient home (Family Caregiver Alliance, 2006a, 2006b). Connected by formal and informal relationships, caregivers are people that form a safety net for the individual who needs assistance. Their role in health care is vital in the quality of life for the person who receives their help.

The need to support someone within an intimate group can happen in a moment and can be quite unexpected. The ability to live independently can change to depending on others very quickly. Consider the following scenario.

Scenario 10:1

One morning I brought my father to an appointment to get the results from a CAT scan of his head. He had told me he was feeling off balance and weak on one side of his body. I believed the results would reveal the effects of a small stroke; instead, the physician announced to my father that he had a brain tumor and it appeared to be cancerous. The physician gave us many directions about the next steps my father needed to take and then, rather routinely, told my father that he was no longer able to drive because of his now increased risk of a seizure. My caregiving began when I accompanied him to the physician's office and continued when, on our way out of the physician's office, my father handed me the car keys. The loss of his lifelong ability to drive was significant, but the onslaught of health needs and critical decisions left no room for the loss to be a priority.

What are the physical, emotional, or social support acts happening in this scenario? What are the losses being experienced?

Multiple caregiving tasks and pressing need demand families quickly abandon the routine of healthy living and interactions and move from significant losses to the immediate needs associated with developing a plan for the future.

In a critical moment, individuals become caregivers and are socially expected to assume responsibilities for tasks that are often totally unfamiliar to them. Caregiving often means accepting accountability for many new jobs, including financial and insurance issues, providing transportation, appointment-making and -keeping, filling medical prescriptions, organizing and giving medication, and providing assistance in medical treatments. Caregivers, in many ways, lose the primary relationship role they once shared with the patient. Wives become nurses or adult children become parents. The family system reels from the shifts in roles and power (Pitsenberger, 2006). These movements in relationships represent a significant loss in how the family once functioned for both patients and for family members.

The emotional loss and the physical and social additions in responsibility often throw the most intact and well-intentioned family systems into disarray and disorganization, at least temporarily. While in some cases, there is a predictable need for supportive care, purposeful planning, and preparation, in some cases the announcement of need is sudden and unexpected and the support system must quickly rally to respond to the urgent changes in the patient's needs based on developing news from medical test results and other sources of health information. These dramatic alterations occur at the same time that caregivers try to maintain some form of equilibrium in their personal lives.

The health care system relies on the presence of caregivers. This is true in the United States and in many other countries in the world. However, due to changes in many societies in the world, reliance on family caregivers is no longer the conventional solution. Although families are culturally still viewed as the resource people rely on in an emergency, it is no longer predictable that family members reside in one geographic area. In addition, the role of women has changed significantly in many cultures and no longer includes family caregiving as the primary role (Conway-Giustra, Crowley, & Gorin, 2002).

Within families, females are the gender most often expected to offer supportive and nurturing care to family members. Caregivers, both family members and friends, are most often women (Conway-Giustra et al., 2002; Gopalan & Brannon, 2006). The Family Caregiver Alliance (2006a, 2006b) supports this finding and states that 77% of caregivers are female. Roles for women in the United States have changed dramatically, particularly since World War II, when great numbers of women entered the job market. Today it is far less common for the women in families to not be employed outside the home. Women are powerfully challenged when they are expected to be the chief nurturers and caregivers and at the same time accommodate the requirements of their employment and personal schedules.

What would the health system do if there were no family caregivers to help people with advanced chronic illness? Although caregivers are expected to offer support to individuals with health-related needs, sadly, there is often insufficient support for the caregivers themselves. Levine (1999) suggests caregivers are an invisible force in the health care system. Caregivers need support, as a group of volunteers, and personal assistants, as individuals, with seemingly no choice but to commit themselves to caring for a dependent family member. They provide the critically important health care that often operates unrecognized. There is frequently little or no training for caregivers and the expectations for their ability to care for someone may be unrealistic. Caregivers are expected to coordinate, supervise, communicate, provide care, and integrate the health needs of a person they care for with no experience for this kind of work (Gopalan & Brannon, 2006; Pitsenberger, 2006).

Caregivers want training and education to provide effective care and they want their emotional attachment to the patient recognized. There is a great deal of fear and anxiety in caring for a family member. Professionals are often insensitive to this, or at least fail to address it with family members. Recognition of caregivers' contributions or praise of their commitment is rare. Complicated and unfamiliar procedures such as providing injections, changing a dressing, and setting up and operating IVs are intimidating. Caregivers see the effects of disease in the patient in a way the professional health care team does not see. They witness the nausea, pain, sleeplessness, and hopelessness of the patient. Caregivers fear making a mistake or hurting their loved ones because of their inexperience. When the health care system fails to assist in the resolution of caregiver anxiety, the consequence is resistance, failure, resentment, and ongoing feelings of inadequacy (Levine, 1999; Rabow et al., 2004). This is detrimental to the patient and caregiver. Potentially, the emotional pain of the caregiver creates barriers that interfere in his or her contribution to the patient's quality of life.

The two most common challenges to providing support to a family member are (1) the difficulties in communicating with others involved in patient care and (2) the difficulties in providing the practical assistance needed for physical care. Frequently caregivers are not professionally trained to provide health-related interventions and are frustrated by attempts to partner with health care providers (Grbich et al., 2001).

Communication Difficulties

Caregivers, both family members and friends, providing health-related assistance experience difficulties with aspects of communication. There are many ways caregivers are expected to communicate while caring for someone with chronic illness. For instance, they are expected to disclose information to the health care system and with the patient about all issues related to the health condition. In addition, there is an expectation caregivers will also voluntarily share their own needs (Grbich et al., 2001; Rabow et al., 2004)

The health care system looms large and can be intimidating during the treatment of advanced chronic illness. There are many physicians, specialties, medications, treatments, appointments, and needs to coordinate. Communication, despite determination to transmit information clearly and accurately, is rarely as effective as hoped. Medical professionals and other health care providers are frequently located within different offices and often accept responsibility for only the portion of care provided by their area of specialty. The world of medical specialties is daunting and each comes with unique language, treatments, and procedures. For instance, the treatment of cancer includes tests, treatments, medications, labs, and symptoms that the cancer treatment community uses regularly, but is unfamiliar to caregivers and patients. In addition, issues related to medical insurance are frequently complex and overwhelming. Preauthorizations, spend-downs, copays, and submission of forms are simply more than caregivers deserve to face after prioritizing the emotional, physical, and social care needs of the patient.

Some families experience difficulty with family member communication with each other about any aspect of the loss and grief associated with giving care. The inability to communicate with each other and with the patient, while also facing multiple personal losses, makes preparation for future medical crises and end-of-life issues difficult. Maybe families are unready or unable to face the impending death of their family members. Medical crises are unexpected and often present emotional challenges that most are unprepared to handle. Perhaps families commonly avoid expression of painful or hurtful feelings and traditionally avoid difficult decision making. Some families function in very specific and rather rigid ways and the threat of changes based on the new dependence needs of a strong or influential family member is disruptive. The changes in family dynamics result in the redefinition of roles within the family system (Waldrop, 2007). In addition, some cultures consider communication about death and dying within the family system taboo and unfortunately this is reinforced by society's nonacceptance of death and dying as a natural part of life. Perhaps families experience guilt and fear that discussing end-of-life issues will cause death to occur. Many believe that development of a living will or other legal options for health emergencies are a form of "giving up" hope. Emotions are frequently heightened during this part of life for caregivers and patients and communication can be intense. For instance, some patients do not communicate their desire to end treatment because they perceive their family depends on them and wants them to keep fighting the disease (Grbich et al., 2001; Waldrop, 2007).

Practical Assistance Difficulties

In addition to the potential difficulties in sharing thoughts, information, and feelings within the family, some families experience difficulty providing for the actual physical tasks required to care for someone who is no longer independent. The daily living skills of ambulation, toileting, eating, and dressing are frequently impossible to accomplish for someone with advanced chronic illness. To provide these services to someone who is relatively unable to assist takes great physical strength. If an aging woman is caring for her aging spouse, the physical tasks may be either impossible or perhaps dangerous to perform. Additionally, and often for 24 hours a day, caregivers coordinate other health-related care needs: medications, medical procedures, appointments, and treatments. This leaves little time for other family needs or personal time.

While families attempt to meet patient needs, they also deal with their own feelings of inadequacy and grief. They witness the changes in their loved ones and their relationships with them. At the same time, families frequently try to preserve hope for recovery. They try, despite their own pain and helplessness, to be encouraging, to draw attention to the positive and overlook the negative events such as an increase in the symptoms of advancing disease. Patients also experience additional pain, discomfort, or fear at the losses they experience in their health as the illness progresses. Families may feel trapped trying to attend to one another at a time when all are suffering and overwhelmed. Caregivers require attention and assistance for their own needs (Rabow et al., 2004).

Responses to Caregiving

Caregivers often experience forms of stress as a result of providing for a sick family member. As with the patient, feeling overwhelmed is likely to occur within a variety of situations. Caregivers, along with the patient, must adjust to multiple losses in their physical, emotional, and social environments. The potential for experiencing some form of stress is great, but Rolland and Walsh (2005) report the needs related to caregiver stress are often unattended to in health care systems.

Responses to the distress and tension of caring for an individual who is ill vary. Caregivers, who are responsible for the bathing, toileting, feeding, dressing, and ambulation of the patient, experience exhaustion or physical injury. If they experience the emotional assault of sadness and sorrow associated with the advancement of chronic illness in their loved ones, they also experience the physical exhaustion associated with grief. Caregiving interrupts the usual means of emotional support available to the provider through social time with friends and colleagues. They may also miss opportunities to attend their spiritual or religious sanctuaries. Their routine of work and socialization is radically interrupted and they may experience loneliness and abandonment (Figure 10.1).

Caregivers often identify the affect of the stress they experience as influencing their own health. One of the most common pressures is their constant worry for the patient. But it is more than worry about someone's health; it is also the fear that they are doing something wrong. Caregivers are anxious that they are putting the patient in danger or doing something to harm them. The challenge of balancing focus on patient care and at the same

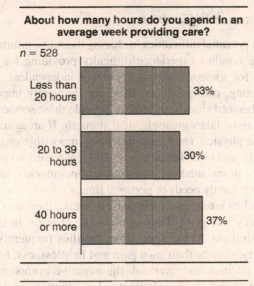

About how many hours do you spend in an average week providing care?

$n = 528$

- Less than 20 hours — 33%
- 20 to 39 hours — 30%
- 40 hours or more — 37%

FIGURE 10.1 *Hours per Week Caregivers Provide Care*

Source: Family Caregiver Alliance (2006b). http://www.caregiving.org/data/Caregivers%20in%20Decline%20Study-FINAL-lowres.pdf

time caring for themselves, other family members, and perhaps a job or career is overwhelming. It is common for caregivers to ask for help, especially when they believe they are unable to do the health care work expected of them. Caregivers identify an inability to sleep, heart palpitations, increase in blood pressure, arthritis flareups, upset stomach, headaches, and other conditions in response to their anxiety (Evercare, 2006; Grbich et al., 2001; Rabow et al., 2004).

Depression stems from a variety of sources. It is related to the gradual or increased rate of deterioration in the patient, the symptoms of anticipatory grief and feeling overwhelmed, and accentuated by the lack of personal time and exhaustion. The caregiver is less able to get away to buy groceries, plan meals, exercise, or rest. Sometimes caregivers must respond to the patient and their medical needs so continuously that it requires interruptions to their sleep. Caregivers are challenged to find others to step in temporarily to allow for respite. At times other family and friends offer to help, but caregivers may be reluctant to ask for assistance and believe others are not really willing to help or will not provide the best standard of care.

Many caregivers have ideas about how the health care system could better support them and wish there were ways to feel connected to health providers in case of an emergency. One way to offer assistance involves face-to-face meetings with health professionals, but many caregivers experience encouragement with their work through interventions as simple as a phone call, a medical emergency plan, or advice with other practical matters (Grbich et al., 2001).

Lack of social contacts with others and an absence of supportive networks develop into a form of isolation and this often acts to reduce or eliminate the positive feedback and encouraging statements caregivers receive in the course of a day. The daily routine is replaced with a pattern that concentrates on patient needs and leaves the caregiver alone and secluded. Even when other family members or caregivers visit, the focus is often on the health needs of the patient and not on those of the caregiver. A daily telephone call from a health care organization to inquire about the health of the patient and the condition of the caregiver is beneficial and allows them to feel linked, remembered, and sustained (Grbich et al., 2001).

Caregiving demands attention to the family member experiencing the advancement of disease-related symptoms such as pain, nausea, vomiting, and delirium. It also demands interrupted sleep and as the family member becomes less mobile, caregivers experience a loss of social connectedness due to their personal commitment to the patient.

Physical Response

Given the increased longevity of U.S. citizens and the medical interventions available to prolong good-quality life, caregiving is frequently administered by aging partners to their aging partners. The physical tasks of moving a patient, assisting patient to move into another position, supporting a patient in and out of a car or bed, and other physical tasks call for special training and skills. Caregivers are physically affected by the role of providing care to a dependent individual. It is common for caregivers to acquire the responsibility for tasks that demand physical effort and strength. In an effort to help a person ambulate, a caregiver, frequently untrained to effectively and safely assist someone with their mobility, can easily become injured. Physical injuries related to physical caregiving can result in pulled muscles, sprains, exhaustion, and other physical pains.

The Family Caregiver Alliance (2006a, 2006b) reports that the most common caregiver health and well-being problems, regardless of culture, are sleep deprivation, poor eating habits, failure to exercise, failure to stay in bed when ill, and postponement of or failure to make personal medical appointments. Common physical responses to these physical stressors include high blood pressure and a weakened immune system (Gopalan & Brannon, 2006).

Caregivers are frequently formidable to support because they may not recognize themselves as needing support. They see caring for their family members as the priority and a personal responsibility; sometimes they believe the work they do is insignificant when compared to the struggle of the patient. Caregivers minimize the incredible physical stress they experience, often while they are suffering emotionally. The best way for social workers to understand the issues of caregiving is to learn from someone performing these duties. It is difficult to understand how physically overwhelming the burden of care is if the work is never witnessed or experienced firsthand (Family Caregiver Alliance, 2006a, 2006b; Gopalan & Brannon, 2006).

There are significant health risks for some caregivers (Figure 10.2). The need to focus totally on the care of the patient may interfere in their self-care. As with any issues regarding self-care, the more fragile one's health, the more important it is to monitor health and when this is ignored, there is increased risk for damage. Caregivers can themselves become at risk for chronic illness and require the services of a caregiver (Family Caregiver Alliance, 2006a, 2006b).

Emotional Response

Families and caregivers for people living with advanced chronic illness experience a significantly increased level of psychological distress (Dumont et al., 2006; Grbich et al., 2001). The most common emotional responses include a feeling of being over-whelmed, depressed, and anxious (Gopalan & Brannon, 2006). The emotional burden is common for a couple of reasons. First, there are few effective supports offered to care providers due to lack of insurance coverage for performing patient care tasks and the very nature of caregiving requires providers spend most of their time with the patient. In addition, care for chronic illness is rarely provided in inpatient settings so people spend more time isolated in their homes. When support efforts are available through hospice and home health agencies, the availability of assistance allows patients to live at home during illnesses and during the end of life. But for those with advanced illness, living at home is impossible without dedicated family caregivers (Waldrop, 2007).

In addition to other hurdles, caregivers often experience emotional and mental health risks. The emotional burden of care provision is clearly great for the caregiver. This person attempts to not only care for the physical, emotional, and social needs of the patient, but also serves as the liaison between medical and health care organizations and the rest of the individuals interested in or involved in the life of the patient. Some may find this role extremely rewarding and view it as an opportunity to serve. Many, however, may find themselves in the caregiving role not by choice, but through a default process. When a

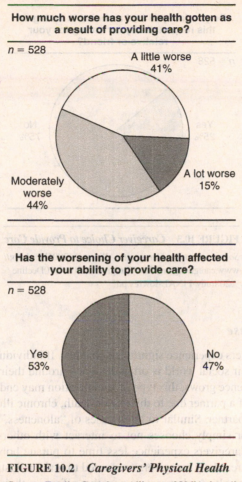

How much worse has your health gotten as a result of providing care?

n = 528

A little worse 41%

A lot worse 15%

Moderately worse 44%

Has the worsening of your health affected your ability to provide care?

n = 528

Yes 53%

No 47%

FIGURE 10.2 *Caregivers' Physical Health*

Source: Family Caregiver Alliance (2006b). http://www.caregiving.org/data/Caregivers%20in%20Decline%20Study-FINAL-lowres.pdf

caregiver tends to a patient due to the absence of others willing or able to serve in this capacity, resentment, anger, helplessness, and feelings of inadequacy may develop. The reality of caregivers may include feelings of entrapment, and escape is unthinkable because it is linked to the absence or death of the person they care for (Family Caregiver Alliance, 2006a, 2006b).

Caregivers can also experience resentment and anger regarding the changes in their lives. The family member receiving care may not show appreciation for the work involved and in some cases may be demanding or aggressive. The caregivers, exhausted, and frustrated may lose their sense of commitment and strike out at the patient. Sometimes angry feelings are directed toward the care recipient and sometimes the caregiver strikes out physically. This is a form of emotional and physical abuse and may be experienced by the caregiver and the recipient of care. The experience and expression of these angry feelings can than lead to additional feelings of guilt (Gopalan & Brannon, 2006).

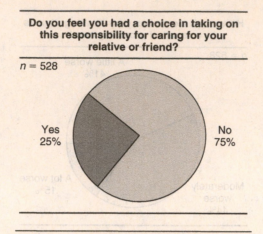

Do you feel you had a choice in taking on this responsibility for caring for your relative or friend?

n = 528

Yes
25%

No
75%

FIGURE 10.3   *Caregiver Choice to Provide Care*

Source: Family Caregiver Alliance (2006b). http://www.caregiving.org/data/Caregivers%20in%20Decline%20Study-FINAL-lowres.pdf

Social Response

Socially, caregivers experience significant changes. If individuals with advanced illness are life partners, their social world is often designed around their interactions as a couple. As physical dependence grows, this type of socialization may end. Like individuals who experience the loss of a partner due to divorce or death, chronic illness also leaves people without their social partner. Similar to other cases of "aloneness," the healthy partner tends to avoid, isolate, or simply chooses not to interact with others without his or her partner (Figure 10.3). Caregivers experience less time to pursue hobbies or other social engagements for pleasure. Many caregivers are forced to make adjustments to work schedules and these adjustments ultimately create a negative effect on their financial status (FCI, 2006; Gopalan & Brannon, 2006; Pitsenberger, 2006).

Regardless of the reasoning, people who cease to interact outside the closed world of caregiving face significant stress. Socialization is a way to take in new information, gain support, and find pleasure through being distracted from overwhelming circumstances. Not only does this time away benefit the caregiver, but ultimately it benefits the patient. New information brought into the home environment is a welcome distraction and adds to the list of things to think, inquire, and care about. Without socialization, the world of both the patient and their partner becomes defined by the illness, symptoms, and care needs. Socialization is limited to doctor appointments and trips to the pharmacist.

Lack of socialization opportunities, both the self-imposed isolation and those forced by lack of options, all damage the independence of the caregiver. The days of picking up and leaving the home for even the simplest of errands is no longer a possibility. Feelings of resentment can occur, quickly followed by feelings of guilt for wanting to escape the situation in which they feel trapped (Grbich et al., 2001; Waldrop, 2007).

Burnout

Burnout is a word frequently associated with individuals who experience the ill-effects of being overwhelmed for too long. Sometimes burnout is a result of the overwhelming demands of professional work, but burnout occurs for caregivers, too. Burnout is the downward spiral of physical and emotional exhaustion, resentment, loss of interest in life, and the inability to sustain positive momentum (Monatague, 1994). The often intense work involved in being a caregiver, the frequent lack of support from professional health systems, and the inability to keep advancing illness at bay, despite best efforts, results in the caregiver's overwhelming emotional fatigue. In the best of circumstances and despite love, affection, and devotion to the patient, advanced chronic illness poses challenges that are long in duration and are difficult to continually manage. The privacy of a home can mask the need for others to offer help (Grbich et al., 2001).

The literature regarding burnout issues for caregivers recognizes that the burden to family in physical, emotional, financial, and social issues is considerable (Hudson et al., 2006). The result of caregiving stress includes symptoms that occur in all areas of caregiver functioning, such as "fatigue, insomnia, weight loss, burn-out, diminished self-esteem, isolation, and general deterioration in health" (Hudson et al., p. 133). Informal caregivers experience anxiety and depression because caregiving takes so much time, limits social interactions, and increases the likelihood of caregivers suffering loneliness and isolation (Dumont et al., 2006; Levine, 1999; Rees, O'Boyle, & MacDonagh, 2001; Waldorp, 2007).

Although there are many cultural variations of response to feeling overwhelmed, there is also some level of predictability for distress based on a number of caregiver variables including age, state of health, relationship to the patient, and the sense of competence and personal sense of accomplishment associated with the caregiving. Younger caregivers, physically unhealthy caregivers, and women tend to experience higher levels of distress than older caregivers, healthy caregivers, and men. In addition, caregivers who feel competent in the care they give and experience some sense of control are more likely to experience a level of protection from psychological distress and burn-out (Dumont et al., 2006; Waldrop, 2007).

It is likely family caregivers will experience psychosocial pain and the need for encouragement and assistance, yet caregivers are rarely recognized by the health care system for their central role in the health management of the patient. As the distress of the patient increases, so does the distress of the caregiver (Dumont et al., 2006). In addition, as the distress of the caregiver increases, it influences the distress of the patient. This is important motivation for social workers to assess and anticipate caregivers' burden. Dumont et al. (2006) suggests that social workers attempt to offer greater attention to family caregivers' concerns and recognize caregivers benefit from health services. Improvement and support for the family ultimately improves the level of care and quality of life for the patient. Social workers recognize the physical, emotional, and social elements for caregivers, but provide additional benefit to caregivers when they support the additional areas of burden often unmentioned, including lack of personal time, logistical challenges, and financial complexities of care (Rabow et al., 2004).

Time and Logistical Challenges

Although sometimes caregiving takes only a couple of hours a week, in many situations caregiving is at least equivalent to the hours of a full-time job, maybe more. Despite the number of hours spent by many caring for a family member, the sense of responsibility never ends. Time previously used for personal and home responsibilities is now used almost exclusively to care for the patient. When caregivers check on medication prescriptions and treatments, review scheduled appointments, and complete other care tasks, they do not have time for personal chores during the course of a day. Caregivers often use "free" time to work with insurance companies and complete the paperwork needed for reimbursement for medical services.

The amount of time and stress in tasks associated with patient care, especially skilled tasks, are overwhelming and seem neverending. Again, it is important to remember many caregivers are retired older adults. Tasks accomplished in their youth, such as driving in busy traffic or climbing up and down steps to do laundry, take more time and energy and are potentially exhausting. Perhaps the most pressing burden on time is the absence of moments in life when there is no worry or concern. Despite well-meaning family members and friends offering moments of respite, most caregivers continue their worry and concern about patient care when they are away (Figure 10.4).

Financial Complexities

In the United States, caregiving remains an uncompensated service. The cost of lost revenue from employment and the expense of health care costs for families are enormous. Rabow et al. (2004) suggest that 20% of family caregivers quit their jobs or make major

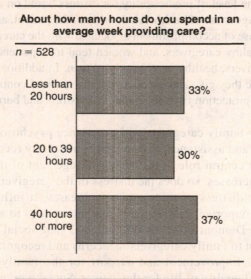

About how many hours do you spend in an average week providing care?

n = 528

Less than 20 hours	33%
20 to 39 hours	30%
40 hours or more	37%

FIGURE 10.4   *Hours per Week Caregivers Provide Care*

Source: Family Caregiver Alliance (2006b). http://www.caregiving.org/data/Caregivers%20in%20Decline%20Study-FINAL-lowres.pdf

life changes in an effort to provide in-home health care and 31% lose most if not all of their family savings as a result of providing care. Most caregivers work for free caring for a family member while incurring care-related expenses.

How to access medical insurance benefits is rarely understood prior to the need to actually access those benefits. Infrequently insurance plans are easy to understand and it is uncommon for the requirements, forms, and processes to receive reimbursement to be simple. Completing financial and medical forms and collecting the necessary documentation to recover reimbursement is maddening to many exhausted and overwhelmed caregivers. If the caregiver is not confident about their ability to read accurately for content, does not understand the technical language of the forms, or can not see the words clearly due to impaired vision, medical insurance–related tasks present an incredible burden. Never underestimate the level of support experienced when someone offers to assist a caregiver with medical insurance tasks. If social workers offer resources or assistance with medical insurance, they are truly freeing the caregiver to respond to needs they believe to be more important: the personal care of the patient (Rabow et al., 2004).

Secondary Trauma

Much of the literature about secondary trauma is connected to the experiences of social workers and other health care professionals who suffer emotional and psychological symptoms caused by work with individuals who survive trauma (Bell, 2003; Bride, Robinson, Yegidis, & Figley, 2004; Geller, Madsen, & Ohrenstein, 2004; Hesse, 2002; Raingruber & Kent, 2003). The experience of secondary trauma is also applicable to the caregivers of patients who live with advanced chronic illness and experience the final stages and end of life while they are helpless to stop it from happening. Additionally, caregivers may experience intrusive imagery, avoidant responses, physiological arousal, distressing emotions, and functional impairment (Bride et al., 2004).

Caregivers are often faced with an overwhelming sense of inadequacy. First, they believe they are inadequate to deliver the care needs of the dependent family member. In many cases this is true. The emotional bond between the caregiver and the patient can lead the caregiver to continue to provide his or her best care, despite knowing he or she is ill-equipped to provide the increasingly complicated assistance required by the patient. Sometimes the caregiver is reluctant to admit he or she cannot provide the necessary care because they know his or her presence and assistance is vital to the patient.

Second, the fear of inadequate care from long-term care facilities and the separation and inability to supervise the care of his or her loved one from afar interferes with the referrals necessary for additional assistance. The caregiver must agree with the need for additional support services or the referral source is bound to fail due to the assessment of the caregiver. Although many caregivers recognize the need for the patient to receive additional specialized or medically technical care and believe that the care is beyond what they can provide, the thought of strangers caring for his or her family member is terrifying. The main issues of concern for caregivers regarding referrals for the patient to long-term care settings include fear about depending on others for his or her family member's care, the quantity and quality of physical care for the patient, the standards of

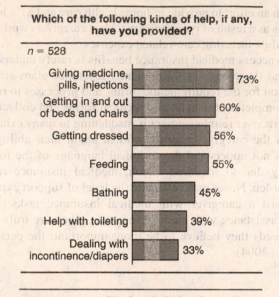

Which of the following kinds of help, if any, have you provided?

n = 528

Giving medicine, pills, injections	73%
Getting in and out of beds and chairs	60%
Getting dressed	56%
Feeding	55%
Bathing	45%
Help with toileting	39%
Dealing with incontinence/diapers	33%

FIGURE 10.5 *Kinds of Help Care Givers Provide*

Source: Family Caregiver Alliance (2006b). http://www .caregiving.org/data/Caregivers%20in%20Decline%20 Study-FINAL-lowres.pdf

care within the physical environment such as staffing levels or staff expertise, and the coordination of medical care with the patient's health care system (Vohre & Szala-Meneok, 2006).

Finally, the caregiver wants to stop this experience from happening, and despite his or her attempts, the advancement continues. The caregiver watches helplessly as disease progresses, despite his or her best efforts. They try to do their best everyday, but the patient experiences little relief and the progression of the disease persists (Figure 10.5). Caregivers experience a sense of failure to save their family members from end of life, and in some cases may truly believe any advancement of disease or eventual death is their fault.

Professional social workers and others who experience overwhelming and unrelenting trauma recognize that it is vital caregivers are given information, education, and referral for debriefing after painful events. Many in-home support services, such as hospice, offer support groups and counseling to caregivers, some for the entire year following the death of a family member (Family Caregiver Alliance, 2006a, 2006b; Waldrop, 2007).

Life's Purpose and Meaning

Perhaps one of the most common experiences of people living with advanced chronic illness is reflection on their purpose in life. A concentration camp survivor, Frankel (1968) discusses how people find meaning in their lives and suggests that the things individuals contribute, the lessons taken, and the values engaged to face circumstances individuals are powerless to change in the world, form purpose and meaning in life (Rappaport, Fossler, Bross, & Gilden, 1993). Perhaps there are similarities in Frankel's experiences with loss as a prisoner in a camp during World War II to the experiences some living with advanced chronic illness experience. Like prisoners in the camps, patients are trying to survive despite the brutal side effects of treatments and watching others die; they may spend time dreaming of the nightmare ending or a return to happier days. Experiencing empathy for patients means that social workers attempt to understand how patients and caregivers experience the sense of powerlessness, continual limitations, and loss and grief.

With the loss of functioning, patients are directed to face the finality and the temporary nature of life in a variety of ways (Rappaport et al., 1993; Waldorp, 2007). Research suggests the death of a spouse, particularly in later life, is a very stressful experience and often changes how the remaining spouse, often the caregiver, continues to live (Minton and Barron, 2008; Stroebe, Schut, & Stoebe, 2007). The spouse/caregiver commonly experiences a considerable reduction in psychological functioning, including depression and loss of purpose for living. As the end of life approaches, there is time when the patient and caregiver must consider letting go of goals for living as they did in the past. Letting go is not loss of hope, but a moment when the family system recognizes the need to make a change from the focus of prolonging life, to the recognition of the nearness of death. Not all families reach this point and some demand health providers continue to medically treat a patient, despite the nearness of his or her death. The Family Caregiver Alliance (2006a, 2006b) states that despite refusal to acknowledge end of life, death does not disappear and sometimes refusal to acknowledge the end of life inadvertently prolongs the death experience and creates a time of increased suffering.

There is a great deal of attention recently to the quality of life for a person living with chronic illness (Goldstein and Fischberg, 2008). Quality of life is difficult to define and measure due to all of the impinging variables, but there is little doubt that the way disease influences life is based on an individual's biopsychosocial circumstances. The quality of life for caregivers is also vital to assess (Gayomali, Sutherland and Finkelstein, 2008; Goldsworthy and Knowles, 2008; Logsdon, 2008). The burden of providing health care to a family member often requires caregivers forfeit their quality of life. A study found caregivers/partners of people living with chronic illness are often physically and emotionally exhausted; in fact, frequently the quality of life for the caregiver was worse than that of the patient. The caregivers reported an increase in worry and concern and displayed signs of anxiety and depression (Rees et al., 2001; Waldrop, 2007).

The Family Caregiver Alliance (2006a, 2006b) reports conversations about the purpose and worth of life with patients reveal that what some think would be worth enduring to live may not be true for others. What makes life worthwhile? When would life definitely not be worth living? Even though things are bad now, what if they get better? The questions and answers reveal that quality of life is complex and contains different elements for different people. These questions are powerful when discussing quality of life with care providers, too. Perhaps patients predict that when they are no longer able to leave their homes they will want their life to end. Yet when the situation or condition occurs, patients recognize an unpredicted variable that adds quality to life. There may be other symbolic moments that patients perceive as representing the onset of advanced disease, such as a hospital bed, commode, or other supportive equipment in their homes. But frequently, the human condition is resilient and people living with advanced illness continue to value their time. Caregivers also adapt to changes and, like patients, anticipate certain events or tasks that will represent an unbearable moment. Caregivers, too, frequently adjust to the same painful losses the patient faces and together they design the best quality of life they can attain. The conversation about quality of life between a patient and his or her caregiver gives both parties peace of mind.

Not all caregiving experiences are completely negative. Rees et al. (2001) suggests the variables that influence how caregivers respond are generally associated with three specific categories: (1) the personal characteristics of the primary caregivers, (2) the personal characteristics of the patient, and (3) the unique characteristics of the care situation. Many caregivers experience increased self-esteem at providing such an important service to their loved one. They may experience feeling closer to their family members and see their commitment to the care provision as part of the meaning of their life. In these cases, the quality of life is improved.

Social workers can recognize and support caregivers and educate others regarding the burden of caregiving. Recognition of the vitally important role the caregiver fills is honored and recognized when caregivers are invited to address the health professionals at team meetings or other forms of consultations. Social workers can ensure that not only patient issues are addressed but can also take the lead to inquire about the needs of the caregiver. The support of the patient and caregiver partnership is overwhelmingly beneficial and results in delays in hospitalizations, assurance of appropriate care within the home environment, and increases in the quality of the care by supporting the strengths of the caregiver. It is essential to recognize this unit as fragile and vulnerable and when simple things like phone calls, written directions, reminders, or resources are offered, it strengthens and enhances the health of the patient and the caregiver (Rees et al., 2001).

Policy Issues

Health care policy in the United States is relatively unsupportive of the role of caregivers and families who provide patient care. Historically this role was taken for granted, mainly when the caregiver role was based on the assumption of women working solely within the home and caring for the needs of nuclear and geographically close extended families. Today, families are less predictably able to provide health-related care, particularly for the long term. The incredible expenses of home health care for things such as treatments, self-care, monitoring, and other procedures is limited at best and rarely fills the need for assistance adequately. The national value of individualism supports the idea of families taking care of their own needs. While many families want and claim this responsibility for their family members due to cultural norms or for psychological rewards, many do so with inadequate resources (Levine, 1999). Others, despite their desire to offer care, are challenged by many barriers including geography, age, disability, lack of money, or loss of employment.

Policies in the United States fail to support caregivers who take personal responsibility for their family members. Many families experience serious financial problems due to the changes necessary for caregiving. It is not uncommon to witness fundraisers and requests for donations to families who are attempting to reduce their financial debt due to health care expenditures. There are significant problems within the national system of health care including the lack of providing inequitable and inadequate coverage for the family support needs, particularly in the care of people living with advanced chronic illness (Levine, 1999).

Social workers can improve their advocacy for the welfare of family caregivers. Caregivers want improved communication from professionals, but also between professionals. They want to be educated and trained to feel empowered to perform the necessary support for their family members. They require emotional support, and want advocacy for the services they cannot provide themselves. Some requests do not require additional money, but they do require a commitment from policymakers and professionals in the health care system, including social workers. Admittedly, health care professionals, particularly working in the managed health care system, are often hurried and are perhaps at times inaccessible (Levine, 1999). Caregivers, however, often remain uninformed about facts like changes in the patient's diagnosis, prognosis, treatment plans, side effects, medications, or the symptoms to look for and what to do or who to call if an emergency happens at home (Grbich et al., 2001). Including caregivers as part of the health team benefits the patient primarily, but also honors the caregiver role and serves to inform the health team of the needs of the caregiver–patient partnership.

Social Work Response

The advancement of medical technology increases the number of people who live longer and better with diagnoses of chronic illness. Children and parents who once died within a short time of diagnosis from diseases like polycystic kidney disease, acquired immunodeficiency syndrome (AIDS), and heart defects now live better and healthier lives. Longer life, however, means that adults nearing retirement now find themselves caring for older parents while trying to maintain their relationships with their children and grandchildren and dealing with finances and other personal responsibilities. Families living with advanced chronic illness face multiple challenges (Rolland & Walsh, 2005).

Although loss, disease, illness, and death are some of the most common of events shared by humans throughout the world, all families are challenged under these circumstances and respond in many ways. There is clearly a role for health care teams to support caregivers and families, particularly for those providing care to patients with advanced chronic illness. Social workers are the best trained professionals on health teams to work with family systems.

The recent changes in the health care system promote a collaborative and systemic model of care that includes biopsychosocial assessment and health team coordination. These types of changes lead to recognition of the family and caregiver needs in addition to the patient needs, rather than a sole focus on the patient (Hudson et al., 2006; Rolland & Walsh, 2005). The implementation of a biopsychosocial assessment instead of the limited biomedical assessment model results in dramatic differences in case planning. Recently a colleague informed me that her father was now in hospice care. She said her father is in the advanced stages of Alzheimer's and his recent physical crisis was so upsetting to him and his wife that the family is requesting there be no more medical emergencies. This kind of intervention is not part of treatment based on a biomedical model, but the plan of care adds to the quality of care and life for the patient, the patient's wife, and the adult children who care for them, by building on the strengths within their family system.

Assessment

Trained to assess and interact with culturally diverse systems, social workers are experienced in attending to the relationships. They identify sources of conflict and recognize the exchange of powerful dynamics between family members. It is good practice to assess patients and their relationships with their family caregivers (Acton & Carter, 2006; Family Caregiver Alliance, 2006a, 2006b). The systems theory interprets all change as systemic. Evaluations using this theory are more likely to predict the changes that occur in families due to chronic illness. Often family modification begins to occur when someone is first diagnosed with a disease, even if changes are rather unnoticeable and the effect on the family unit is subtle. When someone within a family is first diagnosed the changes may be rather simple such as adherence to a recommended diet, exercise changes, taking medications, or maybe periodic blood tests. These changes are frequently first initiated and controlled by the patient, but even these subtle changes are altering and cause changes within the entire family unit.

The Family Caregiver Alliance (2006a, 2006b) challenges health care professionals to regularly assess for caregiver needs as the condition of the patient changes. Social workers recognize the beliefs that interfere with recognition, understanding, and intervention for the needs of caregivers, including the belief that the caregiver is not the patient and it would be meddlesome of the social worker to intrude in their lives. Occasionally, social workers are leery of interacting with caregivers because they worry patients may lose attention if they are not the sole priority. Social workers are also concerned that they will have inadequate answers to caregiver questions and issues. Finally, there is worry that assessment of caregivers' needs will interfere in building a trusting rapport with them and take time away from obtaining the services needed for the patient (Family Caregiver Alliance, 2006a, 2006b).

Families are never spared from the influence of advanced chronic illness. Regardless of the health of family dynamics or the geographic distance between family members, a health crisis affects more than the person with the illness, it affects the family system. Failing to include the strengths and needs of patients' support systems in treatment planning often leads to eventual problems for patients and caregivers. The ability to succeed in the goals of care improves for the patient, the caregivers, and the health care team if all function together at maximum capacity. When social workers link with, encourage, support, and advocate for caregivers, they are listened to, acknowledged, and experience their worth to patient care. When stress is reduced for the caregiver, ultimately the patient experiences a reduction in worry about being a burden to the family.

The Family Caregiver Alliance (2006a, 2006b) suggests when health professionals assess caregivers, they benefit by following the guidelines listed in Box 10.1.

In addition, when completing a caregiver assessment, The Family Caregiver Alliance (2006a, 2006b) suggests the following seven categories of information offers crucial data to best understand caregivers' strengths and the areas that require additional support. The areas that enlighten the social worker through assessment are: (1) history of the caregiver and the caregiving relationship, (2) the caregiver's perception of the health and functional status of the patient, (3) the caregiver's values and preferences regarding everyday living and care provision, (4) the health and well-being of the caregiver, (5) the effects of caregiving on the caregiver, (6) the requirements of care provision, such as the necessary skills, abilities, and knowledge needed, and (7) the resources available to support the caregiver.

BOX 10.1 • *Categories for Assessment of Caregivers*

1. History of the caregiver and the caregiving relationship
2. Caregiver's perception of the health and functional status of the patient
3. Caregiver's values and preferences regarding everyday living and care provision
4. Health and well-being of the caregiver
5. Effects of caregiving on the caregiver
6. Requirements, skills, abilities, and knowledge needed to provide support
7. Resources available to support the caregiver

Source: Family Caregiver Alliance (2006a).

Emotional Support

Family caregivers need emotional support. They often lose their homes to medical equipment and hospital beds. Their lives become a series of appointments and tests. Caregivers no longer enjoy routine or spontaneity in their social lives because every day the goal is to provide the care the family members need. Families need emotional support because the U.S. health care system cannot provide the care necessary to people living with advanced chronic illness without their contribution.

Families are best helped when they are perceived as resilient (Rolland & Walsh, 2005). Instead of an assessment of problems and the damage to the family, social workers recognize families, although challenged, maintain their strengths. A resilient family is powerful and recovers from crisis and trauma (Walsh, 1998). When social workers assess patients and their caregivers, they encourage and motivate the family by identifying areas of strength and deconstructing barriers that lead to reductions in risk (Rolland & Walsh, 2005). Resilience is powerful and social workers create and offer family systems services that assist them to develop hope, opportunities, control, and a sense of power during a very helpless, hopeless, and powerless time in life.

Society often perceives death as the foe and insists on fighting the end of life with every resource possible. Families interact in the end-of-life care experience with patients and represent a critical resource during this exhausting and emotionally painful process. Many patients reach a point in their fight with disease when there is no longer the motivation to continue. Social workers can communicate clearly and effectively with family members around issues of care provision, support, and end-of-life and palliative care issues (Rabow et al., 2004; Way, Back, & Curtis, 2002). Despite the commitment of the family and the planning involved for end of life to occur at home as the illness advances, occasionally the actual end of life occurs in a hospital setting. The social worker communicates with the family as attempts to minimize patient distress occur through adequate pain control and other comfort measures and works to minimize the distress for family and continue to work for patient comfort (Waldrop, 2007; Way et al., 2002).

Caregivers, like patients, benefit by the presence of hope. An acquaintance was in the hospital after a dramatic abdominal surgery for cancer, for example. Later he learned that despite the surgery, tests showed cancer cells remained. The physician stated it was time to consider hospice. While his partner sat in the corner of the hospital room pained and huddled, the patient reported the news and stated, "There is no more hope." This is a frightening place to be in life, a place with no hope. Social workers remind patients and their families that hope should continue. A discussion with my friend, through tears, was about what things could now be hoped for. Hope for pain control, for his family to come together for him, for his partner to be able to accept the news, and for there to be adequate care options for the rest of his health care needs. Hope for the patient and his partner established realistic yet tender mutual goals. No more could they flail against the disease hoping to win health, but they could realistically begin to plan how they would use their time and energy in the most effective way to provide the best end-of-life care.

Evercare (2006) suggests programs developed to support the health and strength of the caregiver are successful if they accomplish one of the following four tasks: "1) preserve and save the caregiver time and energy, 2) relieve them from care giving responsibilities for any period of time, 3) reduce their level of stress, and 4) make them feel cared about and valued" (p. 7). As true with all social programs, interventions are effective only if the implementation of services truly match the needs of the target population. Issues about information, access, cost, and limitations benefit caregivers and offer social workers appropriate resources when they refer caregivers to supportive services.

Self-Care Support

Social workers assist caregivers to think about their own needs for care and support and teach them interventions they can use. For instance, many of the distressing feelings accompanying the provision of long-term caregiving are exacerbated by insomnia, disruptions in sleep, and restlessness. Feelings are perceived as particularly overwhelming when families do not have the emotional strength to put their feelings into context. Social workers assist caregivers to learn techniques that aid them in recognizing the results of sleep deprivation and assist them in finding ways to improve their sleep (Acton & Carter, 2006). Of course all interactions with caregivers must be provided in a culturally competent manner and because each family is a unique system, there is no quick and predictable intervention that effectively works with all families. There are, however, many ways that social workers can provide culturally respectful support to caregivers. The most common area of intervention is encouragement for caregivers to practice self-care. The social worker offers the caregiver information and training in the many ways they can reduce their personal stress, including setting goals, seeking solutions, communicating constructively, asking for and accepting help, talking to the health care team, exercise, and learning from expressed emotions (Family Caregiver Alliance, 2006a, 2006b).

Financial Support

Caregivers also need assistance to determine the most cost-effective ways to provide care. They need an advocate and creative thinker to assist them in understanding the benefits and limitations of the managed care system and to develop ways to access the services needed in an affordable way. Caregivers are expected to provide transportation, nursing care, emotional support, and personal care to family members. Social workers can be aware of new and old programs in the community. More than awareness, social workers can continue to press the issues regarding unmet needs for family caregivers to the service organizations best in position to alter and add to necessary services. Social workers in health care quickly understand the problems about home health care financing from the families' perspective. Frequent denials for various service reimbursements and inconsistent interpretations of policies and eligibility add to the stress of family members already overwhelmed physically, emotionally, and socially (Levine, 1999; Ho Yun et al., 2005).

Summary

Increasingly, there is momentum for health care professionals to integrate the biomedical model with the psychosocial model. Social workers are trained in the biopsychosocial model and ready to assess and provide support and partnership with patients using this holistic perspective. Social workers working in hospital settings, clinics, or counseling centers are more frequently developing specialty areas geared toward the treatment needs of patients and support to the caregivers affected by specific chronic illnesses, including the issues of diagnosis, health maintenance, and grief, loss, and bereavement (Rolland & Walsh, 2005). Families and caregivers require a variety of treatment arenas including hospitals, hospice centers, primary care clinics, and specialty clinics.

Social workers need to understand the needs of families and other caregivers. Family caregivers are at increased risk of physical, emotional, and social health problems. Exhausted family members are more prone to preventable health problems. Social workers must assess the caregivers for their ability to offer care to the family members, train caregivers to gain in their sense of competency, validate the caregiver role, include them in the health team planning, communicate clearly and effectively regarding questions and barriers to home care provision, and recognize the significant role they play in the health of their loved one and validate their grief, loss, and bereavement (Rabow, et al., 2004).

Critical Thinking Questions

1. What would you do if a family member needed full-time supportive care?

2. What area of functioning, physical, emotional, or social, would be most taxing for you if you were a full-time caregiver?

3. What kind of policies would benefit caregivers the most?

References

Acton, G. J., & Carter, P. A. (2006). Health promotion research: Addressing the needs of older adults and their caregivers. *Journal of Gerontological Nursing, 32*(2), 5.

Aneshensel, C. S., Botticello, A. L., & Yamamoto-Mitani, N. (2004). When caregiving ends: The course of depressive symptoms after bereavement. *Journal of Health and Social Behavior, 45*(4), 422–440.

Bell, H. (2003). Strengths and secondary trauma in a family violence work. *Social Work, 48*(4), 513–523.

Bride, B. E., Robinson, M. M., Yegidis, B., & Figley, C. R. (2004). Development and validation of the secondary traumatic stress scale. *Research on Social Work Practice, 14*(1), 27–35.

Conway-Giustra, F., Crowley, A., & Gorin, S. H. (2002). Crisis in caregiving: A call to action. *Health and Social Work, 27*(4), 307–312.

Dumont, S., Turgeon, J., Allard, P., Gagnon, P., Charbonneau, C. & Vezina, L. (2006). Caring for a loved one with advanced cancer: Determinants of psychological distress in family caregivers. *Journal of Palliative Medicine, 9,* 912–921.

Evercare (2006). *Evercare study of caregivers in decline: Findings from a national survey.* Retrieved September 11, 2008, from http://www.EvercareHealthPlans.com

Family Caregiver Alliance. (2006a). *Caregivers count too! A toolkit to help practitioners assess the needs of family caregivers.* Retrieved September 11, 2008, from http://www.caregiver.org/caregiver/jsp/content_node.jsp?nodeid=1695

Family Caregiver Alliance. (2006b). *Caregivers at risk.* Retrieved September 11, 2008, from http://www.caregiver.org/ caregiver/jsp/print_friendly.jsp?nodeid=1003

Frankel, V. E. (1984). *Man's search for meaning.* Boston: Beacon Press.

Gayomali, C., Sutherland, S., & Finkelstein, F. O. (2008). The challenge for the caregiver of the patient with chronic kidney disease. *Nephrology, Dialysis, Transplantation, 23*(12), 3749–3752.

Geller, J. A., Madsen, L. H., & Ohrenstein, L. (2004). Secondary trauma: A team approach. *Clinical Social Work Journal, 32*(4), 415–430.

Goldstein, N. E., & Fischberg, D. (2008). Update in palliative medicine. *Annals of Internal Medicine, 148*(2), 135–141.

Goldsworthy, B., & Knowles, S. (2008). Caregiving for Parkinson's disease patient: An exploration of a stress-appraisal model for quality of life and burden. *Psychological Sciences and Social Sciences, 63B*(6), P372–P377.

Gopalan, N., & Brannon, L. A. (2006). Increasing family members' appreciation of family caregiving stress. *Journal of Psychology, 140*(2), 85–94.

Grbich, C., Parker, D., & Maddocks, I. (2001). The emotions and coping strategies of caregivers of family members with a terminal illness. *Journal of Palliative Care, 17*(1), 30–42.

Hesse, A. R. (2002). Secondary trauma: How working with trauma survivors affects therapists. *Clinical Social Work Journal, 30*(3), 293–309.

Ho Yun, Y., Sun Rhee, Y., Ok Kang, I., Suk Lee, J., Mee Bang, S., Sup Lee, W., et al. (2005). Economic burdens and quality of life of family caregivers of cancer patients. *Oncology, 68,* 107–114.

Hudson, P. L., Hayman-White, K., Arand, S., & Kristjanson, L. (2006). Predicting family caregiver psychosocial functioning in palliative care. *Journal of Palliative Care, 22*(3), 133–141.

Levine, C. (1999). The loneliness of the long-term care giver. *New England Journal of Medicine, 340*(20), 1587–1591.

Logsdon, R. G. (2008). Dementia: Psychosocial interventions for family caregivers. *The Lancet, 372*(9634), 182–184.

Minton, M. E., & Barron, C. R. (2008). Spousal bereavement assessment: A review of bereavement-specific measures. *Journal of Gerontological Nursing, 34*(8), 34–49.

Mitrani, V. B., Lewis, J. E., Feaster, D. J., Czaja, S. J., Eisdorfer, C., Schulz, R., et al. (2006). The role of family functioning in the stress process of dementia caregivers: A structural family framework. *The Gerontologist, 46*(1), 97–105.

Montague, J. (1994). Averting burnout crucial to health of caregiver, hospital survival. *Hospitals and Health Networks, 68*(15*)*, 178.

Pitsenberger, D. J. (2006). Juggling work and elder caregiving: Work-life balance for aging American workers. *American Association of Health Nurses, 54*(4), 181–187.

Rabow, M. W., Hauser, J. M., & Adams, J. (2004). Supporting family caregivers at the end of life: "They don't know what they don't know." *Journal of the American Medical Association, 291*(4), 483–491.

Raingruber, B., & Kent, M. (2003). Attending to embodied responses: A way to identify practice-based and human meanings associated with secondary trauma. *Qualitative Health Research, 13*(4), 449–468.

Rappaport, H., Fossler, R. J., Bross, L. S., & Gilden, D. (1993). Future time, death anxiety, and life purpose among older adults. *Death Studies, 17,* 369–379.

Rees, J., O'Boyle, C., & MacDonagh, R. (2001). Quality of life: Impact of chronic illness on the partner. *Journal of the Royal Society, 94*(11), 563–566.

Rodway, M. R. (1986). Systems theory. In F.J. Turner (Ed.), *Social work treatment* (3rd ed., pp. 514–540). New York: Free Press.

Rolland, J. S., & Walsh, F. (2005). Systemic training for healthcare professionals: The Chicago center for family health approach. *Family Process, 44*(3), 283–301.

Stroebe, M., Schut, H., & Stroebe, W. (2007). Health outcomes of bereavement. *The Lancet, 370*(9603), 1960–1974.

Vohre, J. U., & Szala-Meneok, K. (2006). The last word: Family members' descriptions of end-of-life care in long-term care facilities. *Journal of Palliative Care, 22*(1), 33–39.

Waldrop, D. P. (2007). Caregiver grief in terminal illness and bereavement: A mixed-methods study. *Health and Social Work, 32*(3), 197–207.

Walsh, F. (1998). *Strengthening family resilience.* New York: Guilford Press.

Way, J., Back, A. L., & Curtis, R. (2002). Withdrawing life support and resolution of conflict with families. *British Medical Journal, 325,* 1342–1345.

Part III

Social Work, Health Care, and Professionalism

Health care policies determine the ways people access health care and provide the guidelines for the practice of health care. Policies determine the kind of care, the degree of care, the care provider, and the patient. Although policies never guarantee that the services provided through the health care programs solve the social problems they seek to address, they may improve health care when the people who provide the services work together as committed and ethical professionals.

Social workers in health care settings attempt to provide care to the populations the setting is designed to help. Unfortunately, there are frequently barriers to the transmission of services, such as inadequate or unpredictable funding and failure to accurately assess the needs of the community at risk. But social workers often create positive change, despite the barriers. Sometimes positive change occurs due to alteration of political or programmatic actions, and sometimes the changes are measured by one patient with improved quality of life. A professional social worker seeks opportunities to improve social systems despite the challenges. Social workers are trained to access a variety of professional skills that enable them to treat the patient, provide support to the caregivers, and influence social systems to provide the community resources needed for improved health.

The social work profession has the heart, the mission, the skills, and the commitment that is necessary to challenge and offer leadership for change to the health care system in the United States. Social workers advocate and continue to challenge systems to institute ethical change while at the same time they continue to care for those who face the reality of fractured care.

There are some very clear strategies for social workers to maintain their professionalism in the face of a daunting dysfunctional delivery system. This part examines the ways social workers achieve relief from despair and improve practice during times of relentless systemic change. Social workers benefit from a strong code of ethics and maintenance of boundaries.

They practice critical thought and assess situations and people with an understanding that systems, cultures, and values influence the way people believe, feel, and act. Supervision is an invaluable resource to assist social workers to practice self-care and self-assessment, challenge unrealistic goals, and assist in the incremental progress that will result in positive professional change. Social workers attempt to be acquainted with the growing body of knowledge regarding methods and interventions that achieve positive results. They accomplish this through sharing research and assessment results with other health professionals and by examining and practicing methods of intervention shown to be beneficial through the work of colleagues.

Social workers must continue to educate health care teams about the role of social work and ensure their professionalism through licensing and certification. Despite an academic degree, professionalism is not a guarantee, but social workers committed to the important work associated with making change stand ready to think and act in ways that empower others to experience the best health care possible.

11

Ethical Considerations

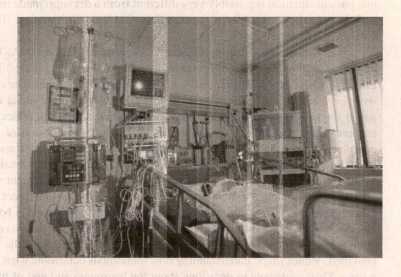

Teaching and Learning Goals

- Recognize how the National Association of Social Workers Code of Ethics shapes professional social work
- Understand the need to resolve conflicts in an ethical manner
- Recognize the role of personal and professional values in decision making

The role of ethical decision making is the foundation of professional social work. Attention to ethical practice is growing in all professions throughout the United States and seminars and conferences on topics such as patients' rights and ethics are conducted regularly (Davidson, 2005; Haas & Sheehan, 2008; Heifetz, 1996). Training on these topics is often required content for continuing education for professional licensure. Professional social work education requires the ethical training necessary before students begin their field education classes.

Education and training in the practice of professional ethics is essential to build and maintain healthy relationships with clients and colleagues (Landau, 2008; Reamer, 2003). Ethical practice and professional codes guide decision making and play a key role in the professional standards applied to social work conduct codes. Using professional ethical standards improves professional awareness and helps social workers recognize when personal values interfere with professional values (Marsh, 2003).

The development and standardization of professional conduct and decision-making codes attempts to ensure health professionals make good, sound, and safe professional decisions that preserve the rights of patients. In the profession of social work the process of assessment and evaluation may reveal challenging moral or legal issues that require an intelligent and rational approach. The ability to think critically is essential because there are never two practice situations that are exactly the same. An ethically sound decision in one patient situation is possibly very different from a decision made in another patient situation, regardless of apparent similarities (Giddens, Ka'opua, & Tomaszewski, 2000; Gossett & Weinman, 2007).

The National Association of Social Workers Code of Ethics (NASW; 1999) is the standard used by professional social workers throughout the United States. The NASW Code of Ethics serves several clear purposes for professional development. The code identifies social work core values, summarizes broad ethical principles to guide social work practice, helps social workers identify relevant considerations when faced with ethical conflicts, provides accountability standards, assists in the retraining and socialization of social workers, and articulates the standards necessary to monitor and regulate the social work profession.

Social workers in health care must be aware of their professional commitment to the Code of Ethics and recognize the need for sound principled judgment when dilemmas and conflicts arise. Practice with culturally diverse populations guarentees that social workers must be prepared to recognize and honor the differences in values based on a variety of cultural norms. Values influence how professionals, patients, caregivers, organizations, and communities see the world, including the values associated with the ways health care is provided. Values shape understanding how individuals determine what is right, and what is wrong. They contribute to decisions about the beginning and end of life and relationships with technology and other health-related services and products (Cagle & Kovacs, 2009). Social workers must be prepared to resolve professional conflicts through clearly designed and systematic steps.

Ethics

Simply stated, ethics are the rules of conduct for moral behaviors. Personal ethics are shaped through the values regarding human behavior taught within cultures. Because values and experiences vary among and within cultures, there are conflicting interpretations about what is right and what is wrong. Families socialize, teach, model, and reinforce values and are influenced by many unique cultural variables. Ethical decision making is not following a system of rules, but is a prism of the ideal used to help individuals and groups make determinations. Values inform individuals about the morals, integrity, and scruples embedded in the situations they encounter and results in the imposition of principled decision making (Corey, Corey, & Callahan, 1998; Heifetz, 1996).

Ethics are based on a code of conduct that recognizes that the beliefs and attitudes people hold result in innumerable yet credible ways to resolve a conflict or solve a problem. People have vastly different opinions about what is considered ethical behavior. Although unique values are taught within cultures, decisions based on those beliefs do not necessarily apply to others and application of personal values do not guarantee ethical behaviors. Following a code of ethics does not necessarily resolve the conflicts inherent within a dilemma. For instance, social workers value the right for patients to decide their course of health, illness, and healing; however, there are certain circumstances when supporting patients' decisions can lead to an ethical conflict for social workers.

The NASW Code of Ethics (1999) is an attempt to capture the goals, principles, and standards that guide social work practice. A common foundation of knowledge, cultures, values, and experiences unites individuals through a code of philosophical principles for the profession.

The challenges associated with ethical practice are part of social work history and were discussed by some of the earliest social workers. Jane Addams witnessed the failure of society to protect children from the "sweating system" of child labor and clearly understood that the torturous systems of child labor were at odds with the cultural values shared by the working families in Chicago and with social work values. Addams (1910) stated, "While we found many pathetic cases of child labor and hard-driven victims of the sweating system who could not possibly earn enough in the short of the year, it became evident that we must add carefully collected information to our general impression of neighborhood conditions if we would make it of any genuine value" (p. 200). Recognizing the injustice, Addams was ethically challenged by the practice of child labor. The ethical dilemma challenged societal principles and Addams took action by reporting child labor conditions and advocating for the legislative changes that led to the first Child Labor Act.

As advocates for social justice, particularly for populations that are often disenfranchised and abused by society, social workers possess firsthand knowledge of the ethical challenges faced by individuals and communities. Health care is a societal issue charged with emotion and driven by the values associated with conditions that determine life and death. The seemingly powerful and privileged health care institutions, combined with societal values that can reveal an indifference to the growing number of under- and uninsured millions in the United States, further ignite dialogue about health care. Ethical dilemmas are often associated with extremes, or a distance in the continuum of moral values in society. In the health care debate, the differences in cultural or individual values influence the availability of medical technology, growing health care costs, and rationing of health-related goods and services (Haas & Sheehan, 2008).

An understanding of the beliefs and values that influence the practice of medicine are important in the discussion of delivering health care. Divisive personal and political debates about moral topics in society regularly steal media attention. Battles about the "rights and wrongs" on issues such as abortion, right to die, euthanasia, beginning of life decisions, and stem cell transplantation are value-laden and very emotional for individuals and communities. Heifetz (1996) notes these debates are especially difficult because the U.S., while promoting the separation of church and state in its government, continues to develop policies strongly influenced by a variety of religious dogmas and doctrines. Although the population of the United States is culturally, religiously, and socially diverse, federal legislative bodies, the judicial system, and the executive bodies that create laws and develop important political positions are primarily influenced by a homogenous group with similar intersections of cultures: white, Christian, male, and economically secure.

The role of ethics emerged in the medical systems during the 1960s. The advancement in dialogue regarding ethical decision making was in response to the growth and widespread success of the medical research community, particularly in response to new technologies. The apparent neverending development and selection of medications, treatments, and other medical machinery demanded new ways to make decisions regarding patients' care and growing costs. The new era offered multiple options for patients' treatment and challenged the health care system to consider the dilemma: If a medical intervention exists, under what circumstances should it be considered? Decisions about using limited and expensive medical resources, or rationing, called for the development of a consistently applied set of guidelines to influence the decisions.

Provision of ethical health care must also consider the cultural beliefs associated with the cost of health care. Health care in the United States is not a national right and is not equally distributed among citizens. The ability to pay for health care strongly influences who gets medical treatment and the type and quality of the interventions received. People living in poverty may have little to no access to health care and middle-class and upper-middle-class families stand to lose all of their savings and resources if faced with the cost of life-saving interventions (Cagle & Kovacs, 2009). While managed care attempts to curb the relentless rise of health care costs, some important ethical dilemmas remain about the decisions made regarding insurance reimbursement for health interventions.

Society wrestles with some very difficult questions about health care. Who decides if someone receives a high-cost/high-risk treatment? Who pays for expensive treatments? How do we make fair decisions about access to limited medical resources? Who defines quality of life for a patient? The avalanche of medical possibilities for treatments creates a dizzying array of options, but does everyone have the same choices? Is equity ever possible?

Making ethical decisions is complicated. For instance, when someone is considered for an intervention using a scarce resource, such as in the case of many organ transplants, most do not want to consider that the variables of age, disease, risk, or potential of the patients' success are part of medical decision making. The decision about who receives the organ transplant determines the individuals given a chance to live longer and better. This form of ethical equation, to give or to withhold medical treatments, is a collision of cultural values (Johnson, 2006). Decisions that determine how limited resources are used poses serious challenges to the decision-makers found in hospital and medical ethic committees and reflect the challenges society faces.

There is no way that every treatment of potential benefit possible can be provided to everyone. The limits on medical intervention options are determined by costs; this is one of the most challenging situations for health legislators to resolve. Ironically, most professionals attracted to work in health care systems chose their profession because they want to design and offer care to improve the health of everyone. Physicians, nurses, and social workers do not enter health care to "sell" their professional care to those with adequate financial resources. Most health care practitioners are personally uninterested in the economic status of their patients. However, health care workers today, particularly in professional private practice settings, must know and care about the insurance and the financial resources of their patients, because without these payments, the practice will go bankrupt. Frequently the expectation to pay for medical services is vital in medical offices and this can place family doctors and other private office physicians in the unenviable position of appearing to discriminate based on a patient's ability to pay. All health care systems practice forms of care based on the patient's ability to pay.

Beneficence and nonmaleficence are two unfamiliar words that are most frequently used in the medical profession, but the words serve as a guide to physicians and are applicable to social workers, too. Beneficence is the ethical commitment that health treatment will provide some measure of good to the patient, and nonmaleficence is the ethical commitment to not harm a patient. These professional conduct commitments are simplistically stated but clarify the basic principles expected when treating patients. Values define what a patient considers "good" or "harm" so if health service delivery is insensitive or unaware of the context of the patient's cultural definitions, the treatment or care is apt to leave the patient feeling unsatisfied. Expectations of good health care are not interpreted the same way in all cultures and only by the assessment of the unique needs of patients and their support systems will health care social workers accurately identify the potential struggles between conflicting values of professional care providers and the personal values of the patients. This knowledge best supports the health providers' commitment to ethical behavior (Giddens et al., 2000).

Health care workers recognize the vulnerability of patients as one of the chief unifying issues within all ethical dilemmas. Physicians and other health care workers must practice within their professional principles and seek to do the best for patients and caregivers while protecting the patient from experiencing harm. For instance, social work values include the commitment to the patient's right to confidentiality, self-determination, and informed consent. Offering patients the information necessary to make "good" decisions about their medical treatments and pain control is essential to ethical care (Latimer, 1998), yet the culturally right choice for the patient may dramatically differ with the choice of the health care system.

National Association of Social Workers Code of Ethics

Social workers witness potential ethical dilemmas emerge every day in the health care system. It is tempting to believe all health care professionals assess and intervene in ethical conflicts in homogenous ways, but within a short period of time, social workers in health care soon realize all of the variations in problem solving that exist (Gossett & Weinman, 2007; Murdach, 2009; Sparks, 2006). Social workers are members of health teams comprised of health care professionals and they offer valuable and unique perspectives while recognizing each discipline brings valid issues to consider in the resolution of ethical conflicts.

Values are as personally unique as any human experience. For instance, even if two people are members of the same family, their experiences, memories, and relationships are never exactly the same. Similarly, no two people ever believe exactly the same thing, even if there are strong similarities. So when there is a question about the "right" and "wrong" regarding a set of circumstances within a health-related situation, there are many points of disagreement and agreement; differences may be minor or extreme. Circumstances are never exactly the same between similar situations, so values and professional conduct codes advise and inform the decisions. A professional code of ethics is not a set of rules that can be applied to any situation, but instead serves as a source to decision-makers for interpretation of the dilemma. Ethical decision making is a process and does not guarantee the unity or equal satisfaction of individuals making the decisions. Making an ethical decision relies on the thoughtful examination of all problem-solving options and an application of an informed and strategic process to determine resolution (Sparks, 2006).

The professional code of ethics for social workers is intended to guide all decision making and professional behaviors, from the most seasoned professional to the bachelor-level social work student. The professional code is applicable to all fields of social work practice and steers professional behavior within all forms of relationships. The code offers social workers leadership and direction when practicing both routine social work practice or when confronted with ethical dilemmas. As with any application of a framework for conduct, there are no easy answers or precise rules that offer social workers perfect solutions. Instead, the code of ethics depends on the social worker to honestly, accurately, and critically assess a situation in context (Gossett & Weinman, 2007; Murdach, 2009). Conflicts occur, in part, due to the wide variety of cultural standards within human relationships (NASW, 1999).

The NASW Code of Ethics (1999) contributes a valuable asset to the social work profession by concisely defining the profession's unique purpose as well as identifying the core values of the profession: service, social justice, dignity and worth of the person, importance of human relationships, integrity, and competence. These values are powerful and complex concepts and support the need for social workers to give thoughtful and considerate attention to the responsibilities associated with each value.

One significant ethical issue for social workers is the concept of boundaries. Boundaries are closely connected to the social work core value regarding the importance of human relationships (Davidson, 2005; Landau, 2008; Reamer, 2003). Social workers are in a powerful professional position that allows them access to private and personal information. Through contact with patients, social workers often know and understand the vulnerabilities and circumstances regarding the patient they interact with. This level of relationship and communication is intimate, yet the level of vulnerability is not equal. The patient does not have equal access to information about the social worker. How do social workers interact with patients on such an intimate level and maintain ethical and professional behavior? The Code of Ethics (1999) states clearly that sexual relationships between a social worker and patient are inappropriate under all circumstances, but there are many other forms of relationships that develop, and exactly what does "sexual" mean? How does a social worker determine the appropriateness of a professional relationship with a patient? When is a relationship "right" and when is it "wrong"? Read the following scenario and consider the ethical issues within the relationship.

Scenario 11:1

Beth worked as a social worker in an Acquired Immunodeficiency Syndrome (AIDS) clinic for 10 years. Mark was one of the first clients she met and the first to tell Mark he tested positive for human immunodeficiency virus (HIV). Beth interacted with Mark for many years. Occasionally a physical or emotional challenge in Mark's HIV status would propel him to schedule an appointment or series of appointments to talk to Beth about his challenges with psychosocial issues. Over the years, Beth learned a great deal about the personal life of Mark. She knew about his sexual relationships, family members, family history, and his struggle with being gay and HIV-positive. Eventually Beth left her position at the clinic for other employment.

Several years later, Mark saw Beth at a grocery store and asked her if she wanted to have lunch. Beth considered her past relationship with Mark, but because 4 years had passed, she agreed to meet him for lunch. At lunch Mark briefly talked about his health, as he did openly with everyone he knew, but most of the conversation was reciprocal. Mark taught Beth about a cell phone option she was interested in and they shared conversation about other casual and friendly topics. The next week Mark called Beth and offered to bring her with him to the telephone store to teach her about her cell-phone options. Beth and her husband and children knew Mark since he annually brought Halloween candy to their home for the children. Mark's partner knew Beth and her family from accompanying Mark on these visits. Beth and Mark also saw each other at the big urban church they both attended. Mark and his partner called one day and asked if Beth and her husband wanted to accompany them to a musical performance the following weekend.

Are there ethical issues in this scenario? How do you ethically assess this relationship? Is there information about this relationship that you still need to know? What additional information would better inform your evaluation? Would you challenge this relationship as being inappropriate? Defend you answers.

As you consider the answers, remember, Beth knows much more about Mark than Mark knows about Beth. Beth was the recipient of years of confidential information and history about Mark and the power relationship between them is not equal. Beth is not in a professional relationship with Mark now, and has not been for many years. Beth and Mark enjoy each other's company. The exact circumstances of this case are unique but are relevant for understanding the subtleties of ethically challenging situations.

Human Rights

Humans are more globally connected than ever before. The methods of communication drive radical new sources for information-sharing that results in exposure to remote and unfamiliar cultures throughout the world. New communication methods reveal the inequities of circumstances for people in ways that were previously unknown. This is particularly true in the area of health. The poorest in the world possess the least amount of social power and as a result are least able to influence their relationship with health. People with the highest socioeconomic status are most likely to experience the best levels of physical, emotional, and social health and as a result are most likely to live the longest (Benatar, Daar, & Singer, 2003; Mann, 1997).

United States citizens tend to limit their understanding of health and health care to the services provided by the nation's medical community. Unfortunately, this ethnocentric perspective regarding the relationship between health and medicine is also used to shape the national and global health care debate. Throughout the world, including the U.S., medical services represent only a small portion of the health care support and interventions that influence the lives of individuals. Public health conditions strongly rely on the environmental, political, and social conditions that exist within societies. For instance, conditions such as poverty, access to uncontaminated water, and exposure to natural disasters influence community health. Countries that experience the most poverty are likely to experience the most health problems. Richer countries are more likely to spend money on disease prevention, health promotion, access to medical care, and other infrastructure-related strategies to support the health of citizens. The reality is, many factors influence the health of national populations, but poverty remains a significant contributor to poorer health and shorter life (Hessler & Buchanan, 2002; Mann, 1997).

There are many international organizations that monitor and advocate for the ethical issues related to global health. The practice of international health advocacy is a principled imperative based on the values that recognize the priority of human relationships with individuals and within the global community. Some international health organizations use strategic guidelines to monitor and influence access to health care on behalf of people living with inadequate resources and no power or privilege to change these conditions. Three international organizations that advocate for global health issues include the United Nations, the International Organization of Medical Services, and the World Health Organization.

The ethics pertaining to human rights and to health care access form a natural relationship. The United Nations offers leadership on the international stage with the creation of the Universal Declaration of Human Rights and it expounds the principles of health and well-being for all. The declaration reflects unifying principles regarding human rights that are shared by many cultures, traditions, and values. Eleanor Roosevelt passionately advocated for countries to take responsibility for the poor health of disenfranchised populations throughout the world. International conventions bind participating governments of member countries that commit to protect the basic right of health. The declaration advances the recognition that health and medical care are not synonymous, and health is the public and community value invested in the prevention of disease and preservation of the human spirit (Gruskin & Dickens, 2006).

When the Declaration of Human Rights was created in 1948, it served to form a statement of the shared values for international powers regarding the assumptions pertaining to the human condition. Ethical health care is broadly defined as recognition of the complex blend of individual, community, national, and international environments affecting the biological, emotional, and social factors of human beings. However, much of the world is challenged to provide such support to improved health even when the values and ethical significance of this commitment is recognized. Many people continue to suffer from poverty, environmental, and political assaults.

The responsibility of health care is not regulated to one profession or one country, yet globally, health care is affected by the actions of all who have power and privilege. Social workers can be part of the core changes needed to create more equitable global health care as a tenant of basic human rights. Currently, the goals of the Universal Declaration of Human Rights remain unrealized, so calls for international powers to recognize their shared values and make ethical global health policies remain vital (Benatar et al., 2003; Gruskin & Dickens, 2006).

The International Organization of Medical Services provide an additional perspective on the ethical issues regarding global health. In the organization's five-point agenda, Gruskin and Dickens (2006) identify a guideline for the ethical review of the global patterns and development of disease. The five points include the identification of nations' investment in the following mandates: (1) promote population health, (2) strengthen public health systems and recognize the power of public health, (3) finance public health,

(4) demand health services provide both prevention and successful responses to preventable disease, and (5) monitor the human right implications of all policies that influence global health conditions.

Social workers understand that the application of health, in the many ways health is understood, includes the recognition that poverty, stigmatization, and other cultural and environmental factors influence health. The power of global public health efforts to improve health conditions is powerful in the prevention of unhealthy conditions such as unsafe drinking water, unhealthy sewage disposal, and unsafe work environments. However, public health is only effective if empowered through political support and funding. All nations struggle with conflicting values, priorities, and needs that compete with the significant resources required to fund and sustain health improvements. For instance, when public health efforts are supported and successful, there is an improvement in the prevention of acute and chronic illness resulting in better quality of life and increased longevity. The ethical dilemma is often implementation of public health measures that improve the life of the community or spending money and resources to combat other significant barriers to improved life such as politics, war, cultural marginalization of groups, ignorance and suspicion of disease prevention methods, and poverty. Underlying all global health efforts, monitoring of health-related policy is critical. This means all health policy must be created to influence and improve global health including environmental policies, agricultural developments, political affiliations, economic globalization, and international trade (Gruskin & Dickens, 2006).

In addition, the World Health Organization (WHO) is another well-known and active participant in the movement toward improved global health. The organization was established in 1948 as a result of the formation of the United Nations in 1945 and the shared national interests in improved global health. Discussions about a global health organization eventually led to the development of WHO. International membership in WHO is voluntary and the invitation is extended to all nations with membership in the United Nations. Members of WHO accept the constitution of the organization and are approved by a majority vote by the World Health Assembly. In 2007, there were 193 member States (WHO, 2006).

The WHO Constitution explicates the organizational values pertaining to the international recognition of the rights to health for all. The Constitution's Preamble states; "The enjoyment of the highest attainable standard of health is one of the fundamental rights of every human being without distinction of race, political belief, economic or social condition" (July 22, 1946). This value is the foundation for the existence of WHO and drives the organization's commitment to recognize all national policies have the potential to influence global health. WHO monitors and supports the values and mission of the organization and through the goals of a six-point agenda: (1) promoting development; (2) encouraging health security; (3) strengthening health systems; (4) harnessing research, information, and evidence; (5) enhancing partnerships; and (6) improving performance (WHO, 2006).

The World Health Organization educates the world about the role poverty plays in dismal health outcomes and works to promote economic and social progress. Equity, a critical ethical principle, drives WHO to promote quality and quantity of life by improving health care access for populations frequently denied access to prevention, treatment, and attention to the development of disease. The organization acts as a resource for the collection of research and information with the understanding that no nation is capable of stopping health threats in isolation. The threat of disease is most significant for the nations least able to provide trained medical professionals, collect data, and finance the resources necessary to access the necessary drugs and technology. The organization connects needs to services and works to nourish partnerships between nations, international organizations, charities, foundations, and other interested partners. They offer a vital role as a centralized point to share supplies and resources, both financial and human, and offer education and information about evidence-based practice and best standards for health practices. As WHO monitors the ethical practice of global health, it also evaluates the ethics of internal organizational policies and processes to ensure efficient and effective responses to global health concerns (WHO, 2006).

International or global ethics provide a basis for broad agreement that a basic and shared human value is a right to health. From a human rights perspective, the global ethics pertaining to health reflect a philosophy that charges all nations with the responsibility to provide access to the vulnerable and recognizes the effect of global and national actions on the health of the poor and disenfranchised around the world.

Ethical Conflicts

The practice of ethics is not as simple. Jayasundra (2004) defines ethics as the philosophy of morality. Ethical practice is an attempt to determine if actions are just in terms of obligations to individuals, groups, and communities. When an ethically challenging set of circumstances is identified as a dilemma, it is frequently a situation that offers two or more choices for action, often represent opposing, competing, or rival values. Dilemmas appear to offer no clear plan of resolution that will result in a satisfactory answer (Loewenberg, Dolgoff, & Harrington, 2000). Ethical dilemmas occur with regularity in the emotionally charged field of health care.

Despite the incredible progress of medicine to improve health, society is still lagging behind in how to interpret the results and repercussions of the innumerable treatment options and opportunities (Sparks, 2006). Progress in the efficacy of medical treatments has increased the ethical challenges of society to make decisions that determine how, when, where, why, and what to do regarding patients' treatment. Ethical dilemmas are at the heart of treatment decisions. The potential for ethical issues exist in all health care settings for social workers, particularly when working closely with patients and their families. There are frequently decisions made regarding quality of life issues, privacy, confidentiality, interpersonal conflicts, disclosure, value conflicts, rationing of health care and medical treatment options (Csikai, 2004).

It is common for hospitals to rely on institutional ethics committees to aid with decisions when value dilemmas are identified (Csikia, 2004; Heifetz, 1996; Johnson, 2006). Although ethics committees are not mandated for hospital accreditation by the Joint Commission on the Accreditation of Health Care Organizations (JCAHO), hospitals form these professional groups to exhibit compliance with ethical practice standards and offering professionals a forum for the review of hospital policies, review of cases, and educational opportunities to staff on the process of ethical decision making. Ethics committees are important in their influence on quality of care decisions (Csikia, 2004).

Dilemmas are assigned to an ethics committee for resolution, particularly when there is no recognition of a common solution recognized. The lack of consensus is sometimes due to inadequate policies or other guidelines for decision making. Ethics committees assist in formulating standards and help professionals determine ways to resolve ethical dilemmas. The committees convene regularly to determine the balance between the possibilities and compassion (Johnson, 2006). Frequently hospitals appoint staff from a variety of disciplines to serve on ethics committees and encourage discussions from multiple perspectives to inform decisions about medical challenges. The multidisciplinary blend of committee members strengthens the discussion about ethics and values because it represents a variety of principles and ways of knowing. The professional disciplines, all with unique ethical codes for conduct and the provision of patient care, are represented and their input considered. Social workers are commonly members of health organizations' ethics committees. The utilization of ethics committees is considered an excellent way to increase the likelihood of reaching the best possible ethical decision (Csikia, 2004; Johnson, 2006).

Cultural Differences

Values influence all that individuals do and despite attempts at consensus, the uniqueness of individuals makes this impossible. The distinctive multicultural makeup of individuals is never reduced to one common set of predictable ways to understand morality. There are significant challenges to the appreciation of cultural pluralism in the United States and threats and challenges to equality for anyone who acts, appears, believes, or thinks in ways that are unique. Individuals may offer verbal respect for differences, but discrimination, stigmatization, and racism remain significant threats to equality. This inequity is particularly true when examined in light of access to health care and is often recognized in the treatment of individuals within the health system.

Many variables influence how people interpret ethical behavior and at minimum the cultural traits of religiosity, spirituality, ethnic culture, geographic region, gender, and age influence how personally "right" decisions are made. People believe and prioritize the elements of life that vary by family, class, and the many other cultural memberships (Miley, O'Melia, & DuBois, 2009). When discussions about ethics take place, the dimensions of decision making are framed within varying beliefs, attitudes, and opinions. Ethical discussions require clear communication about personal values on issues, the rationale for positions, and most importantly, the ability to hear others' interpretations and values regarding their positions. Without shared dialogue the development of a plan to respect the rights of the patient is impaired (Healy, 2003).

Ka'opua (1992) offers guidelines for social workers to move through a decision-making process with individuals that do not share personal values. The DIVERSE model offers simple yet essential steps for providing respect to others to practice self-determination and suggests the essential ingredient to making decisions is to understand and respect the patient's worldview. The steps of this model follow the acronym of the word DIVERSE: Do take time, Involve cultural consultants, Vary strategies, Elicit differences, Reserve judgment, Seek to negotiate, Everyone has a culture (Ka'opua, 1992).

When social workers take the time to ask and listen, they increase the opportunity to learn about the unique values of the patient. The values of the patient are the values that most inform the health care system in resolution of ethical dilemmas. In addition, the model offers an opportunity for social workers to check with others within unfamiliar cultures and honors their expertise to interpret and educate social workers about what they are hearing and observing. Social workers recognize that routine ways of intervention are not effective or desired by members of all cultures. Understanding the cultural fit of interventions assists social workers to think creatively and critically about the needs of patients and caregivers. When differences are discovered between the cultures of social workers, patients, and caregivers, there is an opportunity to discuss differences, share perspectives, and listen to the values of the patient (Ka'opua, 1992).

When assessments are done strategically and respectfully, the interactions can serve to strengthen relationships and communication. Social workers bring their unique personal and cultural values to their work in health care and those values are influenced by the professional code of ethics. But cultural differences between patients and social workers do not require moral judgments regarding cultural values, ethics, and accompanying decisions. Often frank and safe discussions about culturally related value differences are open to some mutually agreeable options, especially when information and options are presented in a way that further empowers the patient and caregiver. The cultural diversity within the health care system is staggering when one considers the staff, patients, and caregivers as intersecting, each with unique cultural values (Ka'opua, 1992).

Attention to the diversity in values is a significant part of social work care. International conflicts give evidence of the conflicts that occur when people interact with others based on disrespect, suspicion, fear, and anger due to the differences in values. Social workers are in a role that offers opportunities to model respect for the different behaviors, beliefs, and values that exist in both health professions and patients and to advocate for new and improved methods of collaboration despite value differences (Heifetz, 1996).

Well-intended social workers risk treating patients and caregivers in paternalistic ways when their personal values to "do good" interfere with the ability to listen to the values of the patient. Ignorance of others' beliefs increases the risk of imposing personal values on others. The imposition, although presumably born from good intentions, is offered as a gift, but results in patients and caregivers experiencing substandard care and leaves both social workers and patients unsatisfied with the interactions. The imposition of personal values wastes an incredibly valuable opportunity to design culturally effective interactions and interferes with ethical social work practice (Heifetz, 1996).

Value Differences

One important way to understand the values of others is to understand personal values. This is a reoccurring theme in social work education, regardless of the field of practice. By understanding how personal values developed and how they continue to influence your life takes careful consideration and thoughtful and honest reflection (Miley, et al., 2009). The discovery of those values is important, but so is the journey. When social workers understand their values and why those values exist, they are more likely to understand why they react to situations the way they do. For instance, when a patient chooses to continue with a high-risk pregnancy despite overwhelming odds of severe disability, perhaps the social worker believes the pregnancy should be terminated. What personal values is the social worker responding to? Without further reflection, they risk interacting with the patient from their personal set of values. Ethical decisions are emotional and evoke strong feelings, both for patients and social workers. Social workers can provide patients with equal access to all relevant information and address concerns and considerate ways that allow patients to make their own best decision (Sparks, 2006).

An additional way to understand the value differences in health care is to examine the nature of the relationships within the system. The relationship between health professionals, patients, and caregivers is not equal. Physicians particularly, due to the traditional biomedical model, are trusted to act on the behalf of "their" patients. Patients may believe that attention to their personal values is an imposition to treatment decisions and the imposition may put them at risk for not receiving quality care. Patients may attempt to please the physician to preserve the relationship because they depend on the physician to care specifically about the physical, emotional, and social needs related to their disease. In recent years the relationship between physicians and patients has changed and there is less confidence that the physician will always know what is best. Patients are often more self-educated about their condition and if financially able, more likely to seek multiple physicians' opinions (Heifetz, 1996). Patients are increasingly interested in taking an active role in their health care management. It is less common for patients today to see the same doctor for their entire lives, so the personal aspect of a patient–health care provider relationship is often replaced with the provider being dictated by the managed care insurance plan.

Ethical values exist on a continuum and most people share a level of agreement about many issues. Unfortunately the points of difference in ethical decision making seem to be the most obvious and frequently the areas of understanding or compromise are missed. It is vital to listen to others express their values without interrupting, especially when their disagreement is the chief message. People are invested in expressing their values. Heifetz (1996) suggests that individuals use three potential frameworks to support and influence their ethical values: religious dogma or philosophy, cognitive reasoning and the desire to avoid harm. When social workers understand what others value and why it is valued, it enhances opportunities for mutual respect and results in appropriate and effective health care.

Informed Consent and Confidentiality

Everyone has a right to know about the risks associated with medical treatments and procedures. Individuals cannot make the best decisions if they are uninformed or if some of the information necessary for decision making is withheld. Legally and ethically, health care workers must receive signed permission from an informed patient to accept medical care. The health care worker must explain the treatment and answer patient questions about the risks and benefits of the intervention. The process also serves as an opportunity to develop a relationship between the health care worker and the patient. The professional value of trust, based on shared and accurate information, is arguably more important than a signature on the appropriate form (Heifetz, 1996).

Informed consent to treatment is a significant patient right in the United States. The requirement controls health care workers from arbitrarily making decisions about the best treatment for patients and obligates them to inform patients about options for treatment, the circumstances of risk surrounding those options, and recognizes their choice to not receive treatment. There is no law requiring competent adults to receive medical treatment against their will. In the United States, people have the right to die and can choose not to accept life-supporting treatment (Heifetz, 1996). Social workers value the patient's right to self-determine and respect and support the ethical and legal commitment to informed consent (Reamer, 1990).

Another significant patient right is the expectation of confidentiality. For trust to exist, patients must believe what they relate to medical staff is confidential and is not for publication to a broader audience. Today, in a world of computerized medical records, email attachments, image-sending telephones, and fax machines, there are many concerns about the privacy of medical information. In addition, health insurance companies and other second-party payers frequently request access to medical information prior to payment. Without signed patient permission, medical information must remain confidential. The Federal Health Information and Privacy Accountability Act (HIPAA) requires patients to be guaranteed privacy of records, but there remains concern that in this era of communication explosions, there continues to be unethical ways for patients' information to be procured without their permission. The value of confidentiality and the right to expect privacy potentially raises ethical issues when a confidence puts others in danger, as in the case of an infectious disease. Health care professionals are faced with ethical decisions regarding sharing information and must seek guidance and supervision from appropriate resources (Reamer, 2005).

Patients also have the right to read the organization's documentation regarding their care and treatment. Social workers follow case documentation guidelines as presented in the professional code of ethics and recognize the ethical implications of record-keeping. Documentation serves an important function as a historic record of services and must include accuracy, timeliness, appropriateness, and privacy. Social workers respect patients' rights to access their medical records and protect the confidentiality of the record (NASW, 1999; Reamer, 1990, 2005).

Technological Advances

The advancement of technology allows people once forced to be dependent of family, friends, and community services to remain in their homes longer and with improved quality of life. While new mechanization is not the sole reason for ethical challenges in health, many technologies present new tests for ethical decision making about medical care (Mann, 1997). Increasing numbers of medical staff, patients, and caregivers are faced with decisions about disease and the sometimes extensive and expensive menu of treatments available.

Technology offers ways to support home care, but it does not make decisions regarding the appropriate and safest setting for the patient. It is common for adults to want to stay in their homes for as long as possible and sometimes the challenge is to determine if they are capable of living independently. Social workers value patient autonomy and self-determination. It is also common for families to be challenged to choose between decisions that offer a family member prolonged independence with complications that may challenge the quantity and possibly the quality of life, or providing care in a dependent setting and potentially adding to patient longevity (Healy, 2003).

Diseases once offered predictable, even dire, courses of life and end of life, but new technologies frequently make extended life possible for both adults and children. For instance, premature babies, once expected to die if their birth weight was low and organs were underdeveloped, today live and grow due to technological systems of life support.

These babies survive, but some may face a lifetime of immense and grueling physical and neurological challenges. Organ transplantation is taken for granted today, but before transplantation people living with diseases such as polycystic kidney disease lived significantly shortened lives and experienced poor quality of life. Today, kidney transplantation is relatively common and many other major organs such as the lungs and the heart can be replaced if damaged. But the ethical questions remain. Should everyone, regardless of age or health, receive access to transplantation? How does society determine allocation of limited resources? Who gets a transplant and who doesn't? Who decides?

Additional ethical issues continue to emerge. For instance, stem cell transplant research remains very controversial in the United States, yet many nations support this research and view it as another promising opportunity for effectively changing the treatment or elimination of some diseases. The ethical issues in support or in suppression of technology are all based in cultural and personal values.

End of Life

End-of-life care remains a hotly debated issue in health care circles in the United States and in other countries (Johansen, Hølen, & Kaasa, 2005). Even seemingly simple decisions about end-of-life support services as familiar and as respected as hospice care are filled with emotional and value-laden issues. For instance, principles associated with end of life include direct patient care issues such as legalization of euthanasia, assisted suicide, and the disparity in access to end-of-life care. Social workers are commonly involved in the ethics related to policy and education of end-of-life decisions (Csikai, 2004).

The two most significant issues of conflict regarding end of life include euthanasia and physician-assisted suicide (Fort Cowles, 2003; Latimer, 1998; Manetta & Wells, 2001; Sparks, 2006). Both of these procedures contribute to the hastening of the end of life. Physician-assisted suicide is when a physician gives a patient the means to end his or her life but the patient is actually the person who administers the lethal medication (Csikai & Chaitin, 2006 Mandetta & Wells, 2001; Johansen et al., 2005). Euthanasia is a means to end life and is different than physician-assisted suicide because the physician is the person who administers the lethal dose of medication to the patient (Csikai & Chaitin, 2006; Johansen et al., 2005).

Social workers need to listen and support patients regarding their thoughts of end of life. For many in our society, the priority is to preserve life and to value living. It is challenging for many to understand that some forms of health deterioration can lead individuals to want to end their lives. It is important for social workers to recognize and understand the dilemma people face when extended life promises poor quality of life. Due to increased treatment methods and technology that increases longevity, sometimes health staff and caregivers fail to recognize the accompanying burdens of poor quality of life, despair, pain, hopelessness, increasing dependence, and continual medical interventions. Professional social workers temper personal reactions of shock or judgment when patients share intimate thoughts about their desire to shorten their lives. Social workers listen and practice empathy: What would I want if I were them and lived with the same set of circumstances? What would I consider doing to solve this problem?

Physicians often play a prominent role in the care of people who are dying from advanced chronic illness. Many physicians and other health care providers are challenged with end-of-life issues and find it difficult to discuss matters regarding death and dying

(Manetta & Wells, 2001; Rubinow, 2005). When patients express an interest in ending their lives, it is vital they be offered an opportunity to express their concerns with professionals and possibly with caregivers. Sometimes pain and depression is overwhelming, but temporary, or perhaps the patient's health staff missed an opportunity to treat a symptom in a way that reduces the patient's pain. In other words, new information shared between patients and staff can alter the patient's assessment of quality of life. Individuals with a desire to shorten their lives also benefit from a professional assessment for depression and possible treatment if depression exists (Manetta & Wells, 2001).

During end-of-life discussions, it is vital social workers monitor their personal values regarding death, dying, and the meaning of life and clearly understands the patient's right to alternative values. Although some medical treatments provide patients with an opportunity for a meaningful and acceptable quality of life, assess the immensity of medical decisions through a social and emotional lens, as well. Be aware of the nondisease elements supporting the patient's thoughts. Social workers offer opportunities to support and problem-solve regarding the nonmedical aspects of advanced chronic illness and offer creative resources necessary to enhance the patient's decision to proceed with treatment. When the patient is empowered to accept or refuse treatment, the decision should be made with all of the information considered, regarding all of the options available.

Rationing

Everyone who needs health care deserves to have health care, but should everyone receive the same medical treatments? This is part of the health care debate in the United States and currently reality suggests that while all people are free to seek medical treatment, not all will receive it. Those who receive it will experience vastly different access quality and treatment options and the options will most likely hinge on issues related to payment.

The concept of the right to health care is particularly challenged during times of limited resources. The national discussion regarding health care rationing is frequently missing from the headlines, but the U.S. practices health care rationing daily. Rationing is practiced when resources are limited and expensive. Resources are allocated based on criterion that makes treatment available to some and not to others. The practice of deciding who and under what circumstances some receive a level of care or treatment superior to others is not always called rationing, but allocation processes influence decisions about access to limited resources for some, and not others (Solovy, 2006).

The decisions to make a human organ of limited availability accessible for transplant to one person, despite the fact that four individuals require the organ to survive, demands ethical discussions. Ultimately a decision needs to be made and based on a consistent and ethically sound reasoning process. Who is the best person to receive an available lung or heart? If increased equality in access to health care is a societal goal, there will be challenges about how already taxed resources will be accessed if demand increases. If more people demand already limited medical resources, tough decisions will become even tougher. If health care systems are legislated to offer equal assess to affordable health care for everyone, how will equitable access to limited resources change? There are many barriers to the equity of health care; some barriers are the challenge of providing service to people who live in isolated geographic locations where there is no access to specialized treatments, but some individuals do not receive access to health care or treatment due to the practice of racism and other forms of discrimination. There is no doubt that the cost of equitable and totally inclusive treatment to all would be staggering (Heifetz, 1996; Solovy, 2006). Issues of cost are relevant to ethical discussions, particularly when offering costly interventions for a few means limiting other, more affordable resources to others.

Unfortunately, the most successful and least expensive form of health care—disease education, health promotion, and disease prevention—seems to be less valued in society. Although disease prevention efforts and provision of food and shelter for the poorest and most vulnerable populations improves quality of life, social improvement efforts in those areas are often not linked to the debate to provide improved health care (Heifetz, 1996; Mann, 2002).

As with all resources in the world, the wealthy have the best access to the best medical care. This is a global reality. Socioeconomic status is a good predictor of the quality and quantity of health care received. Not all need the same health resources, but affordability and access to a basic standard of care for everyone is a laudable goal. Nowhere on the globe is there a nation offering total equity of health and medical care for all citizens (Heifetz, 1996; Menzel, 2002).

Rationing of health care is a significant global issue and is related to issues of social injustice. Some of the drugs available for people living with HIV offer inexpensive ways to extend life for many, but only for those that can afford them. People living in poverty in the United States and in impoverished countries die of HIV without access to even the most basic and affordable HIV medications.

Some medications and treatments are effective in some cases and under certain circumstances, but not for everyone. Is it unethical to proceed with the treatment when the treatment appears to be ineffective? If an intervention is effective, is it worth the price when it extends life only briefly and would possibly extend it longer for someone else? What if a treatment is not proven effective or harmful? These kinds of value-centered debates are necessary to allocate limited resources (Hope, Reynolds, & Griffiths, 2002).

The NASW policy statements promote individuals' right to health care. Social workers promote the responsibility of the national government to promote public health through prevention of disease, promotion of health, and the treatment of disease. In addition, social workers support a national health care policy that provides access to mental health and physical health care for everyone regardless of their cultures. Social workers prioritize patient needs over financial considerations and promote all attempts to act and advocate for patients' health care rights (NASW, 2003).

Resolving Ethical Conflicts

There are many ways to examine ethical conflicts and social workers benefit by familiarity with several models. Corey et al. (1998) suggest a model of ethical decision making that includes eight steps, outlined in Box 11.1.

Sparks (2006) suggests an informed decision be made considering the following factors: (1) the consideration of personal, professional, collegial, institutional, and societal values; (2) examination of relevant ethical decision-making theories and models; (3) social work theories, research, and best practice standards; (4) social work and other professional ethical codes; (5) relevant federal, state, local, and agency policies, regulations, and laws; and (6) the impact of the decision on patients, caregivers, and practitioners.

BOX 11.1 • *Model of Ethical Decision Making*

1. Define the problem or dilemma
2. Identify the potential issues involved
3. Complete review of the relevant ethical codes
4. Know the laws and regulations pertaining to the problem
5. Consult with experts or others with knowledge about this or similar situations
6. Consider and identify the most possible and probable options
7. List the consequences associated with various options
8. Fully consider these options
9. Implement the apparent best option

Source: Corey, Corey, & Callahan (1998).

Giddens et al. (2000) suggest ethical decisions are improved when social workers are guided by the following steps: (1) assess the current situation accurately and completely, applying a biopsychosocial perspective; (2) determine the clinical, physical, legal, cultural, and systemic issues influencing the patient; (3) determine the issues that present an ethical problem; (4) consider the options available for implementation; (5) consider the positive and negative consequences of each option; (6) move forward with confidence about your decision; and (7) evaluate the decision with the patient to learn if the decision offered a successful approach.

Ethical decisions attempt to take a concept that is unclear and challenging and bring it to consensus through a process resulting in mutual endorsement (Johnson, 2006). The challenge is to create an endorsed compromise, especially when there is no identifiable right answer. Compromise is reached as a result of challenges, study, thought, and the critical consideration of options. This process is most successful when it follows a series of discussions by a serious and conscientious group of health care practitioners committed to ethical resolution of an issue (Sparks, 2006).

Many theories are used to direct and inform the process of ethical decision making. Social workers can begin the process by recognizing the power of patients and interact with them about their values and experiences, what they understand, and in particular, to listen to their concerns. Consideration of patients' values are done best when social workers understand their own values and beliefs and support the patients' desires over their own (Sparks, 2006). Ethical decisions can often be complicated by discussions and considerations that interfere in the primary decision-making process. When this occurs, it is beneficial to clearly reestablish an identifiable definition of the ethical problem under consideration and recognize the complexity of issues influencing the decision-making process (Corey et al., 1998; Heifetz, 1996; Sparks, 2006).

Make every attempt to seek appropriate supervision when faced with ethical dilemmas. Every situation regarding a health-related conflict is unique. Supervision offers social workers an opportunity to communicate concerns about the situation and gain insight, suggestions, or review of relevant policies to guide further action. The health setting may offer policies covering certain health-related incidents or an identified process to resolve essential issues.

Summary

Health care team members share the desire to treat patients ethically. Frequently social workers are faced with ethical problems that require an immediate response. Resolve to follow sound procedural steps toward ethical decision making. Know the NASW Code of Ethics (1999) well enough to know and practice social work within these professional parameters and remember the code exists to inform social workers about the ethics related to decisions, provides standards for quality patient care, and is used to evaluate professional practice. Make the integration of sound ethical decision making vital to social work professional practice in all interactions and in all fields of practice.

Critical Thinking Questions

1. Is there a difference between unethical behavior and unprofessional behavior? Give an example.

2. From a global perspective, what are some differences in how health care is defined?

3. Nationally, how does the U.S. define health care? If there are various definitions, how does this assist or impede changes in health care policy?

References

Addams, J. (1910). *Twenty years at Hull-House.* New York: MacMillan.

Benatar, S. R., Daar, A. S., & Singer, P. A. (2003). Global health ethics: The rationale for mutual caring. *International Affairs, 79*(1), 107–138.

Cagle, J. G., & Kovacs, P. J. (2009). Education: A complex and empowering social work intervention at the end of life. *Health and Social Work, 34*(1), 17–28.

Corey, G., Corey, M. S., & Callahan, P. (1998). *Issues and ethics in the helping professions.* Pacific Grove, CA: Brooks/Cole.

Csikai, E. L. (2004). Social workers' participation in the resolution of ethical dilemmas in hospice care. *Health and Social Work, 29*(1), 67–76.

Csikai, E. L., & Chaitin, E. (2006). *Ethics in end-of-life decisions in social work practice.* Chicago: Lyceum.

Davidson, J. C. (2005). Professional relationship boundaries: A social work teaching module. *Social Work Education, 24*(5), 511–533.

Fort Cowles, L. A. (2003). *Social work in the health field: A care perspective* (2nd ed.). New York: Hayworth Press.

Giddens, B., Ka'opua, L., & Tomaszewski, E. (2000). Ethical issues and dilemmas in HIV/AIDS. In V. Lynch (Ed.), *HIV/AIDS at year 2000* (pp. 33–49). Boston: Allyn & Bacon.

Gossett, M., & Weinman, M. L. (2007). Evidence-based practice and social work: An illustration of the steps involved. *Health and Social Work, 32*(2), 147–150.

Gruskin, S., & Dickens, B. (2006). Human rights and ethics in public health. *American Journal of Public Health, 96*(11), 1903–1905.

Haas, B. A., & Sheehan, J. M. (2008). Developing and retaining a successful interdisciplinary law and ethics course for professional health care students. *Journal of Nursing Law, 12*(1), 38–41.

Healy, T. C. (2003). Ethical decision making: Pressure and uncertainty as complicating factors. *Health and Social Work, 28*(4), 293–301.

Heifetz, M. D. (1996). *Ethics in medicine.* Amherst, NY: Prometheus Books.

Hessler, K., & Buchanan, A. (2002). Specifying the content of the human right to health care. In R. Rhodes, M. P. Battin, & A. Silvers (Eds.), *Medicine and social justice: Essays on the distribution of health care* (pp. 84–96). New York: Oxford University Press.

Hope, T., Reynolds, J., & Griffiths, S. (2002). Rationing decisions: Integrating cost–effectiveness with other values. In R. Rhodes, M. P. Battin, & A. Silvers (Eds.), *Medicine and social justice: Essays on the distribution of health care* (pp. 144–155). New York: Oxford University Press.

Jayasundra, C. C. (2004). Ethical issues surrounding the use of information in health care. *Malaysian Journal of Library and Information Science, 9*(1), 69–86.

Johansen, S., Hølen, J. C., & Kaasa, S. (2005). Attitudes towards, and wishes for, euthanasia in advanced cancer patients at a palliative medicine unit. *Palliative Medicine, 19,* 454–460.

Johnson, P. F. (2006). Preserving our values: Habermas, hospital ethics, and the business of health care. *Midwest Quarterly, 47*(4), 393–411.

Ka'opua, L. S. (1992, January). *Training for cultural competence in the HIV epidemic.* AIDS Education Project, Hawaii Area AIDS Education and Training Center.

Miley, K. K., O'Melia, M., & Dubois, B. (2009). *Generalist social work practice: An empowering approach.* Boston: Allyn & Bacon.

Murdach, A. D. (2009). Discretion in direct practice: New perspectives. *Social Work, 54*(2), 183–186.

Landau, R. (2008). Social work research ethics: Dual roles and boundary issues. *Journal of Contemporary Social Services, 89*(4), 571–577.

Latimer, E. J. (1998). Ethical care at the end of life. *Canadian Medical Association, 158*(13), 1741–1747.

Loewenberg, F. M., Dolgoff, R., & Harrington, D. (2000). *Ethical decisions for social work practice* (6th ed.). Itasca, IL: F. F. Peacock.

Mann, J. M. (1997). Medicine and public health, ethics and human rights. *Hasting Center Report, 27*(3), 6–13.

Mann, P. (2002). Health-care justice and agency. In R. Rhodes, M. P. Battin, & A. Silvers (Eds.), *Medicine and social justice: Essays on the distribution of health care* (pp. 121–133). New York: Oxford University Press.

Manetta, A. A., & Wells, J. G. (2001). Ethical issues in the social worker's role in physician-assisted suicide. *Health and Social Work, 26*(3), 160–166.

Marsh, J. C. (2003). To thine own ethics code be true. *Social Work, 48*(1), 5–7.

Menzel, P. T. (2002). Justice and the basic structure of health-care systems. In R. Rhodes, M. P. Battin, & A. Silvers (Eds.), *Medicine and social justice: Essays on the distribution of health care* (pp. 24–37). New York: Oxford University Press.

National Association of Social Workers (NASW). (1999). *Code of ethics.* Washington, DC: NASW Press.

National Association of Social Workers (NASW). (2003). *Social work speaks: National Association of Social Workers policy statements, 2003–2006.* Washington, DC: NASW Press.

Reamer, F. G. (1990). *Ethical dilemmas in social service: A guide of social workers* (2nd ed.). New York: Columbia University Press.

Reamer, F. G. (2003). Boundary issues in social work: Managing dual relationships. *Social Work, 48*(1), 121–133.

Reamer, F. G. (2005). Documentation in social work: Evolving ethical and risk-management standards. *Social Work, 50*(4), 325–334.

Rubinow, A. (2005). The physician and the dying patient: A question of control? *IMAJ, 7,* 3–4.

Solovy, A. (2006). Different people die. *Hospital and Health Networks, 80*(6), 32.

Sparks, J. (2006). Ethics and social work in health care. In S. Gehlert & T. A. Browne (Eds.), *Handbook of health social work* (pp. 43–69). Hoboken, NJ: Wiley.

Stone, L. C., & Balderrama, C. H. (2008). Health inequalities among Latinos: What do we know and what can we do? *Health and Social Work, 33*(1), 3–8.

World Health Organization (WHO). (2006). *Constitution of the World Health Organization.* Retrieved September 11, 2008, from http://www.searo.who.int/EN/Section898/Section1441.htm

12

Supervision

Teaching and Learning Goals

- Understand what supervision is and why it is beneficial
- Recognize ways to provide beneficial supervision
- Recognize the topics best suited for discussion in supervision
- Understand why supervision benefits patients, social workers, and health care systems

When the relationship between social work policy, practice, and professionalism is examined, it is clear social work is more than well-meaning individuals offering their expert advice to vulnerable people. Social workers are professionals. They follow a professional code of ethics, educated by accredited universities, and are licensed and certified by state legislative bodies. In addition, professional social workers in all fields of practice, including health care, are required and expected to receive professional, appropriate, and regularly scheduled supervision.

Issues requiring supervisory feedback develop as a social worker interacts with the health system. Work experiences include a variety of challenging situations and social workers benefit from experienced mentoring and guidance. Health-related social work demands interactions with a variety of systems: (1) health care teams; (2) culturally diverse groups of professionals, patients, and caregivers; (3) political systems and the policies of the international, national, state, and local communities; and (4) vulnerable populations regarding issues related to chronic illness, loss, grief, dying, and death.

Social workers practicing in health care without some form of supervision will not only offer inferior services to patients, but also risk harm to themselves. Supervision requires prioritizing time to become centered, despite the chaos of a high-stimuli, fast-thinking, and decision-demanding job. Reamer (1989) states, "No competent professional questions the appropriateness of supervision" (p. 447). Important decisions are frequently made through the course of a day that influences both the quality of life for patients and their longevity. Social workers risk experiencing burnout, secondary trauma, and unhealthy boundaries. Supervision offers social workers an oasis, however brief, to reflect, to learn self-care, and to refine and develop their professional skills. Social workers require skillful supervision, and as social workers become more experienced and educated, they are frequently asked to give supervision to others. There are many benefits as a result of good supervision, so it is vital to be deliberate about supervision, both in the receiving and in the giving.

Supervision

All professional social workers benefit from supervision, particularly from other social workers. Receiving supervision from another social worker who shares the same values, beliefs, and skills related to the profession is often the best match. Supervision is a widely recognized way to nurture the professional development of a social worker and plays a central role in increasing a social workers' professional and personal awareness of both strengths and areas that require additional growth. Social workers who provide social work supervision to others in their profession model professional knowledge and skills (Itzhaky & Lipschitz-Elhawi, 2004; Reamer, 1989) and offer a contributing role in positive job satisfaction (Egan & Kadushin, 2004).

Although supervision is offered in many different formats: one-to-one, group supervision, weekly scheduled appointments, or on an "as-needed" basis, there are some approaches that are beneficial to all forms of supervisory relationships. The supervisory occasion between the social worker and supervisor must be formulated in a way that guarantees time is spent effectively, prioritizes professional and personal need for input, looks for ways to increase quality of care for the patient, and improves the quality of services provided by the social worker.

The field of health care practice provides social workers with many unique challenges that make receiving supervision a priority. Frequently, social workers interact with people who are experiencing crises. Although crises are not always life-threatening, individuals with medical issues and their caregivers experience circumstances causing feelings of helplessness, dread, or loss. In health environments, social workers often witness others

BOX 12.1 • *Challenges in Health Care Requiring Supervision*

1. Coping with the knowledge that medical care does not always cure
2. Witnessing that medical advances do not treat all illnesses
3. Frequent and repeated exposure to end of life and death
4. Interactions with patients during times filled with grief and loss
5. Witnessing the deterioration of patients living with chronic illness

Source: Itzahaky & Lipschitz-Elhawi (2004)

experiencing pain, stress, frustration, and panic and these emotions can add to the challenges of the work. In addition, health organizations often experience repeated policy changes. Consequently work environments suffer frequent organizational instability leading to reorganizations, cutbacks, and ultimately reductions in the workforce. The rules managing a health care system change repeatedly and, combined with practice and policy instability, add to the necessity of supervision to ensure professionalism (Colby & Dziegielewski, 2004; Dziegielewshi, 2004).

When social workers interact with patients living with advanced chronic illness and end-of-life issues, there are professional and emotional assaults. Challenges include those listed in Box 12.1.

Social workers are emotionally affected by the constant onslaught of chronic or terminal illness in a way other health professionals do not experience. Patients often look for ways to protect family, friends, and the professionals providing them with medical care. But social workers are not family and they are not medical personnel. Instead, social workers are professionals who encourage patients and caregivers to acknowledge and verbalize their honest emotions. This often results in hearing the intimate expression of painful or sorrowful feelings that accompany loss and grief. Social workers experience a heightened sense of vulnerability due to their own pain and grief, but if no one within health organizations inquires about or understands the presence of these feelings, this pain may be absorbed into their personal lives. Confidentiality keeps many social workers from discussing the details of their work experiences in traditionally supportive ways, such as conversations with family and friends. Unresolved and unexpressed emotions can develop into unhealthy coping strategies. Pent-up emotions can also lead to negative views of the job or an inability to make sense of their professional or personal imbalance. Living with unrecognized and untreated emotional pain can lead to adoption of maladaptive coping techniques. These are good reasons for social workers in the field of health care to seek supervision from professional social workers.

Receiving Supervision

All too often supervision is perceived as just one more task to try to schedule into an already busy week of work. In some settings, it becomes one of the first appointments likely to be cancelled or rescheduled as the pressures of the work week overwhelm the actual hours of the day. This is an unfortunate reality about the participation in consistent supervision: the time for supervision is not always prioritized. Admittedly it is difficult to find time to actually step out of the constant busy pace of the health care setting, but the complexity and potential need for supervision demands it occur. Consider supervision time a gift, a safe place where one can seek advice, support, and renewal. Although not all supervisory relationships model this embracing environment, there remain ways to still receive the information and feedback needed to continue to work in a professional manner.

Supervision is not always easy or pleasant to receive. Although supervision is frequently a validating and supportive experience, it is also an opportunity for the social worker to receive honest and perhaps critical feedback about their work performance or their professional behavior. At times supervisors must use the supervision time to address problems noted in work performance. Identified work issues may call for different forms of corrective action such as setting goals for developing mutually agreeable solutions or, in more extreme cases, some formal corrective measure. At times supervision is used to challenge, teach tasks and skills, or perhaps to introduce new changes in organizational protocol. Some social workers may perceive supervision as the highlight of the week, but sometimes they experience a sense of dread, knowing there are uncomfortable issues on the agenda. Social workers may need time to readjust from a supervisory event and reframe the seemingly negative feedback in a way that assures them that their efforts are noted and appreciated but there is a need for readjustment. Good supervision can be very personal.

Other Professional Supervision

All supervisory relationships are not equal. There are supervisors who stand out as mentors and people who help shape the professional self. Years after the relationship ends a social worker may still recall some statement or piece of wisdom that continues to be used to shape and improve professional practice. This experience is not consistent, however. Health care settings are, as mentioned earlier, a host setting for social workers. This means social work is in a setting where the predominant discipline is not social work and social workers are not consistently afforded the luxury of a social worker as their supervisor.

There is a trend within health organizations to save money by offering social workers supervision provided by a professional from a nonsocial work discipline; frequently the choice is supervision by nurses. Regardless of the discipline of the supervisor, it benefits both the social worker and the supervisor to find ways to learn about the differences in each other's education, ethics, values, and skills. When the person designated as supervisor is not a social worker, it can lead to misunderstandings or unclear communication. This is not totally unexpected given the cultural differences between disciplines, but with mutual respect and acknowledgment of the opportunities for misunderstandings by both parties, these issues do not need to stand in the way of a supervisor's ability to advocate and represent the needs of the social worker within the host setting. The best situation is when both members in the relationship ask, listen, and learn about the unique strengths of each profession and find the strong areas of mutual commitment to the patient's overall welfare.

Health care social workers have many venues allowing them professional interactions with other health care social workers. The access to professional relationships is vital, especially if they are not available at the work setting. These organizations offer membership at the national, state, and local levels. Joining an organization of health care social workers allows for the development of relationships supporting the same skills, values, beliefs, and code of ethics.

In addition to supervision from another discipline, there are other potential challenges to the relationship between the social worker and the supervisor. Sometimes supervisors are selected or hired due to strengths that meet the needs of the health care system as a whole. These strengths may not include the ability to supervise. Sometimes social work colleagues with the most experience, the most years on the job, or the best intrapersonal and practice skills are not necessarily the ones promoted to supervisor. There is a chance that the new social work supervisor has less experience than the person they supervise. This can be very challenging for many social workers. Many wonder how they can ask for advice from someone who does not know the work, workers, or health environment. Again, this kind of situation demands social workers use their ability to look for the strengths in the situation. What other skills does the supervisor possess that assist social workers to do their work in the best way possible? It may be as simple as the need to acknowledge that this supervisor has access to information and power they need to do their work.

Finally, there are times when the social work supervisor is not empowered by the health care system. While this is not common because of the cost associated with such an ineffective business practice, it is still possible a health care system withholds total support from the supervisor. Some health systems misunderstand and suspect the profession of social work. If the social work supervisor is not respected by the health care system, the supervisor lacks any real power to advocate or to represent the profession within the larger system. This is an opportunity for social workers and the supervisor to find creative ways to advance and improve their professional reputation and leads to occasions to educate the system about the important tasks social workers contribute to quality and cost-effective patient care. Social workers contribute more to health care than the completion of an assessment and discharge planning. They work to educate the health care system about the real cost savings that result from their work. Social workers can point out the smooth and uncomplicated discharge plans, the less expensive and more effective care plans due to efficiently made support referrals, the increase in patient and caregiver confidence and satisfaction, and the more efficient use of other disciplines within their areas of expertise. Continued use or the development of evaluation tools show that these services result in cost savings and contribute to the less expensive health services. It is important for social workers to claim and publish these facts and be assertive about the value of social work.

Cost Savings

There is ample professional literature that supports the claim that social workers who experience a positive supervisory relationship also experience increased job satisfaction (Cole, Panchanadeswaran, & Daining, 2004; DeLoach, 2003; Fleming & Taylor, 2006; Hyrkas, 2005). Job satisfaction supports cost-effectiveness. The attributes of positive supervision include employee support, effective communication, and reliability. The benefit of job satisfaction is obvious for an employee, but the satisfaction is also a valuable benefit to the agency or organization. When supervision is supportive and job satisfaction is high, the combination results in (1) increased effectiveness on the job, (2) increased creativity for problem solving, (3) less absenteeism, (4) less job burnout, and (5) less employee turnover. Good supervision is a worthy investment for an organization and represents a notable cost savings (Finn, 1997; Noblet & LaMontagne, 2006).

In addition, cost savings also occur when social workers help patients find adequate coverage for their medical charges and demonstrate the important role they play in attending to the bottom line of the health care organization. Understanding the intricacies and changing requirements and plans associated with Medicaid and Medicare is challenging for the most experienced of social workers, and frequently few others within a health organization have sufficient knowledge to provide information or advice to patients attempting to determine coverage. Social workers are in a good position to educate supervisors and hospital administrators about the obstacles that influence the acquisition of adequate insurance coverage. This form of organizational advocacy can lead to successful recovery of costs, previously uncollected, for patient services (Egan & Kadushin, 2004).

It can be frustrating for social workers to locate the support necessary for them to resolve their conflicts and dilemmas. They can be stereotyped into the limited role of patient supporter and are not recognized as having the power of medically trained professionals. The difference in the power of health disciplines results in social workers experiencing less influence over the decisions and this affects their strength within health organizations (Egan & Kadushin, 2004).This is another vital reason to maintain a relationship with a supervisor that advocates within the system on social work's behalf.

Preparation

Supervision is both a gift and a responsibility. Assume there is a competent and caring supervisor consistent in offering social workers time to talk about their work. It is the social worker's responsibility to arrive promptly at the appointment, prepared to use the time allotted in a way that benefits them most. The best supervisor may only ask, "What can I do for you?" If a social worker has no agenda, the supervisor can share information about organizational issues or new assignments. But if an agenda is prepared and ready to refer to when supervision begins, the social worker is more likely to receive the support and counsel necessary to do his or her job. During the week social workers can develop a list of clinical, procedural, ethical, or professional questions. Supervision is something social workers can prepare for and take responsibility for its success. Supervisors may refer their colleagues to books, articles, workshops, and other resources they are unfamiliar with. Supervision time can be very satisfying and offers supervisors a chance to witness a colleague's interest in improving their skills. When a social worker is ready for supervision and arrives with an agenda of the issues or resources they need, the value of supervision increases. Whether or not the supervisor organizes the time for supervision around those issues or not, social workers will know they did not waste an opportunity to attempt to find the support and information they need.

Assessment of Practice

Supervision is a way for social workers to develop professional goals and objectives and to consider the concrete evidence of growing professionalism. Most supervisory roles require the social workers to develop goals and objectives used later to measure work performance.

Depending on the setting, the accomplishment of these goals is connected with salary increases or promotion. The goals are typically created in draft form by the social worker and then further developed with the aid of the supervisor. The goals are placed in an employee file with an advanced date set for review of the goals and reaching goals is evidence of accomplishment.

Social workers can consider the development of a professional portfolio. While not traditionally a method used in social worker evaluation, other health disciplines use this method of maintaining documentation of professional growth and accomplishment. There are a couple of good reasons why this might be useful for social workers as well. First, an evaluation using a portfolio when working with other professional disciplines that do the same creates a sense of teaming and oneness regarding a similar professional project.

Second, a portfolio is a way to creatively put together the evidence of professional development. A portfolio is typically a notebook that holds evidence of attending team meetings, attendance and participation in conferences and trainings, and perhaps letters of thanks from referral sources, patients, or caregivers. It is amazing how easily these pieces of evidence can disappear and are forgotten unless a concerted effort to save this information is made. Social workers can start by designating a file where they place all evidence of how they spend their time and later organize it into a viewable history of their work. The portfolio is a great way of introduction to new supervisors and new employers or a mechanism to show evidence worthy of promotion. It is also a resource to examine when updating a resumé. Often it is difficult to remember everything done over the years and the portfolio is a very helpful tool in sequencing accomplishments and supporting faulty memory. Most importantly, the portfolio reminds social workers of their successful professional work and can result in a sense of professional satisfaction.

Job Satisfaction

Increasing the knowledge that social workers are successful and benefit others through their work is fundamental to their ability to experience job satisfaction. Research confirms that if a social worker believes they make a positive contribution to patient care, they are more likely to experience job satisfaction (Cole et al., 2004; DeLoach, 2003). Job satisfaction, in turn, is effective in delaying or avoiding burnout. Social workers who believe they make a positive difference in the life of patients and caregivers are more likely to stay in their job and experience less emotional and physical exhaustion. A supportive supervisor is believed to be an important link between social workers and job satisfaction. The support of a supervisor does not necessarily end the conflicts and challenges for a social worker in health care, but supervision represents a reliable resource decreasing the influence of the damaging events and experiences (Noblet & LaMontagne, 2006).

Giving Supervision

It is uncommon for a social worker to begin a professional job in health care with the explicit goal of becoming a supervisor. However, regardless of professional goals, sometimes the task of supervision is required and you are the person required to take this responsibility. Sometimes a "promotion" to the supervisor role is a competitive process and the health system seeks to hire the best person for the role. At other times, the administration determines the person to supervise based on criteria other than the ability to supervise and supervisory responsibilities are not expected or welcomed.

The role of supervisor is commonly offered to an individual within the system who exhibits loyalty to the organization, effective and valued contributions to the interdisciplinary workload, and personal and professional respect to those within the organization. If the hiring of a social work supervisor is a competitive process and invites applications from outside the health system, the qualities of working well with other disciplines, good communication, organization, and creativity are highly valued. Often supervisors of social workers in health care have a master's degree in social work, but occasionally supervisors are bachelor-level social workers.

Social workers need to receive supervision specifically from a certified or licensed social worker to meet the requirements of licensure. Continuing to develop and upgrade skills is part of the profession's ethical commitment to social workers, colleagues, and patients. Supervision provided by a social worker to a social worker offers an important contribution to the acculturation and socialization of the worker to the profession (Harkness & Hensley, 1991).

Social work supervision in health care offers informed and professional quality support. The history of social work concurs regarding the importance of supervision, but acknowledges the exact tasks of supervision have varied during the course of the profession (Brashears, 1995; Dziegielewski, 2004). Supervisors fulfill multiple roles: teacher, enabler, administrator, and with the advent of managed care, there is also a business manager component to supervision. They must attend to the quality, quantity, and cost of social work interactions. Supervisors must also be aware of their own experiences and their personal need for supervision. A supervisor can feel overwhelmed by repeatedly hearing the same painful experiences of the supervisees and experience a form of secondary trauma. In addition, supervisors often face the challenge of being limited in the ability to advocate within the system and at the same time supervisors are expected to use their power to make positive change for the colleagues they supervise. This leads to a sense of helplessness and is often maddening to supervisors who try to alter a system that is frequently uneasy to change (Dziegielewski, 2004).

Social workers employed in the health care system understand they work in a host setting that potentially interferes in the formal and informal power they experience. The health care system prioritizes the roles of disciplines trained in medicine and in the provision of medical services. Social workers trained to contribute to the emotional and social welfare of patients and caregivers are ethically committed to patient empowerment and social justice. They continue to educate colleagues that biological, emotional, and social goals are compatible and find ways to communicate effectively and nondefensively.

Social workers are trained to advocate within systems and may find they are frequently involved in situations that appear to challenge the health care system that employs them. The medical system, based on a hierarchy of power, can be a conflictual setting for social workers. Supervisors may be perceived as undermining the system when they question, negotiate, or contest decisions regarding patients that other disciplines accept. Supervisors, whether nurses or social workers, are perceived as most helpful when they are effective advocates for the staff and use their administrative skills and position to assist them to effectively work in the health organization (Egan & Kadushin, 2004).

Good Supervision

What does good supervision look like? Some social workers may state effective supervision is positive emotional support. The supervisor provides feedback resulting in improved morale and feelings of collaboration and encouragement. When this kind of supervision is provided, it is communicated through genuine warmth and respect for the individual (Egan & Kadushin, 2004).

Some social workers find a positive supervisory relationship provides them with a resource for expert knowledge when they are faced with a complex or overwhelming task. This form of supervision enhances the social worker's confidence and lessens feelings of isolation. If a supervisor is aware of the tough situations a social worker is attempting to resolve, the social worker's level of empowerment increases and they know they have an ally if there are questions or problems. Egan and Kadushin (2004) suggest that both forms of supervision, emotional and instrumental, enhance social workers' freedom to be effective, motivated, and mobilized on the job.

Supervision is a complex task because supervisors must be able to discuss ethical and value conflicts with health administrators, social workers, and patient support systems, such as families and other caregivers. They must also recognize opportunities to strengthen the social work role that can result in the social workers' ability to effectively offer the best care to patients. Supervisors understand the pressures of health administrators to maintain fiscal management and help find ways to demonstrate how social workers serve the health organization's goals for cost-effectiveness. But the role of assisting social workers to recognize their important contribution to the quality of life for patients and caregivers is perhaps one of the most important offerings (Egan & Kadushin, 2004).

Establishing Goals

Supervisors are prepared to assist social workers to establish realistic and achievable goals toward their professional development. It is easy to establish goals that match the innumerable needs of the system, but when social workers create goals that are unrealistic for them, there a risk they will fail to reach the goal and the social worker believes they are ineffective. The ability to successfully accomplish tasks is vital to job satisfaction, so regardless of how many other problems are successfully resolved on the job, failure to meet the evaluative goals agreed to as a measurement of success interferes with the intrinsic reward of success. Daily successes are frequently and easily ignored or forgotten and when this happens, workers can believe they are unappreciated and unsuccessful (Kurland & Salmon, 1992).

Supervisors are in a strategic role to assist social workers to set realistic and achievable goals for both their professional development and for the tasks assigned them. Supervisors assist social workers in focusing on the tasks they are trained and skilled to accomplish. Even the most overwhelming and intimidating social work tasks benefit from the attention and intervention provided by a well-trained and focused social worker. They make a positive difference in some of the most demanding situations. So the supervisor must balance the requirement to focus on what needs to be accomplished, without discouraging the creative and energetic aspirations of the social worker considering what could be accomplished.

Supervisors help social workers recognize the incremental steps they make toward improving health care system barriers for individuals, groups, and communities. Most social workers are aware social improvement is a result of community efforts and their professional efforts join the efforts of many other social change advocates. However, when a supervisor identifies the unique role an individual social worker makes to attain positive change, there is a sense of great reward that enhances the motivation, attitude, and morale of the worker. Seemingly simple, a message that acknowledges a job well done reduces burnout in health care workers and challenges pessimistic thoughts about personal and professional failures. Verbal rewards and recognition of accomplishments is believed to reduce job turnover and premature departure from their employment (Kurland & Salmon, 1992).

Work in a health care environment, such as a hospital or long-term care facility, frequently means social workers, while part of a larger interdisciplinary team, work rather independently, perhaps isolated from other social workers. Unless experienced, lone social workers can experience disorientation from the expected outcomes of their role. Supervisors are vital in offering social workers professional grounding and a resource to assist them to set appropriate job-related boundaries. Social workers, similar to other cultures, are nurtured by cohesiveness in an environment where the practice, language, ethics, and expectations of the professional group are known and supported. The cultural environment represents a place where social workers assist each other with professional growth, supporting each other cognitively, emotionally, and physically through difficult experiences and assignments. Colleagues also serve to share in the development of creative ideas toward problem resolution (Kurland & Salmon, 1992).

Supervisors must also attend to the issues of professional documentation. Social workers are aware of this requirement and recognize accurate and professional documentation is vital not only for the processing of insurance claims, but for good patient care, evaluation, research, and potential resolution of ethical dilemmas (Reamer, 2005).

Topics for Supervision

Social workers employed in health care are guaranteed that every working day will be different than the previous one. It is a stimulating career and there are many unpredictable events occurring throughout the course of a day that offer social workers many opportunities to think, collaborate, and assist patients in reaching their goals.

The systems theory supports the understanding that every individual is a part of some form of relationship and lives within or in response to other environments. In addition, interactions with patients are complex because each patient is a culmination of their cultures. A patient is influenced by multiple cultures, and experiences with health, illness, and healing that uniquely influence their worldview. National health care policies also affect interactions with patients (Dziegielewski, 2004). The community, the health care organization, multidisciplinary colleagues, and the patient's support systems all function in ways that influence how interventions are considered. Finally, the medical diagnosis and the patient's physical, emotional, and social response to the condition ensure lack of predictability. This is the work environment of the health care social worker.

The potential complications of assignments highlight the reason supervision is so important. The ethical dilemmas, the challenges to social work values and ethics, the overwhelming pace, the loss and grief witnessed and perhaps experienced, the conflicts with alternative theories of health care, and the increasing size of caseloads lead all social workers to need the expertise, guidance, and support of supervision. The social work supervisor is in a key role to enable and empower social workers to experience success. Supportive supervision contributes to a social worker's sense of stability.

Stress

Unfortunately, most forms of social work demand working with a certain degree of stress. There are a variety of reasons for stress on the job, particularly for social workers. But there are constructive ways to deal with stress, including regular and honest supervision. Corey and Corey (1998) suggest the stress social workers experience while working is related to one of two sources: personal stress or the stress of the environment. Realization that the work-related stress experienced is from potentially two different sources, internal or external, highlights the need and the benefits of periodic self-assessment. As with any good assessment, a clear understanding of the source of stress is vital to developing a plan to reduce or eliminate the stress.

Stressors experienced from internal sources include the times when personal values are in conflict with patient values, frustration with lack of control, a personal history of pain, or unmet personal needs (Corey & Corey, 1998). Cultures and personalities influence how social workers express emotions and how they react to situations. Self-awareness helps them predict their weaknesses or reaction tendencies so they can better plan ways to avoid or reframe stressful situations. However, because social work seldom offers predictable situations, supervisors must assist in the design and adoption of techniques to help reduce stress. External or environmentally produced stressors include work-related policies, overwhelming work responsibilities, personal or professional conflicts with colleagues, or unrealistic workloads (Corey & Corey, 1998).

Stress is a part of most forms of professional employment, but at times organizational policies and procedures add to employee tension (Finn, 1997; Noblet & LaMontagne, 2006). For instance, when health care systems provide health care to individuals with little or no insurance, managed care reimbursements pressure systems to work faster, do more and do better with less, and may result in reorganizations to reduce the expenses related to the workforce. Unfortunately, doing more with less is a threat to social work roles and supervision.

The tasks of social work are potentially stressful. Patients weakened by emotional, social, and physical pain expect partnership to find a meaningful way to live with pain, grief, or loss, yet interaction time with each patient is short. Many drawn to social work take work very personally and experience frustration when time with the patient is reduced because this challenges their relationship with the patient, resulting in environmental stress (Corey & Corey, 1998). Some stress improves creativity and energy, but too much tension interferes and damages these powers. Social workers are required to attend to many details such as building relationships, engagement and assessment with people in crisis, and the development of quality service plans (Corey & Corey, 1998). Supervision can help social workers maintain their balance.

Burnout

Burnout is not a unique phenomenon for social workers. Since the term "burnout" appeared in professional literature in the mid-1970s, many professions report on and explore the effects of burnout. Burnout is of particular risk for social workers and other human service workers, however, because of the lack of control over the successful accomplishment of ultimate goals and the frequently stressful events experienced by patients, caregivers, and social workers. In addition, social work often attracts individuals who are naturally empathetic and subsequently anxious to make things better by helping others. When efforts to help others consistently fail, social workers experience burnout (Siebert, 2005).

The field of health care and social work is stressful in many unique ways, but the most obvious is that patients are seeking help for complicated, if not grim, situations. Social workers are often helpless to solve health-related problems in a way that provides patients and their families with the resolution or ultimate result they desire (Badger, Royse, & Craig, 2008).

Burnout is a negative and progressive process in reaction to job-related stress. It is associated with the continual pressure of working in intense and unrelenting relationships with people in crisis. It does not appear suddenly, but instead happens in stages or incrementally. There is not one form of burnout, nor is there a finite list of defining symptoms. Symptoms of burnout can be subtle or obvious. Unrelenting frustrations enhance the likelihood of the eventual damage and disappearance of the passionate resolve once present in the social worker. The progressive loss of physical, emotional, and social strengths may be replaced with pessimism and cynicism. An individual experiencing burnout may report feeling unappreciated and unnecessary. They may experience depersonalization and seem increasingly mechanical and automated in nature, expressing less emotion and less spontaneity. Eventually burnout can lead to physical, emotional, or social maladaptive feelings and actions (Corey & Corey, 1998; Davis, 2005).

Although the concept of burnout is viewed as primarily emotional, it also affects the physical and social characteristics of an individual. The symptoms vary by individual but include emotional symptoms such as exhaustion, depression, poor self-esteem, inability to concentrate, hopelessness, and helplessness. Physical symptoms consist of headaches, fatigue, lack of appetite, and interrupted or inability to sleep or feel rested. Social symptoms often result in difficulty with interpersonal relationships, disengagement from social contacts, substance abuse, rigidity, blaming others, and social isolation (Acker, 1999; Corey & Corey, 1998; Siebert, 2005).

Some of the conditions identified as influencing burnout include large and unreasonable workloads, the quality and amount of time spent with patients, unclear work responsibilities, and missing or inadequate supervisory support. Working with terminally ill patients takes a particularly heavy toll on social workers. One of the results of burnout is job dissatisfaction, particularly when difficult work seems to make no positive difference. At this point, social workers can feel trapped and consider leaving their job and sometimes the profession. Professional supervision is essential in assisting in the reduction of these negative responses (Itzhaky & Lipschitz-Elhawi, 2004; Noblet & LaMontagne, 2006; Um & Harrison, 1998).

Supportive supervision means different things to different people and depends on an individual's style and his or her personal and professional characteristics. Many look for features in supervision that offer them a sense of support or challenge and some social workers want to develop a relationship with a supervisor to safely share their feelings. Emotional support from someone who understands is the most vital part of supervision for some. Sometimes that support is expressed between individuals, but it can also be expressed through a supervisory style that functions to promote attention to the needs of patients within the health care system and an advocate who enhances and improves the work with patients. Social workers respond to the tension of the job differently based on personal characteristics and how they experience the barriers and challenges faced while working (Siebert, 2005).

There are great advantages in being educated about the causes, symptoms, and the prevention strategies related to burnout. Believing burnout will not affect you or those you supervise is naive given the stressful factors associated with the job. Many supervisors are part of the hiring process of social workers and this is an ideal time to be frank with prospective employees about the rigors of the job and the potential to feel overwhelmed and overtaxed (Corey & Corey, 1998). Hiring is also an opportunity to learn about the candidate's knowledge and prevention techniques regarding burnout.

Supervisors are instrumental in recognizing burnout, but are also vital in supporting others to prevent the onset of burnout. If social workers are equipped with the knowledge of how and why burnout occurs, they are more likely to adjust their style of professional interactions and assess their emotional reactions to job-related stress in a cognitive and thoughtful way (Badger, et al., 2008). Supervisors can offer ways to prevent burnout by encouraging periodic self-assessment, assisting social workers to examine the effects of their work on their overall health, and exploring the possibility of altering maladaptive personal and professional work styles (Siebert, 2005). Supervisors can reassure symptomatic social workers that burnout is not a result of personal or professional weakness, but an opportunity to alter practices to reduce the immense level of stress that exists and can eventually harm patients (Siebert, 2005). Burnout impairs workers. Those experiencing burnout are in untreated pain. The pain is contagious, and although unintentional, is passed to others. Some social workers recognize their symptoms of burnout, but not all (Badger, 2008). It is common to hide the pain and sometimes supervisors must confront this disguise (Corey & Corey, 1998).

The profession of social work is rewarding because there are times when a positive disposition or outcome is visible. The result is often a rewarding and positive emotion for all working toward the achievement of the goal, particularly the patient. Social workers experiencing positive outcomes regularly within their employment are rewarded with feelings of confidence and competence. However, some environments offer few moments when the positive outcomes of work are perceived, and with no positive feedback from patients, caregivers, colleagues, or supervisors, they experience less job satisfaction and increased frustration and hopelessness (Rothman, 1999; Um & Harrison, 1998).

The organizational structure of the environment also influences the working environment and the relationship of social workers to their job. Organizational structure is primarily designed to implement power regarding internal and external relationships, finances, and structural decision making. If organizational values are in conflict with social work values, social workers may face ethical conflicts. If an organization practices discriminatory treatment toward certain patients or removes resources from the medically underserved, these actions can contribute to professional burnout and serve as evidence of helplessness and isolation from organizational support (Um & Harrison, 1998).

As with all health problems, prevention is the best and most cost-effective way to deal with burnout (Noblet & LaMontagne, 2006). Knowing the support and leadership qualities found in good supervision serves as an important barrier to the onset of social worker burnout. Um and Harrison (1998) suggest that in addition to supportive supervision to prevent burnout, new social workers also benefit from clearly understanding the roles and tasks of their work and the potential emotional challenges inherent within the tasks. Discussing burnout potential and symptoms before they are apparent provides the supervisor and social worker with an opening for continued assessment of stressors during ongoing supervision and an opportunity to prevent the damage of this condition (Noblet & LaMontagne, 2006; Um & Harrison, 1998).

Simply telling a social worker to stop feeling burnout is like telling someone with chronic depression to stop being depressed. There is no benefit in telling someone to stop experiencing the pain of burnout, but there are benefits to understanding its causes. Sometimes supervisors can reduce work stress and provide some relief to the social worker through job adjustments or reassignment. There are many reasons why working with people living with chronic health issues is emotionally stressful. Grief and loss routinely witnessed leaves little room for optimism, hope, or professional satisfaction (Davis, 2005; Um & Harrison, 1998). In addition, the build up of loss, grief, guilt, accumulated accounts of patients' emotional and physical pain, paperwork, organizational politics, and an unbalanced personal perspective on life are experienced as powerful stressors (Davis, 2005).

Secondary Trauma

Secondary trauma is a rather new concept in the health professions. It is also referred to as compassion fatigue or secondary traumatic stress (Geller, Madsen, & Ohrenstein, 2004). Secondary trauma is the affective reaction of people who witness crisis and trauma in others. Trauma is the extreme emotional shock associated with war, terrorism, violence, disease, environmental disasters, and other forms of overwhelming loss. The physical, emotional, and social results of trauma are well documented and are occasionally diagnosed as posttraumatic stress disorder (Badger, et al, 2008; Fullerton, Ursano, Vance, & Wang , 2000). Frequently the symptoms of secondary trauma are similar to the symptoms of the individual experiencing the trauma. Social workers in health care are at risk of secondary trauma when they work with people experiencing extreme and distressing shock (Bride, Robinson, Yegidis, & Figley, 2004).

Often people who experience trauma are overwhelmed and sometimes trauma results in some positive growth, but continual waves of helplessness are overwhelming (Castle & Phillips, 2003). Everyone possesses coping strategies, but during a traumatic event, most experience a sense of emotional paralysis and difficulty interacting with their environment (Geller et al., 2004). Social workers in health care experience trauma regularly. Trauma occurs as people learn of new diagnoses and the serious or terminal prognoses associated with disease. The experience of repeatedly witnessing the reactions to traumatic news or the harsh reality of disease or treatment can traumatize members of the health care team. Social workers stand alongside patients and caregivers through the suffering of advanced chronic illness, end of life, and during emergent, acute, and unexpected injuries; they intimately witness the pain of others (Hesse, 2002). Social workers believe their presence contributes to the healing and alleviation of suffering, but in reality, they can be overexposed to pain.

People who experience trauma and secondary trauma often share similar symptoms, such as anger, anxiety, fear, depression, avoidance, reoccurring and intrusive thoughts and images, distress, and feeling unsafe. These feelings lead to impairment in actions, thoughts, and feelings. When a social worker is impaired by symptoms of secondary trauma, they are less able to think clearly and more likely to make errors, provide substandard interactions, avoid conflictual work assignments, miss work, or in some cases, may resign (Bride et al., 2004; Geller et al., 2004; Itzhaky & Dekel, 2005; Noblet & LaMontagne, 2006).

However, sometimes social workers involved with ongoing trauma work with patients experiencing significant and life-threatening crises develop an enhanced level of competence and expertise that contributes to job satisfaction; they experience making a vital contribution (Itzhaky & Dekel, 2005). For instance, during the early days of HIV/AIDS care, health care professionals were overwhelmed by the traumatic experiences of communities devastated by unbelievable losses. Many workers felt empowered and effective in their ability to offer support and understanding to patients experiencing significant discrimination and daunting life crises. Social workers who develop an area of expertise in a challenging area of health care often believe that despite the pain, they make a difference—and they do. Familiar with the biopsychosocial ramifications of disease, social workers are educated in ways that integrate care resources that respond to all areas of trauma.

Professionals, or trauma teams, that experience the same or similar conditions frequently work as a close and intimate unit. Similar to military units that share experiences of terror, helplessness, adrenalin, and purpose, they are united in ways others do not understand. Experiences of trauma are very personal and intimate events that often reveal significant levels of vulnerability to others. The team members become important to each other by normalizing feelings, sharing memories, and offering support. When trauma is shared, the experience becomes more concrete and objective and offers team members an emotionally safe and supportive place to speak about the experience and feel understood (Fullerton et al., 2000; Geller et al., 2004).

It is important for social workers experiencing trauma to be aware of this phenomenon and research suggests there are strategies to reduce the negative effects of secondary trauma (Badger, et al., 2008; Bride et al., 2004; Strom-Gottfried & Mowbray, 2006). These strategies include trainings, supervision, and additional emotional support for workers as well as adequate preparation for traumatic conditions, self-care, institutional support, review and debriefing, and mourning or memorial rituals to assist individuals to cope (Castle & Phillips, 2003; Fullerton et al., 2000; Romanoff, 1998; Strom-Gottfried & Mowbray, 2006).

Preparation

Preparation is an important step to prevent secondary trauma. There are unpredictable events in social work, but acknowledging the possibility or inevitability of pain is important. Supervisors share their practice experiences and can empathize with workers' personal reactions to stress. When supervisors withhold this information, they miss an opportunity to normalize situations or interfere with an opportunity for the individual to express painful feelings. If the supervisor shares their experiences, the social worker is more likely to do the same (Strom-Gottfried & Mowbray, 2006).

Similar to the effect of organizations contributing to employee burnout, organizations can also be a powerful influence in preventing the conditions that contribute to secondary trauma. Institutions that prioritize resources to employees that work in stressful circumstances experience greater worker retention, job satisfaction, and patient satisfaction (Noblet & LaMontagne, 2006). Organizational support is possible in many ways, such as offering support groups, continued education, supervision, grief and loss support, and work coverage for exhausted employees (Strom-Gottfried & Mowbray, 2006).

Supervision time is an appropriate place to talk about and review the details of loss, grief, and death (Strom-Gottfried & Mowbray, 2006). Debriefing is a powerful method to help social workers find perspective and offers a systematic process to support traumatized workers. The process serves to normalize and encourages ownership of emotions, yet honors their response to an experience (Fullerton et al., 2000). Debriefing assists the social worker to experience an increased sense of personal strength and input from others who face similar traumas.

Self-care is recognized as a vital way to prevent the symptoms of secondary loss and begins with an intentional and honest process of self-assessment by evaluating feelings, thoughts, and behaviors. This is an important part of prevention, but the objectivity of feedback from supervisors and colleagues validates or challenges self-perceptions. Self-care can develop from honest self-assessment and serve to reinforce the balance between the professional environments and the support found in the personal environment.

Self-Care

Supervision is a great place for social workers to be reminded about ways to preserve their strength and to continue to stay physically, emotionally, and socially balanced (Noblet & LaMontagne, 2006). With regular supervision, an individual is reminded to create ways to deal with potentially painful work.

Social workers must be encouraged to set realistic goals for themselves and to be honest about what is possible. There are many concrete ways to assist patients and caregivers, but the result is, at best, often an improvement to patients' quality of life, and not a return to optimum health and strength. Supervisors remind social workers to take the time to see and celebrate the interventions that make a positive contribution to good quality of life for patients or caregivers, despite the advancement of chronic illness. Social workers need to recognize small successes, appreciate patient empowerment, and celebrate the positive change that takes place. Realistic goals also clarify, in writing, the tasks expected for successful attainment of a goal.

Supervisors encourage social workers to develop ways to grieve. Rituals associated with grief are personally helpful ways to attend to losses in a symbolic, honorable, and intentional way (Castle & Phillips, 2003; Romanoff, 1998). Perhaps the social worker benefits from the luxury of attending the services for mourning offered by family or the health organization. Some hospice organizations conduct quarterly memorial services for all of the staff and family members who experienced a recent loss. Other forms of ritual are also very beneficial. Privately or within a team, social workers develop moments of memorializing patients and clients that allow for the loss to be recognized goodbyes to be said. For instance, I used my caseload list of HIV-positive patients as a way to say goodbye to patients. At their death, I closed my office door and intentionally and respectfully read the patient's name and then highlighted it with a marker. While the event only took a couple of minutes, the time spent thinking about each person, marking the name, and remembering the relationship and the death moved me to grieve in a very intentional way. The individuals did not just disappear, but their highlighted name remained on my caseload.

Others ritualize when they burn incense and meditate. Some visit a beach, lake, or comforting natural setting to reflect. There are many ways social workers can find to quiet themselves for a moment and to deliberately acknowledge their loss (Castle & Phillips, 2003). Supervision helps direct, respect, and support the ways workers grieve. The NASW "Standards for Palliative End of Life Care" is a great resource for social workers seeking strategies for coping with the grief and loss associated with chronic illness and eventual death (NASW, 2006; Strom-Gottfried & Mowbray, 2006).

Other self-care strategies include setting professional and personal boundaries and recognizing the limits of the professional role to save patients from disease. As social workers expand their view of life, they recognize new ways to measure worth. Social workers need to be reminded, by others and self, of the many ways life is improved by their partnership with others. They need to be encouraged to balance the thoughts, feelings, and activities of the professional day with the appropriate interactions of their personal lives. Continuing to be active in emotional, physical, or social work tasks outside the work setting blurs professional and personal lives in a way that can eventually result in no clear emotional safe haven. Self-care demands social workers acknowledge the vital role their emotional health contributes to competent and professional social work and invest in their most important resource: a healthy and balanced life.

Conflicts

Conflicts are a part of many jobs and unfortunately conflicts can affect work performance. Social workers experiencing conflicts risk missing opportunities to fully complete their tasks, but they also risk hurting their professional reputation. Eventually ongoing conflicts decrease the level of job satisfaction, and if the conflicts continue, the interference in work potentially threatens professionalism and the quality of interventions and outcomes for patients (Acker, 1999).

Employment conflicts exist for many different reasons. Conflicts occur as a normal part of life, but when the problem interferes with the ability to perform work, it is important to attend to resolving the conflict. Often disruptions happen in regard to the politics and policies of an organization or due to personal or professional differences. When conflicts are due to interactions with specific individuals, if left unresolved, they endanger professional and eventually personal relationships. The distraction of personal and professional conflicts with colleagues is risky and potentially dangerous for patients. Sometimes individual differences interfere in vital team relationships and pollute working relationships so that instead of the team functioning together, members circumvent or possibly undermine each other's work. When these situations occur with a social worker, there may be increased scrutiny due to the nonmedical nature of the profession. This increases the need for timely resolution and supervisors are in a position to assist social workers to construct an objective perspective on issues and implement constructive problem-solving strategies (Acker, 1999).

One of social workers' roles is advocacy and the nature of advocacy commonly challenges the accepted norm, particularly if normal practice interferes with the rights and resources necessary to support the best standard of patient care. But conflict also occurs when the expectations of the social worker and support for his or her work is missing. Conflicts are particularly evident when values within the team, or other professional relationships, differ regarding the patients' rights and when personal or professional goals do not match the goals of the organization. Given the inequalities within the health care system and the conflict inequity poses to the social worker, some degree of conflict will always remain. However, there are many ways social workers can improve conditions they cannot immediately change. Supervisors are helpful when they can assist others to see this broader perspective and work toward incremental progress.

If conflicts continue without resolution or individuals lose sight of a more balanced perspective, the issues become inflamed, causing emotional pain, an increase in dread, anger, and helplessness. These are the very emotions that contribute to an increased risk for burnout. Burnout can be contagious and a social worker with unresolved conflicts spills unhealthy symptoms onto others. Issues of disagreement can grow into a situation that risks hurting the morale of colleagues. Supervisors are a valuable resource to help evaluate the conflict, identify the causes, and assist in designing possible solutions to minimize the negative effects (Acker, 1999).

Healthy Boundaries

Social workers in health care, regardless of the actual responsibilities of the job, encounter situations that challenge boundary issues of the profession's ethical standards. Attention to boundaries is important in all relationships, but some of the most problematic boundary issues are when social workers are conflicted within the relationship limits described in the NASW Code of Ethics (1999) regarding social, sexual, religious, or business relationships (Davidson, 2005; Landau, 2008; Reamer, 2003).

Maintaining healthy boundaries is an essential part of relationship building with patients, caregivers, and colleagues. Healthy boundaries are weakened when social workers interact with others despite the possibility of potential professional conflicts. When relationships exist with others and roles within the relationship are unclear due to unusual or additional alterations to the original role, there is a dual relationship (Kagle & Giebelhausen, 1994; Reamer, 2003). Dual or multiple relationships exist when social workers engage in more than one form of relationship with a patient or colleague. For instance, a social worker is planning a discharge for a patient to a facility and the social worker's brother is a manager at the care facility. The manager of the care facility is a relative, and as a service provider, benefits from referrals from the hospital social worker, who is also her sibling. Social workers remember that the professional role is always primary. Boundaries are blurred and dangers increase when social workers are both the professional and attempt to also act in a personal role, such as a friend or partner (Reamer, 2003).

Dual relationships are potentially exploitative, particularly to a patient (Reamer, 2003). Fracturing boundaries is clearly unethical and is an obvious violation of the NASW Code of Ethics (1999). But sometimes dual relationships are very subtle and unintentional. For instance, when patients and social workers all contribute to community disease prevention efforts, this community of volunteers often know each other, share work on boards, volunteer for education and speaking engagements, and participate together in community fundraising. These types of small groups exist to support many health-related causes, including the research, treatment, and prevention of chronic illnesses. Social workers involved in these community efforts must be applauded but also educated about the potential conflicts associated with dual relationships. Reamer (2003) suggests that social workers differentiate between "boundary violations" and "boundary crossings" (p. 122).

When social workers disrespect the personal boundaries of a patient, it is abusive. The action exploits professional power and clearly violates professional ethical codes. Boundary violations hurt patients, their families, the social worker, and the profession. Many professional ethics codes share the recognition that boundary violations are unethical. However, ethical standards are intended to serve as a way to "translate" professional interactions and so dual and multiple relationships are evaluated for the specific circumstances of a situation and the level of vulnerability experienced by the patient. Boundaries are violated when a patient is hurt or taken advantage of due to the unequal power between the social worker and the patient (Reamer, 2003).

Unfortunately, the absence of intention to harm does not always protect the social worker, the colleague, or the patient from getting hurt. Social workers in health care frequently engage with vulnerable individuals experiencing a life crisis, such as the diagnosis of a serious disease or condition, mental and physical health complications, a sense of desperation for help, or loneliness and isolation. Attempts to offer supportive measures beyond employment responsibilities are frequently misunderstood and interpreted as affection, intimacy, or other emotions inappropriate within a professional relationship. Offered as support, interactions of caring are easily misinterpreted and result in unintended harm and confusion for all parties (Reamer, 2003). This is why the objective perspective of supervision is so beneficial.

When a social worker experiences a situation where a dual relationship exists, such as serving on an organizational board with a former patient, evaluation and monitoring of the relationship can lose perspective if done in isolation. Reamer (2003) suggests six strategies to help minimize the potential of ethical conflicts, listed in Box 12.2.

BOX 12.2 • *Six Strategies to Help Minimize the Potential of Ethical Conflicts*

1. Truthfully assess the potential or actual conflicts of interest and understand who benefits and why.
2. If a conflict of interest is identified or possible, communicate this to your employer, supervisor, or colleague and explore potential solutions.
3. Seek supervision and professional opinions by examining the NASW Code of Ethics and professional literature for standards, regulations, and policies regarding the boundary conflict to identify possible solutions.
4. Design a clear plan of action addressing boundary issues and be sure all participants are protected from actual or potential harm.
5. Carefully and thoroughly document the steps taken to evaluate and monitor the relationship including discussions, research, and consultations.
6. Monitor and evaluate the strategy to ensure the safety of all parties.

Source: Reamer (2003)

Abuse of boundaries is undeniable when social workers engage in a sexual relationship with a patient, but there are many other forms of violations that are less obvious. The NASW Code of Ethics (1999) directs social workers to be on guard when it comes to dual relationships, and to avoid them whenever possible. Social workers must make decisions about personal and professional interactions with patients and rely on professional consultation with a knowledgeable supervisor. All decisions regarding all forms of relationships with patients must be motivated by the goal to protect the patient from any kind of harm (Reamer, 2003). Supervisors are essential in assisting social workers to examine and to interrupt unprofessional and unethical relationships with patients.

Benefits of Good Supervision

A well-trained supervisor is invaluable because the benefits of good supervision extend beyond the relationship with the social worker. Professional supervision influences the quality of many systems and leads to improvements in the profession, the host agency, the staff, caregivers, and the patient (Acker, 1999; Harkness & Hensley, 1991; Noblet & LaMontagne, 2006).

Support from supervisors is essential for social workers in health care as they attempt to cope with stressful work situations in a host setting. While there are many opportunities for great satisfaction in health care, the challenges and isolation can present a risk. Social workers must recognize the work they perform results in a positive difference in the lives of patients and caregivers. Many professionals mature to a stage that reduces the quantity of supportive and positive feedback needed from others to recognize the benefits of their role to others, but everyone benefits from outside support occasionally. Creative supervisors implement inventive and productive ways to support social workers and add to the satisfaction experienced in their accomplishments. This form of supervision offers many rewards: the social worker experiences improved emotional health and continued commitment to their job, patients and their families continue to benefit from the support of an experienced and emotionally healthy social worker, the profession of social work is represented by committed and confident social workers, and health care organizations experience the cost savings of low turnover and money-saving social work interventions (Acker, 1999).

The best supervision improves the social worker's ability to provide the best quality of care. A social work supervisor who listens, offers honest and constructive feedback, and challenges the social worker to remain healthy and balanced provides an invaluable service to the care of patients. Social workers in health care face challenges from all systems: individual, families, caregivers, community resources, health systems, and social policies. Social workers experience some of the frustrations and grief many experience, but social workers witness the frustrations repeatedly. Good supervision upholds social workers by setting realistic goals, teaching coping skills, and pointing out success. Supervisors, who use the strengths perspective, assist social workers to see the difference they make, ways they can improve their work, and encourages them to continue to develop professional skills (Cole et al., 2004; Kurland & Salmon, 1992).

Summary

Supervision is perhaps the single most important method assisting social workers in health care to effectively resolve frustration and exhaustion. The isolation of social workers from their colleagues and the misunderstanding of social work responsibilities can challenge social workers to find the rewards in the practice of their profession. The health care system in the United States remains severely underfunded and given the prominence of addressing the biological needs of people with health care needs, the emotional, social, and spiritual needs are also often underfunded. The lack of adequate resources adds to the frustration of social workers that attempt to provide the best psychosocial resources to the patient and caregivers. At times the social worker is not only challenged to provide the best service, but is a witness to individuals who have no insurance or live underinsured. Sometimes social workers are unable to help provide the access to patients necessary for accomplishing their health care goals; this is a challenge to professional ethics.

Because health care systems are not likely to begin an investment in additional social work supervision, social workers must resolve to find the best ways to meet their professional support needs within the supervisory relationship, regardless of the supervisor's professional discipline. Finding the common ground of quality patient care draws health professions together and social workers educate other professions about teaming and cooperation for the good of the patient as a feature of their profession.

Critical Thinking Questions

1. Why is supervision so important?

2. What are some of the chief benefits of supervision?

3. What can you do if you do not have a supervisor?

References

Acker, G. M. (1999). The impact of clients' mental illness on social workers job satisfaction and burnout. *Health and Social Work, 24*(2), 112–119.

Badger, K., Royse, D., & Craig, C. (2008). Hospital social workers and indirect trauma exposure: An exploratory study of contributing factors. *Health and Social Work, 33*(1), 63–71.

Brashears, F. (1995). Supervision as social work practice: A reconceptualization. *Social Work, 40*(5), 692–699.

Bride, B. E., Robinson, M. M., Yegidis, B., & Figley, C. R. (2004). Development and validation of the secondary traumatic stress scale. *Research on Social Work Practice, 14*(1), 27–35.

Castle , J., & Phillips, W. L. (2003). Grief rituals: Aspects that facilitate adjustment to bereavement. *Journal of Loss and Trauma, 8*, 41–71.

Colby, I., & Dziegielewski, S. (2004). *Introduction to social work: The people's profession* (2nd ed.). Chicago: Lyceum Books.

Cole, D., Panchanadeswaran, S., & Daining, C. (2004). Predictors of job satisfaction of licensed social workers: Perceived efficacy as a mediator of the relationship between workload and job satisfaction. *Journal of Social Service Research, 32*(1), 1–12.

Corey, M., & Corey, G. (1998). *Becoming a helper* (3rd ed.). Pacific Grove, CA.: Brooks/Cole.

Davidson, J. C. (2005). Professional relationship boundaries: A social work teaching module. *Social Work Education, 24*(5). 511–533.

Davis, M. P. (2005). Integrating palliative medicine into an oncology practice. *American Journal of Hospice and Palliative Medicine, 22*(6), 447–456.

DeLoach, R. (2003). Job satisfaction among hospice interdisciplinary team members. *American Journal of Hospice and Palliative Medicine, 20*(6) 434–440.

Dziegielewski, S. F. (2004). *The changing face of health care social work: Professional practice in managed behavioral health care* (2nd ed.). New York: Springer Publishing Company.

Egan, M., & Kadushin, G. (2004). Job satisfaction of home health social workers in the environment of cost containment. *Health & Social Work, 29*(4) 287–296.

Finn, P. (1997). Reducing stress: An organization-centered approach. *FBI Law Enforcement Bulletin, 66,* 20–26.

Fleming, G., & Taylor, B. (2006). Battle on the home care front: Perceptions of home care workers of factors influencing staff retention in Northern Ireland. *Health and Social Care in the Community, 15*(1), 67–76.

Fullerton, C. S., Ursano, R. J., Vance, K., & Wang, L. (2000). Debriefing following trauma. *Psychiatric Quarterly, 71*(3), 259–276.

Geller, J. A., Madsen, L. H., & Ohrenstein, L. (2004). Secondary trauma: A team approach. *Clinical Social Work Journal, 32*(4), 415–430.

Harkness, D., & Hensley, H. (1991). Changing the focus of social work supervision: Effects on client satisfaction and generalized contentment. *Social Work, 36*(6) 506–512.

Hesse, A. R. (2002). Secondary trauma: How working with trauma survivors affects therapists. *Clinical Social Work Journal, 30*(3), 293–309.

Hyrkas, K. (2005). Clinical supervision, burnout, and job satisfaction among mental health and psychiatric nurses in Finland. *Issues in Mental Health Nursing, 26,* 531–556.

Itzhaky, H. & Dekel, R. (2005). Helping victims of terrorism: What makes social work effective? *Social Work, 50*(4) 335–343.

Itzhaky, H., & Lipschitz-Elhawi, R. (2004). Hope as a strategy in supervising social workers of terminally ill patients. *Health and Social Work, 29(1),* 46–54.

Kagle, J. D., & Giebelhausen, P. N. (1994). Dual relationships and professional boundaries. *Social Work, 39*(2) 213–220.

Kurland, R., & Salmon, R. (1992). When problems seem overwhelming: Emphases in teaching, supervision, and consultation. *Social Work, 37*(3) 240–244.

National Association of Social Workers (NASW). (1999). *Code of ethics.* Washington, DC: NASW Press.

Noblet, A., & LaMontagne, A. D. (2006). The role of workplace health promotion in addressing job stress. *Health Promotion International, 21*(4), 346–353.

Reamer, F. G. (1989). Liability issues in social work supervision. *Social Work, 34*(5), 445–448.

Reamer, F. G. (2003). Boundary issues in social work: Managing dual relationships. *Social Work, 48*(1) 121–133.

Reamer, F. G. (2005). Documentation in social work: Evolving ethical and risk-management standards. *Social Work, 50(4)*, 325–334.

Romanoff, B. D. (1998). Rituals and the grieving process. *Death Studies, 22*(8), 697–711.

Rothman, J. (1999). *The self-awareness workbook for social workers.* Boston: Allyn & Bacon.

Siebert, D. C. (2005). Personal and occupational factors in burnout among practicing social workers: Implications for researchers, practitioners and managers. *Journal of Social Service Research, 32*(2), 25–44.

Strom-Gottfried, K., & Mowbray, N. D. (2006). Who heals the helper? Facilitating the social worker's grief. *Families in Society: The Journal of Contemporary Social Services, 87*(1), 9–15.

Um, M.Y., & Harrison, D. F. (1998). Role stressors, burnout, mediators, and job satisfaction: A stress-strain-outcome model and an empirical test. *Social Work Research, 22*(2), 100–115.

Index